Forsaken, Forgotten
AND
Forgiven

A Devotional Study of
Jeremiah and Lamentations

WARREN HENDERSON

Forsaken, Forgotten and Forgiven
– A Devotional Study of Jeremiah
  and Lamentations (second edition)

By Warren Henderson
Copyright © 2016

Cover Design by Benjamin Bredeweg

Editing/Proofreading: Randy Amos, David
    Dunlap, Kathleen Henderson, Laura
    Dunlap, Dan Macy, and David
    Lindstrom

Published by Warren A. Henderson
3769 Indiana Road
Pomona, KS 66076

Perfect Bound ISBN: 978-1-939770-36-3
eBook ISBN: 978-1-939770-37-0

Available through many on-line retailers

Table of Contents

Second Edition

This edition of *Forsaken, Forgotten and Forgiven* also includes a devotional study of the book of Lamentations.

Preface

Many Christians have read the books of Jeremiah and Lamentations, but few (including myself, until recently) have made these a topic of thorough study. Some contend that the prophetic narrative of Jeremiah and its epilogue, Lamentations, have Jewish historical significance only and no application for the Church today. Others choose to merely skim these texts because their "doom and gloom" format is distressing; they may glean little from these books other than gratitude to God that they did not have Jeremiah's calling. Others might lack the discipline to stick with the topic to the end; after all, Jeremiah is the second longest book in the Bible.

In regards to excuses for ignoring these texts, I had many, but now have none. The burden of the Lord is upon me; my meditations are full and my conscience swollen. My deepest conviction is that the Church today should heed the spiritual principles disclosed by Jeremiah, especially his warnings against idolatry and ignoring revealed truth. Paul confirmed that the writings of the Old Testament are pertinent for Christians today: *"For whatever things were written before were written for our learning"* (Rom. 15:4). He told the Christians at Corinth that the Church should learn from Israel's mistakes: *"Now these things became our examples, to the intent that we should not lust after evil things as they also lusted...Now all these things happened to them as examples, and they were written for our admonition, upon whom the ends of the ages have come"* (1 Cor. 10:6, 11). Much of what happened to Israel 2,500 years ago is directly applicable to the modern Church, as William Kelly also explains:

> There is some analogy in moral character between the last days of Judah and the last days of the Church, and as the various truths delivered by Jeremiah were chosen by the Spirit to suit the condition of the Jewish people, this Book has great practical value in the present times. Many salutary lessons of faithfulness and obedience

1

amid prevailing weakness and confusion may be gathered from the prophet's own experiences and from the messages he received from the Lord. These are as needful today as then.[1]

Accordingly, many of the warnings in the book of Jeremiah are applicable to the Church today. If the Lord so severely judged His covenant people for their willful idolatry and wickedness, why would He not hesitate to chasten those committing the same offenses who are but mere second benefactors of the New Covenant confirmed with Israel (Heb. 8:8)? This is the essence of Paul's warning to the Christians at Rome:

> For if God did not spare the natural branches [the Jews], He may not spare you [the wild branches grafted in] either. Therefore consider the goodness and severity of God: on those who fell, severity; but toward you, goodness, if you continue in His goodness. Otherwise you also will be cut off (Rom. 11:21-22).

In Paul's olive tree analogy of Romans 11, the Abrahamic covenant is the root of the tree from which all nations of the earth shall be blessed (Gen. 12:3). The olive tree represents the Lord Jesus Christ, through whom all the blessings of God flow up from the root to the branches. If the Church is to be restored to a testimony of power and vibrancy, she must repent, return to the Lord, and obey His Word. The Lord Himself said, *"I am the vine, you are the branches. He who abides in Me, and I in him, bears much fruit; for without Me you can do nothing"* (John 15:5). Without abiding in Christ, the Church is powerless and is nothing more than dried up branches clattering in the secular winds of humanism. Unfortunately, this is a depiction which describes much of Christendom today.

If this warning is not heeded, the Church, like the Jews of Jeremiah's day, will eventually *forsake and forget* the Lord! In this situation, those the Lord loves will turn on Him and break His heart. Paul foretold that this will be the spiritual condition of the professing Church just before the Antichrist is revealed and the Tribulation Period begins (2 Thess. 2:3). Let us have no part in it! The days before us are evil; may God enable the true Church to hold fast to Christ and His Word. The greatest of tragedies would be for us not to learn from God's stern dealings with the Jews and to willfully repeat their offenses.

Forsaken, Forgotten and Forgiven is a "commentary style" devotional which upholds the glories of Christ while exploring the books of Jeremiah and Lamentations within the context of the whole of Scripture. As in *Seeds of Destiny* (Genesis) and *Out of Egypt* (Exodus), I have endeavored to include in this book some of the principal gleanings from other writers. *Forsaken, Forgotten and Forgiven* contains seventy-five brief devotions. This format allows the reader to use the book either as a daily devotional or as a reference source for deeper study.

Jeremiah

Overview of Jeremiah

From a statistical point of view, Jeremiah is the longest of the prophetic books and is the second longest book in the Bible, after Psalms. Psalms has 150 chapters, 2,461 verses, and 43,743 words, while Jeremiah contains 52 chapters, 1,364 verses, and 42,659 words.

Setting

Although at the time just prior to the Babylonian captivity Habakkuk and Zephaniah had crucial prophetic ministries, Jeremiah was the primary prophet God used to preach against Judah's wickedness. Jeremiah was God's main mouthpiece to warn the Jewish nation to repent and to announce impending judgment upon them if they did not. After Jerusalem was destroyed in 586 B.C., God raised up the prophet Ezekiel to minister to Jewish captives in Babylon, while Jeremiah continued to encourage Jewish survivors in Jerusalem.

Outline

The majority of the book of Jeremiah, the first 45 chapters, contain prophecies related to Judah, while chapters 46-51 record prophecies against other nations, such as Egypt and Babylon. The portion of Jeremiah pertaining to Judah (chapters 2-45) can be further subdivided by subject matter: Chapters 2-25 contain thirteen prophetic messages to Judah. Chapters 26-29 review Jeremiah's personal difficulties in delivering these messages. Chapters 30-33 provide comfort and hope to God's people. Chapters 34-45 provide a historical record of the fall of Jerusalem and the social conditions afterwards.

Chapter 52 is a historical appendix detailing the overthrow of Judah and the release of Jehoiachin from Babylon in 561 B.C. This chapter was likely added to the book after 561 B.C. by the writer of Kings, as portions of 2 Kings 24-25 are nearly identical to Jeremiah

52. It is noted, however, that Jewish tradition ascribes the writings of Kings (1 and 2 Kings in the Christian Bible) to Jeremiah. The last chapter of Jeremiah shows the fulfillment of Jeremiah's pronouncements of judgment and recounts Jehoiachin's release from prison in Babylon and his privileged place at the king's table; this foreshadows the Jewish nation's future release from Babylon and their restoration with Jehovah at the end of the Tribulation Period, after which time they will return to Israel and He will bless them.

Topical Arrangement

The book of Jeremiah is topical in arrangement, rather than chronological. There are thirteen distinct messages of warning to Judah and twenty-two specific interactions with various individuals, but few of these are in sequential order. In fact, speaking as to chronology, Jeremiah's messages switch back and forth seventeen times throughout the prophetic record. Appendix 1 contains an attempt by H. A. Ironside to put dates to each of Jeremiah's prophecies. It is likely that Jeremiah organized all his prophetic statements in this final form at the end of his ministry, perhaps after he was taken to Egypt as a prisoner (51:64).

There are four main, reoccurring themes in the book of Jeremiah: an admonition against sin, a warning of impending judgment, a call to repentance, and a promise of future restoration. The general theme of the first half of this book can be summarized by Romans 6:23a, *"The wages of sin is death."* Oswald Chambers once said, "Sin enough and you will soon be unconscious of sin."[1] Such was the spiritual state of God's covenant people at the time of Jeremiah's ministry. The long-suffering nature of God would be restrained no longer – justice would be served. Jehovah was jealous for the hearts of His people who had either forsaken Him for other gods or were engaged in religious exercises devoid of true devotion.

The book of Jeremiah is more autobiographical than any other prophetic book, although Hosea and Ezekiel follow closely behind. All of Scripture is remarkable, but because the prophet projects himself into the pages of his prophecies, this book possesses a special uniqueness in the canon of Scripture. Zachary Macaulay said the following concerning Jeremiah:

It is difficult to conceive any situation more painful than to watch the lingering agony of an exhausted country, to tend it during the alternate fits of stupefaction and raving which precede its dissolution, and to see the symptoms of vitality disappear one by one, till nothing is left but coldness, darkness, and corruption.[2]

His prophecies broke his own heart (9:1); so difficult was his ministry that he wanted to resign, but God would not allow him to do so (20:9). It was his place to stand in the pathway of a nation rushing headlong to its destruction.

The Author

Jeremiah's name means "Jehovah will lift up" or "Jehovah will exalt" and is frequently mentioned throughout the book (some 130 times). This is in stark contrast to Isaiah, whose name is mentioned sixteen times in his prophetic account, and to Ezekiel, who is referred to by name only twice in his respective narrative. As Jeremiah had a difficult calling, perhaps hearing the frequent mentioning of his name would serve to encourage him to not give up. Every utterance of his own name would remind Jeremiah that God would exalt Himself in every part of Jeremiah's ministry, whether the people heeded his message or not.

Jeremiah was informed at the onset of his ministry that he would suffer much to complete God's calling for him. In fact, he was warned not to take a wife because of the terrible destruction God would levy on Jerusalem (16:2). This may have been distressing for Jeremiah; he would have no wife, no children, no legacy or posterity to follow after him. Comparatively speaking, he suffered more than any other Old Testament prophet because of his unpopular message of condemnation and judgment. Many wanted to kill him, but they did not succeed until his ministry was finished, for God was with Jeremiah. Tradition records that Jeremiah was stoned by the rebellious Jewish remnant who had taken him to Egypt as a prisoner.

The life of Jeremiah serves as a reminder to every servant of God that while on earth we are immortal and invincible until the Lord's work in us and through us is complete. On this point, Paul wrote: *"For we are His workmanship, created in Christ Jesus for good works, which God prepared beforehand that we should walk in them"*

9

(Eph. 2:10). May each believer be faithful to walk the course to which he or she is called, so that at the end of our sojourn on earth each one may be able to echo the words Paul spoke just before his death, *"I have fought the good fight, I have finished the race, I have kept the faith"* (2 Tim. 4:7).

Meditation

O tempted one, look up, be strong; the promise of the Lord is sure,
That they shall sing the victor's song, who faithful to the end endure;
God's Holy Spirit comes to thee, of His abiding love to tell;
To blissful port, over stormy sea, calls Heaven's inviting harbor bell.

— John Yates

Devotions in Jeremiah

Called to Serve
Jeremiah 1:1-10

Jeremiah's hometown was Anathoth, one of the forty-eight cities designated during the days of Joshua for the dwelling places of the priests (Josh. 21:18). Anathoth was a small village located in the land of Benjamin, just three miles northeast of Jerusalem. Jeremiah was a priest, the son of Hilkiah, who was also a priest. Whether Jeremiah's father was the high priest who found the Book of the Law during the reign of Josiah is unknown; Hilkiah was likely a common name. Priests were esteemed among God's people, but prophets were often despised. Priests represented the people before God, while prophets conveyed God's will to the people. As Jeremiah was going to be speaking to a backslidden nation, his message from God would not be popular. The knowledge of God's Word in Hilkiah's day brought revival to a wayward nation, but this would not be the case during Jeremiah's ministry.

As a young man, Jeremiah probably thought that being a priest would be a respectable profession; being a prophet could be an entirely different matter. The words the Lord Jesus spoke concerning a prophet being without honor in his own country (Luke 4:24) were certainly proven true in Jeremiah's case. He was despised and generally hated by his own people.

Jeremiah's ministry spanned the reigns of five different Judean kings: Josiah, Jehoahaz, Jehoiakim, Jehoiachin, and Zedekiah. His ministry began in the thirteenth year of Josiah's reign (627 B.C.) and continued well past the destruction of Jerusalem in 586 B.C. Thus, Jeremiah prophesied for forty years before the Jews were exiled and then for several more years afterwards. After the fall of Jerusalem,

Jeremiah was allowed to remain in Jerusalem to continue his ministry to the suffering Jews during the Babylonian captivity.

The number *forty* is used repeatedly in Scripture to symbolize a time of trial or a probationary period of testing. It was no accident, then, that Jeremiah preached to Judah forty years before the nation's probation ended and judgment was executed. Accordingly, brother Lightfoot observes an interesting correlation between the forty-year teaching ministries of Moses and Jeremiah:

> [Just as] Moses was so long with the people, a teacher in the wilderness, till they entered into their own land, Jeremiah was so long in their own land a teacher, before they went into the wilderness of the heathen; and he thinks that therefore a special mark is set upon the last forty years of the iniquity of Judah, which Ezekiel bore forty days, a day for a year, because during all that time they had Jeremiah prophesying among them, which was a great aggravation of their impenitency. God, in the prophet, suffered their manners, their ill manners, forty years, and at length swore in His wrath that they should not continue in His rest.[1]

In summary, the Lord taught His people for forty years to suitably prepare them to enter the Promised Land by faith, and He worked with them for the same duration of time to properly usher them out because of their stubborn disobedience.

God divinely chose Jeremiah to be a prophet before he was conceived, before he was formed by God in his mother's womb (v. 5). God thoroughly knew everything about Jeremiah. The English phrase, *"I knew you,"* (v. 4) is derived from the Hebrew word *yada*, which means "to intimately know." *Yada* is used in Genesis 4:1 to describe the sexual union between Adam and Eve – *"Adam **knew** Eve, his wife, and she conceived."* In the process of creating Jeremiah, God intimately knew him inside and out. David understood this truth, which prompted his praise, *"For You formed my inward parts; You covered me in my mother's womb. I will praise You, for I am fearfully and wonderfully made"* (Ps. 139:13-14). God, foreknowing Jeremiah, made a sovereign choice to use him as His representative to Judah and the nations. What God creates a man for is what He calls him to do;

accordingly, Jeremiah was commissioned as soon as he came of age to engage in the work he had been designed to fulfill.

Jeremiah was aware of the poor spiritual condition of Judah and was understandably fearful of conveying God's displeasure with them. Initially, he excused himself from the appointment, pleading with the Lord that he was but a child (v. 6); this was probably to highlight his perceived inadequacy to speak for God. The humility of Jeremiah is noteworthy, but God does not summon those who cannot effectively serve His purposes. It is noted that the Hebrew word *naar* translated "child" in verse 6 is rendered "young man" in Zechariah 2:4, where it speaks of the man who was measuring Jerusalem. It is also translated "young men" in 1 Samuel 21 in reference to the soldiers who accompanied David as he fled from King Saul. Jeremiah was likely in his late teens or early twenties; he was not a young child.

Accordingly, God told Jeremiah not think of himself as a child, for all that he spoke would be under His authority: *"For you shall go to all to whom I send you, and whatever I command you, you shall speak"* (v. 7). In response to Jeremiah's fear, God told him twice not to be afraid because He would be with Jeremiah every step of the way (vv. 8, 18). *"'I am with you to deliver you,' says the Lord"* (v. 8). Oswald Chambers comments to what God did and did not promise to do:

> God promised Jeremiah that He would deliver him personally – "Thy life will I give unto thee for a price." That is all God promises His children. Wherever God sends us, He will guard our lives. Our personal property and possessions are a matter of indifference, we have to sit loosely to all these things; if we do not, there will be panic and heartbreak and distress. That is the inwardness of the overshadowing of personal deliverance.[2]

After decreeing His pledge of protection, God touched Jeremiah's lips with His hand to affirm that He had put His own words in Jeremiah's mouth (v. 9). Jeremiah need not worry any longer about what he should say; when he opened his mouth God would speak through him. It would be an arduous ministry, but also a spectacular one. Jehovah's supernatural dealings with the nations (i.e. "overthrowing" and "building," v. 10) would be initiated by

13

Jeremiah's utterances (these being symbolized by the less severe gestures of uprooting and planting).

We are left to wonder why God chose a tender and compassionate man like Jeremiah to preach to a stiff-necked people engaged in gross sin. Why not send a hard-nose, battleaxe of a man who would have no qualms about delivering a harsh message? We are not told why Jeremiah was chosen, and it is probably best not to speculate, but certainly if we were the ones dead in trespasses and sin, would we not want to sense the forbearing love of God in the call to repentance? As Jeremiah pleaded with the Jews, sincerity and compassion were woven into every word that was spoken; this is a good pattern for us to follow today as we share the gospel message with the lost.

Moses was comforted with similar words before the burning bush after God summoned him to deliver the Jews from Pharaoh's hand (Ex. 3:12). Like Jeremiah, Moses excused himself from God's calling for his life by reminding God of his own speaking inadequacies. God informed Moses that He knew all about his lips, for He had formed them in his mother's womb. In full knowledge of all Moses' strengths and weaknesses God had chosen him for the task at hand. The fact that he was slow in speech only meant that God would be glorified in whatever Moses spoke to Pharaoh. Moses was to learn that it would not be his own fancy words or eloquent speeches that would pry the Jews from Pharaoh's clutches. He was to convey to Pharaoh only the words that God put into his mouth. It would be God's word of power alone which would defeat the enemy.

Like Jeremiah, Paul found the comfort of God's presence a great help amidst difficulties. Shortly after Saul's conversion on the road to Damascus, the Lord told Ananias that Saul was *"a chosen vessel of Mine to bear My name before Gentiles, kings, and the children of Israel. For I will show him how many things he must suffer for My name's sake"* (Acts 9:15-16). During Paul's third missionary journey he served the Lord in hostile and wicked Corinth for eighteen months. It was during this time that the Lord Jesus comforted Paul with these words in a night vision: *"Do not be afraid, but speak, and do not keep silent; for I am with you, and no one will attack you to hurt you; for I have many people in this city"* (Acts 18:9-10). Shortly after this pronouncement, Paul was delivered from a Christ-hating mob – the

Lord had kept His word. The Lord was on Paul's side and, as Martin Luther once said, "One with God is a majority."

Maintaining the abiding presence of the Lord is essential if we are to complete His will for our lives. Solomon put the matter this way: *"Trust in the Lord with all your heart, and lean not on your own understanding; in all your ways acknowledge Him, and He shall direct your paths"* (Prov. 3:5-6). Is the Lord beckoning you to know Him and learn of His calling for your life? The promise of His abiding presence will safeguard your mind in times of trouble: *"'I will never leave you nor forsake you.' So we may boldly say: 'The Lord is my helper; I will not fear. What can man do to me?'"* (Heb. 13:5-6). Jeremiah found God's abiding presence to be a wonderful source of comfort during the many difficulties he faced throughout the remainder of his life. This provision of peace only resulted from his earlier obedience to the Lord's command, *"For you shall go to all to whom I send you"* (v. 7).

Meditation

Who is on the Lord's side? Who will serve the King?
Who will be His helpers, other lives to bring?
Who will leave the world's side? Who will face the foe?
Who is on the Lord's side? Who for Him will go?
By Thy call of mercy, by Thy grace divine,
We are on the Lord's side—Saviour, we are Thine!

— Frances R. Havergal

The Called Protected
Jeremiah 1:11-19

In his first discussion with the Lord, young Jeremiah learned that he was to be a prophet to backslidden Judah. Shortly thereafter, the Lord again spoke to him, employing two signs to confirm Jeremiah's calling and to foretell of His judgment upon Judah. The Lord concluded His message to Jeremiah with the promise of His abiding presence and protection throughout Jeremiah's ministry.

The confirming signs were presented to Jeremiah through two different visions: the almond tree (v. 11), and the boiling pot (v. 13). The almond tree is one of the first trees to bud in the spring – this symbolized that God's judgment would fall soon. Jeremiah was to sound the alarm and attempt to wake a backslidden nation from its spiritual slumber. God's patience was coming to an end; the time of judgment was at hand, as shown in the next vision.

Jeremiah then saw a boiling pot, facing from the North. This was another picture of judgment, conveying not only its imminency, but also its severity. Boiling water is turbulent, as God's judgment was to be upon His people. Additionally, we note that when one removes a boiling pot from its heat source, the pot continues to boil for a time; this might indicate that Judah's judgment would have on-going, residual effects of chastening beyond its initial, most severe ramifications. History has shown that this certainly characterized the devastating fall of Jerusalem and the aftermath of the following seventy-year Babylonian captivity.

How would God punish His people? God would use a kingdom from the North (Babylon) and allow it to set up a throne in the very gate of Jerusalem (v. 15). In those days, whoever controlled the gate of a particular city, ruled it; the conquest of Jerusalem was clearly in view. We may wonder why God would use such a wicked nation as Babylon to chasten His people. The prophet Habakkuk had this quandary. When God informed Habakkuk that He was about to use Babylon as an instrument to chasten His people for their wickedness, a baffled Habakkuk then asked the Lord how He could use such an outright pagan nation to punish His people (Hab. 1:6). Although backslidden, the Jewish people could be considered more righteous than the Babylonians (Hab. 1:13).

Understanding God's response to this question is foundational to comprehending the workings of God among humanity. He told the prophet, *"The just shall live by faith"* (Hab. 2:4). This verse is repeated three times in the New Testament (Rom. 1:17; Gal. 3:11; Heb. 10:38) and conveys one of the central themes of the Bible. It suffices here to say that trusting in God and His Word results in life and that pride and rebellion lead to death. The lesson for Habakkuk was not to trust in his feelings or emotions, but rather to have faith in God's choices and doings – He would chasten Judah, judge Babylon, and in the process exalt His great name in all the earth. The greatest good is accomplished when man lives for God by faith and trusts God with his fate.

Through personal experience, Jeremiah knew this to be true, but Judah was not living for Jehovah; in fact, they had forsaken Him. Four times in the first two chapters, God bemoaned that His people had "forsaken Him" (1:16, 2:13, 17, 19). Indeed, they had *"burned incense to other gods, and worshiped the works of their own hands"* (v. 16). Like an adulterous wife who had violated her marriage covenant, the Jews had broken their covenant with God (Deut. 28). Rather than expressing love for Jehovah, they crafted images to honor false gods and burned incense before them. The sin of misplaced affection is a grievous sin against the Lord. The Jews were about to learn of God's righteous jealousy in a very painful way (Jer. 3:8; Ezek. 16:32).

The Lord Jesus warned that having more than one master would keep believers from committing to live their lives for Him: *"No one can serve two masters; for either he will hate the one and love the other, or else he will be loyal to the one and despise the other. You cannot serve God and mammon"* (Matt. 6:24). Divided allegiance is not possible, for ultimately a slave can be devoted to only one master. The Lord states that there can be no middle ground; He is either the believer's first love or He is not the Master of the believer's life.

The Lord Jesus demands that He have the first place in our hearts: *"He that loves father or mother more than Me, is not worthy of Me; and he that loves son or daughter more than Me, is not worthy of Me"* (Matt. 10:37). The church at Ephesus was solemnly warned by the Lord Himself concerning their diminishing love for Him – He was no longer their first love (Rev. 2:4). Twice He tells them to repent of that offense. Examine your own heart today. Is the Lord Jesus your first love?

The first chapter ends on a positive note; God uses three metaphors to convey His sustaining power and protection for His prophet. Jeremiah would be like a fortified city, an iron pillar, and bronze walls (v. 18); he would be able to resist the attack of the enemy. Those addressed in Jeremiah's message would inevitably oppose him, but they would not prevail (v. 19). Like Elijah, Ezekiel, Hosea, and many other prophets, Jeremiah would drink from his own ministry, but God would sustain him during the difficult days ahead.

Meditation

> More love to Thee, O Christ, more love to Thee!
> Hear Thou the prayer I make on bended knee;
> This is my earnest plea: More love, O Christ, to Thee.
> More love to Thee, More love to Thee.
>
> Once earthly joy I craved, sought peace and rest;
> Now Thee alone I seek, give what is best;
> This all my prayer shall be: More love, O Christ, to Thee.
> More love to Thee, More love to Thee.
>
> — Elizabeth Prentiss

I Remember You

Jeremiah 2:1-12

Chapter 2 begins the first of thirteen prophetic messages of judgment to be issued by Jeremiah and contains the first of the book's thirteen references to the Jews as God's "backsliding" people. When used metaphorically in Scripture, each of the numbers from one to forty holds a particular meaning; the following are a few examples of how the number thirteen is used in Scripture to show rebellion. The number thirteen is first mentioned in the Bible when five Jordanian kings rebelled against Chedorlaomer (Gen. 14:4). There were thirteen years of silence after Abraham doubted God's promise and fathered Ishmael, after which God reminded Abraham of His covenant thirteen times (Gen. 17). There were thirteen judges who ministered to Israel during the time when *"every man did what was right in their own eyes"* (Judg. 17:6). Haman's plot to destroy the Jews was set for the 13th day of a particular month (Est. 3:13). Satan, or the Dragon, is spoken of thirteen times in Revelation. Throughout Scripture, the number thirteen is associated with rebellion, and this is likely the determining factor in the number of specific prophetic judgments that Jeremiah would speak to Judah.

Albert Barnes provides the following outline for Jeremiah's first message (2:1-3:5):

The prophecy consists of three parts, of which the first (2:1-13) contains an appeal from God to all Israel (i.e. the whole twelve tribes), proving to them His past love, and that their desertion of Him was without ground or reason. In the second (2:14-28) the prophet shows that Israel's calamities were entirely the result of her apostasy. In the last (2:29-3:5) we see Judah imitating Samaria's sin, and hardening itself against correction.[1]

Keeping this overview in mind, the passage begins with God reminiscing about the early years with His people. He remembered the birth of the nation. Though at times they grumbled and complained against Him, overall He had their allegiance and devotion during their forty years in the wilderness. For this reason, Israel was holiness to the Lord and His first fruits among the nations (v. 3). But that had all changed – Israel's sin of idolatry had ruined the blessing of divine fellowship. Kyle Yates explains:

> The honeymoon is over. God reminds rebellious Israel of the fervor and the warmth and the purity of the love streams in the early days. She was desperately in love with her Lover and the tender love made life full of music and joy and hope. She was pure and clean and holy. No disloyalty or unclean thought marred the beauty of her devotion. But now the picture is heart-rending. God's heart is crushed with grief and disappointment. Israel now is living in open sin. She is unfaithful to the covenant vows. Other gods have stolen her affection. She has ceased to love Yahweh and her conduct is shameful in the extreme.[2]

God's faithfulness to His covenant was unquestionable; there was no evil in Him that He should be abandoned by the house of Jacob. The "house of Jacob" (v. 4) and the "house of Israel" (5:15) normally refer to the entire Jewish nation, but depending on the context these terms may only speak of Judah (i.e. that part of the Jewish nation still in the land, as the Northern Kingdom was in exile at this time). Like the Northern Kingdom, Judah was also guilty of deserting Jehovah and His way. They were venturing down a pathway of vanity and pride to their own destruction (v. 5). God had kept His word and greatly blessed the Jews. He had brought them from Egypt to a fruitful land, which was not originally theirs (v. 7). But the Jews had defiled the land that God had graciously bestowed to them; they had polluted it with abominations and idolatries.

Yet, because of His covenant, Jehovah would protect Israel from annihilation, even though they deserved His wrath (v. 3). The nations which oppose Israel and her scattered people should heed this warning! Zechariah proclaimed, *"For thus says the Lord of hosts: 'He sent Me after glory, to the nations which plunder you; for he who touches you touches the apple of His eye'"* (Zech. 2:8). The Jews are the apple of God's eye and any nation which persecutes the Jews will ultimately be judged by God.

The Lord had provided Judah with priests, leaders, and prophets that they might have the means to know divine truth, experience His grace, and enjoy His communion. Yet, these human instruments were guilty of great offenses. Four classes of people are specifically identified and rebuked in verse eight: the priests, those who handled the law (scribes, who also belonged to the priestly class), the shepherds of Israel, and the prophets. God knew His people, but His people no longer knew Him or called upon Him. Instead, they prophesied in Baal's name and wasted time doing things which had no profit. The Lord would severely judge those who had neglected to care for His people properly.

Although God was grieved over the rejection of His people, He pled with them to return to Him and He would continue to do so from generation to generation (v. 9). The longsuffering nature of God is a good reminder to us to continue to plead with those who have stumbled morally or who have displaced God with vain activities. Paul exhorts, *"Brethren, if a man is overtaken in any trespass, you who are spiritual restore such a one in a spirit of gentleness, considering yourself lest you also be tempted"* (Gal. 6:1). It should be the desire of every believer not to allow fallen soldiers of the Cross to remain missing in action, but rather to remind them of God's goodness and their need for restoration with Him. The believer will be miserable if he or she is out of fellowship with God.

Jeremiah rebukes Judah, declaring that no *pagan* nation would ever exchange their gods for gods that were not their own (vv. 10-11). The word "Kedar" indicated the lands to the East, the isles of Kittim (Cyprus), the West, meaning that if one transversed all the regions from the East to the West, one would not find another nation guilty of such apostasy. The Jews had once been a glorious people, but now they had become unprofitable; they had traded their prosperity, God's reward for their obedience, for the destruction which always accompanies idolatry. God was appalled by Israel's rebellion, the consequence of which would be their desolation (v. 12). The heathen blindly worshipped their idols, but the Jews had left the one true living God to bow down before images of wood, metal, and stone.

21

God was gone from their midst and they did not even miss Him or the blessings associated with His presence.

It is important that we as believers keep a biblical perspective of our relationship with the Lord, otherwise our intimacy with Him will slip. First, we must understand that the only reason we know God and are able to love Him is because we were first known by Him and have experienced His love: *"But if anyone loves God, this one is known by Him"* (1 Cor. 8:3); *"We love Him, because He first loved us"* (1 Jn. 4:19). Second, the security of our relationship with God rests, thankfully, in the fact that He knows us: *"But then, indeed, when you did not know God, you served those which by nature are not gods. But now after you have known God, or rather are known by God, how is it that you turn again to the weak and beggarly elements, to which you desire again to be in bondage?"* (Gal. 4:8-10). Though we may temporarily forget the Lord, it is impossible for Him to forget us and we should understand that He will not allow us to remain in that state of fruitlessness. We must abide in Him to experience His joy, peace, and power.

When the Lord Jesus first appeared to His disciples as a collective group on resurrection day, the first words from His lips were, *"Peace be unto you"* (Jn. 20:19). Two verses later, He used the exact same expression again, this time with a lesson adjoined: *"Peace be to you; as My Father has sent Me, even so send I you."* Why did the Lord Jesus repeat His own words? He was acknowledging that the only way one can obtain peace with God is through Himself; likewise, He is the only way one can acquire the divine peace necessary to practically represent Him in the world. If the unsaved are going to be brought to Christ, they must see Christ's peace within our lives. We must know Him and abide with Him to experience His peace. Do you know the presence and peace of Christ?

Hudson Taylor, a pioneer missionary to China, was once asked by an undergraduate student at a training conference, "Are you always conscious of abiding in Christ?" "While sleeping last night," he replied, "did I cease to abide in your house because I was unconscious of the fact? We should never be conscious of not abiding in Christ." In other words, we should be so near to the Lord, that there is never a time that we are conscious of being out of His presence. Accordingly, when he was asked how he could speak at so many different meetings, Taylor responded, "Every morning I feed upon the Word of God, then I pass on through the day messages that have first helped me in my own soul."[3] Hudson's ongoing communion with the Lord was his only source of strength to serve Him. To forget the Lord and His goodness is the first step into a life of emptiness. We need His abiding presence, and He appreciates someone to abide with too.

Meditation

> I need Thee every hour, in joy or pain;
> Come quickly and abide, or life is in vain.
> I need Thee, Oh, I need Thee; every hour I need Thee;
> Oh, bless me now, my Saviour, I come to Thee.

> — Annie Hawks

Forsaken
Jeremiah 2:13-37

Brilliant people sometimes forget elementary things. The famous physicist Albert Einstein once forgot his home address after moving to the Institute for Advanced Study in Princeton, NJ; he had to phone a dean for help. The great inventor Thomas Edison once forgot his own name while standing in line at a financial institution to pay his property taxes; unable to settle his account on time, he received a stiff penalty for the amount past due. Putting proper names and street addresses aside, how can a once God-fearing people forget their God? With a more modern application, we might ask: why do nations which were founded on the teachings of Christ now forsake Him for humanism? What causes a nation who at one time put "In God We Trust" on their currency to trust in themselves and, in time, abandon God? Is it possible for any one man to turn such a nation back to God? This was Jeremiah's seemingly impossible task. Matthew Henry describes the spiritually bankrupt condition of the Jewish nation that had forgotten the Lord:

> Having forsaken God, though they soon found that they had changed for the worse, yet they had no thoughts of returning to Him again, nor took any steps towards it. Neither the people nor the priests made any inquiry after Him, to any thought about their duty to Him, nor expressed any desire to recover His favor.[1]

One can only wonder whether this 18th century Presbyterian minister would say the same thing of the modern Church, if he still were alive. When God's Word is not revered, when it is of little importance to those who identify with Christ, an immoral, lethargic, carnal Church is the result. As the Jews would learn, there are deep consequences for forsaking the Lord. Regrettably, it is only those who are near to the Lord who dread this condition; the remainder need extreme measures to be awakened from their spiritual slumber.

Jeremiah used the expression "you have forsaken" four times in the first two chapters of this book (1:19, 2:13, 17, 19) before switching to the phrase "you have forgotten," which he used twice (2:32, 3:21). The progression is important to note – forsaking the Lord leads to forgetting Him. The Jews had not just recently deserted their God; the Lord bemoaned that He had been forgotten days without number (v. 32). Jeremiah identified four forsaking activities which eventually resulted in the Jewish nation forgetting Him altogether.

The first action of forsaking was that the Jews gave their loyalty and devotion to false gods of wood and stone (v. 27). They turned from Jehovah to worship the works of their own hands. The Jews created not just one or two false gods, but many; they were as numerous as the cities in Judah (v. 28). It is one thing to be a pagan; it is an entirely different matter to be a pagan after having known the one true God, experienced His goodness, seen His glory, and received His promises. The worst part of it was that the Jews did not even miss Jehovah's presence; it was an offense worthy of immense judgment. God loved His people too much to allow them to continue living a vain existence. In application, we recall that an idol is anything that draws us away from the Lord; believers should be wary of them, especially of those things which are associated with the doings of our own hands.

Israel's first error centered in misplaced affections; their second step in forsaking the Lord was to seek satisfaction from that which could never satisfy. Broken cisterns can neither hold water nor supply it when needed. The "broken cisterns" spoken of in this chapter refer to Judah's idolatry (vv. 12-13) and to the foreign alliances they had established in an attempt to insure their protection (vv. 17-18). Idols would not provide Judah with spiritual power, and alliances with other nations would not protect them against God's judgment. They had forsaken God, *the fountain of living water* (v. 13), seeking rather to be satisfied by the Nile (i.e. their alliance and friendship with Egypt). Such behavior from His people always provokes God's chastening hand.

At Calvary, Christ died and passed out of this world. Three days later His body was raised from the grave. The Lord Jesus was then

25

highly exalted by His Father to the right hand of majesty on high (Heb. 1:3). The world crucified His Son, and thus Christ is no longer in the world – to enjoy spiritual life with Him we must by faith come along to where He is. Believers are privileged to sit at His table, and to receive from Him and commune with Him there (1 Cor. 10:16-21). How offensive it must be to the Lord Jesus to desert Him in order to party in the world with demons. Paul warns, *"You cannot drink the cup of the Lord and the cup of demons; you cannot partake of the Lord's table and of the table of demons. Or do we provoke the Lord to jealousy? Are we stronger than He?"* (1 Cor. 10:21-22). In principle, the Jews had committed the same offense in Jeremiah's day. They had forgotten how Jehovah labored to deliver them from Egypt and how He had satisfied them at His table in the wilderness centuries earlier. Throughout Scripture, Egypt is commonly used to symbolize the world; "the way of Egypt," then, denotes worldliness. Jehovah's fellowship with His people was a private matter and solicitations from Egypt (i.e. the world) would not be allowed to interfere with His fellowship with them.

In their unhappy downward progression of forsaking the Lord, the third slip the Jews had was that they rejected God's way of righteousness for the way of Egypt (vv. 18, 36). The Jews had tasted of the Lord and His goodness, yet departed from Him to indulge in the filth of the world (vv. 17-18). They were no longer satisfied with heavenly provisions and divine communion, but rather lusted after what God had prohibited them from having.

The fourth and final indictment, *"you have forsaken the Lord"* (v. 19), is tied to Judah's lack of fear for Jehovah. The fear of the Lord involves a proper understanding of who God is and a proper reverence for Him. This was sorely lacking among the people, and was a matter that would presently be remedied by devastating judgments – God would soon have their respect again. To summarize these four "forsaking" sins, the Jews had misplaced affection, they were looking for satisfaction in other sources than God, they were misdirected from the way of righteousness, and displayed disrespect for God Himself.

The Jews were immersed in sin, but they denied their polluted condition (v. 23). In response, Jeremiah told them that even if they used a strong detergent made from *natron*, an alkaline mineral found in the Nile valley, or *sope* (now called "potash" because it is an alkali compound derived from the ashes of plants), they would not be able to bleach out the stains of their apostasy (v. 22). God knew all about Judah's sins. He stated that He had smitten their children in an attempt to gain their attention, but they would not repent (v. 30). God also sent prophets to call Judah to repentance, but they murdered His messengers (v. 30). And yet, they were righteous in their own eyes and proclaimed their innocence before God (v. 35). Because the Jews had drifted so far from God, they had no true reckoning of their spiritual state.

Measure your growth in grace by your sensitivity to sin.

— Oswald Chambers

Our sense of sin is in proportion to our nearness to God.

— Thomas Bernard

The Jews had slipped so far away from the Lord that they could obtain no bearing of righteousness on their spiritual compass. Like many in Christendom today, the Jews thought they were good people, but had no idea what "goodness" really was.

In verse 21, God says that He had planted Israel as a noble vine (a holy nation), but they had degenerated into a strange vine. The Jews had broken their promise of faithfulness to Jehovah and played the harlot with false gods (v. 20). Consequently, there was no fellowship between Jehovah and His people; in fact, they had become strangers to Him.

In days long past, Moses, just before his death, reminded the people of God's Law and the lessons that they had learned through their wilderness experience with God. Moses knew the rebellious nature of God's covenant people and severely threatened them with destruction if they forsook the Lord:

The Lord will send on you cursing, confusion, and rebuke in all that you set your hand to do, until you are destroyed and until you perish quickly, because of the wickedness of your doings in which you have forsaken Me. The Lord will make the plague cling to you until He has consumed you from the land which you are going to possess (Deut. 28:20-21).

Centuries later, the prophet Isaiah resounded the warning, saying, *"They that forsake the Lord shall be consumed"* (Isa. 1:28). Now, just two generations later, God's anger could no longer be tempered with mercy, and Jeremiah declares, *"Your own wickedness will correct you, and your backslidings will rebuke you. Know therefore and see that it is an evil and bitter thing that you have forsaken the Lord your God"* (Jer. 2:19). Moses had warned them, *"You have sinned against the Lord and be sure your sin will find you out"* (Num. 32:23). A forsaken God would not forsake His people, and His raised rod would be the proof of His love for them (Heb. 12:6).

The English word "backsliding" occurs thirteen times in the book of Jeremiah and is rendered from three Hebrew words *meshuwbah* (noun), *showbab* (adjective), and *showbeb* (adjective), which are all drawn from the same root *shuwb*, a verb which implies the action of sliding backward. The first reference is found in Jeremiah 2:19. Considering there are only eighteen occurrences of these three Hebrew words in the entire Bible, its frequent usage in Jeremiah is significant. As mentioned in the previous chapter, the number thirteen is used metaphorically in the Bible to speak of rebellion. It should be noted that God never referred to His people as "being backslidden," instead, when appropriate, He said His people were "backsliding;" it is an action and not a state. Backsliding is not a matter of ignorance; rather, it results when God's people willfully and actively turn from understood truth. Backsliding, then, is a conscious choice of a child of God to discontinue fellowship with God, to become fruitless, and to invite God's chastening hand.

The writer of Hebrews conveys the same truth to believers in the Church Age:

> *For it is impossible for those who were once enlightened, and have tasted the heavenly gift, and have become partakers of the Holy Spirit, and have tasted the good word of God and the powers of the age to come, if they fall away, to renew them again to repentance, since they crucify again for themselves the Son of God, and put Him to an open shame* (Heb. 6:4-6).

This passage can be difficult to understand; however, as we will see, a look at the original language of the text indicates the writer is saying that as long as someone willfully chooses to fall away (backslide), it would be impossible to renew that person through repentance to a state of spiritual fruitfulness. In fact, trying to please God while in such a rebellious state mocks the power of the Lord's redemptive blood and puts Him to open shame. All of the Greek verbs in Hebrews 6:4, "enlightened," "tasted," and "become partakers" are aorist passive participles, which indicates that these actions have already occurred. The word "tasted" is exactly the same Greek verb used in Hebrews 2:9 to acknowledge the fact that Christ tasted death for every man; the word does not denote a partial experience, but a complete one. The Greek word for "enlightened" is the same one translated as "illuminated" in Hebrews 10:32, where it is employed to speak of the spiritual sight God gives to believers. The third Greek word in this description, "partakers," is rendered "companion" in Hebrews 1:9 (NKJV). The meaning is much more absolute than just a taste of truth limited to some pre-conversion work of the Spirit. Hebrews 6:4 states that those who had tasted and were enlightened were also companions with the Holy Spirit – the writer was clearly speaking of believers.

Considering that the subject of this discussion is believers, not unsaved apostates, how are we to understand the statement that if these people fall away, it is impossible to renew them again to repentance? Again, a look at the original language of the passage aids in its understanding. In Hebrews 6:6, "falling away" is an aorist, active participle verb meaning that these backsliding believers caused themselves, as indicated by the active voice, to fall away in the past, and that condition still continued. The Greek verb *parapito*, not *apostasia*, is used in Hebrews 6:6 to indicate the action of falling. Its root *pipto* is employed to describe the Lord Jesus falling to the ground in the garden to pray (Mark 14:35). The remaining verbs translated "to renew," "they crucify again," "put Him to an open shame" are present, active participles which indicate an active, ongoing process is in view. If perfect tense verbs had been used, then the subject would be engaged in an "unchangeable activity," but the use of present tense verbs conveys the idea that as long as the subject engaged in the stated activities they would suffer ongoing consequences.

What the writer of Hebrews is saying is that as long as backsliding believers fall away, they actively put Christ to shame and cannot be brought to repentance or fruitfulness. One cannot turn back to the Lord (i.e. repent), if he or she is actively backsliding away from Him. Those living in a falling away spiritual condition are "near to cursing," but are not cursed (Heb. 6:8). Backsliding believers are not fruitful, nor can they be; yet, fruit *should* accompany salvation (Heb. 6:9). A believer in this condition has a burned up testimony which ruins their ministries and disgraces Christ (Heb. 6:8; John 15:4-6). Those who are actively falling away from the truth are said to be "rejected" according to Hebrews 6:8. The same word is translated "castaway" in 1 Corinthians 9:27 (KJV), where Paul was surely not speaking of losing his own salvation; rather, the term refers to the loss of one's testimony and one's opportunity for profitable ministry that occur as a result of giving in to the flesh nature. The bottom line: Any child of God who willfully forsakes the Lord will be miserable, fruitless, and cause the name of Christ to be disdained. James Vernon McGee writes the following on this passage:

> In Hebrews 6, we find genuine believers, because they are identified as such in many ways. ... You will notice that it is said of these people that they are dull of hearing (Heb. 5:11) – it does not say that they are dead in trespasses and sins (Eph. 2:1). And in Hebrews 5:12 it says that *"when for the time ye ought to be teachers, ye have need that one teach you...and are become such as have need of milk...."* They need to have milk because they are babes. An unsaved person doesn't need milk; he needs *life*. He needs to be born again.

> The whole tenor of the text reveals that he is speaking of rewards which are the result of salvation. In verse 6 he says, *"If they shall fall away, to renew them again unto repentance"* – not to salvation, but to *repentance*. Repentance is something that God has asked believers to do [e.g. the Lord told five of the seven churches of Asia Minor to repent (Rev. 2-3)]. So the writer of Hebrews is talking about the *fruit* of salvation, not about the *root* of salvation. Notice verse 9 again: *"But, beloved, we are persuaded better things of you. And things that accompany salvation"* [he hasn't been discussing salvation but the things that accompany salvation]... the whole

tenor of the passage is that he is warning them of the possibility of losing their reward.[2]

The Jews in Jeremiah's day were actively backsliding; they were forsaking the Lord and consequently fruitless. With this historical example in mind, Paul warned the Church against making the same mistake, using the figure of an olive tree whose branches were pruned away and other branches from a wild olive were grafted into it. If God did not spare the natural olive branches (speaking of rebellious Jews), how much more likely would He be to punish, as needed, the wild branches (i.e. Gentile believers) that were grafted into the blessings of the Abrahamic covenant (Rom. 11:17-21). God's severe dealings with His covenant people serves as a solemn warning for the Church to take heed and not to duplicate the backsliding ways of the Jewish nation. Our God is a consuming fire (Heb. 12:29), and He is very jealous of where we place our affections (1 Cor. 10:22). Thankfully, He loves us too much to permit us to forsake Him without consequences!

Meditation

Among the nations He shall judge; His judgments truth shall guide;
His scepter shall protect the just, and quell the sinner's pride.

— Michael Bruce

Roadside Lovers
Jeremiah 3:1-5

Jeremiah concluded his first message by acknowledging His people's obstinate persistence in sin and the gross nature of Judah's present harlotries. God's judgment was looming and Jeremiah was faithful to use both messages and prophetic illustrations to call the nation to repentance. Apparently, there was still time to return to the Lord (3:1, 12, 14, 22; 4:1, 4, 14; 5:1). Yet, this opportunity seems to have been lost by Jeremiah's third message beginning in chapter 7. God instructs Jeremiah, *"Therefore do not pray for this people, nor lift up a cry or prayer for them, nor make intercession to Me; for I will not hear you"* (7:16). The people refused to receive divine correction and return to God (5:3), therefore, He was determined to punish them.

E. Paul Hovey once wrote that sin has four characteristics: "self-sufficiency instead of faith; self-will instead of submission; self-seeking instead of benevolence; self-righteousness instead of humility."[1] It is observed in Jeremiah 2 that the Jews exhibited each of these four qualities of sin. They were self-sufficient (2:31), self-willed (2:18), self-seeking (2:25), and self-righteous (2:23, 35). In Jeremiah 3, the Jews are likened to a harlot who sits by the roadside eagerly waiting for anyone to venture by her. No questions were asked; any act of spiritual harlotry was acceptable, and repeated occurrences were customary. Spiritual union with any false god was the status quo. As a result, the land was full of spiritual uncleanness and immorality (v. 2). As G. Campbell Morgan explains, this is the natural fallout of idolatry:

> When a man makes a god according to the pattern of his own being, he makes a god like himself, an enlargement of his own imperfection. Moreover, the god which a man makes for himself

will demand from him that which is according to his own nature. It is clearly evident in Mohammedanism. Great and wonderful and outstanding in his personality as Mohammed was, yet the blighting sensuality of the man curses the whole of Islam today. Men will be faithful to those gods who make no demands upon them which are out of harmony with the desires of their own hearts.

When God calls men, it is the call of the God of holiness, the God of purity, the God of love; and He demands that they rise to His height. He cannot accommodate Himself to the depravity of their nature. He will not consent to the things of desire within them that are of impurity and evil. He calls men up, and even higher, until they reach the height of perfect conformity to His holiness. God's call to humanity is always first pure, and then peaceable; first holy, and then happy; first righteous, and then rejoicing."[2]

At the beginning of Jeremiah's second message, God asked Jeremiah a question: "Do you see the backsliding of Israel?" The Hebrew noun *meshuwbah*, rendered "backsliding," is quite strong; it describes the Jews as a "turning away" people and is synonymous with "apostasy" in the New Testament, which means "to forsake" or "to fall away" in an ongoing manner. The severity of their sin explains the acuteness of Israel's judgment. Previously, Jeremiah informed the Jews that God had punished them by smiting their children (2:30). At this time he said that God had also withheld rain from them (v. 3). Yet, God's correction had been ignored.

Spiritually speaking, Judah was a married woman who shamelessly slept with anybody and then publicly bragged about it without any regard for the hurt and disgrace she was causing her husband. The Law forbade a divorced wife from returning to her previous husband after being joined to another man (v. 1), but Judah had no remorse about being blatantly unfaithful to Jehovah and then returning to Him under false pretense (i.e. in religious rote only).

This text can be better understood by considering the actions of Judah, the head of this tribe, centuries earlier. In Genesis 38, we read that Judah, the fourth son of Jacob, had isolated himself from his brethren and married a Canaanite woman, who gave him three sons. Judah gave his oldest son in marriage to another Canaanite woman named Tamar. But he was a wicked man and God slew him. Judah then gave his second son to Tamar in marriage, but God slew him also. Judah's third son was too young to marry at the time so Judah instructed Tamar to wait in her father's house, in widow's attire, until his youngest son was of marrying age. However, Judah did not keep his promise to Tamar.

Seeing that she had been lied to, Tamar played the harlot to obtain her right and opportunity to bear children in the name of her husband. Tamar knew that Judah had gone to Timnah to shear sheep and that his own wife had just died. She used this information to selectively lure Judah to lie with her by masquerading as a prostitute. Her plot worked. Judah agreed to the price of her services (a young goat) and presented her with a pledge that he would pay her the agreed price. His pledge was his seal that hung about his neck on a cord and his staff. Tamar knew that, if she was not to be put to death for fornication, she would need recognizable proof of the identity of the man who was responsible for her pregnancy.

Although we do not approve of Tamar's actions, she was no mere prostitute for hire. She simply wanted her entitlement. So after their encounter, she returned home without collecting the goat kid. Judah sent the goat via a friend to where Tamar had been posing as a temple prostitute, but the friend could not find her, and the inhabitants of the area did not know of any harlots in that place. Not only was Judah a liar (Gen. 38:11, 14), and immoral (Gen. 38:16), but now he would also be shown to be a hypocrite.

The Hebrew word *qedeshah* means "devoted one" and is used three times in Genesis 38:21-22 to describe what Judah and his Adullimite friend believed Tamar to be – a temple prostitute. *Qedeshah* is used to describe a harlot engaged in pagan rituals in Hosea 4:14. Claus Westermann notes, "Religious prostitution had played a role among the peoples of the Near East from ancient times."[3] In the ancient Near East, it was customary in many places for married women to give themselves to strangers because of some kind of religious pagan oath. This is slightly different than ordinary prostitution. Both types were strictly forbidden later by the Law of Moses.[4] Because Tamar was standing by the road and had her face covered, Judah thought her to be a harlot (Gen. 38:15). The appearance of a harlot on the roadside was obviously not a surprising spectacle. Tamar is not posing as a common prostitute, but rather a married woman indulging in the practice of cult prostitution (i.e. temple prostitutes were veiled, while common harlots were not). This is affirmed by the use of *qedeshah* to describe Tamar as the "devoted one."[5]

Judah was ready to have Tamar burned alive when he found out that she was pregnant three months later. Legally, she was under his authority, engaged to Shelah, and guilty of adultery. But his rage soon turned to guilt when he learned that she was his mystery harlot and was carrying his baby (actually, babies – twins). Judah confirmed that he had been the dishonest one, and Tamar was acquitted on the matter.

Just as Judah had carelessly lain with a supposed Canaanite temple prostitute, his descendants, centuries later, were continuing in frivolous religious harlotries. Judah had been self-reliant, self-seeking, and self-righteous, yet after his sin was exposed, he did acknowledge his wrongdoing. His descendants, however, had no intention of relinquishing their harlotries – they enjoyed their sin and were proud of it. What was initially the character weakness of one man, Judah, had in time become widespread sin within an entire tribe.

In the time of Jeremiah, the people of the tribe of Judah cried out to God as a familiar friend and begged Him to cease being angry with them, but their words were hollow. Jehovah would not be manipulated by pleasant words; He wanted a change of heart. Love is motivated by what is best for another, and in this situation, genuine love required stern measures, not pity. Wrongly applied pity endorses sin, and Jehovah is not a sin-enabling God.

For those of us who are parents, this story serves as a good reminder that many of the bents we observe in our children are merely learned behaviors that they have witnessed in us. We often joke about idioms such as: "the apple didn't fall far from the tree" or "like father, like son," but the fact of the matter is that our sin has consequences that affect our children. The more they witness the righteousness of Christ, His will, and His sufficiency in us, the more they should want to seek after Him also. Staying near and dear to the Lover of our souls will keep us from being abused by roadside lovers (i.e. idols in our hearts).

Meditation

God of all power, and truth, and grace, which shall from age to age endure,
Whose Word, when heaven and earth shall pass, remains and stands forever sure;
Purge me from every sinful blot; my idols all be cast aside;
Cleanse me from every sinful thought, from all the filth of self and pride.
Give me a new, a perfect heart, from doubt, and fear, and sorrow free;
The mind which was in Christ impart, and let my spirit cleave to Thee.

— Charles Wesley

Two Sisters
Jeremiah 3:6-25

Jeremiah's second message (3:6-6:30) reinforced the conclusions of his first message. Both messages were delivered early in Jeremiah's ministry and during the early reforms of Josiah, but before the Book of the Law was found in the Temple and read to the king and the people. Though Josiah's initial reforms were honorable, there cannot be a true revival in the hearts of men unless it is rooted in God's Word. The first message confirmed that Judah had forsaken God's way; the second message would use a familiar analogy to summon her to repentance.

The story pertains to two sisters, Israel and Judah. Both had pledged their loyalty to Jehovah through a marriage covenant. Israel was the first of the sisters to commit fornication. She embraced false gods and worshipped their idols in various high places throughout the northern kingdom. The cover of every green tree became the canopy over her bed of adultery (v. 6). God called Israel to repentance, but she would not forsake her idols and return to Him. God responded by writing her a bill of divorcement and sending her away to Assyria in 722 B.C. (v. 8).

Even though the other sister, Judah, had witnessed firsthand God's harsh judgment of Israel, she also committed spiritual fornication by worshipping images of stone and wood (vv. 7-9). But as Jeremiah explains, God was more angry with Judah than He had been with Israel:

> "So it came to pass, through her [Israel's] casual harlotry, that she defiled the land and committed adultery with stones and trees. And yet for all this her treacherous sister Judah has not turned to Me with her whole heart, but in pretense," says the Lord. Then the Lord said to me, "Backsliding Israel has shown herself more righteous than treacherous Judah" (Jer. 3:9-11).

Judah would experience greater judgment than Israel did, for two reasons. First, Judah, having seen the harsh consequences of the sin of adultery, deliberately chose to be unfaithful despite this understanding. Second, Israel was blatantly idolatrous, but two-faced Judah embraced other lovers while still sweet-talking the Lord with vain pleasantries. The people of Judah acted religious, but their hearts were not with God. They pretended to be devout but embraced pagan gods whenever they thought they could get away with it. Israel did not try to hide her adultery, but Judah disguised her treachery in order to appear righteous; thus, she deserved greater judgment.

Which of us would have any compassion on an adulterous wife that continually and willfully broke the heart of her husband? "She deserves whatever she gets!" would be the response of most of us. Yet, before rebuking Judah's treachery too loudly, we should examine ourselves to ensure that we are not making the same mistake. On this matter, H. A. Ironside provides the Church with something to think about:

> Backsliding was not so much her [Judah's] continual sin as was her treachery. A strict attention to the outward ordinances of the temple worship, but the heart going after the filthiness of the nations, was generally her course; as it had been even in the days of Solomon – who built the house of Jehovah, and erected altars to the gods of his heathen wives! This is what markedly characterizes much of what is called Christendom today. There is talk of devotedness to the Lord, a prating of loyalty to Christ; but alas, how little is known of separation from that which dishonors Him. In fact, the position of Jeremiah in this book must be very much that of the man today who would stand for Christ and walk in the truth.[1]

Having seen God's stern dealings with Israel for idolatry and with Judah for religious fraud, this author wonders how much longer the Lord will tolerate the same in Christendom today.

The Lord Jesus once encountered a group of self-righteous, religious zealots who were demanding the death of a woman caught in the act of adultery. Their demands were hypocritical; the fact that the guilty man had been set free demonstrated their lack of reverence for God's Law (Deut. 22:22-24). The Lord told them, *"He who is without sin among you, let him throw a stone at her first"* (John 8:7). He successfully appealed to their consciences, and they all departed from the guilty woman. It is relatively easy for us in the Church Age to fling a cold stone at adulterous Judah and miss the application of the illustration. Do we allow idols in our hearts to displace our love for the Lord Jesus? Do we flirt with the world and feast on immoral things, and then draw near to our Lord and pray sweet-nothings into His ear, fully playing the part of a chaste virgin awaiting her wedding day? Is our bridal attire stained with unconfessed sin and religious pride?

The immense love of God for His covenant people, even in their backsliding condition, is shown five times in Jeremiah 3 in His call for the Jewish nation to repent and to be restored to Him (vv. 12-14, 20-24). While the message is directed at Judah, God still longed to be reunited with Israel also, even after a hundred years of dispersion and captivity. Both the marital relationship (v. 12) and the parent-child relationship (v. 14) are used by the Lord to convey to the Jews a twofold certainty of their relational acceptance with Him, though their sinful practices had severed their fellowship. Although their hearts were not with Jehovah, God's heart was still with them, as Isaiah informed Israel:

> *You whom I have taken from the ends of the earth, and called from its farthest regions, and said to you, 'You are My servant, I have chosen you and have not cast you away: Fear not, for I am with you; be not dismayed, for I am your God. I will strengthen you, yes, I will help you, I will uphold you with My righteous right hand'* (Isa. 41:9-10).

In application, the same truth of security exists for all true Christians, though the enjoyment of our relationship with Christ is dependent on our behavior. Sometimes it seems as if the Lord is far away, but when we come to our senses and turn back to Him, we find that He was right there with us all along. The abiding presence of the Lord Jesus Christ is a great defense against entering into sin. His nearness repels evil from our minds and strengthens our wherewithal to overcome the lusting of our flesh. Frustration, edginess, and anxiety are warning signs that we have lost His presence of mind and that we need to realign our thinking with His in order to gain His peace again.

Jeremiah affirms that Israel will again enjoy this situation in the future Kingdom Age: *"At that time Jerusalem shall be called The Throne of the Lord, and all the nations shall be gathered to it, to the name of the Lord, to Jerusalem. No more shall they follow the dictates of their evil hearts"* (v. 17). At that time, Jeremiah says, Jerusalem shall be called the throne of Jehovah and all the nations shall be gathered to it. The Lord Jesus is the only one entitled to a universal spiritual monarchy. He will have this kingdom upon the earth: Jerusalem, His center, and all the nations, His sphere.

Presently, the Lord sits on His Father's throne (Rev. 3:21) and waits to receive His bride. After the Church is with Christ in heaven, He shall return to earth at the end of the Tribulation Period to defeat the Antichrist and his armies who gather to battle Israel (Zech. 14; Rev. 19). Shortly after this battle, Christ will separate those who are able to enter His kingdom from those who cannot; this is called the Judgment of Nations (Matt. 13:47-50, 25:31-47; Rev. 19:21). Then, the Lord Jesus will establish His righteous kingdom on the earth. Satan and demonic forces will be contained within the bottomless pit during this one thousand-year period (Rev. 20:1-3), and the world will be governed by Christ from Jerusalem (Isa. 60:12-14, 66:10-14; Zech. 14:9). The curse that was placed on the earth in Adam's day will be lifted and the earth will be returned to her full fruitfulness (Ps. 72:16; Isa. 11:1-10; Rom. 8:18-22). Peace, prosperity, righteousness, justice, holiness, and the glory of God will be known throughout the planet.

During the Kingdom Age, the Jews may remember the tabernacle and temple, but they will not place any value on these, for a mere type cannot surpass its antitype, the real thing. Christ will be known as the fulfillment of all the Feasts of Jehovah, every article of priestly attire, each sacrifice and offering, every aspect and furnishing of the tabernacle/temple. The spiritual realities conveyed through these Old Testament patterns will be understood and appreciated – Christ's character and work will be vindicated, and all His enemies will know that He is the eternal Son of God. He who has already been highly exalted and has a name above all others will be honored by all who remain on the earth!

Jeremiah prophesied that Judah and Israel will no longer be two nations when they come into their inheritance in Christ's Kingdom, but that they would be one (v. 18). Isaiah foretold the same event (Isa. 11:12), as did the prophet Ezekiel (Ezek. 37:16-21), Ezekiel adding that at the restoration the united nation would be called "Israel." These prophecies refer to God's dealings with the Jews just prior to and then during the millennial kingdom, when Christ will rule over them as their king (Ezek. 37:22). Accordingly, as we approach the end of the Church Age, the initiation of these prophecies will be apparent, especially the regathering of Jews back into the land of Israel after centuries of global exile. Recent events seem to indicate that God has begun the process of bringing His covenant people home.

On May 14, 1948, while Egyptian fighter-bombers flew overhead and the last remaining British troops prepared to depart Palestine, Ben Gurion and his cabinet gathered at the Tel Aviv Museum where they proclaimed the independence of the state of Israel. After nearly 2,600 years of being a dispersed people scattered throughout the world, the miracle birth of the Jewish nation occurred. Considering most conquered or displaced people simply blend into the fabric of the society that is forced upon them, the fact that the Jews maintained their distinction as God's covenant people for all that time is miraculous.

The Jews formed one autonomous state called "Israel," just as the Bible had foretold. The next day, the armies of Egypt, Transjordan, Iraq, Syria, and Lebanon invaded Israel and the War of Independence began. Israel emerged victorious, but not without great cost. Thousands of Israeli and Arab soldiers died and approximately 600,000 Palestinians fled their homes, thus creating a "refugee problem" that continues to trouble the region to this day.[2] Isaiah prophesied that the nations would marvel that such a feat could happen in a day (Isa. 66:7-9). This event occurs shortly before the initiation of Christ's millennial kingdom (Isa. 66:10-18).

The chapter closes with Jeremiah's prayer of confession. Like Daniel (Dan. 9:5) and other prophets, Jeremiah identified himself with his backsliding people, confesses their sins as his own before God, and hoped for national repentance. He knew that idolatry was unprofitable (v. 23), indeed ruinous (v. 24), but he prayed as one

41

among many needy souls. Judah's continued sin against the Lord had resulted in their confusion and shame: *"Righteousness exalts a nation, but sin is a reproach to any people"* (Prov. 14:34). A nation that rebels against the Lord cannot expect His blessing and a nation that does so under the guise of reverence should anticipate His condemnation.

Meditation

> Thy righteous judgment, Thou hast said, shall in due time appear,
> And Thou Who didst establish it will fill the earth with fear.
> Jehovah holds a cup of wrath, and holds it not in vain,
> For all the wicked of the earth its bitter dregs shall drain.
> The God of Israel I will praise and all His glory show;
> The righteous He will high exalt and bring the wicked low.

> — From Ps. 75 (unknown author)

Break Up Your Fallow Ground
Jeremiah 4:1-3

The phrase "fallow ground" is found only twice in the entire Bible, in this chapter and also in Hosea 10. Both Jeremiah and Hosea had similar prophetic ministries, though Hosea preceded Jeremiah by a century. According to Hosea 1:1, this prophet ministered to Israel during the reigns of four Judean kings and during the reign of Jeroboam II in Israel. Throughout this time, he continued to warn idolatrous Israel of the captivity that would be forthcoming, unless they repented. After the Assyrian invasion of Israel, Hosea continued to encourage the survivors.

A century later, God spoke through Jeremiah with a call of repentance that was not only to the Southern Kingdom of Judah, but also the house of Israel; they were instructed to forsake their idols and return to Him (v. 1). Doing so would result in God's blessing (v. 2). Unfortunately, the preaching of Jeremiah, and other prophets such as Habakkuk and Zephaniah, was largely rejected; the result was that Judah experienced similar repercussions under the hand of the Babylonians as Israel had suffered earlier from the Assyrians. Like Israel, Judah had refused to break up their fallow ground as well.

Israel had been unfaithful to Jehovah and had forsaken Him for other lovers. God's anguish over the matter is conveyed through the allegory of Hosea's experiences with his own adulterous wife Gomer. In many respects, Hosea was made to feel the pain Jehovah suffered because of the desertion of His people. Hosea's plea to the nation of Israel was heartfelt and genuine:

Sow for yourselves righteousness; reap in mercy; break up your fallow ground, for it is time to seek the Lord, till He comes and rains righteousness on you. You have plowed wickedness; you have reaped iniquity. You have eaten the fruit of lies, because you trusted

43

in your own way, in the multitude of your mighty men (Hos. 10:12-13).

The Jews were a nation composed of shepherds and farmers. So when Hosea sternly warned them to plow up their fallow ground, they knew what he meant. Fallow ground is soil that was once cultivated, but now lies waste and is completely fruitless. The longer it remains uncultivated, the harder it becomes. In order for it to be made profitable again it must be broken up with a plow; only then can it be planted again and made fruitful. The purpose of the soil analogy was to call Israel to repentance.

Jeremiah's message to adulterous Judah, though very similar to Hosea's, contained the additional warning against sowing among thorns (v. 3). In Matthew 13, the Lord Jesus likened the ground in which seed (identified as the Word of God) is sown to the spiritual disposition of various human hearts. In the same parable the Lord used the imagery of thorny ground to describe how worldliness chokes out the impact of God's Word in a person's life (i.e. the acceptance of the gospel message). A similar spiritual consequence is true for believers also; lingering complacency to obey God's Word causes our hearts to become hard, cold, and dry; the only solution is to plow them up. Living under the shade of briars and thistles will block the light necessary for growth and fruit-bearing; it will amount to a wasted existence. For revival to occur in the Church we must be open to God's Word and shun worldliness. God's Word must penetrate our minds and take root before we can bear fruit. Revival must start in the Church before it can spill over and affect the unregenerate. Much of the Church today has become unprofitable. If there was ever a time for spiritual revival within the House of God, it is now; Oh God, may it start with me!

Speaking of the Jews, H. A. Ironside concludes, "No real fruit for God could be expected where they were sowing on unbroken and thorn-choked ground (4:3). The plowshare of conviction must overturn the hardened soil of the heart."[1] How can the heart be spiritually plowed? First, each believer must examine his or her own heart to determine his or her own spiritual state. Second, we must ask the Holy Spirit to search our hearts and expose sin, whether it be hidden or blatant, sins of commission and sins of omission. Hidden sins might include pride, hypocrisy, unloving attitudes, and disrespect for God's order and authority. Sins of omission may include a lethargic prayer-life, an absence of faith, a lack of concern for the lost, or a deficiency of love for the Church. All sin grieves the Lord, but His dealings with Israel and Judah show us that when His people engage in willful sin without guilt or remorse, He is moved to severe measures to correct the problem.

The story of Hosea and Gomer presents us with a vivid picture of how God is offended by the worldly indulgences of His people. Hosea was an honorable man, but his wife Gomer was lascivious and actually conceived children that were not Hosea's. In time, Gomer abandoned Hosea to pursue a fast-life with her various lovers. It was not long before Gomer found herself in a poor and desperate situation. Hosea demonstrated sacrificial love for Gomer and sent supplies to her. With Hosea looking on from a distance, his wife Gomer praised her lovers for the very provisions he had sent to assist her (Hosea 2:5-8). Later, Gomer was abandoned by her lovers and sold into slavery. The redeeming love of God is exemplified when Hosea bought his own adulterous wife during a public slave auction. After experiencing the magnitude of Hosea's love, she would never depart from him or play the harlot again.

Paul reminds believers that they are the espoused bride of the Lord Jesus (Eph. 5:22-25; 2 Cor. 11:2). If believers could understand Christ's redeeming love in even a small measure, they would not commit adultery by fraternizing with the world. In the face of such love, how could a person break the heart of God? The ideologies of the world oppose God and God opposes them. Gomer's lovers did not care for Gomer or about the pain they were causing Hosea; they used and abused Gomer until the thrill of the moment was gone. This was what the prodigal son learned in Luke 15; the world does not offer anything that has lasting value; it only takes what is valuable to God.

Worldliness is any sphere from which the Lord Jesus is excluded. James likens worldliness to the sin of spiritual adultery: *"Adulterers and adulteresses! Do you not know that friendship with the world is enmity with God? Whoever therefore wants to be a friend of the world makes himself an enemy of God"* (Jas. 4:4). Worldliness is the love of passing things, and things have no eternal value, except in how they are used to please God. Worldliness opposes God, and God hates it.

May the Church learn from Israel's and Judah's idolatrous past and not invoke the chastening hand of God – it is time to break up our fallow ground! *"Return, you backsliding children, and I will heal your backslidings"* (Jer. 3:22).

Meditation

With one consent we meekly bow beneath Thy chastening hand,
And, pouring forth confession meet, mourn with our mourning land;
With pitying eye behold our need, as thus we lift our prayer;
Correct us with Thy judgments, Lord, then let Thy mercy spare.

— John Hampden Gurney

Circumcise Yourself
Jeremiah 4:3-31

Two metaphors are used in this chapter to illustrate Judah's need for repentance: one, as previously discussed, is breaking up fallow ground; the other is circumcision. The Jews were still practicing male circumcision as a sign of the covenant God made with Abraham centuries earlier; however, their compliance with this was superficial, and did not reflect the condition of their hearts. To carry out the physical act of circumcision and yet neglect one's spiritual condition made a mockery of the symbol, in much the same way as adultery mocks a wedding band. The deeper ramifications of circumcision, as explained to Abraham in Genesis 17, had been largely lost.

In that chapter, Abraham was told that he would receive a token of the covenant God had made with him. Contrary, perhaps, to what the patriarch was expecting, the sign given was not a wonder in the sky or some spectacular miracle; it was circumcision. The chapter ends with 99-year-old Abraham, and all the males of his household, circumcised; in fact, the procedure was performed on the same day God had commanded it (Gen. 17:26-27). Paul tells us in Romans 4:11 that circumcision was *"a seal of the righteousness of the faith which he had yet being uncircumcised."* Circumcision was a token of Abraham's righteous standing gained by faith in God's promise. Abraham's descendants continued this symbolic ritual in acknowledgement of God's covenant with them.

Why would circumcision be given as a sign? What is the organ of the body that best identifies an individual as a man? Right – that's it. So, by stripping away a piece of foreskin from this organ, God was symbolizing the stripping away of an old identity. Abraham's new identity would remind him to rely on God; accordingly, the act of circumcision in Genesis 17 neatly corresponds with the name changes given in the same chapter: Abram became Abraham; Sarai became

47

Sarah. God was about to enact His covenant with them by giving them a son. It was only fitting that they realize their new identities as God's chosen people and as human instruments to bless the entire world. Abraham had already been declared just by God before male circumcision was instituted (Gen. 15:6; Rom. 4:11). However, the physical act would be a constant reminder to him to live a "circumcised life" before God (i.e. Abraham was to live by faith in accordance to revealed truth, rather than rely on his own wisdom and strength).

Unfortunately, by Jeremiah's day, circumcision had become merely a badge, a mark that identified the Jews as a distinct people. They were identified with Jehovah in name only, and thus much of the spiritual significance of circumcision had been lost. The same attitude existed during the Lord Jesus' sojourn on earth (John 7:21-23). The apostle Paul was led to affirm the deeper spiritual meaning behind the practice of circumcision: *"For he is not a Jew who is one outwardly, nor is circumcision that which is outward in the flesh; but he is a Jew who is one inwardly; and circumcision is that of the heart, in the Spirit, not in the letter; whose praise is not from men but from God"* (Rom. 2:28-29). Symbolically speaking, circumcision speaks of a life that has no confidence in the flesh (Phil. 3:3). To have no confidence in the flesh means to have no glory in it either. The circumcised life has an inner spiritual reality which is manifested in daily life. It is a quality of life that law-keeping could never accomplish; it requires nothing less than the power of God to live in such a way.

If Judah wanted God's blessing, they would need to quickly circumcise their hearts and return to Him. Jeremiah warned Judah that if they did not sincerely repent, God's fury would come upon them like fire (v. 4). He would bring an invader from the north to punish them (v. 6). Messengers from Dan (some Jews still remained in the far North of Israel) would send advance warning of the approaching Babylon army. The sound of alarm would be heard throughout Judah, but even though the people would flee to fortified cities (especially Jerusalem) they would not escape destruction (v. 5). Babylon, the destroyer of nations, would be like a devouring lion that has come up out of his thicket (v. 7). The land would be laid waste and the destroyed cities would remain uninhabited. Once God's fierce anger was unleashed, it would be relentless, even if the Jews wailed before Him in sackcloth (v.8). The devastation of the land would weigh especially heavy upon the king, his officials, the priests, and the false prophets, for they would be made to realize how they had failed to lead the people towards God (v. 9). A condensed version of Jeremiah's message would be this: "Now is the time to repent and turn to the Lord; later will be too late."

As Jeremiah became more fully aware of what God intended to do to Jerusalem, he became overwhelmed with sorrow. He cries out to the Lord, *"Ah, Lord God! Surely You have greatly deceived this people and Jerusalem, saying, 'You shall have peace,' whereas the sword reaches to the heart"* (v. 10). This is a difficult verse to understand. Obviously, God cannot sin and does not deceive anyone (Num. 23:19; Jas. 1:12), though at times He may not fully reveal a particular truth until He deems it necessary to do so (1 Cor. 2:8-9). So what is the proper interpretation of Jeremiah's statement? Jeremiah may have been complaining to God for allowing the false prophets to preach a message of peace to the people, or he may have thought that God had previously deceived him because the full ramifications of Judah's judgment had not been fully revealed to him. In either case, the fault was not with God, but rather with Jeremiah's comprehension of God's sovereign design in a difficult time.

Jeremiah's accusation is not explained, so we can only guess at what he meant by it. What is evident is that as he gained understanding of God's plan of judgment, his resolve to call Judah to repentance increased. Like Ezekiel, Jeremiah likened the coming Babylonian invasion force to the strong east winds that rolled off the hot desert (v. 11; Ezek. 17:10). These winds (the sirocco) withered vegetation and caused severe discomfort to humans and livestock. In four verses, each beginning with the phrase "I beheld," Jeremiah relates his vision of the forthcoming destruction of land, the cities, and the people of Judah and of the surrounding nations.

I beheld the earth, and indeed it was without form, and void; and the heavens, they had no light. I beheld the mountains, and indeed they trembled, and all the hills moved back and forth. I beheld, and indeed there was no man, and all the birds of the heavens had fled. I beheld, and indeed the fruitful land was a wilderness, and all its

49

cities were broken down at the presence of the Lord, by His fierce anger (Jer. 4:23-26).

The scene reminded Jeremiah of the chaotic state the world must have been in during its infancy. So catastrophic were God's actions that it seemed as if creation itself had been undone, that the commands of Genesis 1 had somehow been reversed. Imagine the effect that witnessing such a scene had upon God's prophet! Everything that he had been accustomed to was gone; that is, except his God, who remains forever the same.

God was going to severely judge Judah's paganism. His wrath would be so extensive that there would be no place for the Jews to hide from it; not even rocky cliffs and dense thickets would provide adequate cover (v. 29). Paganism originated in Babylon and had spread into Judah, thus Jeremiah referred to the Babylonians as a past lover. Some in Judah would dress up like harlots and try to lure the Babylonians from their attack through flattery and enticing gestures. This ruse, however, would fail, for the Babylonians now despised Judah; they would not fall prey to her seductive trickery (v. 30).

But though the heavens would be blackened and the earth shaken with violence, God's mercy would temper His vengeance; He would not make a full end of Judah (v. 27). The reason for this is that, as of yet, He had not fulfilled many of His unconditional promises to Abraham. God called Abraham out of idolatry to be the father of a nation – His own people. Abraham's faith was demonstrated by obedience to this call, and God promised to give him a special son of promise, to make a nation from him, to give him a land, and, through him, to bless all the families of the earth (Gen. 12:1-3). To date, Israel has never obtained all of the land which God promised Abraham in Genesis 15, nor has He made an end of Israel's enemies. Yes, God would severely chasten His people by the hand of the Babylonians, but there is a coming day in which they will be fully restored to Him and greatly blessed – for God always keeps His promises.

Jeremiah's anxiety in this situation poses a good lesson for all believers to consider. Through sanctification, the believer is separated and carved out of the world to be like the Lord Jesus, to be used by Him, and to glorify God. In this manner the Holy Spirit saves the believer from being ruled by his or her inherent depraved nature and from the clutches of the corrupt world system. Although God uses a host of ways to conform the believer to the likeness of His Son, two general means are employed. First, an individual must invest time in God's Word to know Him and His will (John 15:3, 17:17). Second, God will orchestrate various trials, tests, sufferings, persecutions, and other circumstances in our lives in order to fashion holy character in us and to bring us closer to Him. Both of these activities enable the believer to better understand the will of God in our lives.

Indeed, the Bible exhorts us to understand the will of God and to submit to it (Eph. 5:17; 1 Thess. 4:3, 5:18; 1 Pet. 2:15). The will of God is not some abstract concept that is variable for different believers, but rather the Bible expresses God's will in terms of the proper conduct and holy living which is required of all Christians. God's will for the believer's life has already been declared; what we need now from the Lord is day by day guidance: *"Trust in the Lord with all your heart, and lean not on your own understanding; in all your ways acknowledge Him, and He shall direct your paths"* (Prov. 3:5-6). If you are toiling in the Word to know God's will and submitting to what you do understand, you need not be anxious about the daily specifics of your life; His faithful hand will guide you.

Meditation

> Lord, circumcise our hearts, we pray,
> Our fleshly natures purge away;
> Thy Name, Thy likeness may they bear:
> Yea, stamp Thy holy image there!

> — Sebastien Besnault

51

Foolish Pagans
Jeremiah 5:1-9

To show the utter corruption of His people, God told Jeremiah to thoroughly search out the land to see if there was even one Jew who was treating his fellow man with honesty and was diligently seeking the truth (v. 1). If Jeremiah could find such a person, the Lord would spare Jerusalem from destruction. Jeremiah's diligent search did not identify anyone that was living for the Lord. In fact, he found that the Jews had no remorse or grief about their sin; at His correction, they had only hardened their hearts further against the Lord. A character sketch of the people was presented back in chapter four: *"For My people are foolish, they have not known Me. They are silly children, and they have no understanding. They are wise to do evil, but to do good they have no knowledge* (Jer. 4:22). The Jews had become foolish, not knowing the way of the Lord or His Law (v. 4).

At first, Jeremiah thought it was only the poor and the dregs of society that were uneducated in the ways of the Lord. However, he soon learned that the problem of ignorance and rebellion was much more widespread; even the leaders of the nation *"had broken off the yoke"* of service to Jehovah (v. 5). In the previous chapter, Jeremiah likened the invaders of the north to a lion, a hot wind, a whirlwind, and eagles. Now the prophet portrays Babylon as a lion boldly leaving the cover of the forest, as a wolf lurking in the twilight ready to attack its prey, and as a leopard lying in wait to suddenly pounce upon its quarry. Judgment would be all-encompassing; the Jews would not escape the clutches of their enemy (v. 6).

God then asked Judah two rhetorical questions. First, why should He forgive her (v. 7)? Second, why should He not punish Judah for her sin (v. 9)? The Lord proceeded to answer His own questions. He cannot forgive a nation that has forsaken Him and sworn in the name of false gods, nor can He forgive a fornicating people with animalistic behavior (v. 8). God's people had become like animals driven by natural instincts instead of a people ruled by His Law. The Jews were now nothing more than foolish pagans, and Jehovah would punish them for both their immorality and their idolatry.

The Jews had failed to pass down the Law of God to their children and, consequently, over the generations they had become foolish pagans, polluting God's land. The harsh reality of divine recompense for the neglect of parental stewardship is witnessed repeatedly in Scripture. After Joshua died, the people ceased to teach their children about the Lord, and as a result, the next generation did not know Him. Consequently, they forsook the Lord and embraced other gods. How would God respond to a nation that was called by His name, but refused to teach the next generation about Him and His Law?

Now these are the nations which the Lord left, that He might test Israel by them, that is, all who had not known any of the wars in Canaan (this was only so that the generations of the children of Israel might be taught to know war, at least those who had not formerly known it) (Judg. 3:1-2).

God would use war and invasion to teach the new generation in Israel who He was and what He demanded of His covenant people.

The situation in Israel after the death of Joshua illustrates the fallacy of depending upon any spiritual influence outside the family to maintain the family's spiritual welfare. The Israelites probably relied too much on Joshua and the priests, and neglected their personal responsibility to train their children. In response, God seized the role of the parent in order to teach the new generation about Himself. He loves His people too much to leave them void of truth and ignorant of His presence. What was God's instrument for making His presence known? The disciplinary rod of military invasion and conquest. Israel did not remember God's awesome means of delivering them from slavery and from Egypt, so God used death, invasion, and servitude to awaken them again to His presence. All this occurred because Jewish parents did not uphold God's Law before their children.

What is the lesson in this for us? In the New Testament, Paul used Israel's past foolishness as an object lesson to teach the Corinthian believers about proper behavior. He warns, *"now these things were our examples"* (1 Cor. 10:6); Christians should learn from the mistakes of Israel. Human history inevitably repeats itself when man fails to acquire wisdom from his past failures. The application, then, is that Christian parents must teach the Scripture to their children so that they might intimately know God for themselves. If we neglect this duty, the Lord will resort to harsher methods to ensure that He is known by our children! Children must be trained up for the Lord.

Untrained children remain foolish (Prov. 22:15), and predictably, absorb from outside influences whatever seems appropriate to fill their lack of understanding. The evil sons of Eli serve as a good example of how wicked uncorrected children can become (2 Sam. 2:12). Children are natural sponges – they are compelled to learn and to develop an understanding of the world in which they live. Billy Graham highlights the danger of neglecting the spiritual aspects of a child's development, especially in the modern era in which we live: "Parents have little time for children and a great vacuum has developed, and into that vacuum is going to move some kind of ideology."[1] Peter Marshall acknowledges the unfortunate outcome: "Let us not fool ourselves—without Christianity, without Christian education, without the principles of Christ inculcated into young life, we are simply rearing pagans."[2] Jehovah would not allow His people to become a nation of pagans.

The new generation in Israel grew up without knowing God, so they embraced false gods, and God had to judge His covenant people – a bitter chastening resulting from parents' neglect to raise spiritual children (Mal. 2:15). The same travesty is occurring today. The nation of Israel was to be a lampstand to the world of God's grace and righteousness, yet they failed miserably in this task. Today the Church is to display the greatness of God to a lost world and to principalities and powers (Eph. 3:10). How are we doing? May we fulfill the Great Commission (Matt. 29:19-20), train the next generation to do the same (Eph. 6:4), and pray that they will continue to walk with the Lord.

Meditation

> Oh, you that are spending your leisure and powers,
> In those pleasures so foolish and fond;
> Awake from your selfishness, folly and sin,
> And go to the regions beyond.

To the regions beyond I must go, I must go,
Till the world, all the world, His salvation shall know.

— Albert Simpson

The Unknown Tongue
Jeremiah 5:10-31

Jeremiah repeatedly told the Jews that God would use the Babylonians as a rod of reproof against them for their continuing idolatry. One of the aspects of Jeremiah's preaching, which especially infuriated the final four Judean kings, was his message to submit to the Babylonians (Jer. 27). He warned that if they did not do so, Jerusalem would be destroyed and the nation would be exiled to Babylon (22:5-10; 25:8-11). This demonstrates that God was willing to temper His discipline, if the Jews accepted His chastening without offering resistance. The Jews hated this message and in time plotted to kill God's messenger, Jeremiah (26:7-24).

Babylon would destroy Judah's best fortifications and battlements. In the hands of rebels these devices of self-preservation would utterly fail. Without the Lord's assistance to preserve them, the Jews had no hope of thwarting God's justice against them. What good is a high wall or a catapult against the God of the universe? But the people would not listen; they accused Jeremiah and the other godly prophets of being full of wind (v. 13). In response to this accusation, God declared that His words would instead be like a fire that would consume both the people and the land. The people would know that judgment was near when they heard a language that they did not recognize (vv. 14-15).

The sign of the unknown tongue is used throughout Scripture as a warning to Israel of imminent judgment. Moses told the people that if they rebelled against the Lord, He would punish them through a nation whose language they would not understand (Deut. 28:49). This meant that God would use an army from a distant land instead of a neighboring nation. Isaiah warned Israel by this sign just prior to the invasion of Assyria (Isa. 28:11-12) and Jeremiah now referenced the same sign as a final warning to Judah of imminent judgment (v. 15). The terms "house of Israel" and "house of Jacob" normally refer to the entire Jewish nation, but with the Northern Kingdom in exile, "house of Israel" is used in verse 15 to speak of that which remained in the land to represent it (i.e. Judah). But the Jews ignored Jeremiah's messages and the sign of the unknown tongue and judgment ultimately came, yet, this was not the last time God would use the sign of an unknown tongue to alert the Jews of impending judgment for their unfaithfulness.

According to Acts 2:9-11, ten specific languages were heard in Jerusalem at the Feast of Pentecost, just after Christ's ascension into heaven. This was the day the Church Age began. The Holy Spirit came to the believers as promised by the Lord Jesus and baptized them into the life of Christ, bestowed them with spiritual gifts and enabled them to supernaturally serve the Lord. This event served two main purposes. First, it verified in the sight of the Jews that the apostles were continuing the ministry of Christ and were doing so by His power (Acts 2:22). Second, it served as a final warning to the nation of Israel to repent and turn to God through Christ. As a nation, they had rejected and crucified their Messiah, but as individuals, they now had the opportunity to be saved – unavoidable judgment was coming upon the nation of Israel and trusting Christ for salvation was the only way for them to obtain God's forgiveness.

In 70 AD judgment came. A large Roman army led by the future Emperor Titus besieged and conquered Jerusalem. The temple that had been built towards the end of the sixth century B.C. by the Jewish captives who returned from Babylon, and that had then been renovated by Herod the Great some five centuries later, was destroyed. There were to be no more offerings, sacrifices, Levitical priesthood, or stench of humanized religion in the nostrils of Jehovah. Even to this day, although the Jews are back in their land and are a self-governing nation, they have no temple or priesthood to reinstate what God put away. Why? The writer of Hebrews explains:

> For if that first covenant had been faultless, then no place would have been sought for a second. Because finding fault with them, He says: "Behold, the days are coming, says the Lord, when **I will make a new covenant with the house of Israel and with the house of Judah** – not according to the covenant that I made with their

fathers in the day when I took them by the hand to lead them out of the land of Egypt; because they did not continue in My covenant, and I disregarded them, says the Lord. For this is the covenant that I will make with the house of Israel after those days, says the Lord: I will put My laws in their mind and write them on their hearts; and I will be their God, and they shall be My people.... In that He says, "A new covenant," He has made the first obsolete. Now what is becoming obsolete and growing old is ready to vanish away (Heb. 8:7-13).

About three to five years after these words were penned God completely removed the religious practices of the Old Covenant from Israel. In reality, these had been replaced by the New Covenant sealed with Christ's blood forty years earlier, but the Jews had rejected the terms of this covenant which required them to receive Christ as their Messiah. Through the destruction of Jerusalem and the temple, God put an end to the Levitical order established by the Old Covenant, a system that the Jews had developed into their own religion (Gal. 1:13-14). No more ceremonial lip service, devoid of all spiritual value, could be offered to God. Through the New Covenant, and it alone, God would forgive the sins of Israel and Judah, pour out His Spirit upon them, and restore them to Himself. Although during the Church Age some Jews have certainly come to faith in Christ, the nation as a whole will not turn to Him until His second advent to the earth at the end of the Tribulation Period (Joel 2:18-3:21; Hos. 3; Isa. 11:1-16; Ezek. 36:16-38; Zech. 12:10, 14:1-21; Rom. 11:7-25).

Jeremiah warned that when the Babylonian invasion force arrived in Judah, they would despoil the Jews of their crops, flocks, vineyards, and fruit trees. The Jews would have no food supplies left to sustain themselves. The Babylonians would lay siege to their fortified cities and use starvation to cause their inevitable surrender (v. 17). Yet, God would not completely destroy His people (v. 18), but rather teach them submission by forcing them to render service to their conquerors in Babylon (v. 19). Jeremiah was to announce this message throughout all the land of Israel so that everyone could hear it (v. 20).

However, the spiritual problem in the house of Israel ran deep; the entire nation was guilty of spiritual fornication and wickedness. They were a foolish people without understanding (v. 21). They had no fear of God (vv. 22, 24). They were rebels by nature (v. 23). They resisted the Lord even after being severely punished (v. 25). They had become an immoral, uncaring, and deceitful people (vv. 26-28). It was not that the rains did not fall or that the time to gather the harvest had been shortened: God's goodness was readily apparent, only their wickedness prohibited them from enjoying it (v. 24-25). Jeremiah's concluding description of Judah's spiritual condition might well describe Christendom today:

> *An astonishing and horrible thing has been committed in the land: The prophets prophesy falsely, and the priests rule by their own power; and My people love to have it so. But what will you do in the end?* (Jer. 5:30-31).

From God's perspective, there was no other option but to severely punish His people and avenge His holy name for their appalling and horrible deeds (v. 29). Hearing the unknown language of the approaching invasion force was God's final warning to His people of impending doom, but they ignored this sign! Before the Church Age draws to a close, might each believer use his or her tongue to sound the warning of imminent danger and destruction. As in Jeremiah's day, there are many deceivers proclaiming false messages, and many more who only listen to what they want to hear. God's Word tells us that judgment on the wicked is imminent, thus, the Church cannot remain silent on such an important matter as eternal life and death. Every second of each day, many souls pass into eternity without knowing Christ, and yet, the fires of hell are never quenched.

Meditation

O for a thousand tongues to sing my great Redeemer's praise,
The glories of my God and King, the triumphs of His grace!
My gracious Master and my God assist me to proclaim,
To spread through all the earth abroad the honors of Thy name.
Hear Him, ye deaf; His praise, ye dumb, your loosened tongues employ;
Ye blind, behold your Saviour come; and leap, ye lame, for joy.

— Charles Wesley

Full of Fury
Jeremiah 6:1-30

Jeremiah's second message, recorded in chapter six, was delivered during the days of Josiah (3:6). This prediction as to how Jerusalem would be destroyed was given around forty years before the actual event took place. Babylon was not a great power at that time, so Jeremiah's prophesy must have seemed out of place to the people.

In the near future, alarms would sweep throughout Judah announcing the approach of the invasion force from a great nation to the North, that is Babylon (vv. 1, 22). Trumpets would sound the alarm in Tekoa, which was located on the edge of the desert some 10 miles southwest of Jerusalem, while signal fires on the high ground of Beth Hakkerem, just south of Jerusalem, would be lit. The people of Benjamin, who lived just north of Jerusalem, were instructed to flee to the far south without stopping in the capital. The people were warned not to flee to Jerusalem for safety since it would be so decimated by the Babylonians that in days to come shepherds would pitch their tents upon its ruins and there graze their flocks (v. 3).

The Babylonian armies would be ruthless and eager to conquer Jerusalem. Rather than waiting to start the battle at daybreak, Babylon would begin their assault on the city at night (vv. 4-5). Apparently, the Lord Himself would direct and enable the Babylonians to construct siege mounds or ramps to breech the city's fortifications (v. 6). God planned to punish Jerusalem for her wickedness unless His people repented and turned back to Him (vv. 7-8). Jeremiah likens Jerusalem to a vine full of grapes that God would allow the Babylonians to glean if they did not repent (v. 9).

Although Jeremiah was faithful to sternly warn Judah of her impending doom, the people would not listen. He was amazed at their lack of response to God's word; indeed, it was odious to them (v. 10). This is the first of nearly forty times that Jeremiah acknowledges the resistance of the people to God's Word. Their rejection of divine truth (what they needed for life) seems to be directly tied to their propensity to covet what they did not have (which could not enhance life) (v. 13). The entire nation was obsessed with covetousness – the irony was that they were lusting for what they did not need, while rejecting the only One who could satisfy their true needs! This marked them for God's judgment. Full of holy fury, swelling with righteous jealousy, Jehovah would vindicate His name (v.11).

His judgment would be all-encompassing: young and old, men and women would suffer, and houses, fields, and esteemed possessions would be lost (vv. 11-12). Those who falsely prophesied in the name of Jehovah would be particularly punished (v. 13), for the priests and prophets had soothed the anxiety of the people with their false message of "Peace, Peace." Certainly, there was future hope for the nation, but at the present moment, Jeremiah could only offer the people a choice in the severity of God's judgment. Judgment was inevitable and inescapable, but if the people yielded to God's message, they would live, howbeit in exile; there they could wait for the forthcoming era of restoration and blessing.

A similar false message of "peace, peace" will be powerfully proclaimed at the beginning of the Tribulation Period, when under the Antichrist a false peace will engulf the world. At that time, the Jews, who will have taken back their land through war (Ezek. 38:8) will sign a peace treaty with the Antichrist (Dan. 9:27) and then dwell safely in unprotected villages (Ezek. 38:11). It is in this time of "peace and safety" that the Antichrist will strike; before the Tribulation Period is over, two-thirds of the Jews in the world will be slaughtered (Zech. 13:7-8). In this sense, the events surrounding the Babylonian invasion are a precursor to the more devastating period yet to occur during the Tribulation Period.

False prophets have plagued the Jews throughout their history. The problem is compounded by the fact that God's prophets always seemed to be greatly outnumbered at any given time by their counterparts. The ministries of Elijah (1 Kings 18), Micaiah (1 Kings 22), and Jeremiah (Jer. 20) serve as good examples. All of this goes to say that, time and again, God's prophets have suffered greatly for their faithfulness to be one voice for God among a throng of dissident and often hostile people.

The message of a true prophet is correct: what God's prophet says will happen, will occur with one hundred percent accuracy (Deut. 18:20-22), and this is confirmation that the message indeed is from God. The false prophets in Jeremiah's day had no shame about lying to the people (v. 15). Indeed, their spiritual disposition towards God had become so hardened that they did not even know how to blush when their sin was exposed. The Lord has always dealt sternly with false prophets, and Jeremiah's contemporaries would be no different; they would perish when Jerusalem was destroyed (v. 12).

Drawing his second message to a close, Jeremiah concludes by expressing God's disgust for ceremonial rituals void of genuine devotion. Although the Jews were secretly engaged in idolatry, in public they continued to observe the feasts, sacrifices, and offerings as demanded by the Law. Yet, the Lord had no pleasure in these things – action without conviction is hypocrisy. The Jews would be punished severely for their false pretenses and rebellious dispositions. They had been shown the right way, but would not continue to walk in it (v. 16). This situation reminds us that what we will be in the future is determined by the choices we make today. Judah was about to reap the repercussions of years of wrong choices. With judgment looming, Jeremiah's heart was full of sorrow for the nation; he wished that they would dress themselves in sackcloth and wallow in ashes (v. 26), but this was not to be.

Jeremiah was likened to a tester of metals (v. 27), and Judah to unrefinable ore (v. 28). He knew the hearts of his rebellious countrymen; they were hardened and had not been softened by the refining efforts of his prophecies (v. 29). In this verse, Jeremiah was also compared to the worn-out bellows of a furnace; though divine inspiration burned hissing hot within him, all his efforts to declare God's message had emotionally exhausted him. Commenting to this word-picture, Albert Barnes writes:

This then is the end. The smelter is God's prophet; the bellows, the breath of inspiration; the flux, his earnestness in preaching. But in vain does the fervor of prophecy essay to melt the hearts of people. They are so utterly corrupt, that no particle even of pure metal can be found in them. All the refiner's art is in vain. They have rejected all God's gifts and motives for their repentance, and therefore

62

Jehovah has rejected them as an alloy too utterly adulterated to repay the refiner's toil.[1]

The people of Judah were corrupt through and through; the desired precious metal could scarcely be found in their composition. So far, God's attempts through prophetic utterance to remove the stubborn components of bronze, iron, and lead from their makeup were unsuccessful. God wanted purified silver, but His people were so full of impurities, that He must utterly reject them (v. 30). Refuse silver has no value; it must either be cast away or exposed to intense heat to remove its dross. On this point Kyle Yates comments:

Perhaps someday we may see clearly how unattractive, how loathsome, how useless sinful men are in the sight of a holy God. How we need to look objectively at ourselves to see the miserable emptiness that is so clearly visible to God! There is no point in keeping refuse silver. It has no worth. Can it be that God has already marked off as valueless many who consider themselves useful?[2]

God knew how to remove the wicked dross from Judah: Babylon would be the flame, Jerusalem the chaff, and God's prophetic word the catalyst for the Refiner's fire. Any living soul emerging from that great conflagration would assuredly be genuine silver.

Meditation

Fear not, I am with thee, O be not dismayed,
For I am thy God and will still give thee aid;
I'll strengthen and help thee, and cause thee to stand
Upheld by My righteous, omnipotent hand.

When through fiery trials thy pathways shall lie,
My grace, all sufficient, shall be thy supply;
The flame shall not hurt thee; I only design
Thy dross to consume, and thy gold to refine.

— John Rippon

The Temple of the Lord?
Jeremiah 7:1-16

Jeremiah's third message was delivered at the temple gate (v. 2), probably around fifteen to twenty years after the previous two messages, which were given during the reign of Josiah. In continuation of the theme of Jeremiah's second message, the third message confirmed God's judgment on Judah for her vain religious practices. Of particular offense to God was the Jews' notion that they were invincible because they had the temple (v. 4). The temple was viewed as a "good luck charm" which would protect the nation. Apparently, the structure, having been disassociated from Jehovah, was itself regarded as a bastion of safety (i.e. the people trusted in a man-made building to protect them rather than the One it honored).

Jeremiah set the matter straight: God valued obedience more than the temple, a fact He would soon demonstrate by destroying it. The people were exhorted to amend their ways (vv. 3, 5). Three examples are given in verse six to illustrate the behavioral changes God desired from His people; each of these also relates back to a particular instruction in the Law. First, the poor and helpless in their society should be cared for and protected (Deut. 14:29). Second, innocent blood should not be shed (Deut. 19:10-13). Third, no idolatry should be permitted; the Jews were to worship God alone (Ex. 20:3-4). God was ready to reward His people for genuine reform. If they concluded that the temple would not protect them from conquest, and would honor the covenant that they had made with Him, He then would preserve them in their own land (vv. 7-8). William Kelly seizes the principle articulated by Jeremiah 2,500 years ago and applies it in respect to modern Christendom:

> He shows them that their boast in an uninterrupted succession of national privilege was a vain trust.... The delusion was equally destructive to them as it will be to Christendom. There is nothing

64

more certain to bring destruction upon Christendom than the notion of an indefectible security.

I do not mean security for the soul, for the believer. This assurance is quite right. We cannot too strongly hold the eternal life of the believer; but to apply to the state of Christendom the notion that it will go on indefectibly when God, on the contrary, has warned us in His word that Christendom will fall just like the Jewish state before it is to be caught by the wiles of the wicked one. Such a notion is precisely the delusion by which Satan brings about its total departure from God.

What is perfectly true for the soul in Christ is thoroughly ruinous for the general collective state in religion. There is nothing finer than the faith that gives God credit for grace to the soul; but there is no greater pit of delusion than to predicate generally of the apostate state of things in Christendom what is only true of and for the individual soul; because the one is real genuine faith, and the other is most arrogant and lofty presumption, which God will judge.[1]

Though all true believers are secure in Christ forever, the believer should never think too highly of humanized Christianity; all that is associated with the name of Christ, but yet does not bear His seal of approval will be severely judged and put away. The Lord Jesus said that *"every plant which My heavenly Father has not planted shall be uprooted"* (Matt. 15:13). The writer of Hebrews confirms that only the unshakable portion of the kingdom of God will be left standing after God's consuming fire removes what does not represent Him (Heb. 12:27-29).

The temple had become a social center for practicing immorality and pagan rituals (vv. 9-10). Did the Jews not think that Jehovah would take action? The temple had been erected in His name and was to be a place of prayer and worship to Him. It was not to be a lair for thieves and idolaters (vv. 10-11)! God would take action to remove the disdain associated with His name, as He had done five centuries earlier in a similar situation (vv. 12-14). Before the temple was constructed, the Ark of the Covenant was kept in a tent at Shiloh. With the Philistine army advancing towards them, the Jews decided to bring the Ark of the Covenant out to the battlefront, thinking that it would help them achieve a great victory. As in the days of Jeremiah, the Jews trusted in a tangible object more than the One the object stood for. God allowed the Israelites to be slaughtered and the Ark of the Covenant to be captured by the enemy. Later, it was returned and was eventually brought to Jerusalem by David, and years afterwards it was placed in the temple that Solomon constructed, where apparently it remained until the Babylonian invasion.

The Lord was much more concerned that what occurred in the temple was an expression of His holy character rather than whether it remained standing or not. How an individual reveres the Lord in personal conduct validates the sincerity of his or her worship. Accordingly, H. A Ironside ties the spiritual desecration of the temple in Jeremiah's day to the then future condition of Israel at Christ's first advent:

> Nothing can be more abhorrent to Him than the dreadful state described in verses 8-10. It is the divorce of position from condition – the making much of ecclesiastical place, while the walk is utterly at variance with the truth connected with it. Position is important. Nothing, in fact, is more so; but let us be careful to maintain the corresponding practice. Those who, through grace, have been gathered out of unscriptural systems to the precious name of the Lord Jesus Christ alone should see to it that their walk is consistent with their privileged place. The next verse, it will be noted, is referred to by our Lord when He made a whip of small cords and drove the money-changers and venders from the courts of the temple (Matt. 21:13). On that occasion He connected two scriptures together. The first was from Isa. 56:7 – *"My house shall be called a house of prayer for all people."* This shall yet be true when Christ's kingdom is set up in power; but when the King appeared in lowliness, His judgment was, *"Ye have made it a den of thieves,"* as Jeremiah had said before: *"Is this house, which is called by My name, become a den of robbers in your eyes? Behold I, even I, have seen it, saith the Lord."* As a result, like Shiloh, it was to be left desolate, and the false worshippers were to be cast out from their land.[2]

Whether in sixth century B.C., at the time of Christ's First Advent, or today, worship of God that willfully ignores revealed truth cannot please God; in fact, as Judah was about to learn, it is worse than blatant idolatry.

If the Jews did not regain proper focus, Jehovah would remove their "good luck charm" and also remove them from the land of their inheritance (v. 15). We see that as He reviewed the specifics of Judah's sin. God's anger swelled. He foreknew that His people would not repent. With this known and the fact that they valued a stone structure over the Lord of Glory provoked Him to charge Jeremiah not to weep or pray for His people (v. 16). This request seems to be in contrast with the previous two messages, in which the people were extended a genuine offer of restoration contingent upon their repentance.

Although the call to repentance still resounded throughout Jeremiah's ministry, the time for it had expired – the door of opportunity was closed. Though he knew that the Jews would not heed his message, he continued to announce the certainty of punishment and the means to escape it, that the righteousness of God might be upheld in the matter. Perhaps a modern day example will assist in understanding this concept. The floor lighting in a commercial aircraft is designed to assist passengers to find their way to an emergency exit when the cabin is full of smoke and the cabin lighting system has failed. To remain in such a dangerous situation when one can see the way of escape is foolish. It will not be the aircraft designers' fault if someone ignores the emergency lighting and chooses to perish in the aircraft. Neither could anyone accuse God of wrongdoing in judging Judah – the Jews had chosen to be chastened, and it was now an unavoidable fact. Unfortunately, throughout their history, the Jews have often been guilty of appreciating religious things more than the Lord.

Six centuries after the Babylonian invasion, the Jews again returned to the same pattern of emphasizing material things rather than the Lord. As a part of His pungent message of "woes" to the Pharisees, the Lord Jesus addressed this misplacement of honor, specifically as demonstrated by hypocritically swearing in a way which degraded the name of the Lord:

"Woe to you, blind guides, who say, 'Whoever swears by the temple, it is nothing; but whoever swears by the gold of the temple, he is

obliged to perform it.' Fools and blind! For which is greater, the gold or the temple that sanctifies the gold? And, 'Whoever swears by the altar, it is nothing; but whoever swears by the gift that is on it, he is obliged to perform it.' Fools and blind! For which is greater, the gift or the altar that sanctifies the gift? Therefore he who swears by the altar, swears by it and by all things on it. He who swears by the temple, swears by it and by Him who dwells in it. And he who swears by heaven, swears by the throne of God and by Him who sits on it" (Matt. 23:16-22).

The Jews of Christ's day not only valued the temple more than the Lord, but they valued the gold band that adorned the pinnacle of the temple more than the temple itself. The Pharisees had apparently slipped further into the sin of valuing things associated with Jehovah more than the One who gave those things value. By using the temple and the altar as an illustration, the Lord Jesus taught the Jews that things only have value as based on their connection with God. Is it the gold or the temple that is valuable? Does the offering sanctify the altar or is it visa versa? Is it the temple or the Lord that is important? The Lord bluntly told them that the altar gave value to the sacrifice, just as the temple bestowed significance to the gold. The altar and the temple were patterned after holy heavenly realities (Heb. 9:23); each was directly connected with God. In placing the value on the offering and the gold, which were earthly things, the Pharisees had disassociated themselves from God. The Lord clarified that only that which is connected with God has value; their traditions were just human nonsense and an insult to God.

The highest honor possible for a piece of gold was to be used in the house of God. The highest honor for a lamb in Judea was to be used as a sacrifice on the bronze altar. If gold and sheep had ambition, this would have been their highest calling. Christ was teaching that man apart from God is nothing; ambition apart from God is nothing; abilities apart from God are nothing! The only reason a believer can be honored before God is because of his or her association with Jesus Christ. Spurgeon once said to a believer, "The greatest thing about you is your connection with Calvary [Christ]."

The Lord Jesus wants our motives, our abilities, and our entire lives to be connected with Him; only in this way will they have any true value. It is possible for us to ignorantly commit the same form of blasphemy that the Pharisees did (i.e. undervaluing our association with Christ). For example, the reader might have a brilliant mind. Some might say, "The Lord would be fortunate to have a mind like yours in His service." Wrong! The right thinking is, "My greatest privilege in life is to lay hold of the mind of Christ and use my talents for Him." Your intellect does not sanctify Jesus Christ; it is Jesus Christ who sanctifies your mind for His purpose and glory. Only those abilities that are submitted to the Lord can be used to honor Him and to bless the body of Christ. The Jews of Christ's day had drifted into the same mindset of those whom Jeremiah spoke to: their identity as a people was rooted, not in the Lord, but in the social practices and religious traditions they had developed. In this rebellious condition, the Jews could not represent God as a holy people; nevertheless, they would be a testimony of His longsuffering nature.

The rebel heart will never experience the loving-kindnesses and tender mercies of the Lord, beyond the fact that God permits it to beat one more time and, by abundant grace, one more day. Peter puts the matter this way: *"The Lord is not slack concerning His promise, as some count slackness, but is longsuffering toward us, not willing that any should perish but that all should come to repentance"* (2 Pet. 3:9). God had chosen the Jews to stand forth as *"a light to the nations"* (Isa. 49:6), that is, as a great witness to the entire world of God's faithfulness, mercy, and patience. In the future, when His covenant people are restored to Him once and for all, the entire world will marvel at God's longsuffering nature and His steadfast faithfulness to His word.

Thankfully, at this time, the Jews will look back over ruined centuries stained with blood and tarnished by rebellion and idolatry and gladly declare, *"The Lord shall be King over all the earth. In that day it shall be – 'The Lord is one,' and His name one"* (Zech. 14:9). It will not be any temple or any man-made article that attracts their devotion then, but the Lord Jesus Christ, the King of kings.

Meditation

Crown the blessed Saviour King of kings.

69

Forsaken, Forgotten and Forgiven

Soon He is coming back again,
A thousand years on earth to reign;
We'll see Him by and by, we'll see Him by and by;
All the redeemed with Him He'll bring,
Who in their hearts have crowned Him King,
And they shall live and reign with Him on high.

Crown Him! Crown Him! Crown the Saviour King of kings;
In your hearts enthrone Him, Lord and Master own Him;
Crown Him! Crown Him! While heaven exultant rings.

— Leila Morris

The Queen of Heaven
Jeremiah 7:17-20

In Jeremiah 7:16, God instructed the prophet not to intercede for Judah. God further explains the reasons for this "prayer ban" by noting two specific examples of their dreadful idolatry. First, families throughout Judah were uniting for a festive celebration in honor of the goddess Ishtar, the so-called "Queen of Heaven." The event included preparing special cakes that bore her image and were offered to her in a sacrificial rite (v. 18). Second, these same families were pouring out drink offerings, probably wine, before various idols (v. 18). The Jews did not seem to care who they honored through these casual social traditions; apparently, they did not consider these celebrations idolatrous, but just an opportunity for families to enjoy doing something together (i.e. children gathered the wood, fathers kindled the fires, and women kneaded the bread).

The false gods were not a threat to Jehovah; human imaginations cannot hurt Him or diminish His glory. However, God's anger was provoked by the confusion of truth among His people. They no longer had clear distinctions between what was right and what was wrong, between what was holy and what was unholy. Yet there was no reason for them to have "confused faces" (v. 19); the Lord had expressly revealed the way of righteousness to them, and had also commanded them to walk in it.

The same confusion of face is common today among those who associate themselves with the name of Jesus Christ. It is caused by a blurring of what is righteous and what is not. For example, many families gather to commemorate various "Christian" holidays which have pagan origins (e.g. Christmas, Easter, Halloween, etc.). Over time, various traditions have developed around these celebrations, which sound very similar to the practices of the Jews in Jeremiah's day. In these supposed Christian holidays, cookies, cakes, breads,

71

chocolate figurines, etc. are often shaped after ancient pagan images. Fictitious personalities are honored through various traditions and gift-giving practices. A full investigation into the history of these customs would be beyond the scope of this book, but a brief review of the "Christian" holidays of Easter and Christmas will suffice to show their pagan roots.

We begin with Easter. Bunnies and decorated eggs were symbols the ancient Babylonians used to honor their fertility goddess *Astarte*, also called *Eastre*. In 325 AD, the Roman Catholic Church (under Constantine) created a yearly religious holiday to commemorate the resurrection of Christ, setting it for the first Sunday after the first full moon on or after the vernal equinox. This was to align the new holiday with the ancient spring celebration of *Eastre* (i.e. Easter). Although the word "Easter" appears once in the King James Version of the Bible (Acts 12:4), it is an inaccurate translation, no doubt due to centuries of Roman Catholic influence. The appropriate rendition of the Greek word *pascha* in Acts 12:4 is "Passover," as it is translated elsewhere in the New Testament. There is absolutely no trace of the Easter celebration in the New Testament. The early Church did not hold a yearly remembrance of the Lord's resurrection; rather, they kept the Lord's Supper weekly (Acts 20:7) in obedience to the Lord's command to regularly remember Him and to proclaim the value of His death (Luke 22:19-20). Today, much of Christendom is ignoring the commands and patterns of Scripture to practice social traditions which actually honor pagan deities.

Although the Christmas holiday has become something entirely different than what it was when first instituted by the Roman Catholic Church in 350 AD (by Julius I), its tie with Easter is unmistakable. There is no biblical or extra-biblical evidence that points to December as being the date for the birth of Jesus Christ. Rather, the date was chosen to honor the ancient sun-god *Mithras*. The son of *Isis*, *Mithras* (or *Horus*) was claimed to have been born on December 25th, which is nine months (human gestation period) after the spring equinox in late March – the time of the pagan fertility celebrations. The pagan tie between the dates of Easter and Christmas is unmistakable. Neither observance was commanded in Scripture, but was developed by the Roman Catholic Church in association with existing Anglo-Saxon pagan rituals, derived from still more ancient cultures. Today, these have become mere social events in which Christians, professing Christians, and non-Christians alike participate. Although traditions vary widely, one aspect that has never changed is the fact that these man-made traditions draw attention away from the Lord. Idolatry, in any form, draws people away from the truth and causes them to engage in activities that God does not commend. This fact is demonstrated to us in the life of the first pagan mentioned in the Bible, Nimrod. What started with Nimrod long ago affected the Jews during Jeremiah's day and still influences the Church today.

The tenth chapter of Genesis identifies Babylon [Babel] as the fountainhead of all pagan worship. The human founder of this city was Nimrod, whose name means "rebel." First century Jewish historian Josephus regarded Nimrod as the father of the pagan Babylonian and Assyrian cultures. The Babylonians called their rising kingdom *Babel*; in their own estimation, they were "the gate of God" (Gen. 10:10). Through human achievement, they believed they could obtain divinity. Nimrod's quest for deity would hinge upon his success in constructing an enormous tower intended to bridge earth with heaven and close the eminence gap between man and God. Obviously, such a tower would be an affront against God, who is holy and separate from sinful man. Any attempt to bridge the distance between a Holy God and fallen mankind must be righteous in nature and God-ordained. Only the cross of Christ can bridge the spiritual chasm between fallen humanity and a holy God. Accordingly, God brought the construction of Babel's tower to an abrupt halt by diversifying the language of the people.

Babylonian history records that Nimrod met with a sudden and violent death. After this, his beautiful wife, Semiramis, who had ascended by marriage from a common social class to the throne, gave birth to what she claimed was the essence of Nimrod (accomplished through soul transference). The developed Chaldean story states that Nimrod willingly gave us his life in order to further bless the Babylonian kingdom. In any case, Semiramis' son, Bacchus, meaning "the lamented one," was said to be her deified husband.[1] Classical history refers to him as Nimus, meaning "the son," while Scripture calls him "Tammuz" in Ezekiel 8:14.[2] The Lord God is addressed as *Adonai* in the Old Testament; worshippers of Tammuz would later refer to their false deity as *Adon* or *Adonis*, a clear effort to affirm the son as deity. Under the name *Mithras*, he was worshipped as the "Mediator."[3] As Zoroashta, he was worshipped as "the seed of the woman."[4]

Semiramis was licentious and gave birth to several children, though she had no husband.[5] The story concocted around Nimus' birth not only secured her throne, but in time the people reverenced her as *Rhea*, "the great goddess Mother" or *Beltis*, "the Queen of Heaven."[6] She derived all her glory and claim to deification through the very son she held in her arms. Ancient art of the mother and son has the glow of the sun positioned behind each of their heads to indicate sun divinity, but the glory of Semiramis was accentuated even above that of her son.[7] Ancient idols have been excavated showing a mother-god and child-god that bear a strikingly resemblance to modern-day images of Mary and Jesus.[8] The Roman Catholic Church refers to Mary as "the Queen of Heaven" and the "Mother of God." Many have ascribed glory to Mary in the same way Semiramis was deified in the eyes of her people – through the glory of her son. The veneration of Mary has its roots in Babylon; indeed, it is simply a repackaged pagan lie.

The Lord stopped the work on the tower of Babel and spread mankind throughout the region by confounding their speech (Gen. 11:7-8). When the people dispersed, they also carried their developed pagan traditions with them. Consequently, the story of the death (or sacrifice) of the father, to be reincarnated as deity in the womb of a mother goddess is found in many ancient cultures, but with different names:

Babylon: Semiramis and Nimrod (Ninus, or Yule, as son)

Assyria: Ishtar and Tammuz

Egypt: Isis and Osiris (Horus as son)

India: Iswara, or Isa, and Isani, or Isisi

Asia: Cybele and Deoius

Syria: Astarte and Bel, or Baal (Marduk, or Adonis, as son)

Greece: Aphrodite and Adonis

Rome: Kybele, or Venus, and Attis, or Adonis

In the pagan myths of all these ancient cultures runs a central theme: a goddess gives birth to a deified son, the essence of her dead husband. This early Babylonian legend has propagated all over the world! This brief history highlights the main rudiments of paganism, which were eventually incorporated into the Roman papal system and, thus, infiltrated and perverted much of the professing Church.

Roman Catholicism was forged in paganism and through the centuries has culminated in blatant goddess worship of Mary, worshipped and adored as the Queen of Heaven. The Roman Catholic Catechism proudly proclaims that Mary "was exalted by the Lord as Queen over all things" (1994; line 966), a position gained after her supposed assumption into heaven. It is further taught that it is through Mary that all divine blessings, and even salvation, are obtained. The motive for *earning* heaven becomes obvious: it is to join Mary, not to be with the Lord Jesus Christ. Goddess worship has replaced the reverence of the Lord of glory, and ancient Babylon is where it began. It was the influence of Babylon that enticed the Jews to depart from the Law and the Lord in Jeremiah's day and same effect can be witnessed in Christendom.

Some 2,600 years ago, the prophet Jeremiah warned the Jews of God's anger towards them because of their unrepentant idolatry (v. 18). His warning against worshipping the Queen of Heaven could never be more appropriate for mankind to consider than now. Love for the supposed Queen of Heaven has supplanted proper allegiance to the declared Head of the Church – Christ (Eph. 1:22; Col. 1:18). Babylon is alive and well in the Church, and God hates it! We wonder how the Jews were so blind to their social paganism, yet the Church has been entrusted with much more divine revelation and is committing the same sin. What will be God's wrath against those who invoke the name of Christ in superficial rituals, but will not receive Him as Lord and Savior? At the Judgment Seat of Christ, what excuses will believers offer to the Lord for dabbling in pagan rituals which honored others, but not Him?

Meditation

Praise, my soul, the King of Heaven; to His feet thy tribute bring.
Ransomed, healed, restored, forgiven, evermore His praises sing:
Alleluia! Alleluia! Praise the everlasting King.

Praise Him for His grace and favor to our fathers in distress.
Praise Him still the same as ever, slow to chide, and swift to bless.
Alleluia! Alleluia! Glorious in His faithfulness.

— Henry Lyte

Cut Off Your Hair

Jeremiah 7:21-34

God acknowledged that the Jews were correctly offering all of the temple sacrifices; unfortunately, they had failed at the deeper matter of obedience to His Law. As the prophet Samuel confirmed to King Saul centuries earlier: *"Has the Lord as great delight in burnt offerings and sacrifices, as in obeying the voice of the Lord? Behold, to obey is better than sacrifice, and to heed than the fat of rams"* (1 Sam. 15:22). Like Saul, the Jews whom Jeremiah was confronting felt that the sacrifices were more than obeying the Law. However, Jeremiah reminds them that the command for burnt offerings and sacrifices was not given to the Israelites until after they had broken the Law (Ex. 32). God's commandments were established to guide their relationship with Him and with others; thus, only by obeying the Law would they be blessed (Ex. 20).

Jehovah wrote down His Law in tables of stone so that the Israelites would have a permanent record of what He expected of them. Moses instructed them in all the precepts of this Law, and from that time on God had sent numerous prophets to call the Israelites' attention to their negligence of it (v. 25). Consequently, Jeremiah was not to expect a response of repentance from the people (v. 27); apparently, the only way God would get their attention would be through drastic measures (v. 28).

To illustrate that the time of pleading for repentance was now over and that imminent judgment loomed over Judah, Jeremiah was to cut off his hair (v. 29). The cutting off of one's hair was a sign of deep mourning (Isa. 15:2-3; Ezek. 7:18). Jeremiah was also *"to take up a lamentation on high places"* (v. 29). He was to mourn over Jerusalem as one would express deep sorrow in a funeral dirge for the passing of a loved one. At this point in time, the catastrophic consequences Judah's sin demanded were unavoidable: *"For the Lord has rejected and*

77

forsaken the generation of His wrath" (v. 29). Though God had not forgotten His people, He had abandoned them to the mercy of His chastening hand.

Jeremiah 7 is one of the most detailed accounts of the specific offenses that Judah was committing against the Lord. The Lord, acutely knowledgeable of every sin, spelled them out so that the people might know He knew about their iniquities. Besides honoring the Queen of Heaven with cakes and pouring out drink offerings to various gods, the Jews were sacrificing their own children in burnt offerings to false deities. They had built the high places of Topheth, located just southwest of Jerusalem in the Hinnom Valley (v. 31). God vowed that He would change the name of this place to "The Valley of Slaughter" (v. 32). The very place that they had sacrificed their own children would be the slaughtering ground for countless Jews during the Babylonian invasion. The fowls of the air and wild beasts would feed upon their carcasses in that place (v. 33). There would be so many dead and so few who survived that it would not be possible to frighten the birds and beasts from devouring their rotting flesh.

Scripture states, *"Behold, children are a heritage from the Lord, the fruit of the womb is a reward"* (Ps. 127:3). Though the Lord had smitten the Jewish children as a disciplinary action (Jer. 2:30), He had not left them without a posterity to maintain their generations. Yet they had chosen to sacrifice the children He had given them for a heritage to Himself to false gods: to Baal (Jer. 19:6), and perhaps others (2 Chron. 33:6). For God's people to offer their own children in sacrifice to the god of this age is perhaps the greatest insult that can be committed against God.

What was given as a reward to parents, what was to be an earthly testimony of God's goodness (Mal. 2:15) was instead wasted in worthless pagan rituals. Such practices would not be tolerated; the day was coming when there would not be any gladness or joy in the streets of Jerusalem – the city would be desolate (v. 34).

In application, we learn from this chapter that God is not impressed by religious ritual, developed church tradition, sanctimonious form, or denominational smugness, but rather He is interested in personal living that conforms to divine truth (Col. 2:20-23). Christianity, therefore, is not a religion; however, when a person properly lives out Christian doctrine, this produces the right kind of religion that pleases God (Jas.

1:27). When one comes into a right relationship with God through the Lord Jesus Christ, then, and only then, is he or she able to please God by doing sincere, God-empowered good works. As the Jews in Jeremiah's day have shown us, world religion is an exhaustive system of *doings* apart from God's truth and God's enablement. They were quite zealous in all their doings, but they had forgotten God's Law and their covenant relationship with Jehovah. As C. I. Scofield explains, it is this same religious blindness that continues to plague Christendom today:

> It may safely be said that the Judaizing of the Church has done more to hinder her progress, pervert her mission, and destroy her spiritually, than all other causes combined. Instead of pursuing her appointed path of separation from the world and following the Lord in her heavenly calling, she has used Jewish Scriptures to justify herself in lowering her purpose to the civilization of the world, the acquisition of wealth, the use of an imposing ritual, the erection of magnificent churches, the invocation of God's blessing upon the conflicts of armies, and the division of an equal brotherhood into "clergy" and "laity."[1]

The main distinction between Christianity and all the religions of the world is that biblical Christianity teaches that man has a vital need to be saved from spiritual death by trusting in the Savior alone, whereas the world's religions pose a system of *doing* to merit salvation or to obtain an improved afterlife. Religion equips man with a "do it yourself" manual and workbook through which he may impress himself as to how well he is *doing* by completing religious exercises and checklists. Christianity, however, is not a *religion*; it is a *relationship* with Jesus Christ. Apart from Christ, there is no forgiveness of sins, no life, and no hope.

Although this gospel message may be expressed in various ways, in different dispensations of God's working with mankind, it is the only message of everlasting life presented in the Bible. Although the Jews of Jeremiah's time did not know the name of their Savior, if they would have repented of their sins and turned to God, they would have experienced complete forgiveness and the full love of Christ, just as every repentant sinner does today.

Meditation

There is a fountain filled with blood drawn from Emmanuel's veins;
And sinners plunged beneath that flood lose all their guilty stains.

The dying thief rejoiced to see that fountain in his day;
And there may I, though vile as he, wash all my sins away.

Dear dying Lamb, Thy precious blood shall never lose its power,
Till all the ransomed church of God be saved, to sin no more.

— William Cowper

No Balm in Gilead
Jeremiah 8:1-22

The main theme of this chapter is conveyed in verse 6: *"No man repented of his wickedness, Saying, 'What have I done?' Everyone turned to his own course."* Sin was so deeply seated into Judah's daily enterprises that it had become commonplace. The Jews had lost their sensitivity to sin and they had forgotten that, as Jehovah's representatives to the nations, they were to be a holy people. They were tolerant of what displeased God and their ears were dull to His appeal, delivered by the prophets. They had become perpetual backsliders that held to deceit and refused to embrace the Lord (v. 5).

The people had slid so far into spiritual anarchy that they did not even blush when committing the grossest abominations (v. 12). Though they had been often pleaded with, they would not repent, but rather *"everyone turned to his own course, as the horse rushes into the battle"* (v. 6). They consoled each other with words of *"peace, peace,"* but there would be no peace in Judah. The Jews would realize this later: *"We looked for peace, but no good came; and for a time of health, and there was trouble!"* (v. 15). One can marvel at the similarities between ancient Judah and our own immoral western society.

God lamented the fact that the various creatures of the air and sea know the laws of nature (e.g. seasonal migration), but His own people did not know His Law that He had directly delivered to them (v. 7). They had willful amnesia – they had rejected God's Law (v. 9). They were stubborn, willing to trip and fall down an unknown path rather than walk with the Lord in the way they should go (v. 4). Jewish leaders were likened to a field medic, who after dressing a mortal wound, tells the wounded not to worry because it is only a superficial injury (v. 11).

Consequently, severe judgment was inescapable; the time of harvest (signifying repentance and restoration) was past (v. 20). God warned the men of Judah that He would allow other men to possess their wives and lands (v. 10). Those rebels who died before the Babylonian conquest would have their bones exhumed and cast out as refuse on the ground (vv. 1-2). Living conditions would be so bad in Judah that those who survived the siege and attack would wish they had died (v. 3); God's indignation would consume them (v. 13).

Jeremiah then paused from speaking on behalf of Jehovah to reveal his own personal thoughts and sorrow concerning the spiritual state of his people (Jer. 8:18-9:2). He wondered why they refused to be healed and be restored to God: *"Is there no balm in Gilead? Is there no physician there?"* (v. 22). Balm was made from the resin extracted from the storax tree; it was used for medicinal purposes. Albert Barnes explains Jeremiah's questions:

> Balm used to grow in Israel for the healing of the nations. Her priests and prophets were the physicians. Has Israel then no balm for herself? Is there no physician in her who can bind up her wound? Gilead was to Israel what Israel spiritually was to the whole world.[1]

However, Israel had ceased to be *"holiness unto the Lord"* (2:3) and consequently they could not be healed of the deadly sickness they refused to recognize they had. The Great Physician had examined them, but they had ignored His findings and only He could cure their debilitating spiritual condition (v. 22). Why would a desperately ill person not want to be made well, when the remedy was readily available? As a spiritual man, Jeremiah could not understand the illogical nature of the carnal man, especially when God's provision for their healing was so clearly evident and easily obtainable. But the people would not repent and receive it.

Commenting on Jeremiah's quandary, H. A. Ironside writes:

> From verse 14 of chapter 8 to the end of chapter 10 we have a most touching lamentation over the fallen estate of the people who have been "put to silence" by God; that is, who are so clearly proven to be guilty before Him that they are speechless in His presence.

Jeremiah enters most deeply into all their feelings, even wailing with them, *"The harvest is past, the summer is ended, and we are not saved"* (8:20). It is a temporal salvation that is referred to, of course. The day of God's patience with them as a nation is ended, and all hope is now vain. How striking is the impassioned cry, *"Is there no balm in Gilead? Is there no physician there? Why then is not the health of the daughter of My people recovered?"* (See also chap. 46:11). Alas, too deep is the wound for Gilead's balm to heal![2]

Naturally speaking, the balm of Gilead could not heal Judah's deep spiritual problem; they needed to trust the Great Physician to be made well again. Only He could restore His covenant people to the prosperous relationship He longed for them to enjoy.

We must remember how the Jews came to such a depraved spiritual condition. God's people had identified with things connected to Jehovah without associating with Him personally. In time, religious things became more important to them than the Lord. Jeremiah states that after the temple's destruction the deported Jews living in far away countries would wonder, *"Does not God dwell in the temple?"*, *"Where is Jehovah?"* (v. 19). It would take the demolition of the temple for the people to finally miss God's presence. How sad. When God's people fail to identify with Him, they soon cease to live for Him and to be a testimony of His goodness. Unfortunately, this same error is prevalent in the Church today. One of the ways the Church fails to fully identify with Christ is through the use of casual terminology which does not bestow to Him His proper due. The modern Church finds it difficult to revere Christ, and thus, has become spiritually pathetic – a condition similar to Judah's before the destruction of Jerusalem.

The Lord Jesus considered the accurate manifestation of His Father's name to be an essential aspect of His ministry; He would do nothing to bring disdain or disgrace upon it. This is the example that the believer is to follow. The Bible refers to believers by various names, but one term, "Christian," specifically relates the *identity* of all believers in Christ to their *calling* in Christ. As believers we are not to identify ourselves by fanciful titles, or with religious causes, or with some denomination/organization, but rather with Him that died for us.

We read in Acts 11:26 that *"the disciples were first called Christians in Antioch."* "Christian" simply means "Christ-one" and refers to those who have trusted Christ alone for salvation.

Unfortunately, the term "Christian" has come to mean something quite different from its original meaning as found in Scripture. Today, many think that they are Christians because they have Christian parents or grandparents, or because they went to a church once in their life, or because they were baptized as a baby, or because they know something about Christ. The Lord Jesus makes it clear that it is not by knowing about Him that one becomes a Christian, but rather by knowing Him personally as Lord and Savior (Matt. 7:21-23). The Jews knew all about God's temple and the sacrifices they were to offer there, but they did not know the Lord personally and thus did not value His Law. This is why the Lord's primary emphasis in training the disciples was for them to learn of Him.

The word "disciple" is derived from the Greek word *mathetes*, meaning "a learner." What is a disciple to learn? The Lord Jesus answers this question:

> *Come unto Me, all ye that labor and are heavy laden, and I will give you rest. Take My yoke upon you, and **learn of Me**; for I am meek and lowly in heart: and ye shall find rest unto your souls. For My yoke is easy, and My burden is light* (Matt. 11:28-30, KJV).

The disciple of Christ is to learn *Him*! This is the only passage in the New Testament where the Lord personally informs His disciples of what He is like and tells them that they should learn of Him. Believers learn of the Lord's gentle and humble spirit when yoked with Him in service, and they enjoy the peace of His presence when they rest in Him.

> Thou hast made us for Thyself and our souls can never be at rest until they rest in Thee.
> — Augustine of Hippo

The goal of discipleship emphasizes again that the Holy Spirit's work of sanctification in a believer's life is crucial to effectively serve the Lord. To learn and to know Christ are integral to the sanctification process.

Consequently, doing important tasks in the name of Christ without bringing honor to His name is hypocrisy, not biblical discipleship. To be a true blessing to others requires us to impart the loveliness of the Savior in what we do for them. Consequently, our fruitfulness increases as we learn of Christ and allow Him to be witnessed in what we do for Him. By spending time in God's Word, the believer learns of Christ and becomes increasingly more like Him (2 Cor. 3:18).

To completely identify with Christ, to learn of Christ (Matt. 11:29), and to be like Christ (Matt. 10:25) is the essence of biblical discipleship. It is in this manner that the called can know the One who calls. The extent to which this identification occurs will directly reflect how well the believer manifests the nature of Christ to the world.

A Christian is an ambassador for Christ (2 Cor. 5:20). He or she is a representative of Him to the earth (Phil. 3:20). As faithfully as Christ declared the name of His Father during His earthly sojourn, the Christian is now to reveal to the world the name of the Lord Jesus Christ. This was Paul's prayer for the young believers at Thessalonica: *"That the name of our Lord Jesus Christ may be glorified in you, and you in Him, according to the grace of our God and the Lord Jesus Christ"* (2 Thess. 1:12). Learning Christ and identifying with Him in all that we do causes others to appreciate the Lord and to honor His name.

Paul stated what is necessary for Christians to adequately display the name of Christ when he exhorted, *"Let everyone who names the name of Christ depart from iniquity"* (2 Tim. 2:19). Believers cannot pretend to be holy; their conduct will either honor a sin-hating Savior or endorse a Savior-hating system. To declare the name of Christ is a great privilege, but to fully associate with His name is the highest honor. To be identified as a "Christian" is one and the same as acknowledging Christ's call to live as He did. The Jews no longer personally identified with Jehovah, though He still knew them. The balm of Gilead could not heal their desperate spiritual condition; they needed to be one with the Lord again. If you are feeling spiritually dry, why not take steps to further identify with your Savior – *"Oh, taste and see that the Lord is good; blessed is the man who trusts in Him!"* (Ps. 34:8).

Meditation

> There is a balm in Gilead to make the wounded whole;
> There is a balm in Gilead to heal the sin-sick soul.
> Sometimes I feel discouraged, and think my work's in vain,
> But then the Holy Spirit revives my soul again.

> — African-American Spiritual

Guided by Imagination
Jeremiah 9:1-26

Jeremiah continued to disclose his personal remorse and revulsion concerning the plight of Judah. He cried, *"Oh, that my head were waters, and my eyes a fountain of tears, that I might weep day and night for the slain of the daughter of my people!"* (Jer. 9:1). The coming judgment would affect Jeremiah's family, friends, and fellow-countrymen; his tears could not be restrained. Jeremiah made no attempt to hide his empathy or his tears for the people; as a result, he became known as "the weeping prophet" (4:19-26, 8:18-22, 13:17, 15:18, 20:7-18).

On one hand, he prayed that his eyes might be like a well-supplied fountain so that he could weep tears day and night for his people. On the other hand, Jeremiah voices his disgust for the immoral behavior of his people and expresses his desire to be separate from them. Though God had called him to preach to Judah, Jeremiah wanted no close association with adulterers, liars, thieves, slanderers, and deceitful men who continually engaged in evil (vv. 3-8). Paul reminds us that bad companions corrupt good morals and that God's people should be careful of those with whom they have close associations (1 Cor. 15:33). Jeremiah preferred to live in isolation in the wilderness rather than to be numbered with the wicked (v. 2). He knew God would punish Judah to avenge His holy name (v. 9).

The Jews were to be a holy people who honored the one true God, but they no longer knew Him. Our spiritual proximity to the Lord will determine our sensitivity to that which offends Him. Accordingly, a casual association with the Lord permits us to sin without being conscious of the distain we cause to His good name. This is why a believer who remains in sin loathes close interaction with God's people; they remind the errant child of God to whom he or she belongs. Apparently, the only way of escape for the unrepentant is to

87

concoct a religious system which condones his or her sin. This was what the Jews had done – they had departed from the truth and were following their own imaginations (v. 14).

Often when we get caught in sin, our first inclination is to behave like Jacob did after the terrible events at Shechem (Gen. 34) – we are concerned about how our wrongdoings will affect us and what others will think about us. Such a thought pattern in itself indicates contempt for God. We should be more concerned about the glory of God than about the trouble we have brought upon ourselves. For example, when a well-known preacher is found to be engaging in gross moral sin, our first response should be to grieve over the shame levied upon Christ's name. When an assembly of God's people splits over personality issues, we should all grieve for the poor testimony of Christ in that community. It is time that the Church brings the name of the Lord Jesus Christ into the forefront of our thinking and ceases from making religious excuses for our sin and lack of vitality. Fully identifying with Christ, instead of pursuing vain imaginations, prompts spiritual fruitfulness (John 15:4-5).

Why did David engage a giant named Goliath in battle? The honor of God's name was at stake! The people were unconcerned that the name of their God was brought into disrepute, but David felt the matter keenly:

> Then David said to the Philistine, "You come to me with a sword, with a spear, and with a javelin. But I come to you in the name of the Lord of hosts, the God of the armies of Israel, whom you have defied. This day the Lord will deliver you into my hand, and I will strike you and take your head from you. And this day I will give the carcasses of the camp of the Philistines to the birds of the air and the wild beasts of the earth, that all the earth may know that there is a God in Israel" (1 Sam. 17:45-46).

David courageously defended the Lord's name because he understood that *"the name of the Lord is a strong tower; the righteous run to it and are safe"* (Prov. 18:10). Likewise, our conduct must consider Christ and His name first in all things, for we are His saints (Eph. 5:3). Believers compose the household of God, His living temple on earth to shine forth His glory; God forbid that we despise His name before the nations.

Instead of identifying with the Lord, the Jews had forsaken Him and His word (v. 13). A spiritual void exists in the human heart that only God can satisfy; forsaking Him necessitates trying to fill that emptiness with something else. The Jews chose to forsake Jehovah and to walk after *"the imagination of their own heart, and after Baalim"* (v. 14, KJV). The Hebrew word *sheriyruwth*, which means "twisted obstinacy," is translated "imagination" (KJV) in this verse. The NKJV renders *sheriyruwth* as "dictates" and the NASV translates it as "stubbornness." This word is only found ten times in the Old Testament and is rendered as "imagination" (KJV) in each case. Interestingly, eight of those ten occurrences are found in Jeremiah. This highlights the fact that twisted reasoning results in hardened hearts towards God.

The Jews would soon learn that their twisted obstinacy, or stubbornness, would cause them great harm; Baal would not be able to save them from the sword and dispersion (vv. 15-16). The judgment would be so great that the dead bodies on the ground would resemble cut grain at harvest time (v. 22); God would call professional weepers to walk up and down the hills surrounding Jerusalem to lament over it (vv. 17-21).

In the closing verses of Jeremiah 9, the Lord provides the solution to Judah's identity problem: right thinking leads to doing right. If His people were intimately familiar with His character and attributes, they would love Him, and not turn away from Him. There is nothing about God that would not be good for His people to understand and appreciate. Who would not want to bask in His love, grace, mercy, and kindness? Who would not want holiness, justice, and righteousness to fill the earth? The answer to both questions is only those who willfully determine not to know Him.

Accordingly, Jeremiah warned the people not to glory in their own wisdom, strength, or riches, for these things would not last. Instead, they should only boast to the extent that they knew and understood God. God did not want religious fanfare, a form of humanism, but genuine devotion. The fact that the Jews were practicing male circumcision was of no value since they did not understand its spiritual significance (v. 25). They were no longer mindful of the covenant it stood for or of the One who had instituted it. Even though they still practiced the ritual symbol of the covenant, they were no longer under God's protection. Practically speaking, Judah was uncircumcised in heart and had become no different than the surrounding idolatrous nations, who were physically uncircumcised (v. 26).

While it is true that most Christians will not create idols of stone and wood to worship, we engage in mental activities which replace the Lord's rightful place in our hearts. For example, have you ever noticed how some people create titles for others or themselves, presumably in order to serve Christ better? However, no disciple of Christ in Scripture had any title before his or her name. Men covet titles so that they might be honored by others – it is a natural pull of our fallen nature. But those who worship Christ must not dishonor Him by stealing His glory. Listen to the solemn words of the Lord Jesus on this very matter:

> But you, do not be called "Rabbi"; for one is your Teacher, the Christ, and you are all brethren. Do not call anyone on earth your father; for one is your Father, He who is in heaven. And do not be called teachers; for one is your Teacher, the Christ. But he who is greatest among you shall be your servant. And whoever exalts himself will be humbled, and he who humbles himself will be exalted (Matt. 23:8-12).

Disciples of Christ should not seek the praise of men, high positions, or honorable titles – all epithets and all praise are reserved for the Lord Jesus Christ. John the baptizer, speaking of Christ, declared the proper obligation of all true believers: *"He must increase, but I must decrease"* (John 3:30). Elihu put the matter this way: *"Let me not, I pray you, accept any man's person, **neither let me give flattering titles unto man**. For I know not to give flattering titles; in so doing my Maker would soon take me away"* (Job 32:21-22; KJV). Men love religious titles, but lovers of Christ should take none – all titles of position in Scripture belong to Him, not His followers.

Many of the common expressions we use to refer to each other or to Biblical individuals do not conform to the etiquette used in

Scripture to uphold God's honor. For example, we do not read of "Doctor Luke," but "Luke, the beloved physician." Nor do we read of the "Apostle Paul," but "Paul an apostle of Jesus Christ." No titles can be found before any of the disciples' names. We do not read of "Saint Matthew," "Elder Peter," "Deacon Stephen," "Minister Paul," or anything of the kind. Men love titles, yet the New Testament provides the Church none, except for the Lord Jesus Christ – all appellations belong to Him. How we address the Lord and others does matter. May each of us esteem the Lord more and human titles less. His name is Holy, and only He is to be revered and reverenced by men (Ps. 111:9). Let us not be carried away by our imaginations into unprofitable activities that steal glory from the Lord Jesus Christ: "*But 'he who glories, let him glory in the Lord.' For not he who commends himself is approved, but whom the Lord commends*" (2 Cor. 10:17-18).

Meditation

Glory to God on high, let praises fill the sky!
Praise ye His Name. Angels His Name adore,
Who all our sorrows bore, and saints cry evermore,
"Worthy the Lamb!"

To Him our hearts we raise – none else shall have our praise;
Praise ye His Name. Him our exalted Lord,
By us below adored, we praise with one accord.
"Worthy the Lamb!"

— James Allen

Dumb Idols
Jeremiah 10:1-16

Before continuing his prophetic ministry concerning the coming invasion and exile, Jeremiah paused to review the character of God, the One decreeing judgment. As the entire house of Israel is addressed, the first sixteen verses are best understood as a parenthetical statement that interrupts Jeremiah's temple message to Judah. In verse 17, the prophet resumed his prophecies against Judah and then ended the message with a prayer for the people (vv. 23-25). The theme of this interlude is the futility of worshipping the works of one's own hands. This portion of Scripture is filled with satire on idolatry.

Israel was not to follow the idolatrous practices of the nations, nor were they to be directed by signs in the sky (v. 2). The latter were probably naturally occurring events such as lunar and solar eclipses, comets, strange cloud formations, etc., which the pagans believed were caused by their gods. The Lord described the process by which an idol is manufactured; this alone is enough to demonstrate both its own limitations and the utter stupidity of those who trust in it. First, someone would chop down a tree, and then the wood would be carved into an image and fastened to a base so it would not tip over. Idols, as you know, have a poor sense of balance, especially once they have been covered with silver or gold (vv. 3-4). Idols do not walk too well either; actually, they do not move at all, so someone has to carry them to the specific place where they are to be honored (v. 5).

God told His people not to be afraid of something that was lifeless, created by man, and unable to move or even stand upright without help (v. 14). Just in case there was any confusion on this matter, He reminded them that a dumb idol cannot help those who honor it. A scarecrow in a corn patch might frighten away birds, but people realize it for what it is – a lifeless image. An intelligent

92

individual realizes that a rabbit's foot, a four-leafed clover, and good luck charms are nothing more than gimmicks, which are usually sold to gullible patrons. The Jews, on the other hand, did not comprehend this obvious truth; they vainly ascribed honor to inanimate objects.

Jeremiah then contrasts the dumb idols with Jehovah. Jehovah is unique, wise, and powerful (vv. 6-7). He is a living God, not a lifeless piece of wood. He is eternal and unchanging, whereas idols break, tarnish, chip, and even get misplaced (vv. 8-10). All that was created was made by Jehovah and all the forces of nature obey His every whim (v. 12). False gods cannot speak, but God's voice thunders in creation (v. 13). Jehovah is the only true God and will judge all those who worship false gods (vv. 10, 15).

Verse 11 is the only verse in the entire book that was originally written in Aramaic, the common tongue of the day, instead of Hebrew, the language of the Jews. As in the book of Daniel (the middle portion of Daniel is also in Aramaic), this seems to be God's calling card to warn the nations of their accountability to Him. The main purpose of Jeremiah's ministry was to call the Jews to repentance and to announce their judgment for not heeding that call, but verse 11 reminds the nations that they too will answer to Jehovah on Judgment Day. At that time, all that is wicked upon the earth will perish from it. Then everyone will know Jehovah and honor Him as the one true God.

Jeremiah concluded his parenthetical interlude by acknowledging that the Jews belonged to Jehovah because He had created them; thus, His covenant people were like an inheritance to Him (v. 16). This is such a lovely gesture of God, to confirm His love for His rebellious people. Psalm 100 conveys the same message: *"Know that the Lord, He is God; it is He who has made us, and not we ourselves; we are His people and the sheep of His pasture"* (Ps. 100:3). It was not enough for the Jews to merely know they were God's sheep; God wanted them to understand that He Himself knew they were His sheep. He loved them and longed to care for them and He wanted them to rest in that love.

Before we become too critical of the Jews' idolatry, we must recognize our own natural proclivity to create visual stimuli to accentuate religious experiences. Many of the religious symbols that Christendom uses today are simply Old Testament *figures* of what is now reality in Christ. Judaism was full of physical imagery which appealed to the senses, but its purpose was to point forward to the Messiah. Christianity, however, is spiritual and must be appreciated through faith, not our natural senses. Christ has come, and, therefore, has replaced all the types and shadows which were the prelude of the spiritual realities and good things to come (Heb. 8:13). However, much of Christendom has retained these symbols as part of their religious practices. What was meant to point the Jews to Christ's arrival now leads many away from Him. Here are a few examples of how Judaism is intruding into the gatherings of the Church.

Robes and Candles

Just as the Jewish priests wore ephods, many of the clergy in Christendom today have spectacular colored robes. In the tabernacle, the Jewish priests burned incense and kept the lampstand trimmed and bright. Many in Christendom light candles and wave incense canisters to mimic the religious practices of old.

The Sanctuary

In the Old Testament, the word "sanctuary" referred to a location within the temple or tabernacle where the priests officiated worship on behalf of the nation of Israel. In the New Testament, it is never applied to a physical room in which the Church gathers for worship, but to God's dwelling place in heaven. In the Old Testament, access to God was limited. Only the High Priest could gain entry into the Most Holy Place of the tabernacle and temple, and he did so in trepidation and not without the blood of a goat and bullock. After the completion of Christ's work at Calvary, the inner veil of the temple was rent from top to bottom to illustrate that through Christ, God could have full fellowship with man and man could have full access to God.

So all those "Sanctuary" signs we see in church buildings should really be turned to point upwards instead of down the hallway, or one could even tie a string around the sign and hang it from one's neck so that it points to himself or herself, since God dwells within those who have been born again during the Church Age (1 Cor. 6:19). Bricks and mortar cannot contain Him, but those who have responded to His invitation to be saved have His abiding presence forever.

The Altar

Some call the wooden table in the front of the "sanctuary" (already explained to be a misnomer) an "altar." Concerning altars, the Church has none but Christ (Heb. 13:10), and He is in heaven. How demeaning it must be to Christ to ascribe His ministry in heaven to a piece of manmade furniture! Some bow the knee before such religious objects, presumably in reverence for God. But it is through Christ and Him alone that the believer offers worship to God. Using terms such as "prayer altar" and "altar calls" demonstrates an ignorance of God's dispensational truths as revealed in Scripture.

From the time the first man walked upon the earth, God, in order to emphasize that salvation is only received by divine grace through faith, has been proving His greatness, and man's inclination to fail in whatever stewardship God dispenses. Ignorance of dispensational theology allows Judaism to ever so gently creep into Christian practices and effectually mars the clear testimony of Christ. Let us not bow down before pieces of furniture under the guise of being religious; if it supplants Christ, it is an idol!

The House of God

The term "house of God" occurs ninety times in the Bible, with eighty-seven of those occurrences speaking of the Old Testament dwelling place of God among His people in a tent or a temple. All three references to "the house of God" in the Epistles refer to the Church. During the Church Age, God dwells in His people, not a building (1 Cor. 6:19-20). Paul refers to the Church as *the house of God*: *"But if I am delayed, I write so that you may know how you ought to conduct yourself in the house of God, which is the church of the living God, the pillar and ground of the truth"* (1 Tim. 3:15). The NASV actually renders the expression *"house of God"* in this verse as *"household of God."* The "house of God" is not a building, but a *household* of God's people.

Incorrect terminology introduces unbiblical ideas about the Church. The Church is not a dead building; it is a living body. The next time someone welcomes you to "the house of God" (speaking of a building), you might ask, "Through what door does one gain entrance into the house of God?" The answer, of course, is the Lord

Jesus (John 10:1, 14:6). He is the only spiritual entrance into the spiritual house called the Church (Eph. 2:19-22).

Man-made religion appeals to the human senses, not to the human spirit, which is the part of man that God desires communion with. Thus, religiosity has flesh-appeal; it is a humanistic attempt to create something spiritual which is void of God's presence and endorsement. Such meetings will be characterized by the use of religious trinkets, elaborate buildings, fanciful garb, shallow music, and meaningless busyness. A. P. Gibbs summarizes the origin of such erroneous practices:

> One may well ask when attending such a meeting for "public worship:" "Whence came all these gaudy vestments; these tinkling bells; these burning candles; this smoking incense; these crosses; this sanctuary, reserved only for the clergy; this bloodless altar; this ornate ritual, with the sing-song intonation of its ready-made prayers, and ordered responses of the congregation; and this unholy distinction between clergy and laity? By what authority have all these things been introduced? Have they a Divine origin and scriptural foundation?" The answer is an emphatic negative. They are the results of man-made expediency, which has substituted the inventions of men for the scriptural and spiritual worship which God's word so clearly enjoins.[1]

May we learn a lesson from God's dealings with the Jews, and not ascribe spiritual value to sophisticated buildings, stained-glass windows, altars and other furnishings, burning candles, incense, and religious attire. None of these things mean anything to God; rather, they draw us away from the one true God and distract us from honoring His Son. If these things, the works of our own hands, gain spiritual significance in our thinking, have we not committed the same sin Jeremiah confronted in his day? May the Church keep Christ enthroned in her thinking and not allow dumb idols to rob Him of our adoration.

Meditation

Lord, we would never forget Thy love, who hast redeemed us by Thy blood;
And now, as our High Priest above dost intercede for us with God.

96

We would remember we are one with every saint that loves Thy name;
United to Thee on the throne – our life, our hope, our Lord the same.

Lord, we are Thine, we praise Thy love, one with Thy saints, all one in Thee;
We would, until we meet above, in all our ways remember Thee.

— James G. Deck

Correct Me
Jeremiah 10:17-25

The Jews were told to gather up their meager belongings in preparation for the impending captivity – in modern vernacular, the message was "pack your bags – you're leaving" (v. 17). If they wanted to survive, they would have to accept their sojourn in Babylon as their just punishment and not resist their armies. If, however, they chose to remain in Jerusalem (their supposed invincible fortress), they would be slaughtered.

Jerusalem is personified in verses 19-22 as a woman; she would bear the invasion as a grievous wound that would take a long time to heal. Her situation is likened to a collapsed tent and a mother who cannot find her missing children (v. 20). Her people would be scattered like lost sheep because her *"stupid"* shepherds (NASV) did not follow the Lord (v. 21). She would be made desolate by the Babylonians and become the home of scavenging predators (v. 22).

As many preachers still do, Jeremiah ended his message with a prayer to conclude his temple message to Judah. While praying, he acknowledged that a person does not own his or her life; it is to be directed by God: *"O Lord, I know the way of man is not in himself; it is not in man who walks to direct his own steps"* (v. 23). We are to live for the Lord, meaning that He must be the One directing our path in life, that is, if we want to enjoy His blessings and fellowship.

Jeremiah realized that to properly walk God's way in life requires Him to correct our missed steps. This disciplinary principle should have been no surprise to the Jews, as Moses informed them of it shortly after their deliverance from Egypt (Ex. 15:26). It is the same principle that parents must teach their children early in life: obedience brings blessing, but disobedience results in punishment. Accordingly, our children have a choice as to whether they will receive our warm embrace or the rod of reproof. Every child of God has the same choice: *"Be you therefore followers of God, as dear children"* (Eph. 5:1); *"As obedient children, not fashioning yourselves according to the former lusts in your ignorance"* (1 Pet. 1:14); *"For whom the Lord loves He chastens"* (Heb. 12:6). There truly is only one way for a child of God to be happy in the Lord Jesus – to trust and obey!

If one loves the Lord, submitting to His precepts will be a delight. Love for the Lord is a stronger motive for obedience than the fear of consequences: *"There is no fear in love; but perfect love casts out fear, because fear involves torment. But he who fears has not been made perfect in love"* (1 Jn. 4:18). A believer motivated by the love for Christ can venture into each and every day with confidence that God has his or her best in mind; he or she need not fear eternal retribution for every misstep. God is for those who love Him (Rom. 8:28).

This is a fundamental truth that parents must understand if they are ever to enjoy a happy home. If the only way parents are able to control their children is by the constant threat of chastening (fear), there will be problems in the home as the children grow older. Certainly there is a place for chastening; demanding obedience in toddlers develops a heart of submission later. Children (older than toddlers) who truly love their parents will require little discipline. God teaches us through His dealings with His own children that childrearing must focus on changing the heart: win the heart, mold the heart, train the child to keep his or her heart pure – and to God be all the glory.

Thankfully, our heavenly Father's work in our hearts is ongoing also. The divine work of sanctification begins in the believer's life immediately after he or she answers the call of salvation. God begins to fashion the new believer into a holy vessel and each believer is exhorted to cooperate in the working out of what God is working into his or her life (1 Thess. 5.23; IIcb. 13:21). All believers will ultimately be conformed to the moral image of Christ (Rom. 8:29); there is no human choice of involvement in that aspect of sanctification – it is God's will and power that accomplishes this. Yet, there is an ongoing call to each believer to not resist God's working in his or her life, but instead to be yielded to Him. God promises to chasten those who choose not to submit to Him in order that they may be brought to a yielded position and experience sanctification (Heb.

12:6). Consequently, sanctification in a practical sense is happening to every believer, but some are more serious about it than others and, accordingly, will reap a greater blessing of further refinement here and now.

During his prayer, Jeremiah personally identified with His people, pleading *"O Lord correct me"* (v. 24). Why would Jeremiah beseech the Lord's correction? Apparently, Jeremiah felt it was needful, yet he also requested that the Lord correct with a righteous objective, lest His anger consume them. God's anger with His children was justified, but His reproof is always done in love, with the end goal of repentance and restoration. God's love would ensure that what was best for Judah would be performed in such a way that His righteous nature would not be affronted. Jeremiah concluded his prayer by asking God to judge the nations because they did not honor Him and they had persecuted His people relentlessly. Every child of God receives correction now (it is proof of God's love for us), but there is a coming day in which all the enemies of God's people will be judged and removed from our presence forever. With this eternal perspective in mind, we believers ought to walk in the right way, thank the Lord for His correction when we stray from this right path, and look forward to the day when there will be no other way to go, but to walk with the Lord.

Meditation

When we walk with the Lord in the light of His Word,
What a glory He sheds on our way!
While we do His good will, He abides with us still,
And with all who will trust and obey.

Then in fellowship sweet we will sit at His feet,
Or we'll walk by His side in the way.
What He says we will do, where He sends we will go;
Never fear, only trust and obey.

— John H. Sammis

The Broken Covenant

Jeremiah 11:1-17

The timing of Jeremiah's fourth message may have coincided with the temple repairs initiated by King Josiah (about six years after Jeremiah's ministry commenced). It was at this time that the Law of God was found in the temple and read to the king. Josiah was deeply moved and his conviction ushered in an era of sweeping reforms. Unfortunately, the spiritual renovations were superficial; the influence of a single person, no matter how godly or influential, cannot force a change of heart in an entire nation. After Josiah's sudden death in a battle with Pharaoh Neco, Judah quickly reverted back to the dead spiritual state it was in before the reign of Josiah.

Jeremiah may have heard the newly discovered scrolls read aloud; he may have read them himself; in any case, the validity of God's Law was fresh in his mind. Accordingly, he begins his fourth message by reminding the inhabitants of Judah in general, and the people of Jerusalem in particular, of the covenant their forefathers made with Jehovah after being delivered from Egypt:

> Thus says the Lord God of Israel: "Cursed is the man who does not obey the words of this covenant which I commanded your fathers in the day I brought them out of the land of Egypt, from the iron furnace, saying, 'Obey My voice, and do according to all that I command you; so shall you be My people, and I will be your God,' that I may establish the oath which I have sworn to your fathers, to give them 'a land flowing with milk and honey,' as it is this day." And I answered and said, "So be it, Lord" (Jer. 11:3-5).

Jeremiah reminds the Jews that their forefathers did not obey this covenant, and were punished (vv. 7-8). The same motif was occurring again; God's people were rejecting His Word and serving other gods (vv. 9-10). Likewise, God would punish them as He did their

101

ancestors (v. 11). Idolatry had become so rampant that there were altars of incense set up throughout the streets of Jerusalem to honor various false gods, especially Baal. In comparing the beginning of this message with Jeremiah's previous prophecies, William Kelly notes an escalation in intensity:

> In Jeremiah 11 … we find a new and very solemn warning to the men of Judah and Jerusalem. As a rule, in all the prophets of Israel progress may be observed in their messages; there is increasing depth in the appeals of the Spirit of God to the people. Here, then, we have "Cursed be the man that obeys not the words of this covenant."[1]

There also is a correlation between the increasing intensity of Jeremiah's messages and his flow of tears for his countrymen. Inevitable judgment was looming, and the prophet who had been forbidden to pray and to cry for his people could only warn them.

God was infuriated by their blatant disregard for His covenant, so much so that He instructs Jeremiah a second time not to pray or weep for the people. God had specifically shown them through the Law how to offer acceptable worship to Him, and had made it clear that they were to reverence Him alone. Though they were His beloved people, they had brought lewdness into His temple, and consequently their blood sacrifices (i.e. "*holy flesh,*" v. 15) had no value to Him (v. 15). They may have thought that their sacrifices could avert God's judgment, but religious showmanship is not equal to repentance. God wanted changed hearts, not religious sacrifices. He had planted Judah like a man plants an olive tree, but now He planned to ignite (the imagery here may be a lightning strike) that which He planted. The tree would be consumed by His anger (vv. 16-17). God's fury with Judah is reminiscent of His anger towards Nadab and Abihu.

Centuries before the time of Jeremiah, as Israel wandered in the wilderness, Jehovah gave His Law to them, and then He selected Aaron and his four sons (Nadab, Abihu, Eleazar, and Ithamar) to officiate worship in the tabernacle on behalf of the nation. Before the Israelites moved northward from Mount Sinai, Nadab and Abihu would be fatally judged for intruding into God's presence with strange fire (Lev. 10:1-6), an event which demonstrated God's hatred of humanized religion. Man may worship God only according to His revealed order and may offer to Him only that which He says is acceptable. The Jews had been forewarned; if, in time, they developed elaborate ceremonies and religious rituals to offer God their self-approved sacrifices, both their self-righteous doings and their polluted sacrifices would be rejected.

Fallen humanity has a natural propensity for religious pride (i.e. making superficial choices or changes that neither show faith in God nor turn us from a path of sin). Nadab and Abihu offered strange incense to God in worship just after God had given specific instructions as to the proper way for priests to present sacrifices to Him. God struck them both dead for their arrogance, and their father was not permitted to mourn their deaths since they had offended God. Religious doings do not impress God, nor do they have any eternal value.

On this point, the rebuke of the Lord Jesus to the Church at Laodicea is most pertinent: *"You are wretched, miserable, poor, blind, and naked – I counsel you to buy from Me gold refined in the fire, that you may be rich; and white garments, that you may be clothed, that the shame of your nakedness may not be revealed; and anoint your eyes with eye salve, that you may see"* (Rev. 3:17-18). Those in the Church at Laodicea were not living for Christ; consequently, God's righteousness was not displayed in their lives. Though all believers in the Church have been positionally declared righteous in Christ, each believer has the opportunity to labor in righteous acts for Christ. Those things which are done in accordance with revealed truth and in the power of the Spirit have eternal value; these righteous acts are what the believer is adorned with throughout eternity. In heaven, the bride of Christ must have righteous attire; she is *"arrayed in fine linen, clean and bright, for the fine linen is the righteous acts of the saints"* (Rev. 19:8).

Paul explains in 1 Corinthians 15:40-42 that after the resurrection, some saints will shine forth the glory of God more brightly than others, just as some stars in the nighttime sky are more luminous than other stars. This acquired glory directly reflects the good works that are done for Christ by His strength in this present life. Eternal glory, evidently, has a weight to it (2 Cor. 4:17); in other words, its quality is measurable and can be earned by believers through selfless service for Christ now. At the judgment seat of Christ, everyone worthy of God's praise shall receive it (1 Cor. 4:5). While the church at Laodicea was spiritually naked (i.e. they had no righteous acts for clothing), the Holy Spirit does bear fruit in the life of the individual "overcomer" (Rev. 3:18, 21). Though believers will suffer varying degrees of loss at the judgment seat of Christ, all will have the praise of God and thus guaranteed righteous attire for eternity (1 Cor. 4:5).

The appropriate clothing for eternity is obtained now through righteous acts; may all believers work to secure for themselves now a covering of eternal glory. Acts of righteousness done now will endow believers with a corresponding measure of glory in heaven (1 Cor. 15:41-42; 2 Cor. 4:17). Endeavoring to worship God through any means or method other than what His Word authorizes does not contribute to one's eternal attire.

How utterly putrid to God, then, are all the ceremonies, the holidays, and the rituals which the Church has created to obtain some religious experience or to try to impress Him. In the Church Age, believers are commanded to regularly observe the Lord's Supper in remembrance of Christ, to be living sacrifices by mortifying their fleshly desires and yielding to God's will, and to fulfill their work of ministry within the Body of Christ. Anything beyond this is humanized religion and an offense to God.

Thankfully, the Old Covenant which the Jews could not keep was replaced with a unilateral covenant that God would honor despite their failings. How is this possible? God ratified and sealed the New Covenant with the blood of His own Son. The Lord Jesus Christ said on the eve of His death, *"This cup is the new covenant in My blood, which is shed for you"* (Luke 22:20). By punishing His Son for the sins of the people, God could righteously extend them forgiveness and blessing though they were undeserving of it. In a future day, after repenting of their sins and turning to Christ, the entire nation will be saved.

The New Covenant, which was made with the house of Judah and Israel (Heb. 8:8), would end the dispensation of the Law and usher in the age of grace – the Church Age. The blessings of this covenant are received through faith in Christ, and in Him alone. Thankfully, the Gentiles are a second benefactor of this covenant (Eph. 2:11-3:6). The events on Mount Sinai in Moses' day all pointed to a future, incredible event on Mount Calvary in Christ's day. There God would once and for all satisfy His righteous demand for justice concerning human wickedness.

Meditation

O! How I love Thy holy Word, Thy gracious covenant, O Lord!
It guides me in the peaceful way, I think upon it all the day.

Long unafflicted, undismayed, in pleasure's path secure I strayed;
Thou made me feel Thy chastening rod, and straight I turned unto my God.

O! Had Thou left me unchastised, Thy precept I had still despised;
And still the snare in secret laid, had my unwary feet betrayed.

I love Thee therefore O my God, and breathe towards Thy dear abode;
Where in Thy presence fully blest, Thy chosen saints forever rest.

— William Cowper

The Suffering Prophet
Jeremiah 11:18-23

Jeremiah's messages of rebuke and judgment were not popular. The men of Anathoth, Jeremiah's hometown, offered him an ultimatum: "Jeremiah, shut up or die." Apparently, these rebels had already devised a plan to murder Jeremiah (v. 19), but God revealed the entire matter to His faithful prophet (v. 18). Without God's help, Jeremiah said he would have been like a lamb or an ox brought to the slaughter. This was the first of several attempts to snuff out the life of God's ambassador to Judah.

God had promised Jeremiah His protection when He first summoned him to be His prophet. In the following chapters, the Lord's faithfulness to this pledge would be shown repeatedly. David, who also knew what it was like to suffer wrongfully, wrote, *"Many are the afflictions of the righteous, but the Lord delivers him out of them all"* (Ps. 34:19). Certainly, Jeremiah would suffer because of his ministry, but God would be faithful to preserve his life and deliver him from jeopardy.

Besides the plot of the citizens of Anathoth (11:18-13), Jeremiah would suffer much verbal abuse by the people (18:18), he would be assaulted and chained by the priest Pashhur (20:1-3), the priests and prophets would seek to kill him (26:7-24), King Jehoiakim would burn Jeremiah's scroll and then order him to be arrested (36:22-26), Jeremiah would be struck by the priests and then imprisoned (37:15), and in a final attempt on his life, the princes would drop Jeremiah down into a deep pit where he would sink into the mire (37:11-38:13). But though they left him there to die, God had other plans. In each of these threatening situations, Jeremiah would be miraculously sustained and delivered by the Lord. Why? He was God's man doing God's will and was thus invincible until God's will for his life was complete.

Job understood that each of us has a specific number of days on earth to work the will of God: *"Man who is born of woman is of few days and full of trouble. Since his days are determined, the number of his months is with You; You have appointed his limits, so that he cannot pass"* (Job 14:1, 5). Until Jeremiah's ministry was complete, he was immortal. This truth is an immense comfort for those who drink from the bitter cup of their own ministry. God's people living godly lives will suffer in a wicked, sin-cursed world (2 Tim. 3:12), but they cannot be overcome by the enemy until their work is done.

Jeremiah's ministry and the people's response to it illustrate a pattern repeated throughout Scripture: especially in moral and spiritual matters, the majority is usually wrong. In secular movements, numbers are everything, but rarely do vast hordes of people represent God's will. This anomaly is quite evident in the modern Church movement, which equates church attendance with church success. The mindset is that big church meetings are obviously the result of divine blessing. However, it is making disciples of Christ that is the key to Church growth and vitality (Matt. 28:19-20). The Great Supper Parable of Luke 14 teaches us that the Lord is much more interested in the commitment of His disciples to Him than in the hordes of people merely following Him. The Lord longs for the genuine numbers. This means the Church has a responsibility beyond just preaching the gospel to the lost: discipleship. Using crowd-drawing gimmicks to shore up poor attendance is absurd. Biblically speaking, the numbers ideology is erroneous on at least two counts.

First of all, Church history, and indeed biblical history, has shown that the religious majority has rarely aligned with God. Rather, crowds normally translate to doctrinal compromise and shallow spirituality, while a mere "remnant" composes the real thing (Hag. 1:12-14; Rom. 9:27, 11:5). Only eight souls were faithful to God at the time of the flood, Abraham and his family were alone with God in Canaan, later Elijah and 7,000 others were all that remained in Israel who had not bowed the knee to Baal – each of these was the Lord's remnant at a particular time (Rom. 11:4). As we have observed, very few individuals stood with Jeremiah against the wickedness of his day.

Throughout the Church Age, it has been organized religious movements that have persecuted true believers, and they have often done so in the name of Christ. The general counsel of Mark Twain seems pertinent in such matters: "Whenever you find yourself on the side of the majority, it is time to pause and reflect." In spiritual matters, the mainstream is rarely right, so huge attendance does not necessarily confirm the scriptural soundness of the congregation. In fact, if your local church is growing in numbers, it would be a good time to review your evangelistic methods and ensure that they are upright and that the gospel message being preached is accurate; otherwise, the false professors being added to your meeting will only cause havoc later. As anyone with cancer will tell you, not all growth is good; irregular or out-of-control growth leads to the body's destruction.

The second reason the emphasis on numbers is not good is that, though modern Christendom will not admit the fact, the underlying motivation for increasing church membership is to boost revenue. Many of the best-selling books on church growth promote the use of business-like practices to increase organizational numbers. More members translates to more money, which is then used to fund further advertizing campaigns, first-contact incentives, and church programs to entice even more people to join the growing corporation. Yet, the Lord Jesus taught that He would not build His Church by human gimmicks, but rather through the supernatural power of the gospel message (John 6:40, 44).

Only those who have experienced spiritual rebirth are living stones in the great spiritual house that God is building (1 Pet. 2:5). Man seeks to erect a religious facade to mock what God accomplishes by His grace. However, it will be the true Church, not humanized religion, that will testify of the manifold wisdom of God for eternity (Eph. 3:10). In God's perfect timing, He will judge and remove from the earth all that perverts truth and opposes His righteousness. Consequently, Jeremiah prayed that God would judge his adversaries, and execute vengeance upon them (v. 20).

The Lord responded to Jeremiah's prayer by promising the complete judgment of Anathoth during the Babylonian invasion. Either by the sword or by famine (v. 22), none of them would be left (v. 23). God's dealings with the inhabitants of Anathoth would be a warning to all Jews that opposing God's Word and those delivering it had severe consequences. May this truth encourage every believer who has suffered for the cause of Christ.

Meditation

Come, sound His praise abroad, and hymns of glory sing;
Jehovah is the sovereign God, the universal King.

Today attend His voice, nor dare provoke His rod;
Come, like the people of His choice, and own your gracious God.

But if your ears refuse the language of His grace,
And hearts grow hard, like stubborn Jews, that unbelieving race;

The Lord, in vengeance dressed, will lift His hand and swear,
"You that despise My promised rest shall have no portion there."

— Isaac Watts

The Wicked Way
Jeremiah 12:1-17

Even though God had protected Jeremiah from the citizens of Anathoth, he still had some lingering questions about God's dealings with the wicked. Jeremiah was not questioning the righteousness of God, but rather the execution of His justice (v. 1). From Jeremiah's perspective, the wicked looked happy and prosperous. This was impossible apart from God's enablement: it seemed that He had planted them and let them take root in order to experience material fruitfulness (v. 2). Jeremiah wanted to know why this was happening. Why was Jehovah apparently blessing those who had angered Him?

Jeremiah did not want God to bless the wicked; rather, he wanted God to set them apart for judgment in the same way he had been chosen to be prophet (v. 3). He had been faithful to his calling and his opposition had rejected him and his message. Accordingly, Jeremiah requested that they be dragged like sheep to the slaughter. In verse 4, the prophet went on to imply that when God does judge the wicked, the righteous normally suffer along with them. It appeared to Jeremiah that, even when judgment falls, the wicked fare better than the righteous; it seemed that the righteous suffer at all times (i.e. at the hands of the wicked or when the wicked are punished), but the wicked usually prosper. So what benefit was there in living righteously? Why did it seem that God's justice was inconsistent in that it extended both blessing and judgment to the wicked, while the righteous suffered all the time?

The Lord answered Jeremiah's questions, but not in the way that he expected. Instead of defending His dealings with the wicked, He exhorted His prophet. The severity of our difficulties is relative; we might complain about a sore toe, but someone who experiences chronic pain probably would not. God responded to Jeremiah's inquiries with a question of His own: if the prophet thought his present situation was tough, how would he fare in the days to come, which would be more difficult (v. 5)?

Two metaphors were used to illustrate this point. First, how could a person who succumbs to fatigue in a foot race against other men possibly compete with horses later? Second, how could one who stumbles on the smooth walkways ever venture through the thickets by the Jordan? The situation in Judah was going to get much worse before it would get better for Jeremiah. The Lord concluded His response by telling Jeremiah that his own family had turned against him and warned him not to trust them no matter what accolades they might shower upon him (v. 6). God's lesson was that complaining would not resolve Jeremiah's hardship; he must learn to trust the Lord more fully and to rely on His strength.

Now that His prophet had been both protected and admonished (11:18-12:6), God again continued with the pronouncement of judgment on Judah. She was described as a house and an inheritance which He would abandon to the Babylonians (v. 7). God loved His people and wanted to bless them with His intimate presence, but this was not possible. Their opposition against Him had become as bold as a roaring lion (v. 8). So deep-seated was their sinning that Jeremiah likened Judah to a speckled bird (Albert Barnes suggests that the bird is a vulture), which relentlessly threatens other birds in the woods; it deserved to be caught and destroyed (v. 9). H. A. Ironside comments on the lion and bird analogies:

> It is too late to plead for them. Jehovah has forsaken His house and left His heritage. His "dearly beloved" is to be given into the hand of her enemies. Like a lion roaring in the forest, they have proudly defied Him; now, like a speckled bird persecuted of the birds of the wood, the assembled nations shall devote her to destruction.[1]

The people had become wicked because their leaders were wicked. God had planted a beautiful vineyard (Israel), but Israel's shepherds had made it desolate (v. 10). The nation of Israel, as a political reality, is likened to a noble vine (a grape vine; Jer. 8:13), which God planted in the world (2:21, 12:10); Israel was God's vineyard. Vineyards were usually protected by walls to prevent damage from livestock, but in the case of Judah, there would be no hedge of protection. The Jews were a nation of herdsmen so they would understand the devastation brought about by many herdsmen and their livestock entering a vineyard. God would allow the vine of Israel to be trampled. Moreover, the sword of the Lord (exercised through Babylon) would decimate the land. It would have no productivity, bearing only the fruit of sowing to sin, that is, the thorns of affliction and a harvest of shame (vv. 11-13).

When Israel is spoken of as a fig tree in Scripture, the metaphor relates to the religious element of Israel (i.e. Judaism), which normally was fruitless to God (Matt. 21:19-21; Luke 13:6-9). This reality is typified for us during one of the events in the life of the Lord Jesus. After preaching three years to the lost nation of Israel, Christ cursed the fig tree just before His death at Calvary. Less than forty years later Jerusalem and the temple were destroyed and the Jews have not sacrificed since then. The Old Covenant was replaced by the New Covenant, sealed with Christ's blood, and God was determined not to allow the Jews to continue in what was now obsolete.

One of the signs that the Tribulation Period and the Second Advent of Christ is nearing is that the fig tree (i.e. religious Israel) will again shoot forth leaves after a long winter season of deadness (Luke 21:29-31). Leaves must precede fruit, but the fig tree will bear no fruit until the rebirth of the nation occurs in the latter days of the Tribulation Period. What might the new leaves speak of? This is likely a reference to the Jews reviving the old sacrificial system during the Tribulation Period. At that point, there are leaves upon the tree, depicting a religious reality, but there is no fruit. Spiritual fruit can only come through spiritual rebirth which coincides with the Holy Spirit being poured out upon the Jewish nation at the end of the Tribulation Period. At that time they will know and worship Jesus Christ as Messiah (Joel 2:25-3:21; Zech. 12:10-13:1).

Therefore, we see that, during the Tribulation Period, the Jews will again offer sacrifices under the Levitical system. Logically speaking, before the Antichrist can stop these sacrifices during the middle of the Tribulation Period, they must begin again (Matt. 24:15; 2 Thess. 2:4-6). Finally, at the end of the Tribulation Period, the refined Jewish nation will receive the Holy Spirit and obtain spiritual life in Christ.

In this spiritually fruitful state the Jews are known as the olive tree which provides a testimony to the entire world of God's goodness (Hos. 14:6; Rom. 11:17-24). Although we see that individual Jews in the Old Testament were filled by the Holy Spirit in order to serve the Lord effectively, the nation as a whole has never received the Spirit (Zech. 4:4-7), and this will not happen until the eve of Christ's second coming to the earth.

This same reality is illustrated in Ezekiel's vision of the valley of dry bones, when Ezekiel was instructed to preach to a valley of bones and the bones began moving and assembling themselves into standing skeletons (Ezek. 37). This vision symbolizes the fact that the nation will be established again prior to its receiving spiritual life. After 2,600 years of Gentile rule, Israel became its own political reality in May 1948, even though the nation still remains dead in a spiritual sense, coinciding with the figure of the grape vine. As Ezekiel continued to preach, the skeletons took on flesh – this great army now had the appearance of life, but in fact there was no life within them, corresponding to the image of the fig tree. Ezekiel then prophesied to the wind (a type of the Holy Spirit) to come and give life to and breath into the great army, symbolizing the spiritual birth of Israel and relating to symbol of the olive tree.

Jeremiah concluded his fourth message by promising the Jews that God would judge the Gentile nations who seized His inheritance. Though He would uproot His people, He also would bring them back and replant them in the land. Likewise, after judging the wickedness of the nations, He promised to restore them also in a future day: *"If they will learn carefully the ways of My people, to swear by My name, 'As the Lord lives,' as they taught My people to swear by Baal, then they shall be established in the midst of My people"* (v. 16). This is a reference to the millennial kingdom of Christ in which all the inhabitants of the earth will be blessed; those not submitting to Christ will be removed and destroyed (v. 17).

> *Yes, many peoples and strong nations shall come to seek the Lord of hosts in Jerusalem, and to pray before the Lord. Thus says the Lord of hosts: "In those days ten men from every language of the nations shall grasp the sleeve of a Jewish man, saying, 'Let us go with you, for we have heard that God is with you'"* (Zech. 8:22-23).

During the Kingdom Age, Jerusalem will be the religious center of the world (Isa. 66:10-20). At this time, the Jewish nation will not only be restored to God, but they will also be esteemed by all nations. Jeremiah's words must have resounded in the ears of the Jews throughout their Babylonian captivity. The same prophet that had foretold their severe chastening, which had happened, was also informing them of God's promise to restore them back to their homeland and to honor them before their enemies.

The Lord's promises to the nation of Israel have earthly fulfillments, but His promises to the Church relate to a heavenly inheritance which includes His earthly rule:

In My Father's house are many mansions; if it were not so, I would have told you. I go to prepare a place for you. And if I go and prepare a place for you, I will come again and receive you to Myself; that where I am, there you may be also (John 14:2-3).

He who overcomes shall inherit all things (Rev. 21:7).

If we endure, we shall also reign with Him (2 Tim. 2:12).

And have made us kings and priests to our God; and we shall reign on the earth (Rev. 5:10).

Like Israel in Jeremiah's day, the Church has hope for the future, despite the difficult days ahead. We should live our lives *"looking for the blessed hope and glorious appearing of our great God and Savior Jesus Christ"* (Tit. 2:13). The promise of the Lord's return should resonate in each believer's mind: *"Beloved, now we are children of God; and it has not yet been revealed what we shall be, but we know that when He is revealed, we shall be like Him, for we shall see Him as He is. And everyone who has this hope in Him purifies himself, just as He is pure"* (1 Jn. 3:2-3). Living each day as if the Lord could return at any moment to catch up the Church to heaven (1 Thess. 4:13-18) will safeguard our hearts against discouragement and from settling comfortably into a condemned planet.

A believer is an ambassador of Christ who represents the kingdom of God while on earth (2 Cor. 5:20). The world is not the believer's playground, but God's classroom. Those answering God's call of salvation have no ownership in the present perverse world nor have they yet inherited the eternal one to come. Though temporarily living between these two realms, each ambassador of Christ is called to maintain the blessed hope, that is, to recognize the promise of Christ's return as an imminent prospect. Do you long for the Lord's coming? The Lord Jesus will reward all those who love His appearing (2 Tim. 4:8). Those who do not abide with Him and long for Him will most likely be ashamed at His coming (1 Jn. 2:28).

Meditation

See Him, who is gone before us, heavenly mansions to prepare,
See Him, who is ever pleading for us with prevailing prayer,
See Him, who with sound of trumpet, and with His angelic train,
Summoning the world to judgment, on the clouds will come again.

Raise us up from earth to heaven, give us wings of faith and love,
Gales of holy aspirations wafting us to realms above;
That, with hearts and minds uplifted, we with Christ our Lord may
    dwell,
Where He sits enthroned in glory in His heavenly citadel.

So at last, when He appears, we from out our graves may spring,
With our youth renewed like eagles, flocking round our heavenly King.
Caught up on the clouds of Heaven, and may meet Him in the air,
Rise to realms where He is reigning, and may reign forever there.

— Christopher Wordsworth

The Marred Belt
Jeremiah 13:1-11

Jeremiah's fifth message contained two parables, the marred belt and the broken wine jars. What is the timing of this message? The narrative specifically mentions the ruling authority of the queen along with the king in verse 18. As a queen is rarely mentioned in Scripture as having such authority, the timing of Jeremiah's message must have aligned with an unusual social situation. The most probable explanation is that Jeremiah was referring to newly crowned Jehoiachin, the son of Jehoiakim, and his now widowed mother Nehushta (2 Kgs. 24:5-8). Jehoiachin was eighteen years of age when crowned king of Judah and was not likely married. His mother, after eleven years of sitting with her husband on the throne would have been quite comfortable there (2 Kgs. 23:36).

If these assumptions are correct, the date for this chapter would be 587 B.C., as Jehoiachin only reigned three months before being removed from the throne by Nebuchadnezzar. This date would put Jeremiah's message some eight years after the first Babylonian invasion. It was at this time that Jeconiah (Jehoiachin) was taken to Babylon in chains along with thousands of other captives, including the prophet Ezekiel (Ezek. 1:1). Why did Jeremiah act out parables in his fifth message since it would be faster just to speak the prophecy?

The Lord Jesus often spoke in parables; in all, about forty are recorded in the gospels. He used these as a way of illustrating the truth for those who were disinterested in spiritual matters. The idea was to provoke curiosity, which would prompt the serious listener to seek out the meaning of the illustration. In the following chapters of Jeremiah, this prophet uses parables with the same intention. In their poor spiritual condition the Jews were ignoring Jeremiah's prophetic utterances; perhaps they would be more interested in dramatized messages.

116

What is a parable? The word "parable" literally means "to cast alongside." The Lord Jesus used a story format to juxtapose a spiritual truth with a common, everyday activity that the people could relate to, such as sowing seed, using a dragnet for fishing, or watching birds nest in a mustard tree. The Lord Jesus intentionally spoke in parables to reveal truth in a partially-veiled manner, especially when His audience was composed largely of doubters and those who rejected His message.

The parables were not just enjoyable stories but served as a test to the hearers. The casual onlookers, the "spiritual window-shoppers," would hear the message but not comprehend it, nor would they desire any more understanding: "Thanks for the good story," might be all they would say as they continued along their own way. But those who longed to understand the spiritual significance of the parable (often only His disciples) would seek the Lord for further instruction. Jeremiah also spoke in parables, but as in the days of Christ, few Jews would heed the metaphoric warnings.

Jeremiah was to purchase a linen belt and wear it in public to pique the curiosity of the people (v. 1). The belt would be similar to the sash that the priests wore in the temple. It was to be preserved in good condition, and thus, was not to be washed with water. After a period of time, God instructed Jeremiah to travel to *Perath* (i.e. normally understood in Scripture to be the Euphrates River) and hide the belt in a crevice of rocks there (v. 4). As the Hebrew spelling for "to Parah" and "to Euphrates" are exactly the same, we have to use context and sound reasoning to determine which was being referred to. It seems more likely that Jeremiah went to the village of Parah some three miles northeast of his hometown of Anathoth instead of a seven hundred mile round trip to the Euphrates River. This same journey was to be repeated after many days (v. 6). Although it is possible that Jeremiah made two long expeditions to the Euphrates and back, given the hostile conditions at that time and that Jehoiachin's reign was only three months, it seems more likely that he traveled twice to Parah.

At the Lord's command, Jeremiah later returned to the same spot he had previously buried the belt and recovered it. Exposure to the elements had spoiled the belt and made it completely unusable (v. 7). The Lord explained the meaning of the parable to Jeremiah in verses

117

8-11. The belt around Jeremiah's waist pictured Israel and Judah. Around Jeremiah's waist the belt was protected from harm and admired by all that looked upon it. However, when removed from him, the belt would become useless. As God's people, the Jews enjoyed His protection and they had the opportunity to display His greatness to the nations, but idolatry had ruined them:

> *"For as the sash clings to the waist of a man, so I have caused the whole house of Israel and the whole house of Judah to cling to Me," says the Lord, "that they may become My people, for renown, for praise, and for glory; but they would not hear"* (Jer. 13:11).

The once prominent and beautiful sash had become completely unsuitable for adornment and honor. Thus, the linen belt was discarded; it was no longer useful. Likewise, Israel and Judah would be discarded and scattered among the nations by God, their Owner, until such time as He recalled them to their homeland and restored them as His holy people. The sash was a sign of service. Israel had been Jehovah's girded servant since departing from Egypt, but not a faithful one. Close communion with the Lord would enable the Jews to serve Him and be blessed by Him. The Jewish people only had value and security in their proper place of proximity to God: figuratively, as a sash about His waist.

Similarly, the New Testament uses a bride and groom analogy to express Christ's desire for believers to remain near to Him. It is befitting for a bride to be at her groom's side; likewise, the most secure and blissful location for the Church is to be with her Beloved (Eph. 5:22-33). Paul uses this word picture to exhort Christians not to tolerate false doctrines and false teachers in the same way Jeremiah used the parable of the marred belt to warn the Jews against idolatry:

> For I am jealous for you with godly jealousy. For I have betrothed you to one husband, that I may present you as a chaste virgin to Christ. But I fear, lest somehow, as the serpent deceived Eve by his craftiness, so your minds may be corrupted from the simplicity that is in Christ. For if he who comes preaches another Jesus whom we have not preached, or if you receive a different spirit which you have not received, or a different gospel which you have not accepted – you may well put up with it (2 Cor. 11:2-4)!

For the Church to be deceived by Satan *"from the simplicity that is in Christ"* is a serious sin. The Jews of Jeremiah's day had been beguiled into thinking that religiosity was more important than keeping the Law. Five centuries later, Satan was defeated at Calvary by the Lord Jesus Christ (John 12:31-33). Having failed to stop Christ from completing His redemptive work, Satan now concentrates on casting uncertainty upon the Person and work of Christ. Satan continues to slander Christ in the media, and to seduce worshippers into idolatry or heresy. Let us not be ignorant of his devices; if what we are engaged in pulls us away from abiding in Christ or casts disdain upon His name, there is only one course of action – repent and return to Him!

Meditation

I need Thy presence every passing hour.
What but Thy grace can foil the tempter's power?
Who, like Thyself, my guide and stay can be?
Through cloud and sunshine, Lord, abide with me.

Hold Thou Thy cross before my closing eyes;
Shine through the gloom and point me to the skies.
Heaven's morning breaks, and earth's vain shadows flee;
In life, in death, O Lord, abide with me.

— Henry Lyte

Smash the Jars!
Jeremiah 13:12-27

The next parable relates to wineskins or wine jars, and carries a similar meaning to that of the marred belt illustration. The Hebrew word *nebel*, translated as "bottle" in the KJV and NKJV, "jug" in the NASV, and "wineskin" in other Bible versions, has a variety of meanings: bottle, pitcher, vessel, jar, etc. Wineskins were created by sewing animal skins tightly together to create a pouch that could hold fluid. Considering that Jeremiah was later told to smash these vessels together, it seems more likely that these were wine jars, rather than wineskins.

The Jews apparently ridiculed Jeremiah's proverb, *"Every* [wine] *bottle should be filled with wine"* (v. 12). No explanation was needed; in their minds, this was a trite maxim that failed to rise above common sense. Wine jars are created for holding wine, so certainly the jars should be used for that purpose. However, Jeremiah probably caused a quandary among the people after he started smashing the jars together; if they had been filled with wine, this would appear to be a terrible waste of both wine and jars. The empty, broken jars represented the Jews in the land, including both the political and religious leaders. God would allow them to be filled with drunkenness, a symbol of judgment in Scripture (Isa. 49:26, 63:6), and then smash them together. Although pieces of the jars would remain on the ground (a remnant in the land), the jars themselves would be completely destroyed and would not be useful to God.

Sinful behavior is a matter that God cannot ignore in His people. It must be judged. There was a dark and ominous cloud approaching the land, but the Jews ignored Jeremiah's message of impending doom (vv. 16-17). Jeremiah appealed to the king (likely Jehoiachin) and the queen (probably Nehushta, the king's mother and widow of Jehoiakim) to humble themselves by laying aside their regal splendors and accepting God's judgment (vv. 17, 18). If they resisted the Babylonian armies, they were promised that it would not go well with them; even their past allies would side against them. But, if they surrendered to the invasion force, many lives would be saved (vv. 18-21). They were commanded not to question God's chastisement or else He would lift up the skirt of the nation and expose all their secret lewdness and harlotries (vv. 22, 26-27). This was a fitting word picture, for they had abandoned their husband Jehovah to commit spiritual adultery with false gods. If they remained unyielding, He would add shame, sorrow, and death to their disciplinary captivity.

Though the alarm was sounded, God foreknew that His people were in such a pathetic state that they could not spiritually reform themselves any more than an Ethiopian man could change his dark skin, or the leopard his spots (v. 23). Sin was so deeply ingrained in Judah that it was all they knew how to do, and for this reason severe punishment was needed to awaken them from their backsliding behavior (v. 25). They had forgotten God and trusted in a lie. In response, God would scatter them abroad, like a strong wind that blows away the chaff from the threshing floor (v. 24).

Jeremiah's parables of the marred belt and the wine jars convey the same message to the Jews that the prophet Ezekiel would deliver to them a few years later in Babylon:

> Moreover the word of the Lord came to me, saying: "Son of man, when the house of Israel dwelt in their own land, they defiled it by their own ways and deeds; to Me their way was like the uncleanness of a woman in her customary impurity. Therefore I poured out My fury on them for the blood they had shed on the land, and for their idols with which they had defiled it. So I scattered them among the nations, and they were dispersed throughout the countries; I judged them according to their ways and their deeds" (Ezek. 36:16-19).

Ezekiel's message and Jeremiah's parables demonstrate God's revulsion to the pollution of His name among the nation by the very people who were called to honor it. Willful sin and rebellion invokes God's chastening hand, a matter that Paul said the Church should be mindful of:

You will say then, "Branches [i.e. the natural branches are the Jews] *were broken off that I might be grafted in." Well said. Because of unbelief they were broken off, and you stand by faith. Do not be haughty, but fear. For if God did not spare the natural branches, He may not spare you either* [the wild branches are the Gentile believers]. *Therefore consider the goodness and severity of God: on those who fell, severity; but toward you, goodness, if you continue in His goodness. Otherwise you also will be cut off. And they also, if they do not continue in unbelief, will be grafted in, for God is able to graft them in again. For if you were cut out of the olive tree which is wild by nature, and were grafted contrary to nature into a cultivated olive tree* [i.e. the blessings of Christ stemming from the root of the Abrahamic covenant], *how much more will these, who are natural branches, be grafted into their own olive tree?* (Rom. 11:19-24).

Paul argued that it would be much more natural for God to bless His covenant people, than Gentile believers who were only a second benefactor of the New Covenant (Heb. 8:8). This covenant, sealed with Christ's own blood, was the fulfillment of the original covenant made with Abraham. If God did not hesitate to remove His erring people, the Jews, from His covenant blessing, why would He hesitate to remove Gentiles, who were not His people, from it also?

Paul affirmed that God's dealings with Israel are examples that the Church should learn from: *"Now these things became our examples, to the intent that we should not lust after evil things as they also lusted. And do not become idolaters as were some of them. ... Now all these things happened to them as examples, and they were written for our admonition, upon whom the ends of the ages have come"* (1 Cor. 10:6, 11). Paul warned that disbelief leads to rebellion and the loss of blessing and fellowship with God. The fact that the Jews (the natural branches) could be, and indeed will be, grafted back into the covenant blessings (the olive tree) indicates that the focus of the illustration in Romans 11 is not eternal salvation per se, but rather all of the blessings in Christ that God desires to share with those who exercise faith in Him.

The Lord Jesus used a similar illustration in John 15 to convey this same truth. He likened Himself to a vine and those who believe in Him to the vine's branches. The Lord then charged His disciples, *"I am the vine, you are the branches. He who abides in Me, and I in him, bears much fruit; for without Me you can do nothing*" (John 15:5). The message is simple and profound: without Christ, a believer cannot do anything (John 15:5); however, with Him a believer can do all things (Phil. 4:13)! Why then would a Christian ever want to part from the Lord's presence and provoke His chastening hand? May we learn from Israel's mistake; our God is quite jealous for our attention!

Meditation

> I want a godly fear, a quick discerning eye,
> That looks to Thee when sin is near and sees the tempter fly;
> A spirit still prepared and armed with jealous care,
> Forever standing on its guard and watching unto prayer.
>
> I want a true regard, a single, steady aim,
> Unmoved by threatening or reward to Thee and Thy great Name.
> A jealous, just concern for Thine immortal praise;
> A pure desire that all may learn and glorify Thy grace.
>
> — Charles Wesley

Severe Drought
Jeremiah 14:1-22

On the eve of their entrance into the Promised Land, Moses warned the Jews that if they bowed to false gods, Jehovah would punish them with drought (Deut. 28:22-24). Jeremiah previously alluded to the fact that God had already been punishing them with drought conditions (3:3; 12:4), although no explanation of timing was given. What was clear was that a severe drought would accompany the Babylonian invasion and would amplify the suffering during the siege of Jerusalem.

The drought would dry up the cisterns (v. 3), crack the ground (v. 4), cause crop failures (v. 4), wither the pasturelands (v. 5), and even cause the doe to leave her newborn fawn to die (v. 5). The desiccation would prompt the people to cry out to God, the Hope of Israel, as the only One who could deliver them from this hardship. Yet, even when they acknowledged their sins, God would not deliver them; rather, He would be like a disinterested traveler passing through the land (vv. 7-9). Certainly, God was concerned for His people, but He knew that their confession was shallow and temporary. They were inclined to act wickedly; if He relented from judging them, they would just continue committing idolatry (v. 10).

For the third time, Jehovah instructed Jeremiah not to pray for his fellow countrymen; no pleading or intercession on their behalf would be accepted. Until their judgment was passed, God would not regard the cries of His people or ascribe any value to their offerings; His anger would not be appeased (v. 12). Their chastening would include death by the sword, by famine, and by pestilence, and there was nothing that would cause God to avert that decree.

Jeremiah interrupted the Lord by reminding Him that there were many false prophets who were contradicting his message. They were promising the people that God would bless them with peace (v. 13). God informed Jeremiah that these so-called prophets were not appointed by Him, and were in fact speaking lies (v. 14). Those who should have been the best of Judah were the worst, and God had marked them for death; furthermore, anyone listening to these alleged prophets would suffer the same judgment – they would perish by the sword or by famine (vv. 13, 18). The connection between physical drought and the spiritually destitute teachings of the false prophets in the book of Jeremiah is a recurring theme throughout Scripture.

Peter, for example, warns against misleading teachers: *"These are wells without water, clouds carried by a tempest, for whom is reserved the blackness of darkness forever"* (2 Pet. 2:17). False teachers offer falsehoods, which culminate in false hopes. A lie is more than happy to escort those parched souls willing to follow it to the closest open grave. No bubbling fountain of refreshment is there; only a deep dry hole waiting for its next victim. In contrast, the Lord Jesus is God's messenger of truth and offers an abundant life of joy, regardless of circumstances (John 10:10). When one embraces the Savior, a jubilant fountain of refreshing spiritual drink is enjoyed by one's soul, blessings are obtained, and the abundant life is found. Dear believer, like Israel in the midst of the wilderness, we too can sing to the fountain of life, *"Spring up, O well"* (Num. 21:17). Drink, yes, drink abundantly from the everlasting springs of God; for from such the sheep are watered (Gen. 29:2), and God refreshes His sheep through Christ.

After learning the fate of the false teachers and those who listen to them, Jeremiah can no longer contain his tears; God's pronouncement of inevitable and imminent judgment on Jerusalem causes his eyes to well over. His weeping did not subside for many days and nights; the destruction of Jerusalem and the death of its inhabitants was a burdensome heartache with no remedy (v. 17).

As Jerusalem is being decimated in the future, the Jews will cry out to Jehovah and confess their sins, but it will be too late to remedy the situation (v. 20). Accordingly, they would not understand why Jehovah was not moved to intervene on their behalf. They were incredulous: would God really allow the temple, the throne of His glory which bore His name, to be destroyed? Would He break His covenant with them (v. 21)? The people failed to realize that the covenant God made with them was conditional in nature – they had to do their part (i.e. keep His Law) in order to be blessed by Him.

125

Eventually, the Jews would realize that their idols were helpless to end the drought and that only Jehovah could summon rain, but He was not going to. The only solution was to wait upon the Lord, the one who made all things (v. 22). His timing had their best interests in view, though the near-term situation would be brutally hard for them.

Suffering will either harden or soften the human heart towards God's working – the same sun that melts the wax also hardens the clay. Suffering will either cause a believer to draw closer to the Lord or to flee His presence. The determining factor is the quality of his or her faith. Overwhelming circumstances may cause a child of God to lose hope and to lapse into doubt; it takes strong faith to trust the very hand that originates the waves and billows of adversity that crash upon our heads. Sometimes these storms of life are God's chastisement for sin, but at other times, the purpose is merely our edification.

In the case of Job, for example, Satan twice claimed that Job would curse God if Satan were allowed to assault him (Job 1:11; 2:5). As Satan thoroughly enjoys dishonoring God's name, he did everything he could to cause Job to do just that. But even after the loss of all his wealth, his children, and his health, Job would not blaspheme God. Notice that it was God who began the conversation with Satan concerning His servant Job. In other words, God nominated Job for this perfecting storm! The next nominee could be you or me. The fact is that God loves us too much to permit us to remain the way we are. He knows that as we grow in faith we will also increase in holiness and fruitfulness. God obtained glory out of Job's situation, and at the same time, further refined His servant, whom Scripture declares *"was blameless and upright, and one that feared God, and shunned evil"* (Job 1:1). Apparently, perfecting storms are a necessary part of our spiritual growth and, therefore, we should learn to appreciate God's working through them.

Amidst arduous circumstances, it is all too easy for the downcast and disheartened soul to think and speak evil of God's doings, but these are school days for the believer. Just as aggressive chiseling, chipping, sanding, and polishing are required to transform a chunk of granite into an attractive sculpture, God is ever laboring to mold and shape our hearts to beat for Him and Him alone. Our God is a God of promises, and we must simply trust Him in challenging times and not question His character – He does have a plan, and it is marvelous:

For I know the thoughts that I think toward you, says the Lord, thoughts of peace and not of evil, to give you a future and a hope (Jer. 29:11).

And we know that all things work together for good to them that love God, to them who are the called according to His purpose (Rom. 8:28).

No temptation has overtaken you except such as is common to man; but God is faithful, who will not allow you to be tempted beyond what you are able, but with the temptation will also make the way of escape, that you may be able to bear it (1 Cor. 10:13).

If there were no God, our present sufferings would be overwhelming, for we would be a people without hope. But knowing that God is with us in every difficulty, and that He is personally working each one out for our good and His glory, affords joy in tribulations! In trials, let us maintain the heavenward perspective, and not be guilty of hardening our hearts against the Lord and His dealings with us. The hearts of the Jewish people in Jeremiah's day were cold and despondent towards the Lord, but He had devised a plan to remedy that condition. So also God is working with believers in order to refine and edify them.

Meditation

To him that overcomes God gives a crown,
Through faith we shall conquer, though often cast down;
He, who is our Saviour, our strength will renew,
Look ever to the Lord Jesus, He will carry you through.

— Horatio R. Palmer

Famine to Famine
Jeremiah 15:1-21

Jeremiah 15 continues with God's response as to why judgment would not be averted, even after the Jews would confess the futility of idols and that Jehovah was God alone. In such a situation, where sin was so rampant among and deeply ingrained in His people, severe judgment was the only solution for the problem. The Lord declared that not even the intercessory prayers of Moses and Samuel could avert the pronounced judgment (v. 1).

Centuries prior to this time, Moses had interceded on behalf of the Israelites after the golden calf incident, and although three thousand souls died in judgment for that offense, the nation as a whole was spared from destruction (Ex. 32). After the Israelites doubted God at Kadesh-barnea, Moses again prayed to God to spare the nation (Num. 14); accordingly, only those who were twenty years of age and older were judged. The older generation, aside from Joshua and Caleb, expired in the wilderness. After this, during the time of the judges, Samuel successfully interceded on behalf of the Jewish nation to overcome their enemies, the Philistines (1 Sam. 7:5-11). Later, Samuel called his people to repent of their sins and then promised to pray for them, as God was threatening them with imminent judgment (1 Sam. 12:18-25). They had angered God by demanding that they, like other nations, should have a king to reign over them.

These were great prayers of faith by faithful men, but Jeremiah's prayers, however fervent, would not deter God's existing agenda for His people. Accordingly, God told Jeremiah not to pray for the Jews; such prayers would be a complete waste of his energy, as the time for repentance and restoration had passed. The people of Judah would be brought to one of four ends: death by pestilence, death by sword, death by starvation, or captivity (v. 2). The scene of carnage in Jerusalem is graphically described; wild beasts, fowls, and dogs would devour the corpses of the dead (v. 3).

128

Although Hezekiah had been a godly king and had brought much spiritual reform to the nation, his son Manasseh's long, evil reign had thoroughly corrupted the people (v. 4). In her present spiritual state, Judah had moved away from the Lord (v. 6), and would not retreat from her evil ways (v. 8): *"'You have forsaken Me,' says the Lord, 'you have gone backward. Therefore I will stretch out My hand against you and destroy you; I am weary of relenting!'"* (v. 6). "This verse," says Albert Barnes, "gives the reason of the refusal of Jehovah to hear the prophet's intercession. The punishment due has been delayed unto wearisomeness. And this seeming failure of justice has made Judah withdraw further from God."[1] As a result, Jehovah's hand was against His people (v. 6), and He would destroy them (v. 7). Widows would be multiplied in Jerusalem (v. 8), but no one would pity them or the destroyed city (v. 5). Even a mother with seven able sons to protect her from harm would not be safe when the invaders entered Jerusalem – she also would perish with the besieged inhabitants of Jerusalem (v. 9). Onlookers would observe the slain without concern or compassion.

Jeremiah interrupts this scene to complain to the Lord about his own living conditions; he was suffering greatly because of the messages he was proclaiming. He had been careful not to do anything to aggravate the situation (such as borrowing or lending money), but he was still hated (v. 10). God tells Jeremiah that there was a coming day in which his oppressors would beg him for mercy (v. 11). Jeremiah would be vindicated, and indeed, King Zedekiah himself would plead for Jeremiah's help and direction before the city fell to the Babylonians (Jer. 38:14-24).

The Lord illustrates the certainty of judgment and the Jew's inability to escape it with a rhetorical question: *"Can anyone break iron, the northern iron and the bronze?"* (Jer. 15:12). Is it possible for a man to break iron or bronze with his bare hands? The obvious answer is "no." Neither would the inhabitants of Judah be able to thwart their judgment; rather, God's anger would burn like fire against them (v. 14). He was determined to bestow all of their substance and treasures to their enemies free of charge (v. 13); the Jews would be completely despoiled.

Although God had already said that He would protect Jeremiah from his enemies and vindicate him in the future, Jeremiah wanted to see it in his lifetime (v. 15). He knew God's long-suffering nature, and he was concerned that he might not see justice served before his death. The request shows the intimate level of communion Jeremiah enjoyed with the Lord. Jeremiah joyfully ate God's word, which sustained and delighted his soul (v. 16). He shunned the company of evildoers and fools in order to sit alone with the Lord and be guided by Him alone (v. 17). Because Jeremiah was in such close communion with God, he too felt indignation against Judah (i.e. he could identify with God's righteous anger over their sin).

Jeremiah concludes his message by lamenting his deplorable situation. He suffered daily, as someone with an incurable wound (v. 18). He wondered whether or not God would sustain Him in the days to come, or if He would be like a wet spring, which at times provided water, but then ran dry. Jeremiah was not expressing doubt in God's ability, but rather in his own expectations of God's sustaining power. Suffering for righteousness's sake would be unbearable if God did not uphold him, and Jeremiah hoped he would not be disappointed.

One of the amazing things about God is that He is able to work with everyone (the lost, the rebel, the saved, the backsliding believer, the spiritually mature, etc.) through the same situation. By means of the situation in Judah, not only was God dealing with His spiritually destitute people, but He also was refining His prophet. Just as faith cannot be trusted unless it has been tested, character cannot be validated until circumstances affirm it. How else would Jeremiah really know what was in his heart? From a human standpoint, we can certainly understand Jeremiah's anxiety, but from God's perspective, Jeremiah needed to be admonished; he needed to *take the precious from the vile* (vv. 19-21). William Kelly explains God's exhortation to Jeremiah:

> The great concern of believers in an evil day is not to be meddling with the vile but to be seeking to do good to the precious. The gospel seeks the vile because it is God's way of making the vile to be precious. But, the people of God are not to occupy ourselves with what is bad, except to reject it. They are to seek what is good, to proclaim it. This is precisely what is pressed upon Jeremiah: "If thou take forth the precious from the vile, thou shalt be as My mouth." That is, you will be enabled to utter My truth and My

grace. You will be the vessel of My mind, which the mouth is. "Let them return unto thee; but return not thou unto them"; that is, do not meddle with them, but if you love My mind, My words, My truth, you will be made a blessing to them.[2]

Thus, Jeremiah was instructed to repent of his doubts and self-pity if he wanted to serve God. As God's spokesman, he was expected to utter worthy words, not worthless prattle which would have no effect in moving the Jews towards righteousness. Jeremiah was to stand fast in his faith and not water down God's message. He was not to think like the rebels he was preaching to, for then they would not have the opportunity to turn back to God. Jeremiah 15 concludes with God reaffirming His promise to protect Jeremiah from harm in the execution of his ministry (vv. 20-21).

Part of the Lord's message to the vibrant and evangelical church at Philadelphia was "*Behold, I am coming quickly! Hold fast what you have, that no one may take your crown*" (Rev. 3:11). There was no rebuke for this church, but the Lord knows our human tendency to pull back when things get tough; thus, the warning. The meaning of the message is that if you are not willing to do the Lord's bidding, He will find someone else to do it; then, that person will get the reward that could have been yours. This reward refers to the victor's crown. It was bestowed to the winner of a sporting contest, and is generally used in the New Testament to speak of the reward given to properly motivated Christians for faithful service.

The lesson Elijah learns in 1 Kings 19 relates directly to John's exhortation to the church at Philadelphia. Elijah had faithfully declared God's message to evil King Ahab, he had been victorious over the 450 prophets of Baal on Mt. Carmel, and he had lived with a death sentence over his head for three years, but these victories did not hinder him from slipping into spiritual depression. What brought Elijah's ministry to a close? It was his own mental disposition towards the faithfulness of God. He weighed the events of the day according to his own expectations for his ministry and was unsatisfied and thus entered into spiritual depression. When he failed to see revival sweep through the land, he felt that God had betrayed him; he felt defeated, alone, and wished to die. The Lord did not answer that prayer, but He did call a new prophet that would pick up Elijah's mantle and continue the work. Spiritual depression is a real enemy of God's servants – beware of it; fortify yourself against it. God knows what He is doing, and, in the end, we will understand this also.

The circumstances in Jeremiah 14-15 mimic the future scene in Revelation 6. During the Tribulation Period, God will use war, famine, and pestilence to punish the inhabitants of the earth. Yet, during that time many will choose not to follow the Antichrist or take his mark, preferring rather to honor God by suffering death. These faithful souls are seen in heaven under the altar of God (Rev. 6:9-11). The priests of old poured out the blood of the sacrificial animals at the base of the Bronze Altar (Lev. 4:7, 18, 25); in type, these believers had poured out their lives as an offering to the Lord. From beneath this altar, these souls cried out to the Lord to avenge their deaths. The narrative describes how they were given white robes and were told to wait for the Lord's timing; more wrath must come upon the wicked before their final doom and before these believers would be vindicated. At the time of the Tribulation, the rebels on earth will refuse to repent, but rather cry out that the rocks would fall on them and hide them from the face of the Lamb, the Lord Jesus Christ (Rev. 6:12-17). This is part of God's plan that all the wicked should both know their judge and learn to fear Him – those waiting for justice should appreciate God's overall plan.

This future scene demonstrates God's faithfulness to vindicate His people in front of those who opposed them and to honor Himself, and those faithful to Him, in the process of executing justice. The Lamb of God will judge the wicked and vindicate His righteous character and holy name. We think of a lamb as a feeble and defenseless creature; this pictures the Lord Jesus in His first advent to the earth. However, the title of His humiliation will become the title of His exaltation at His second advent. God's Lamb is prominent in Scripture, with one-fourth of all references to the word "lamb" being found in the book of Revelation: *"Worthy is the Lamb who was slain to receive power and riches and wisdom, and strength and honor and glory and blessing!"* (Rev. 5:12). May every child of God honor God's Lamb, who sacrificed Himself for our sins, that we might have ultimate and eternal victory in Him.

Meditation

Crown Him with many crowns, the Lamb upon His throne.
Hark! How the heavenly anthem drowns all music but its own.
Awake, my soul, and sing of Him who died for thee,
And hail Him as thy matchless King through all eternity.

Crown Him the Lord of Heaven, enthroned in worlds above,
Crown Him the King to Whom is given the wondrous name of Love.
Crown Him with many crowns, as thrones before Him fall;
Crown Him, ye kings, with many crowns, for He is King of all.

— Matthew Bridges

Take No Wife
Jeremiah 16:1-21

The next time the word of the Lord came to Jeremiah it was to convey a personal message; God was placing three restrictions on Jeremiah. First, he was not to take a wife (v. 2). Certainly, this must have been a difficult thing for Jeremiah to concede, as no wife meant no lifelong companion and no children of his own. Yet, God reminded Jeremiah that, in the coming days, not only would death (and widowers) be common among the inhabitants of Judah, but the Jews would suffer grievously before dying (v. 4). This was no place for a new bride, and it was certainly a poor time to raise a family. The request was not to punish Jeremiah in any way, but rather to save him grief later. Moreover, Jeremiah's singleness would serve as a sign to the people that the future would be catastrophic to family life; many fathers, mothers, daughters, and sons would die by the sword, famine, or disease.

The second restriction levied on Jeremiah was that he was not to attend any funerals, meaning he was not to console the family of the deceased. He was also forbidden to show sorrow by cutting himself or shaving his head – there was to be no demonstration of sympathy or mourning. This directive may at first glance seem unnecessary. The Law prohibited the cutting and tattooing of oneself during times of mourning because these acts were pagan in origin (Lev. 19:28), and it is not likely that Jeremiah would have done these actions which were expressly forbidden in the Law; however, the prohibition may have been mentioned to show that the Jews of Jeremiah's day were ignoring it and indeed cutting themselves. Jeremiah's lack of attendance of funerals or public display of grief was to illustrate that the Lord had withdrawn His love, pity, and blessings from His people.

The expression *"Nor shall men break bread in mourning for them"* in verse 7 has an important application for believers in the

Church Age. William Kelly notes the unmistakable connection in this passage between the breaking of bread and death:

> This practice of breaking bread in connection with death seems to be the origin of what the Lord Jesus consecrated into the grand memorial of His remembrance. *"Neither shall men break bread for them in mourning, to comfort them for the dead; neither shall men give them the cup of consolation."* There you have the Supper, in both its parts. It was a familiar custom among the Jews, but the Lord gave a unique significance to it, and stamped new truth upon it. It was connected with the Passover, for, as we know, that was the time of its institution. There was a particular reason for its establishment at that and at no other time, because it was to mark the impressive change from the great central and fundamental feast of Israel. A new and different feast was begun for the Christians.[1]

Not only was Jeremiah not to mourn with his people, but the third restriction prevented him from feasting and making merry with them as well. Jeremiah could not attend any parties or festive occasions; this was to demonstrate that Jehovah would remove all joy and happiness from Judah. These three limitations again confirm that Jeremiah drank from his own ministry. Like Hosea before Jeremiah and Ezekiel after him, the daily affairs of God's prophets were themselves a message to the people.

When Jeremiah explained to the people the meaning of his behavior, the people were puzzled: *"Why has the Lord pronounced all this great disaster against us? Or what is our iniquity? Or what is our sin that we have committed against the Lord our God"* (Jer. 16:10)? The Lord responded to these naïve questions. Since the conception of the nation, the Jews had been a stubborn people. God had frequently punished their forefathers for idolatry, but even though they knew this, the present generation behaved even more wickedly. They had not learned from the mistakes of their ancestors, so God would use a more extreme means of punishment to regain their attention. They were sinning continually, but were unconscious of their sin. In response, He would cast them out of the land that He had given them as a possession centuries earlier, and relocate them to a far country full of idolatry (v. 13).

135

Although the time was coming when the Jews would wonder if the God that brought them out of Egypt was dead, the Lord assured them that He would honor His covenant and restore them to their land in the future. In fact, in coming days the people would be more likely to speak of their miraculous return from Babylon than their deliverance from slavery in Egypt (v. 14). But before that restoration, the Babylonians would come; they would catch the Jews like fishermen catch fish in their nets, or like hunters track and kill their prey (vv. 16-18). The people had failed in their stewardship; they had defiled both the Lord's land and His inheritance (their children) and they would be punished. The land was the Lord's and He longed to dwell there with a people who would honor Him and obey His Law.

At this juncture, Jeremiah was prompted to praise God and affirm Him as his Strength, his Fortress, and his Refuge. He longed for the coming day when not only the Jews, but all the nations would know the one true God, and that His name was Jehovah. Then the earth would be full of the glory of God and everyone would agree that false gods are just worthless idols (vv. 20-21). Just as Jeremiah was encouraged to honor the Lord in his day, may each believer live in light of this hope!

Meditation

A mighty fortress is our God, a bulwark never failing;
Our helper, He amid the flood of mortal ills prevailing:
For still our ancient foe doth seek to work us woe;
His craft and power are great, and, armed with cruel hate,
On earth is not his equal.

Did we in our own strength confide, our striving would be losing;
Were not the right Man on our side, the Man of God's own choosing:
Dost ask who that may be? Christ Jesus, it is He;
Lord Sabaoth, His Name, from age to age the same,
And He must win the battle.

— Martin Luther

The Deceitful Heart
Jeremiah 17:1-18

Jeremiah 16 concludes with the prophet foretelling that the Gentile nations would turn to the Lord in a future day. His attention, however, is quickly brought back to Judah's present problem of deep-seated idolatry. The Jews seemed to be unmovable in their wicked appetites; it was as if their sins had been engraved on their hardened hearts by an iron tool with an unbreakable tip. (The KJV refers to the instrument as a diamond-tipped tool.) The people had stony hearts, which directly related to their pagan stone altars. So deeply entrenched was their paganism that even the children worshipped at their altars and before the Asherah poles on high places. Asherah was the Canaanite goddess of fertility.

During Manasseh's reign an image of Asherah had been placed in the temple (2 Kgs. 21:7). Although he later removed it (2 Chron. 33:13-15), the image found its way back to the temple because King Josiah had to remove it again (2 Kgs. 23:6). The stony hearts of the people prevailed, and, despite Josiah's sweeping reforms, idolatry returned to Judah. Idols were worshipped by propping up green trees and branches (Asherah poles) before them on the high hills surrounding Jerusalem. It was likely the image of Asherah that Ezekiel spoke of as "the idol of jealousy" being worshipped in the temple in his day (Ezek. 6:13). There would be no more opportunities for repentance; God's patience had given way to wrath. He was going to severely punish His people by despoiling and deporting them. They would be enslaved by their invaders (v. 4).

A brief contrast is provided between the way of the wicked and the path of the righteous (vv. 5-8), which is quite similar to David's poem in Psalm 1. The righteous are blessed because of their resolve to trust and hope in the Lord – He is their strength. In contrast, the wicked are cursed because they trust in others and in themselves and not in the Lord and His Word. Consequently, the wicked are like a shrub that withers in the desert heat, or like the salt land surrounding the Dead Sea where nothing grew. But the righteous are like a tree planted by a river, which always enjoys an ample supply of water. The tree is deeply rooted, speaking of personal faith in the Lord. Even in times of drought the righteous are sustained by the Lord and bear fruit for Him. Accordingly, the religious beliefs of all humanity fall into but two categories; those who can improve or save themselves, and those who know they need a Savior and will trust in Him alone for salvation.

World religion is an exhaustive system of *doings* apart from God's truth and God's enablement. The main distinction between Christianity and all the religions of the world is that biblical Christianity teaches that man has a vital need to be saved from spiritual death by trusting in the Savior alone, whereas the world's religions pose a system of *doing* to merit salvation or to obtain an improved afterlife. Religion equips man with a "do it yourself" manual and workbook through which he may impress himself as to how well he is *doing* by completing religious exercises and checklists. Christianity, however, is not a *religion*; it is a *relationship* with Jesus Christ. Apart from Christ, there is no forgiveness of sins, no life, and no hope – this is the Christian message as fully revealed in the New Testament. The Jews of Jeremiah's day had God's Law to compel them to rely on Him alone for salvation (Gal. 3:24), but instead, they had abandoned the security of Jehovah's love and way, for the hallow vanities of world religion.

Jeremiah was perplexed: with the respective pathways to cursing and blessing so clearly revealed, why would anyone depart from the Lord? Why would anyone choose sin, which only ensures God's judgment? Did they not know that to rebel against the Lord was like having one's name written in the earth, to be easily erased: *"O Lord, the hope of Israel, all who forsake You shall be ashamed. 'Those who depart from Me **shall be written in the earth**, because they have forsaken the Lord, the fountain of living waters'"* (v. 13, emphasis added). Clearly *all* who forsake the Lord shall be ashamed and *"shall be written in the earth."* What does it mean to have one's name written in the earth? Matthew Henry explains:

They shall soon be blotted out, as that which is written in the dust. They shall be trampled upon and exposed to contempt. They belong to the earth, and shall be numbered among earthly people, who lay up their treasure on earth and whose names are not written in heaven...They deserve themselves therefore to be condemned, as Adam, to *red earth,* to which by the corruption of their nature they are allied [united and related], because they have forsaken the Lord [the fountain of living waters], which is so well-watered. Those that depart from God are *written in the earth.*[1]

However, those with a rebel heart will ignore the warning about being written in the earth, concluding that such talk of accountability and divine retribution is foolishness, and asking how one could be truly assured of such things.

Apparently, this was exactly what the Jews were saying to Jeremiah: *"Indeed they say to me, 'Where is the word of the Lord? Let it come now'"* (v. 15, emphasis added)! David Martyn Lloyd-Jones adds this important insight into the repercussions of pompously calling for the word of the Lord to come immediately:

What the prophet uttered came to pass, and it was not long before these people were in chains marching to Babylon [as slaves]. The Jews said the same thing when they heard Christ's prophetic words, "Let it come." Indeed, they went further, and flippantly, with a shuddering boldness, cried out, "Let His blood be upon us," and it came upon them! In forty years their city was in dust, and those who were left from the terrible slaughter of Titus were being marched to Rome as slaves. So, too, will come an end of this age. Man may speak scoffingly of the second advent [coming] of Christ and of the day of judgment, saying, "let it come," but, oh, it will come.[2]

"Let it come now!" What prompted the Jews to be so arrogant and foolish? Jeremiah could not explain the reason for the Jewish insurrection, but he did understand the source of the problem – the human heart: *"The heart is deceitful above all things, and desperately wicked; who can know it?"* (v. 9). The Lord declares that He knows all about the human heart: *"I, the Lord, search the heart, I test the mind, even to give every man according to his ways, according to the fruit of his doings"* (v. 10). David understood that the Lord knew his thoughts afar off (Ps. 139:2) and his words before he spoke them (Ps. 139:4).

The writer of Hebrews puts the matter this way: *"And there is no creature hidden from His sight, but all things are naked and open to the eyes of Him to whom we must give account"* (Heb. 4:13). We cannot hide from God; He intimately knows what motivates our behavior, the strongholds which exist in our hearts, and the mental gymnastics we perform to justify sin. Even that deep, dark secret that no one else is aware of, the Lord knows all about it. God knows the human heart and just how wicked it is.

The heart of man is referred to four different times in Jeremiah 17 and nearly sixty times in the entire book. What does the "heart" refer to in the Bible? Certainly the heart organ may be in view, but more generally the word speaks of an invisible component of the human soul relating to emotions, desires, moral inclinations, and cognitive abilities. Figuratively, the heart is the hidden spring of the personal and inward life.

Tertullian correctly observed that the New Testament writers focused their instruction on the particulars of the soul rather than upon the soul itself. He writes, "As for 'the man within,' indeed, the apostle prefers its being regarded as the mind and heart rather than the soul."[3] The Old Testament writers certainly referred to the heart and mind, but the Hebrew language is more limited in expressing the same level of distinction as the Greek.

The Hebrew word *leb* and its synonym *lebab* appear 860 times in the Old Testament and are generally translated as "heart." However, ten times *leb* is rendered "mind." While *leb* is applied in various ways to convey different meanings, in the context of our subject, the word focuses on inner feelings, emotions, inclinations, and moral character; these non-physical aspects of our makeup refer to our "heart."

Although the Hebrew word *nephesh* is translated "mind" in Jeremiah 15:1, it is normally rendered "soul" or "life" throughout the book, and indeed, the Old Testament. The soul expresses one's entire personality, including the seat of the affections, desires, emotions, and the will of man. The heart would be the core of man's soul – the seat of moral character, emotions, the will, and reasoning abilities. The mind speaks of reflective consciousness at the center of the heart and includes the ability to perceive, understand, analyze, and determine (judge by rational thought). The mind of man would then be directly influenced by the deceitfulness and wickedness of the heart's depraved state (v. 9). So how is it possible to change the condition of a depraved heart, when the decisions of the mind are being strongly influenced by a wicked heart?

It is observed that the bulk of scriptural exhortation is not focused upon the soul or the heart, but upon the mind. Thus, the mind must be *"transformed"* (Rom. 12:2) before a pure heart can be *"formed"* (Ps. 51:10). A pure heart serves to *"conform"* (Eph. 6:5-8) one's will to God's will. The mind is clearly the area between the physical and spiritual realms where spiritual battles are won or lost. On one side of the window is the physical realm, revealed to us through our senses, and on the other side is the human spirit which is God-conscious and longs to be in communion with Him (Job 32:8; 1 Cor. 2:11). The mind frames the soul's will and emotions. If a believer truly desires the Holy Spirit to have free access through his soul window, the mind must be properly framed. When this happens, the soul becomes a funnel extended to heaven through which spiritual blessings freely flow to earth (i.e. we enjoy communion with God through our spirit). In this sense, a proper scriptural mind-frame provides a corridor for the Holy Spirit to battle evil in the world by relaying spiritual power to human agents. (He literally hinders sin – 2 Thess. 2:7.)

The Lord Jesus decreed, *"And you shall love the Lord your God with all your heart, with all your soul, with all your mind, and with all your strength"* (Mark 12:30). Dear reader, does the Lord have your whole mind, which is at the core of your heart? Who or what controls your mind? If you love the Lord with your entire mind, your heart and body will be constrained to do the same.

In the resurrection, the spirit of the believer will completely rule his or her glorified body, for the physical body will be raised a spiritual body (1 Cor. 15:44). But why wait for that, when the resurrected life of Christ is available now for all Christians to witness and enjoy? When your mind yields to Scripture, even though strongholds in your heart may be leading otherwise, the way of blessing is open. A consistent walk down the path of righteousness will mold the heart, and soften it so it will beat more strongly for God with each passing day. Jeremiah demonstrates a good defense against sin; he focused his mind on the majesty of God and His throne of righteousness in His heavenly sanctuary (v. 12). He wanted to be heavenly-minded and to align his thinking with God's.

Those who would not have the Hope of Israel, the Lord, to rule over them would have their names written in the dust of the earth, where wind and rain would erase their remembrance. Nothing accomplished in their lifetimes had eternal value or deserved God's praise; thus, they vanished from the earth as condemned fools. Indeed, Jeremiah prayed that those who persecuted him and opposed God's message would be confounded, dismayed, and destroyed by the forthcoming judgment (v. 18). In contrast, Jeremiah's own faithfulness to follow the Lord and be a shepherd to His rebellious people demonstrated that the Lord was his Hope (vv. 16-17).

God knows the quality of every human heart and, therefore, will be just to dispense either rewards or judgment to each one. For example, if people acquire wealth dishonestly, God will remove their wealth. Jeremiah likened this principle to a partridge which broods and hatches another bird's eggs; the chicks will soon recognize the ruse and desert their "mother." Similarly, those who come by wealth deceitfully or hoard it selfishly will be exposed as the fools they are (v. 11). God knows the heart of every person and will render accordingly to each one: *"For it is written: 'As I live, says the Lord, every knee shall bow to Me, and every tongue shall confess to God.' So then each of us shall give account of himself to God"* (Rom. 14:11-12). What is the condition of your heart today?

Meditation

A charge to keep I have, a God to glorify,
A never-dying soul to save, and fit it for the sky.
To serve the present age, my calling to fulfill:
O may it all my powers engage to do my Master's will!

Arm me with jealous care, as in Thy sight to live;
And O Thy servant, Lord, prepare a strict account to give!
Help me to watch and pray, and on Thyself rely,
Assured, if I my trust betray, I shall forever die.

— Charles Wesley

Keep the Sabbath
Jeremiah 17:19-27

Jeremiah's sixth message was to be delivered at the various gates in Jerusalem which the Jewish royalty used to enter and exit the city (vv. 19-20). The Jews were ignoring the fourth of the Ten Commandments which pertained to honoring the Sabbath. They were to sanctify that day for the Lord by refraining from labor, as their forefathers had been commanded (v. 22). The prophet was to warn those carrying bundles and transporting goods in and out of the city on the Sabbath Day that they were dishonoring the Lord.

The people were promised that if they humbled themselves, repented of this sin, and began to honor God by setting apart the Sabbath Day, then the descendants of David would continue to sit upon the throne of Judah. The city's gates would continue to be used for the normal affairs of life, and Jerusalem would again be restored as a worship center for all inhabitants of Israel (vv. 24-26). However, if they did not repent, the gates through which they so frequently passed and the very walls which they thought were impregnable would be burned and destroyed (v. 27). The people ignored Jeremiah's warnings and continued to rebel against God's Law (v. 23). It is quite possible that if the people would have yielded to this one commandment, they would have soon submitted to the remainder of the Law and spiritual revival would have spread through the land. But this was not to be.

Moses was given the Law on Mount Sinai, first orally and then in written form (on stone tablets). Although the pattern of sanctifying the seventh day for the Lord was set up at the time of creation by God Himself (Gen. 2:1-3), it was not commanded until the Israelites were alone with God at Sinai. The Sabbath Day, Saturday, was set aside to rest and to honor God. The Jews, their slaves, and their beasts of burden were all to rest on the Sabbath. Albert Barnes notes that the Jews were rewarded in three ways for keeping the Sabbath Day holy: "(1) in great national prosperity, (2) in the lasting welfare of Jerusalem, and (3) in the wealth and piety of the people generally, indicated by their numerous sacrifices."[1] Sometimes God commands that which is right for us to do, while at other times, what we are to do is right only because He commands it. Keeping the Sabbath Day falls into the latter group, but regardless of why the commandment was given, man is always blessed by doing what God says.

Why did God consider the Sabbath Day observance to be an important part of Jewish life? Irving L. Jensen explains that it is for the same reason the Lord commanded the Church to remember Him through the breaking of the bread, and to honor Him through obeying believer's baptism and other such commandments:

> The real test of the heart's relation to God is obedience to His Word. One of the laws of Israel was the hallowing of the Sabbath by not working on that day (17:21-22). The constant pressure of materialism upon the lives of all, including the people of God, made the keeping of such a commandment difficult, and for this reason this one commandment of the ten was a real test of the priority of the temporal or the eternal in the heart. Was the keeping of the Sabbath law that crucial to Judah? The symbolic action of Jeremiah and the explicit words he was told to speak gave an affirmative answer.[2]

God honors those who obey His commandments. Accordingly, the Sabbath day ordinance provided a simple test as to what God's people really valued – their own private affairs (as symbolized by Jeremiah's bundle carrying illustration) or what the Lord deemed as important.

The Israelites were to honor not only the Sabbath day but also the Sabbath year. The Sabbatical year was to remind the Jews that God owned the land they dwelled in and that they were merely stewards of it (Lev. 25:23). Every seventh year the fields, the olive groves, and the vineyards were to receive a full year's rest. Whatever grew naturally during the Sabbath year was to be freely gleaned by the poor, and anything that remained was considered as God's provision for the beasts of the field.

This was God's law of the land; unfortunately, the Jews often ignored the Sabbath year commandment. God was keeping track of the offense, and, in one lump sum of years He gave the land its due – seventy years of rest (i.e. one-seventh of the four hundred ninety years the Jews did not honor the Sabbath year). This judgment was realized during the Jews' seventy-year exile to Babylon, proving that there are no loopholes in God's judicial system (Ex. 23:10-13).

Those who reject God's Word and authority will be punished. The Lord Jesus said that His Father had committed the judgment of all men into His hands (John 5:22). At the Great White Throne judgment, justice will be administered in accordance with His Word: *"He who rejects Me, and does not receive My words, has that which judges him – the word that I have spoken will judge him in the last day"* (John 12:48). God will judge all humanity according to His decrees; therefore, it behooves man to behave righteously now and to uphold what His justice demands.

If God foreknew that the Jews would consistently disobey His Law, why then did He give it to them? God, in every dispensation, has always maintained a testimony of man's need for divine grace and mercy; yet, man in his lost state is ignorant of his destitute condition. Man knows the heartache of his existence, but does not understand that he suffers because of his spiritual failure. The Law would provoke the Jews to search more deeply into such matters, and to gain an awareness of their spiritual state before a holy God and their inadequacy to please God though personal efforts.

Although the Christian is not under the Law, it would be good to remember that the Lord Jesus affirmed each of the Ten Commandments as still valid for the Jews at the time of His earthly ministry (i.e. just prior to the Church Age). So while the Church is not commanded to keep the ordinance of the Sabbath day, the early Church set a precedent for us by gathering on the first day of the week to remember the Lord Jesus Christ through the breaking of the bread (John 20:19; Acts 20:7; 1 Cor. 11:18-20, 16:2). The Lord Jesus was raised from the dead on the first day of the week. All those who have experienced new birth in Christ have received His resurrection life – they have eternal life in Him. Law keeping could never accomplish that feat for the Jews, so the first day of the week has significance for

Christians, which the Sabbath Day could never have for those under the Old Covenant.

The divine pattern of setting aside one day in seven for the Lord (Gen. 2:1-3) is still to be followed. During the dispensation of the Law that day was Saturday (according to the fourth of the Ten Commandments), but during the Church Age, Sunday (resurrection day) is observed as the Lord's Day. In time, the Jews brought reproach upon the name of Jehovah because they neglected the Law of God and ceased to honor Him and His Sabbath; consequently, they were severely punished. May the Church avoid this same offense; let us live as a holy people before the lost and consecrate to God what is His.

Meditation

Take time to be holy, speak oft with the Lord;
Abide in Him always, and feed on His Word.
Take time to be holy, be calm in thy soul,
Each thought and each motive beneath His control;
Thus, led by His Spirit to fountains of love,
Thou soon shall be fitted for service above.

— William D. Longstaff

The Potter's Wheel
Jeremiah 18:1-6

The seventh message to the Jews came in the form of an illustration. Jeremiah was instructed to journey to the potter's house; there, as he observed the potter's skill in action, God would speak to him (vv. 1-2). Jeremiah did as requested and watched the potter work with a lump of clay on his wheel (v. 3). In ancient times, potters' wheels were normally spun by a mechanical apparatus that had to be pedaled by the operator. Albert Barnes explains, "The lower wheel was worked by the feet to give motion to the upper one, which was a flat disc or plate of wood, on which the potter laid the clay, and molded it with his fingers as it revolved rapidly."[1] Consequently, to form pottery was quite a laborious task; the potter had to use both feet to pedal the wheel and both hands to form the clay. In a parallel to this, we note that it required both the hands and feet of our Lord at Calvary to shape us for eternity.

The first lump of clay was marred in the potter's hands, that is, it was not pliable. The potter tossed it aside and began to work with another lump of clay which he fashioned into a beautiful vessel (v. 4). The illustration is then explained to Jeremiah: Israel was like the unworkable clay which God, the Potter, wanted to shape into a secular vessel that all nations would admire (v. 6). The second lump of clay shaped by the potter, after the first was discarded, is likely a reference to the Church. After it is fashioned, as only God can, He will return to work with the first lump, the Jewish nation.

H. A. Ironside notes that the Lord is often presented as a potter in Scripture:

In Psalm 2:9 and Revelation 2:27 Messiah takes the part of the offended potter, dashing in pieces the unworthy vessel. Isaiah in chapters 29:16 and 64:8 of his magnificent prophecy, and Paul in

147

Romans 9:20, 23, use the same figure as this chapter in Jeremiah brings before us. God is the Potter; we are but the clay in His hands.[2]

In time, the divine Potter will put that which was discarded back on His wheel and form it into a useful vessel of His choosing. The shaping of the Jewish nation will be completed during the Tribulation Period when they will be infused with the life of Christ and be restored to Him forever.

One cannot read this portion of Scripture without contemplating God's mysterious ways in each of our lives. When an individual, a lump of clay, so to speak, yields to the gospel message, the molding process begins; until then the clay is marred by sin and cannot be fashioned into a vessel of honor. When a potter sets a lump of softened clay upon the wheel in order to make something of it, the first thing he or she does is to poke into the center of the clay with his or her hand or some other instrument. This reminds us that God molds us from the inside out; He starts by cleansing and shaping the heart. Circumstances in this life then supply the Potter's wheel with the motion and energy to assist the Master's hand in molding our hearts to the pattern of Christ-likeness.

The forming process on the Potter's wheel is a lifelong project. Sometimes the wheel seems to be spinning so fast we may fear we will fly apart. What a delightful promise is expressed to the Christian in 1 Corinthians 10:13: *"No temptation has overtaken you except such as is common to man; but God is faithful, who will not allow you to be tempted beyond what you are able, but with the temptation will also make the way of escape, that you may be able to bear it."* The Master Potter uses one hand to shape our inner man and with the other He keeps us from flying apart. Without the pressures and trials of life, God could not shape us into the vessel He desires; we can safely conclude that He endorses every one of our difficulties in life (Jas. 1:2-3).

Mysterious are God's ways! How is it that He can incorporate both human submission and rebellion into His sovereign design, causing all events to bring about His glory? Before creation, God previewed the corridors of time, considered all the possible permutations of natural cause and effect as well as the future choices of cognitive beings, and made sovereign choices to bless humanity in time and glorify His name throughout time and eternity. As only a triune God existed when the plan of redemption was devised, the plan is solely His – it originated in His mind and He deserves all the glory for it. God's choices ensure that humanity will receive the greatest possible blessing and that He will obtain the most glory as a result.

Man has no choice in being a part of God's plan, but as a moral and a conscious being, he has every choice in how he will answer God's call and be used within God's unfolding design. Whether or not we yield to His call, God will be glorified through our choices; He will use us either as vessels of mercy prepared for glory, or as vessels of wrath fit for destruction (Rom. 9:14-23). God prepares yielded vessels for glory and rebellious vessels to receive His wrath.

For example, God did not force Pharaoh to worship Egyptian gods, but He did intervene to harden Pharaoh's heart on certain occasions in order to accomplish the release of His people from Egypt. The fact that Pharaoh hardened his own heart afterwards (some ten times) demonstrates he still had free choice in the matter. God would have been perfectly just to destroy a pagan like Pharaoh, but instead He designed ten specific plagues to prove to Pharaoh that He was superior to a number of specific Egyptian gods. Pharaoh rejected this revelation and hardened his own heart against the Lord – he proved himself to be a vessel of wrath fit for destruction. God brought glory to His name by honoring Pharaoh's decision, which God already foreknew. This example shows how human responsibility and sovereign design align, ensuring that God will receive all the glory in every situation. Isaiah puts the matter this way:

> *Woe to those who seek deep to hide their counsel far from the Lord, and their works are in the dark; they say, "Who sees us?" and, "Who knows us?" Surely you have things turned around! Shall the potter be esteemed as the clay; for shall the thing made say of him who made it, "He did not make me"? Or shall the thing formed say of him who formed it, "He has no understanding"?* (Isa. 29:15-16).

A vessel is used to hold or to transport something – it is what a vessel does and not what it is that is important. Consequently, Scripture refers to individuals as vessels and states that God will use both the yielded and the rebellious vessels to work His eternal purposes and to uphold His glory. On this point, Timothy was implored by Paul to flee youthful lusts in order to be a vessel of honor fit for God's intended use. While on earth, only those Christians who yield to God's work of sanctification will practically experience the life of Christ in selfless service.

Submitting to God's ongoing work of sanctification enables one to know God's purpose for his or her life. Without the work of sanctification, service to God is impossible. Fanciful words and good intentions do not define a servant; his or her character is the message. A Christian who lacks Christ-likeness will fail miserably in representing Christ to the lost. May the divine Potter have His way with each of us and may each vessel He fashions glisten with sovereign grace for all to see!

Meditation

Have Thine own way, Lord! Have Thine own way!
Thou art the Potter, I am the clay.
Mold me and make me after Thy will,
While I am waiting, yielded and still.

Have Thine own way, Lord! Have Thine own way!
Hold over my being absolute sway!
Fill with Thy Spirit 'till all shall see
Christ only, always, living in me.

— Adelaide Pollard

The Kingdom
Jeremiah 18:7-23

The word "kingdom" is found only three times in the entire book of Jeremiah, and two of these occurrences are in Jeremiah 18. It is used here to explain two parallel thoughts. The Lord is the only one able to pluck up, to pull down, and to destroy a nation and a kingdom (v. 7). He is also the only one who can build up and plant a nation and kingdom (v. 9). The order of words is significant; there must first be a nation before a kingdom can be established, which will have control well beyond its borders.

God had built the Jewish nation in Egypt, and delivered them from bondage and from that land in order to sanctify them and bring them into their promised inheritance. The strength and duration of the kingdom they would establish among the nations would be dependent upon their faithfulness to Him. This is why the Jews fared well and had a wide influence of control in the region during the reigns of David and Solomon. But now, by the time of Jeremiah, the southern kingdom had followed the course of its northern counterpart Israel and declined into open rebellion against God. Jeremiah noted that even the snow-covered slopes of Lebanon and the cool streams which continually trickled down from the mountains were more reliable than fickle Judah (v. 14). By turning to idols and forgetting the Lord, Judah had stumbled from the ancient path of righteousness to wander aimlessly on rough byways (v. 15).

The warning Jeremiah issued to Judah was thus not addressed to a kingdom, but to a ruined nation; even the remnants of the once powerful kingdom of Solomon's day were gone (v. 8). Instead of submitting to God's Law, the people were following every evil imagination of their hearts (v. 12). Their willful sin had constrained the blessings of God, and they were at present merely surviving as a political reality in a hostile world and were soon subjugated to its

151

control. Their land would be desolate and they themselves would be an appalling sight (v. 16); they were to be removed from the land and scattered abroad (v. 17).

At the time of Christ's first advent, the Jews continued to be a people scattered throughout the earth. Though a series of Jewish governors, tetrarchs, and kings presided over the land, these leaders were in reality ruled by whatever world empire controlled the region: first the Babylonians; then the Medes and Persians; then the Greeks; and finally, during the time of Christ, the Romans. At approximately thirty years of age, the Lord Jesus Christ began His public ministry to the lost sheep of Israel with these words, *"Repent: for the kingdom of heaven is at hand"* (Matt. 4:17). In concept, the same kingdom which included God's blessing, God's communion/fellowship, and complete deliverance from oppression was again being offered to the Jews. However, this time, its rightful King, the Messiah, was included in the offer – for only under His leadership and His provision could such a kingdom be established and maintained forever.

This kingdom was foretold in the Old Testament, was announced by John the Baptist and Jesus Christ, but then was rejected by the Jews (i.e. they refused its spiritual aspects and its King). We can learn more about God's kingdom from the seven Kingdom Parables of Matthew 13, which bridge the gap between the first advent of the Lord to earth to become a man to suffer for our sin and His second advent in which His kingdom will be established and all that is wicked will be removed. After the Jews rejected Christ's offer of a literal, earthly, political kingdom with Him as King, the kingdom in its spiritual sense was then offered to the Gentiles. God's rule presently encompasses the hearts of believers, the Church. This interim of God's kingdom will conclude at the end of the Church Age, and then the same kingdom offered to the Jews long ago will be physically established on earth at Christ's Second Advent. The final phase of God's kingdom will be the establishment of a new heaven and a new earth; this will be the eternal state of righteousness – *"that God may be all in all"* (1 Cor. 15:28).

Through the Kingdom Parables, the Lord Jesus foretold that the Jews, who had already been scattered among the nations for 600 years for committing spiritual adultery (Ezek. 36:16-25), would be found again by Messiah for the purpose of offering Himself to them as their

King. However, they would reject Him and, thus, continue to be lost among the nations until their repentance during the last days of the Tribulation Period. In order to retrieve them in the future from the nations and to restore them as His people, the Lord first had to pay the debt of their sin at Calvary.

In the fifth of the Kingdom Parables, Christ alludes to this: *"Again, the kingdom of heaven is like treasure hidden in a field, which a man found and hid; and for joy over it he goes and sells all that he has and buys that field"* (Matt. 13:44). God considers Israel *a treasure* unto Himself (Ex. 19:5; Ps. 135:4). It seems, then, that what is pictured in this parable is the spiritual blindness of the nation of Israel; they were cut off from God for rejecting Christ who then turned to woo a Gentile bride for Himself. This "treasure" was therefore hidden again in a field (i.e. among the nations of the world). However, at the Lord's second coming, He will be accepted by the Jewish nation (Zech. 12:10), and they will then receive the Holy Spirit and be restored unto God as His people. God will regather the Jews to the land of Israel; He will not leave one of them among the nations (Ezek. 39:28-29). In that day, God's *peculiar treasure* will be recovered.

The Jews responded to the Lord's kingdom offer the same way that they responded to Jeremiah's prophecy six centuries earlier – not only did they reject the message, they also sought to kill the messenger. The necessity of the Lord Jesus' death had been specifically foretold a full millennium before it happened (Ps. 22); His substitutionary death would be God's means of reconciling sinners to Himself. Jeremiah, however, would not be killed, as this would have undermined God's promise to sustain and protect His prophet from harm.

Jeremiah's adversaries would first attack him verbally (v. 18). They would attempt to publicly slander Jeremiah and ridicule his important message so that no one would heed it. A verbal lashing was only the beginning of their assault; they planned to silence Jeremiah for good. Jeremiah apparently knew that his oppressors had dug a pit and planned to put him into it, perhaps to bury him alive or else merely leave him there to die (vv. 20-21).

This information greatly disturbed Jeremiah and prompted him to ask God not to show the Jewish rebels any mercy, something he had earlier requested (7:16, 8:20-22). The more Jeremiah communed with the Lord, the more he understood God's anger over sin and accepted the fact that His judgment of Judah was necessary. Jeremiah concluded that he could do no more for his people; judgment was warranted and was, moreover, the only solution to turn this stiff-necked nation back to God. In a future day, with their refining trials all past, Israel will fully repent and turn to Christ and He will establish them in an everlasting kingdom!

Meditation

Come, kingdom of our God, sweet reign of light and love!
Shed peace and hope and joy abroad, and wisdom, from above.
Come, kingdom of our God, and raise the glorious throne,
In worlds by the undying trod, when God shall bless His own.

— John Johns

The Broken Vessel
Jeremiah 19:1-15

In the arrangement of the book of Jeremiah, the message of the broken vessel in chapter 19 was placed directly after the message of the marred clay in the preceding chapter for the obvious connection – the potter. The one who creates also has the right to destroy what he has made. God had fashioned the Jewish nation in righteousness, but now that vessel was full of corruption; it needed to be shattered and scattered.

Jeremiah purchased from a potter a bottle or flask used for carrying water. This vessel would be the prop to illustrate his next message. After gathering a group of Jewish leaders (probably elders and priests), Jeremiah walked through the East or Potsherd (Potshard) Gate to the Valley of Hinnom located directly south of Jerusalem (vv. 1-2). The people used this gate to enter the valley to discard their refuse, such as broken pots (thus, the gate's name). The message was delivered at a place in the valley called Topheth.

The Valley of Hinnom was Jerusalem's garbage dump and piles of burning rubbish smoldered there incessantly. The Jews likely thought of this place when the Lord Jesus spoke of hell as a place of eternal judgment where fire burns continually (Mark 9:43-47). The summits surrounding the valley had become the high places of Baal, the scene of intense idolatry. This was where Jewish children were being sacrificed on pagan altars (vv. 4-5).

With these altars as a backdrop, Jeremiah first explained the message before he dramatized it before his elite audience. Because of Jewish paganism, God would rename the Hinnom Valley to the "Valley of Slaughter" (v. 6). The Babylonians would use the valley as a killing ground for Jerusalem's inhabitants and leave the carcasses of the slain lying on the ground to rot and be devoured by beasts (vv. 7-

155

8). After the future slaughter, there would not be sufficient tombs and graves for the Jewish corpses that would litter the ground (v. 11). The siege of Jerusalem would be so severe that hunger would cause parents to eat the flesh of their own children (v. 9). Topheth would be the location of immense suffering and death.

After delivering this solemn message, Jeremiah shattered the vase which he had purchased. The action was accompanied by these words: *"Even so I will break this people and this city, as one breaks a potter's vessel, which cannot be made whole again"* (v. 11). After pronouncing judgment on Jerusalem and her inhabitants, Jeremiah departed from Topheth to deliver the same message at the temple to the general populace (vv. 14-15). The underlying message of Jeremiah 18 and 19 is that an unprofitable vessel must be broken before God in order to be recreated by Him into a useful form. The process would be painful, but profitable in the end. This same principle is true for the believer today – brokenness is the pathway to fruitfulness.

Normally, when something breaks, it loses value. For example, a collision decreases the worth of an automobile, and a shattered keepsake is remorsefully discarded as a total loss. Within the physical realm the laws of nature work to depreciate the value of our possessions, but this is not so in the spiritual realm – in fact, the opposite is true. Scripture poses a number of metaphoric examples to show that in God's reckoning, things and especially people become more valuable for service after being broken. Each of the following examples testifies of what can be accomplished in the believer's life through brokenness.

To Know Meaning in Life

The donkey's colt, which had never been saddled, became instantly broken in the presence of the Lord Jesus (Luke 19:30). Through brokenness, the colt learned God's purpose for its life and fulfilled it; he was to carry Messiah down the Mount of Olives into Jerusalem before a cheering crowd. It is when we are broken before God that we will be able to learn of Him and, like the colt, find true meaning in life: *"Come to Me, all you who labor and are heavy laden, and I will give you rest. Take My yoke upon you and **learn from Me**, for I am gentle and lowly in heart, and you will find rest for* *your souls"* (Matt. 11:28-30). Learning of the Lord's character is a wonderful privilege of all believers.

To Offer Acceptable Worship

Only days before the Lord would be crucified, Mary took a stone flask of spikenard, broke it open, and anointed the Lord Jesus with its precious contents (John 12:1-11). As the ointment was very costly, some criticized the action as being wasteful, but the Lord was refreshed by her expression of devotion, and said, *"Let her alone; for the day of My burial has she kept this"* (John 12:7). The vessel which contained the spikenard had to be broken for her worship to be appreciated by the Lord and others, and the same is true for the believer: *"The sacrifice acceptable to God is a broken spirit; a broken and contrite heart, O God, You will not despise"* (Ps. 51:17). The Lord hates pride of any sort, but those with broken hearts are welcome to come near Him through Christ's blood (Heb. 10:19-21).

To Be Fruitful

Under his ephod, the high priest wore a blue sleeveless robe which hung down below his knees. Pomegranates, which rattle when dried, and golden bells were to be attached to the bottom hem (Ex. 28:33). The rattling of pomegranates and the tinkling of bells spoke of Christ's continual intercessory work before the throne of grace on the behalf of His people (i.e. every movement of the serving High Priest would be heard by the people). The result of this ministry enables believers to be fruitful (as typified by the pomegranates which were full of seeds) and to have a clear testimony of Him in the world (as pictured in the *pure* gold bells). Yet, for the pomegranate to be fruitful, its hard shell must be broken in order to release its seeds; if no seeds are planted, there will not be any fruit to come. What it was previously had to radically change in order to experience God's creative power and fruitfulness – the same principle is true in the life of the believer.

To Have a Bright Testimony

Gideon was to attack a vast host of Midianites with merely 300 men armed only with trumpets and torches (Judg. 7:9-22). The torches were hidden in jars which were to be broken on command to let their lights shine beyond the jars' confines. The trumpets were blown, 300 torches shown brightly upon the hillsides, and mass confusion swept the camp of the enemy, so much so that they slaughtered each other. Just as the torches shown forth their light after the jars were broken, the believer's testimony for Christ becomes more intensely brilliant through brokenness.

To Be Sanctified

Jehoshaphat was a good king, but he had a tendency of associating with wicked people. He aligned himself with evil Ahab to recapture a religious city, and the endeavor almost cost Jehoshaphat his life. Later, he would enter into a joint venture with Ahab's son, Ahaziah, to sail ships to Ophir for gold; however, God would not have His man fraternizing with the enemy, so He "broke up" all the ships (2 Chron. 20:35-37). Because the ships were destroyed, the unnatural union Jehoshaphat had with the world was severed and Jehoshaphat's only recourse was to draw near to God. Often the Lord will bring us into painful situations to pry us out of the world's grip. God hates worldliness in the believer's life and will take drastic measures to ensure that the believer feels His jealousy (Jas. 4:4).

Summary

The lesson posed by these broken things is that the believer must be broken in order to: know the meaning in life, offer true worship, be fruitful, have a powerful testimony, and be disillusioned with a corrupt world. Spiritually speaking, God puts a premium on broken things, especially on the brokenness of His people: *"The Lord is near to the brokenhearted, and saves the crushed in spirit"* (Ps. 34:18). The Lord will never harm us, but He may hurt us so that we relinquish control of our lives to Him, resulting in our fruitfulness and His glory.

Meditation

> Come, oh come, with thy broken heart, weary and worn with care;
> Come and kneel at the open door, Jesus is waiting there;
> Waiting to heal thy wounded soul, waiting to give thee rest;
> Why wilt thou walk where shadows fall? Come to His loving breast!

— Fanny Crosby

158

Labor and Sorrow
Jeremiah 20:1-18

The message of the broken vessel, delivered in the courtyard of the temple (19:14), was not received by Jeremiah's audience. Whether there was a public outcry against Jeremiah we do not know, but he caused enough of a disruption to temple affairs that the chief governor of the temple, Pashhur, arrested Jeremiah. Pashhur was responsible for maintaining order in the temple and, therefore, had the authority to have Jeremiah beaten, perhaps flogged, and put into stocks. And that is exactly what he did.

Jeremiah was placed in public stocks at the high gate of Benjamin, near the temple (v. 2). Common stocks were extremely uncomfortable as a prisoner's head, hands, and feet were placed through holes in a single board and secured either by ropes or wooden clamps. The person in stocks could not move from this confined, bent-over position, which would be especially distressing if the prisoner had previously suffered a beating.

The next day, Pashhur ordered that Jeremiah be released and brought before him. It is likely that Pashhur had much to say to Jeremiah, but his words are not recorded in the text; however, Jeremiah's are. He informed Pashhur that the Lord had renamed him Magor-missabib, which means "scared to death" or "terror on every side." Jeremiah's message is brief and to the point – the city would be despoiled and destroyed. He also informed Pashhur that he, his entire house, and those who prophesied lies with him would be carried away as captives to Babylon, where Pashhur would die and be buried (vv. 4-6).

Pashhur was a religious man, but his relationship with the Lord was not genuine. Although he publicly represented God's authority in the temple, he did not speak for Him. As Paul explains, this propensity for zealous religiosity ran deep in the Jewish blood: *"For I*

159

bear them witness that they have a zeal for God, but not according to knowledge. For they being ignorant of God's righteousness, and seeking to establish their own righteousness, have not submitted to the righteousness of God" (Rom. 10:2-3). This is a spiritual pitfall to avoid. Self-illuminated fervor for God will never please Him; in fact, Paul affirmed that it kept the Jews in his day from accepting God's truth, as revealed in Christ, that they might be saved (Rom. 9:1-3, 10:1). In application, Pashhur's sin serves as a warning to believers: we should keep our relationship with the Lord open and genuine, and not impose our own thinking when God has clearly expressed His will.

It is utterly understandable that Jeremiah would feel abandoned and deceived by the Lord in this situation. He had been promised to be protected and, yet, he had suffered brutally for his faithfulness (v. 7). Though publicly mocked and derided daily, he had steadfastly declared God's Word to those who did not want to hear it (v. 8). Even when he wanted to hold back from preaching God's word, he found that he could not: *"But His word was in my heart like a burning fire shut up in my bones; I was weary of holding it back, and I could not"* (v. 9). Jeremiah's oppressors were constantly watching him, hoping he would stumble morally and discredit himself as God's prophet, thus making his message void. They wanted to catch him in some misconduct and take revenge on Jeremiah through legal recourse (v. 10).

Jeremiah understood that God was testing the quality of his faith through this trial (v. 12); still, he longed for his time of *"labor and sorrow"* to be over (v. 18). It seems there were two ends which were desirable to Jeremiah: either for him to see God take vengeance on the evildoers (v. 12) or his own death. Jeremiah bemoaned his life and wished he had died shortly after birth (vv. 14-17). He preferred to die rather than to endure these dreadful trials. Have you ever felt like that? In the weakness of the flesh, I have. But praise God, when we look back over the situation later, we can thank the Lord for the peaceable fruit that resulted from it. We find we are the better for the experience, we are more reliant on the Lord, and best of all, God is pleased.

In such circumstances as this, the believer has full access to the throne of grace, and Jeremiah took full advantage of it. He explained his hurts and woes to God. He suffered for righteousness, and for this reason he cried out for help and vindication (vv. 11-12). Jeremiah's only recourse was to exercise faith and bring joy into his situation by singing praises to God and by thanking Him for delivering him out of the hands of his oppressors (v. 13).

> Faith is a deliberate confidence in the character of God whose ways you cannot understand at the time.

> — Oswald Chambers

In a sin-cursed world, suffering is guaranteed. As God's children, we do not seek sympathy from our heavenly Father for our sins or their consequences; the Word of God wields a mortal blow to the former, and the latter is just compensation for our offense. However, we may beseech the Lord for comfort and grace when we suffer wrongfully at the hands of sinners. This was the practice of the Lord Jesus Christ; we are to follow His example (1 Pet. 2:19-21).

Paul instructed the believers at Thessalonica who were enduring persecution for Christ to *"rejoice evermore"* (1 Thess. 5:16). Though this verse is the shortest in the Greek New Testament, the concise command is essential to spiritual vitality. As Tim Hansel explains, joy lifts burdens: "I cannot choose to be strong, but I can choose to be joyful. And when I am willing to do that, strength will follow."[1] God's family should be a happy family, meaning we all must contribute to the atmosphere of joy. There is no room for a "doom and gloom" attitude, for all our difficulties are opportunities to honor God. *"Yet if anyone suffers as a Christian, let him not be ashamed, but let him glorify God in this matter"* (1 Pet. 4:16). As a believer chooses to rejoice in the Lord in the midst of a dire situation, God often glorifies Himself by working a miraculous solution to end the trial. Here are a few examples:

Pagans at Philippi accused Paul and Silas of wrongdoing. They were not extended the right of a fair trial, but instead were beaten, chained, and put into prison. In the inner prison, air circulation was poor, and no doubt the stench of open wounds, feces, and body odor accompanied the smoke from torches. How did these two servants of the Lord respond to this cruel situation? We read, *"But at midnight*

Paul and Silas were praying and singing hymns to God, and the prisoners were listening to them" (Acts 16:25). They prayed and rejoiced in their God through song. How did the Lord respond to their prayers and decision to rejoice? He brought a great earthquake, which released them from their captivity and then provided an opportunity for the jailer and his whole family to hear and believe the gospel of Jesus Christ.

In another example, how did the apostles respond after they had been arrested and beaten by the Pharisees for preaching Christ?

> *And they agreed with him, and when they had called for the apostles and beaten them, they commanded that they should not speak in the name of Jesus, and let them go. So they departed from the presence of the council, **rejoicing that they were counted worthy to suffer shame for His name**. And daily in the temple, and in every house, they did not cease teaching and preaching Jesus as the Christ* (Acts 5:40-42).

Despite the Pharisees' solemn warning against preaching Christ, the apostles continued preaching and teaching, and the Church multiplied. Instead of choosing to be depressed or bitter about their stripes, the disciples determined to rejoice in their Savior. It may be that our rejoicing does not specifically or immediately bring relief or conclusion to our difficulty, but God has promised to work a greater good and glorify Himself through every situation (Rom. 8:28). Rejoicing in the Lord demonstrates a trusting faith in God's sovereign control over every matter of life.

In the writings to the Corinthians, Paul related some of the incredible difficulties he faced in his ministry, but then concludes by declaring, *"As sorrowful, yet always rejoicing"* (2 Cor. 6:10). The Lord had miraculously delivered him from many life-threatening circumstances (2 Cor. 11:23-28). Paul also informed the Corinthians that he had maintained gladness though his labor among them had cost him greatly. Paul had a choice whether to complain or to rejoice in his service for the Corinthians, which in time brought them to maturity. Paul taught the believers at Philippi that rejoicing is a choice (Phil. 1:18). Despite his Roman imprisonment, Paul chose to set his mind on those things in which he could rejoice, and thus, he was not defeated by misery, but triumphant through faith.

Believers glorify God by rejoicing in Him during difficult circumstances. The next time seemingly insurmountable woes threaten to bury you, look up to heaven and say, "Lord, things down here look pretty bad right now, but I am rejoicing in You, and You just do what You think is best." Satan tempts Christians not to rejoice in their God during such times. By rejoicing in dire situations, we demonstrate that we trust God with the big picture, and we declare to those watching us that we know Who is in control and Who will resolve the matter. Rejoicing demonstrates faith without constraining God to act according to our preconceived solutions. So let us rejoice evermore in the here and now.

Meditation

When all my labors and trials are over,
    and I am safe on that beautiful shore,
Just to be near the dear Lord I adore,
    will through the ages be glory for me.
O that will be glory for me,
    glory for me, glory for me,
When by His grace I shall look on His face,
    that will be glory, be glory for me.

— Charles H. Gabriel

I Fight Against You
Jeremiah 21:1-14

Chapters 2 through 20 record nine general prophecies denouncing Judah's sin and threatening judgment against them. The next four chapters contain four more messages of judgment against specific individuals and people groups. Generally speaking, these final four messages brought Jeremiah's public preaching ministry to a close. The prophetic messages of Jeremiah 21 and 22 pertain to God's dealings with Judah's last four kings prior to Jerusalem's destruction. The messages are not presented in chronological order and span some twenty years. Jeremiah's message to King Zedekiah (21:1-22:9) prompted him to request that the priests, Pashhur and Zephaniah, inquire of Jeremiah as to whether or not the Lord would miraculously deliver them from the Babylonian armies which now encompassed the city (v. 2). This particular Pashhur is not the same man of Jeremiah 20:1-6, as the two men had different fathers (i.e. Immer and Malchijah).

Jeremiah must have been dumbfounded by this question as he had been foretelling the destruction of Jerusalem by the Babylonians for over 35 years. Was Zedekiah hoping that God had changed His mind? The Lord would not change the course of prophesied events; in fact, He would personally ensure everything that Jeremiah had spoken on His behalf would come true:

> "I Myself will fight against you with an outstretched hand and with a strong arm, even in anger and fury and great wrath. I will strike the inhabitants of this city, both man and beast; they shall die of a great pestilence. And afterward," says the Lord, "I will deliver Zedekiah king of Judah, his servants and the people, and such as are left in this city from the pestilence and the sword and the famine, into the hand of Nebuchadnezzar king of Babylon, into the hand of their enemies, and into the hand of those who seek their life;

and he shall strike them with the edge of the sword. He shall not spare them, or have pity or mercy" ' (vv. 5-7).

Although Zedekiah's response to Jeremiah's denunciation is not recorded, the pronouncement of destruction (which continues through verse 14) must have greatly disturbed the king. It is one thing to be surrounded by an army of superior strength; it is an entirely different matter to escape the wrath of Almighty God.

Jeremiah had previously rebuked the priests and prophets of the land, and now judgment was declared on the royal house of David; thus, as William Kelly explains, the authorization of Judah's destruction was complete:

> The sin of Zedekiah was more serious. The guilt of the people and the priests and prophets has already been exposed, but now the responsible head of the nation is condemned. There was no exception; the ruin of Judah is complete. Royalty was always the last stem of blessing in the history of Israel. If only the king had been right, though the people and the prophets were ever so wrong, God would still send blessing to Israel. Everything depended upon the king, the seed of David. God might have chastised the prophets and priests and people, but He would have held to them for His servant David's sake. But when not only they went astray but the king himself was the leader of the wickedness, it was utterly impossible to hold to them, and it was the sorrowful task of Jeremiah to pronounce this divine decision.[1]

Zedekiah had hoped that God would perform a *"wondrous work,"* as He had done in Hezekiah's reign when the Assyrians surrounded Jerusalem with a massive army and sought to conquer the city (2 Kgs. 18-19). But God would not act in their immediate favor; instead He would use His vast resources to defeat them. In doing so, God would righteously judge the past and present sins of His people, and open the way for their future restoration. In that sense, God was performing a wondrous work on behalf of His people; the Potter would supernaturally work to soften the marred clay in order to reform it (18:2-3).

The only gleam of mercy to be found in Jeremiah's response to Zedekiah was conditional in nature and had already been mentioned in previous messages: the choices were to surrender the city and live as captives in Babylon, or to resist God's chastening hand and die in Jerusalem (v. 9). Jeremiah then focused on God's contempt for the royal line of Judah who were supposed to execute righteousness in His name, but had instead perverted justice and brought disdain upon His good name (v. 12). Though Zedekiah may have been rattled by this message, he ignored it because he felt quite secure within the high walls surrounding Jerusalem. He pompously proclaimed, *"Who shall come down against us? Or who shall enter our dwellings?"* (v. 13). Those questions would be answered in God's timing.

Simply put, the king had a choice between death and life. Stubborn Zedekiah chose death. That decision had tremendous consequences not only for himself, but also for those he ruled. Before his eyes were put out by the Babylonians, he would personally witness the massacre of all his sons (2 Kgs. 25:7). With those hideous images fresh in his mind, he was chained and hauled off to Babylon like an animal (39:5-7). He never returned to Israel but died a pitiful captive in a strange land.

Each individual who sojourns on this earth is faced with the same choice that Zedekiah was given – to continue traveling down the pathway of death or to choose God's way which leads to life. Concerning the choice between eternal life and eternal death the Lord Jesus warned:

> *Enter by the narrow gate; for wide is the gate and broad is the way that leads to destruction, and there are many who go in by it. Because narrow is the gate and difficult is the way which leads to life, and there are few who find it* (Matt. 7:13-14).

Later, the Lord Jesus told His disciples that He was the only means of obtaining eternal life: *"I am the way, the truth, and the life. No one comes to the Father except through Me"* (John 14:6). Peter declared the same truth, *"Nor is there salvation in any other, for there is no other name under heaven given among men by which we must be saved"* (Acts 4:12). The narrow way is God's way, and the only one that leads to salvation.

Yes, God is a God of love (1 Jn. 4:8), but He could not justly save mankind by love alone – His sense of justice demanded that sin be condemned. Yet, it was God's love which supplied the solution by which mankind could be saved: *"But God demonstrates His own love toward us, in that while we were still sinners, Christ died for us. Much more then, having now been justified by His blood, we shall be saved from wrath through Him"* (Rom. 5:8-9). Thus, God's love found a way to righteously offer salvation by judging His Son for human sin. He can legally offer the gift of eternal salvation to *"whosoever will"* (John 3:16). Those who reject His gracious offer will spend an eternity in the lake of fire, *"for the wages of sin is death"* (Rom. 6:23).

What is the message of salvation today that must be believed in order to receive a full pardon from God? It is that the Lord Jesus Christ, the eternal Son of God, suffered for my sins, died in my place, was buried, and arose from the dead that I might be justified and have eternal life in Him. This is called the "gospel" (literally, the "good news") of Jesus Christ. Paul reminds the Corinthian believers that this was the message he preached to them and the one by which they were saved (1 Cor. 15:1-4).

The message of God's salvation is inclusive in its application; it is offered to anyone who will believe it (Rev. 22:17). However, it is exclusive in nature, for trusting in any other message brings eternal judgment (Gal. 1:6-9). God is *"not willing that any should perish but that all should come to repentance"* (2 Pet. 3:9), but a seeking sinner must trust Christ and Him alone for his or her salvation.

The Lord Jesus extends an invitation to all who understand their miserable spiritual condition and desire to find rest for their souls by being reconciled with God. While on earth, He proclaimed, *"Come to Me, all you who labor and are heavy laden, and I will give you rest"* (Matt. 10:28) and *"He who hears My word and believes in Him who sent Me has everlasting life, and shall not come into judgment, but has passed from death into life"* (John 5:24). Concerning the Lord Jesus, Paul stated, *"There is one God and one Mediator between God and men, the Man Christ Jesus, who gave Himself a ransom for all"* (1 Tim. 2:5-6). The apostles agree; there is salvation in Christ alone.

The solution to sin is found in Christ alone; we must repent and receive Him as Savior. A true believer will seek to practically enthrone Christ as Lord of his or her life because He is Lord over all. Repentance is the first step a sinner must take and without it there can be no salvation. The Lord Jesus said, *"Unless you repent you will all likewise perish"* (Luke 13:3). Repentance means, firstly, that you agree with God that you are a sinner deserving His judgment and that you turn away from all that you ever thought would earn you heaven; such repentance indicates a deep grief over personal sin and a desire to turn from wickedness (Jer. 8:6). Secondly, you must turn to something – that is, you must believe the gospel of Jesus Christ. For example, the Thessalonians turned to God from idols. Their salvation was evident in that they diligently served the living and true God even while being severely persecuted for their faith (1 Thess. 1:5-9).

Mankind has a simple choice: either exercise faith in God's message of salvation, be accredited righteousness, and have the debt of sin erased; or work for salvation and earn a fair wage, which is death. (Spiritual death is to be separated from God.) We cannot please God without trusting Him (Heb. 11:6), and we cannot approach Him except through the Lord Jesus Christ (John 14:6).

Self-reliant Zedekiah chose to disregard God's means of escaping judgment, and he and those he governed suffered the consequences of that decision. Jeremiah chose God's way, the way of life; though it was a difficult path to walk, the Lord accompanied him every step of the way. Dear reader, which path are you on today?

Meditation

Rescue the perishing, care for the dying,
Snatch them in pity from sin and the grave;
Weep o'er the erring one, lift up the fallen,
Tell them of Jesus, the mighty to save.

Rescue the perishing, duty demands it;
Strength for thy labor the Lord will provide;
Back to the narrow way patiently win them;
Tell the poor wanderer a Saviour has died.

— Fanny Crosby

Kings Beware
Jeremiah 22:1-30

Jeremiah was instructed to visit the king's palace, which was located near the temple, in order to deliver his tenth message (v. 1). The king, who is not identified, was to be reminded that those who rule God's people are to reflect God's character in their decisions and judgments. If the king ruled justly and continued in God's Law, then he would be blessed. If, however, he ignored God's commandments and abused his office, the Lord would judge him. God's recompense for such behavior would be the destruction of the royal palace and the removal of rebels from the throne of Judah permanently (vv. 2-5).

As the scene in Jeremiah 22 does not seem to fit the siege situation described in Jeremiah 21, it is possible that this message (22:1-9), though placed after Jeremiah 21, was actually delivered at the onset of Zedekiah's reign. Another indication that this message was given at that time is that there was still the opportunity to receive God's blessing in Jeremiah 22 (v. 4); on the other hand, the only opportunity offered in Jeremiah 21 is to escape death by surrendering the city (v. 9).

William Kelly comments to the general theme of Jeremiah 22:

In Jeremiah 22 the sin of the representatives of the house of David is dwelt upon in further detail. Beside Zedekiah, Shallum (Jehoahaz), the son of Josiah (v. 11), Jehoiakim, also son of Josiah (v. 18), and Coniah (Jehoiachin, son of Jehoiakim, v. 24) are all arraigned as evil rulers in the critical times when the monarchy was drawing to its close. The kings named are out of their chronological order, but the purpose is to bring the separate prophecies against the separate kings of Judah all into a cluster for the moral object of showing that virtually there was no difference. Some might be a little more pronounced in their violence and gross iniquity, but they were all

169

faithless and godless. Hence, the solemn sentence was uttered by Jehovah: *"O earth, earth, earth, hear the word of Jehovah. Thus saith Jehovah, Write ye this man childless, a man that shall not prosper in his days; for no man of his seed shall prosper, sitting upon the throne of David, and ruling any more in Judah."* It is implied, not that the line of David should fail, but that this man's line should.[1]

Thus, Jeremiah's message to Zedekiah was not to him alone; he held the four final kings of the dynasty in contempt – they were wicked. The line of David would be cut off and no descendant of David would rule over Judah again until Messiah arrived to establish His kingdom.

When it was first constructed by Solomon, the royal palace was called "The Palace of the Forest of Lebanon" (1 Kgs. 7:2-5). Apparently, lumber hewn from the forests of Gilead was used in addition to the enormous amount of cedar harvested from Lebanon. The palace was huge and required thirteen years to complete its construction. Jeremiah foretold that the Babylonians would cut it into pieces and burn its timbers (vv. 7-8). The wood from the palace was likely used as fuel for the intense fires that would be needed to crumble rock structures such as the temple and the walls surrounding Jerusalem. What the Jews considered as a beautiful framework would be used by the enemy against them.

Even the surrounding nations would be puzzled as to why Jehovah would allow the temple and the royal palace, which had stood for over four centuries, to be destroyed (v. 8). But in fact, the nations would answer their own question, acknowledging that the Jewish desolation had been brought about *because they* [had] *forsaken the covenant of the Lord their God, and worshipped other gods, and served them"* (v. 9). This was a stinging indictment against the Jews; the pagan nations understood why God was dealing so harshly with His own people, but the Jews could not comprehend the matter. Those who were not associated with the Lord had a better understanding of His character than those who had been entrusted with His written Law! As the professing Church continues to depart from Scripture, one must wonder if the lost have more respect for the Lord today than those who identify with Him. But indeed, such things are predicted and are a sign of the coming Tribulation Period (2 Thess. 2:3).

The message to Zedekiah was a capstone of prophetic judgment against the line of David then on the earth; accordingly, the remaining kings would be addressed in chronological order. The second king to receive a message was Shallum (Jehoahaz), the son of Josiah. Godly King Josiah was killed in battle by Pharaoh Neco in 609 B.C. Jehoahaz reigned only three months before he himself was removed from the throne by Neco and taken to Egypt. Jeremiah penned this prophecy while Jehoahaz was a prisoner in Egypt, saying he would never return to Jerusalem (vv. 11-12). Just as Jeremiah had predicted, Jehoahaz died a captive in Egypt.

Pharaoh Neco put Jehoiakim, also the son of Josiah, on the throne instead of Jehoahaz. Jehoiakim was a selfish and corrupt king. Unlike his father, Josiah, who cared for the poor and championed righteousness, Jehoiakim oppressed the people and perverted justice for his personal gain (vv. 15-17). As a specific example of his poor leadership, Jeremiah noted Jehoiakim's efforts to construct a prestigious palace of cedar panels for himself while forcing his subjects to build it for him without being paid (vv. 13-14).

Jeremiah prophesied that because Jehoiakim had exploited the people, he would not be mourned when he died and would receive the burial rites of a donkey. When domestic animals died, their carcasses were dragged outside the walls of the city and left to rot and be devoured by scavengers (v. 19). Normally, after the death of a Judean king there was a time of public mourning, an elaborate funeral procession, and then a burial ceremony; however, Jehoiakim would receive none of these honors. Although it is possible that Jehoiakim died by natural causes, it seems more likely that he was assassinated by fellow Jews to appease King Nebuchadnezzar who journeyed to Jerusalem with his army to put down Jehoiakim's rebellion in 598 B.C. (2 Kgs. 24:10).

Jehoiakim's eighteen-year-old son, Jehoiachin, ascended to the throne of Judah only three months before he surrendered himself and the city to Nebuchadnezzar (2 Kgs. 24:8-9). He was an evil king, and Nebuchadnezzar took him, his servants, and the queen royal as prisoners to Babylon. Nebuchadnezzar despoiled the temple of its precious vessels and treasure, and then enslaved all the princes, the craftsmen, the blacksmiths, and the mighty men of valor in the land (2 Kgs. 24:11-16). In all, he took some ten thousand captives back to Babylon, the prophet Ezekiel being among them.

Jeremiah foretold that all Judah's surrounding allies would also be defeated by the Babylonians, the result of which would be bitter lamentations throughout the region (vv. 20-22). Those in sorrow would include the "inhabitants of Lebanon," which is a reference to the Jews living in Jerusalem. Apparently, many of Jerusalem's citizens were living comfortably in cedar-paneled houses constructed with wood from Lebanon. Such luxurious living would be replaced by captivity. However, since Jehoiachin surrendered the city to Nebuchadnezzar, Jerusalem, with its plush housing, would not be destroyed at that time.

Jehoiachin was an evil king. Jeremiah likened him to a signet ring, something that kings commonly wore in those days and used frequently to express their authority in legitimizing their edicts. Even though Jehoiachin had a position of importance, much like a valuable signet ring, God would rather remove him from the throne than allow his wickedness to continue. Jeremiah prophesied that Jehoiachin and his mother would not return from Babylon.

Jeremiah's final questions were addressed to the people, some of whom wanted Jehoiachin to return from Babylon to be their king again (v. 27). The answers to the questions were obvious; these were posed for the purpose of proving to the people that God had brought about all these events. The fact that Jehoiachin had been removed from the throne demonstrated that the Lord did not approve of him; in fact, God had pronounced a specific judgment upon him: none of his descendants would ever ascend to the throne of David (v. 30).

Before leaving Jerusalem, Nebuchadnezzar placed the uncle of Jehoiachin, Zedekiah, on the throne of Judah. He would be the last Judean king from the line of Solomon to reign over Jerusalem and would be subservient to Babylon the entire time. Jeremiah's prophecy concerning Jehoiachin is significant, for God had promised David that one of his descendants would be on his throne forever (2 Sam. 7:12-16), but according to Jeremiah, that descendant could not come through the royal line of Jehoiachin, since Jehoiachin had been cursed by God for his wickedness.

This prophecy is used to magnify the incarnation of the Lord Jesus Christ as Messiah. Joseph, the husband of Mary (the mother of the Lord Jesus), was a descendant of Shealtiel who was the son of Jehoiachin or Jeconiah (Matt. 1:12; 1 Chron. 3:17). Therefore, no son of Joseph could sit upon David's throne. Mary, however, was also a descendant of David through Nathan (Luke 3:24-38). Thus, the son of Mary could fulfill both prophecies, if she conceived supernaturally through the power of the Holy Spirit and not by Joseph her husband. Such a child would avoid the curse of Jeconiah, would not be corrupted by the fallen nature inherited from Adam, and would be the rightful heir to the throne of David. Jeremiah's prophecies foretold God's dealings with the last four wicked kings of Judah, but also laid the foundation for the future exaltation of the King of kings.

Meditation

Crown Him! Crown Him! Crown the Saviour King of kings;
In your hearts enthrone Him, Lord and Master own Him;
Crown Him! Crown Him! While heaven exultant rings;
Crown the blessed Saviour King of kings.

Soon He is coming back again, a thousand years on earth to reign;
We'll see Him by and by, we'll see Him by and by;
All the redeemed with Him He'll bring,
Who in their hearts have crowned Him King,
And they shall live and reign with Him on high.

— Leila N. Morris

The Righteous Branch
Jeremiah 23:1-8

Although the vast majority of Jeremiah 2 through 45 deals with God's judgment of Judah and His reasons for judgment, there are brief passages which would inspire hope in God's covenant people while they suffered under His chastening rod. Jeremiah 23 is one of these portions and provides a clear reference to the coming Messiah who would rule over them with power and righteousness forever. Though the kings of Judah in Jeremiah's day were exceedingly wicked (as stated in the two preceding chapters), there would be a future Ruler who would establish a kingdom of righteousness in Judah. Judah's perverse shepherds had scattered God's sheep and turned them away from following the Lord; this unfortunate situation had led to the slaughter of many (vv. 1-2). God promised to judge these evil leaders; Jeremiah spoke of their doom in chapters 21 and 22.

Yet, there was hope for the future! In a coming day God would regather His people who had been scattered among the nations back to their homeland. His sheep would return to His fold and be restored to fruitfulness (v. 3). He would establish godly leadership in the land and His people would never be in lack or dismayed again (v. 4). The wise and righteous king to come would be a descendant of David and be honorable and just in every respect. He would bless His people and protect them from harm. The people would revere Him and call Him "The Lord Our Righteousness," but God would refer to Him as His "Righteous Branch" (vv. 5-6).

Under His leadership the Jews would be more excited about their future return to the Promised Land than they were at their historical deliverance from Egypt and initial entrance into the land under Moses and then Joshua (vv. 7-8). It is likely that verse 8 refers to two different occasions for rejoicing, both future from the prophet's point

174

Devotions in Jeremiah

of view. The first was when the Jews would return to their homeland from Babylon. The second is when both Israel and Judah would return from all nations and be cleansed of their filthiness forever at Messiah's Second Advent to the earth.

The announcement of the Messiah being God's "Righteous Branch" is just one of four similar "branch" declarations in the Old Testament. The number four is used to symbolize earthly order throughout Scripture. For example, there are four seasons, four directions, four divisions of a day, four types of soil, and four realms in which all creatures dwell. It is no wonder then that the New Testament contains four, and only four, gospel accounts which reveal Messiah from four different perspectives and to four unique earthly audiences. These vantage points of Christ declare to us how God the Father wanted His Son to be known. The following table provides a short summary to assist in recognizing more clearly the Old Testament fourfold pictures of the coming Savior to earth.

Gospel	Matthew	Mark	Luke	John
Perspective	King	Servant	Human	God
Audience	Jewish	Roman	Greek	The World

Although there are a number of these fourfold presentations of Messiah in the Old Testament, space constrains us to focus on the one Jeremiah introduces us to, namely, Christ as The Branch of Righteousness. God speaks prophetically of His Son being a Branch in four ways, which align with the unique vantage points of Christ in the four Gospels. These statements were to prepare the way for Christ's first earthly advent, that the Lord Jesus Christ might be recognized as God's Messiah:

*"Behold, the days are coming," says the Lord, "that I will raise to David **a Branch of righteousness; a King** shall reign and prosper, and execute judgment and righteousness in the earth"* (Jer. 23:5; also see Isa. 11:1).

*"Hear, O Joshua, the high priest, you and your companions who sit before you, for they are a wondrous sign; for behold, I am bringing forth **My Servant the Branch**"* (Zech. 3:8).

175

*Thus says the Lord of hosts, saying: "Behold, **the Man whose name is the Branch**! From His place He shall branch out, and He shall build the temple of the Lord"* (Zech. 6:12).

*In that day **the Branch of the Lord shall be beautiful and glorious**; and the fruit of the earth shall be excellent and appealing for those of Israel who have escaped* (Isa. 4:2).

The above "Branch" declarations closely align with four Old Testament commands to "behold." Each emphasizes one of the main Gospel themes. The word "behold" means "to earnestly look upon with regard;" it may convey a connotation of surprise or wonder. These four "behold statements" are God the Father's invitation to Jews, and indeed, mankind, to gaze upon and admire His dear Son.

*Rejoice greatly, O daughter of Zion! Shout, O daughter of Jerusalem! **Behold, your King** is coming to you; He is just and having salvation, lowly and riding on a donkey, a colt, the foal of a donkey* (Zech. 9:9).

***Behold! My Servant** whom I uphold, My Elect one in whom My soul delights! I have put My Spirit upon Him; He will bring forth justice to the Gentiles* (Isa. 42:1).

*Thus says the Lord of hosts, saying: "**Behold, the Man** whose name is the Branch! From His place He shall branch out, and He shall build the temple of the Lord"* (Zech. 6:12).

*O Zion, you who bring good tidings, get up into the high mountain; O Jerusalem, you who bring good tidings, lift up your voice with strength, lift it up, be not afraid; say to the cities of Judah, "**Behold your God!**"* (Isa. 40:9).

These four Messianic titles perfectly align with the four Gospel presentations of Christ:

> Behold your King – Gospel of Matthew
> Behold My Servant – Gospel of Mark
> Behold the Man – Gospel of Luke
> Behold your God – Gospel of John

When the Lord is presented in a position of authority (as King and as God), the possessive pronoun "your" precedes the title, but when the position of a lowly servant is in view, the pronoun "My" appears; Christ is man's King and Jehovah's Servant. When the Lord is introduced as a man, the neutral article "the" is applied. This arrangement demonstrates the various facets and positional glories of the Lord's ministry and how He would relate to mankind. Luke shows us that as a man, the Lord is on an equal footing with humanity, though, only He was spiritually alive at that time. In Matthew and John, the Lord is presented in a position of authority above man. In the record of Mark we see that the Lord, in accordance with the will of the Father, humbly lowered Himself (not in essence, but in the sense of position) below His rightful station of divinity and took on the form of a Servant.

Who, being in the form of God, thought it not robbery to be equal with God: but made Himself of no reputation, and took upon Him the form of a servant, and was made in the likeness of men: and being found in fashion as a man, He humbled Himself, and became obedient unto death, even the death of the cross (Phil. 2:6-8; KJV).

Within the New Testament, we find two exhortations to "behold," framing the beginning and ending moments of the Lord's ministry on earth. John the Baptist, who prepared the way for the Lord's coming, proclaimed in reference to the Lord Jesus, *"Behold the Lamb of God, who takes away the sin of the world"* (John 1:29). Just hours before the death of our Lord, after He had been mocked, buffeted, scourged, and spit upon, Pilate presented Jesus to the Jews, saying, *"Behold, your King!"* (John 19:14). It was a gruesome presentation. Thorns had broken the Lord's brow. His beard had been wrenched from His face as an undesired weed is uprooted and discarded from a garden. Roman fists had pulverized His comely visage in playful sport.

What King is this? The prophet Isaiah, writing seven centuries earlier, foretold the sufferings of the Savior at this moment. He would be so physically marred by human brutality that He would cease to resemble a man (Isa. 52:14). Any movie's portrayal of these events or any artist's conception of this scene will be incredibly sanitized from the gory reality. Isaiah also declared what the Jewish attitude towards their God-sent Messiah would be upon that hallowed day: *"When we shall see Him, there is no beauty that we should desire Him"* (Isa. 53:2; KJV). So, when presented with their king, the Jews emphatically shouted, *"We have no king, but Caesar"* (John 19:15). In accordance with God's sovereign plan, their King was crucified, but would be raised up from the dead to reign over them in a future day.

God's cutting off the branch of David through Jeconiah would serve to assist the Jews in a future day to recognize the Righteous Branch of David, the one who would rule over them in righteousness forever. However, before that kingdom could ever be established, that eternal Branch of the Lord first had to become the Lord's Servant Branch, the Man Branch, who by Himself alone would provide the means of reconciling sinners to a holy God. Jeremiah's declaration of the coming "Branch of Righteousness" was good news indeed for the suffering Jews, but represents only the outcome of the fuller work of God accomplished through Christ!

Meditation

> Great Jehovah, mighty Lord, vast and boundless is Thy Word;
> King of kings, from shore to shore Thou shalt reign forevermore.
> Jew and Gentile, bond and free, all shall yet be one in Thee;
> All confess Messiah's Name, all His wondrous love proclaim.

> — Fanny Crosby

False Prophets
Jeremiah 23:9-40

The future kingdom under Messiah would be wonderful, but Jeremiah was not permitted to write any more about it; instead, his attention was directed to the multitude of false prophets in the land. Jeremiah had already spoken against wicked leadership; now, in his eleventh message, he would address those who claimed to speak for God, but were in reality speaking against Him.

When Jeremiah considered the awesome responsibility of conveying God's Word accurately, he became deeply unsettled. It broke his heart that God's Word was lightly esteemed in Judah; even the leaders of the people profaned God's name by ignoring His messages to them. Throughout the Bible, idolatry is shown to be an open door leading to immorality. This is why John, in his parting exhortation to fellow believers, wrote, *"Keep yourselves from idols"* (1 Jn. 5:21). Idols in our hearts will eventually lead us into moral ruin. Consequently, both spiritual and physical adultery were rampant in Judah. To make matters worse, prophets falsely speaking in Jehovah's name were causing the people to slide further into deepening darkness (vv. 11-12). The language of verse 12 ensures that the fall of the nation was unavoidable; they were being "driven" or "pushed" down "a slippery path" by violence and sin.

Not only had these false prophets caused the people to ignore Jeremiah's preaching and warnings, they had maligned God's holy name through their wicked character. True prophets of God exhibit the character of God in their ministry; their message would be in moral agreement with their lives. The prophet who spoke for the Lord was to be an example to follow; those who were not would be judged severely because they had distained the character of the One they were representing to the people. The fact that God's name had been tarnished by these false prophets greatly grieved Jeremiah. Believers

179

in the Church Age should feel the same way when God's name is blasphemed.

The Church is commanded to *"go therefore and make disciples of all the nations, baptizing them in the name of the Father and of the Son and of the Holy Spirit, teaching them to observe all things that I have commanded you"* (Matt. 28:19-20). When you evaluate the options for living life, two choices become evident: you will either uphold the name of the Lord or live in such a way that causes others to blaspheme His name. Identifying with the Lord but ignoring His Law causes those who are lost to blaspheme God's name (Rom. 2:21-24). Not submitting to rightful authority or God's order for the home is another way to bring disdain upon the name of Christ (1 Tim. 6:1; Tit. 2:3-5). These sins are just a sampling of a much larger list of ways people today who identify with Christ's name cause it to be blasphemed.

Often, when we get caught in sin, our first inclination is to behave like Jacob after the terrible events at Shechem (Gen. 34) – we are concerned about how our wrongdoings will affect us and what others will think about us. Such a thought pattern in itself indicates contempt for God. When a well-known preacher is found to be engaging in gross moral sin, our first response should be to grieve over the shame levied upon Christ's name. When an assembly of God's people splits over personality issues, we should all grieve for the poor testimony of Christ in that community. It is time that the Church bring the name of the Lord Jesus Christ into the forefront of our thinking and refrain from being selfish and blasphemous in our religiosity.

Why did David charge a giant named Goliath? The honor of God's name was at stake! The people of Israel were unconcerned that the name of their God was brought into disrepute, but David felt the matter keenly: *"Then David said to the Philistine, 'You come to me with a sword, with a spear, and with a javelin. But I come to you in the name of the Lord of hosts, the God of the armies of Israel, whom you have defied'"* (1 Sam. 17:45). David courageously defended the Lord's name because he understood that *"the name of the Lord is a strong tower; the righteous run to it and are safe"* (Prov. 18:10).

Likewise, our conduct must reflect that we consider Christ and His name first in all things, for we are His saints and ambassadors on earth. Paul understood the value of this identification: *"But* *fornication and all uncleanness or covetousness, let it not even be named among you, **as is fitting for saints***" (Eph. 5:3). Jeremiah's solemn charge against those claiming to represent God to others, but in fact disgracing His name, is pertinent for us to consider today. Is my life consistent with the gospel message that I am to be declaring to the lost or am I blaspheming the Lord's name by conduct that dishonors Him?

Another behavioral trait of false prophets is that they are morally corrupt; in fact, Jeremiah likens their lascivious nature to the inhabitants of Sodom and Gomorrah (v. 14). Centuries later Peter would vividly describe false teachers: they engage in sexual sins, despise authority, are animalistic in nature, are deceitful, are chronic sinners, are mercenaries, are spiritually bankrupt, use swelling words, and allure the weak-minded through flesh-appealing tactics (2 Pet. 2:10-18). These men have *"eyes full of adultery"* (2 Pet. 2:14); in other words, the first thing they think of when they see a woman is sex! Whether they were workers of iniquity in Jeremiah's day or in Peter's, these spiritual frauds were easy to spot – they were corrupt through and through. No false prophet will escape punishment; God will force all of them to eat wormwood and to drink poison.

Jeremiah explained that false prophets lead people away from the Lord because they preach from the vanity of their own hearts; they do not speak for God (v. 16). In disclosing their own dreams they were leading the people to forget Jehovah in the same way that other false prophets had earlier caused the people to worship Baal (v. 13). These dreams were the delusions of their own minds. The Lord does not regard words spoken in His name which do not come from Him (vv. 17-18). So even though the false prophets had misled the people into believing that they would not suffer judgment, but instead have peace, God promised to pour out His fury upon Judah. Then the inhabitants would know that these supposed prophets were frauds (vv. 19-22) and that their words were just useless chaff, as opposed to real wheat – they did not provide food for God's people (v. 28).

These false teachers obviously misunderstood the character and attributes of God to think that they could hide from Him in order to escape justice or that they could somehow elude His watchful eye. Jeremiah reminded them that God is omnipresent and omniscient.

181

Consequently, there was nowhere to hide from His presence; they were in His sight at all times (vv. 23-24).

True prophets declare their dreams accurately and convey the Word of God faithfully. God's Word is like a consuming fire or a strong hammer that breaks rocks – it will not be overcome through corruption. Commenting on this twofold analogy, Albert Barnes writes:

> *Like a fire:* God's word is the great purifier which destroys all that is false and leaves only the genuine metal. *Like a hammer*: God's word rouses and strengthens the conscience, and crushes within the heart everything that is evil.[1]

Despite Judah's wickedness, God's hammer and fire would eventually remove what was evil from Judah, including its false prophets.

Jeremiah noted that another telltale sign of false prophets is that they often plagiarized each other's prophecies in order to have something to say, since they were not receiving anything from the Lord. Jeremiah concluded that false prophets *"shall not profit the people at all"* (v. 33).

The inhabitants of Jerusalem were asking each other, *"What is the burden of the Lord?"* (v. 33; KJV). The Hebrew word *massa*, which is translated "burden," means "to lift" or "to carry." When a true prophet of God received a message from the Lord, it became a burden on the prophet's heart that must be shared. He carried the word of the Lord within himself and was compelled to share it with those to whom he was sent to warn and rebuke. Messages of rebuke, calls to repentance, and warnings of judgment were not usually heeded, which made the burden of God's Word even heavier. Preaching God's Word to those you know will reject it and threaten you because of it is a hard ministry. This Jeremiah knew full well.

If someone asked Jeremiah, "What is the burden of Lord?" he was to tell them that there was no new message from the Lord (v. 36). What he had already told them is what God wanted them to know. Jeremiah 23 concludes by insisting that only the word of Jehovah had value for His people – the words of the false prophets had none.

William Kelly explains and illustrates the importance of understanding this truth:

> The value of the word of Jehovah is again insisted upon very strongly, and in an interesting way. The false prophets, the profane priests, and all the other dreamers brought forward their words to deceive, but the Lord stands to His own utterances, and how? Why should they take heed to it? Upon what ground? Upon its own intrinsic power. "What is the chaff to the wheat?" (verse 28). Nutritive value decides. I never read a tradition that was not manifestly chaff. I never read a thought that was of man that was not worthless in the things of God. Give me something of God, and the moment my faith lays hold upon the mind of God I have got the wheat. In other words, the truth of God is not a mere question of historical investigation, but it is what suits a plain man much better and straightway. What would become of the poor and the simple if they had to conduct all kinds of long investigations to find out what the word of God was?
>
> There is one capital way of meeting a man when he is hungry. Give him a piece of bread, and he knows right well it is bread. He may never have seen that kind of bread before, and may never have tasted it, but he is convinced it is bread. Give him a piece of board, and he knows this is not bread. Thus, judged by human learning, a man may be exceedingly ignorant, but there is a sort of practical test by which God guards even the simplest of His people. "What is chaff to the wheat?" The truth of God always commends itself to the consciences of those that hear it.[2]

From Jeremiah's lips passed the words to be ruminated by the people. Their divine portion was directly before them, but they would not eat of it that they might be sustained for the future. Consequently, God had vowed to punish them, but He would not forsake them. Jerusalem would be destroyed and all those who had spoken falsely in His name would be judged (vv. 37-39). Jeremiah promised the false prophets that for dishonoring the Lord's name, indulging in wickedness, and misleading the people, they would suffer everlasting reproach and perpetual shame (v. 40). This chapter reminds us that the consequences of neglecting and ignoring God's Word are just too high! May we heed its warning.

Meditation

Jesus, Thy Name I love all other names above,
Jesus, my Lord:
O Thou art all to me; nothing to please I see,
Nothing apart from Thee, Jesus, my Lord.

Thou, blessed Son of God, hast bought me with Thy blood,
Jesus, my Lord:
O how great is Thy love, all other loves above,
Love that I daily prove, Jesus, my Lord.

— James G. Deck

Two Baskets of Figs
Jeremiah 24:1-10

Shortly after the deportation of King Jehoiachin, other Jewish leaders, and skilled tradesmen to Babylon in 597 B.C., Jeremiah saw a vision. In this vision, two baskets of figs were placed in front of the temple: one basket contained excellent fruit, while the other held rotten, inedible figs. What did this vision mean? H. A. Ironside explains what the two baskets of figs represent:

> They set forth the two classes into which Jehovah had divided the people. Those carried away captive by the Chaldeans had been sent away "for their good." He would watch over them in grace, and eventually restore them (the remnant) to their land...These then are the good figs to be treasured up by Jehovah. The evil figs, which were utterly worthless, typified Zedekiah with the residue of Jerusalem remaining in the land, and those dwelling in defiance of His Word in the land of Egypt, They were to be removed into all the kingdoms of the earth "for their hurt" (as the others "for their good"), and should be "a reproach."[1]

The evil figs would be judged in Jerusalem, while God would preserve the good fruit in Babylon for His own good pleasure.

This vision, which formed the basis of Jeremiah's twelfth message, likely prompted him to think of the first fruits offerings that were to be presented before the Lord in baskets each spring. The first gleanings (the best part) of the barley harvest was to be brought to the temple and waved before the Lord as an acknowledgement that He was the Lord of the harvest (Lev. 23:10). This grain was the Lord's provision for His priests who continually served in the temple. The concept of the first fruits offering was first introduced to the Israelites by Moses; after Joshua led the Israelites to possess Canaan, each family was to prepare a basket of the first fruits of the land and

185

present it to the Lord (Deut. 26:11). God demanded the best part, which was the first part of everything the Jews had.

Nebuchadnezzar had taken the best part of the Jewish society to Babylon as a result of Jehoiachin's surrender. The city of Jerusalem was thus spared, and the first fruits of the Jews had been reserved for God's refining and future restoration (v. 5). God had allowed this to happen for the good of the Jews, so that He could purge their idolatrous ways and give them a new heart (vv. 6-7). When they returned, they would follow God with a whole heart and not depart from Him again. This prophecy has only been partially fulfilled as, to date, only individuals, not the entire nation, have received the Holy Spirit.

The Jews who remained in Jerusalem probably thought they had been the lucky ones because they had been spared from exile, but this was not the case – they were the basket of bad fruit. Baskets are used to transport things from one location to another. Although a remnant of Jews would be carried to Babylon to be preserved, the prophet Zechariah informs us that God would use a basket to return something else to Babylon at that time also. Zechariah's seventh vision, occurring some seventy years later, illustrated that paganism originated in Babylon (Gen. 10) and that God was removing it from Israel and sending it back to that location (Zech. 5:5-11). When the Jews left Babylon to return to their homeland, their idolatry would remain in the land from which it originated.

King Zedekiah and all those remaining in Jerusalem (excluding God's prophets) were the basket of bad fruit. These would resist God's chastening hand and not be spared, whereas those taken in the second invasion (the good figs) had yielded to His chastening rod of authority, the Babylonians. The bad figs would be judged and most would die by the sword, famine, and pestilence during Nebuchadnezzar's third invasion after Zedekiah's rebellion (vv. 8-10). The rebels were a basket of bad fruit which, good for nothing, must be thrown out.

On several occasions the Lord Jesus told His disciples that only good trees bear good fruit, and, likewise, that bad trees produce according to their nature (Matt. 7:17). His point was that a true believer is known by his or her fruit in the same way as *a tree is known by its fruit"* (Matt. 12:33). Apple trees do not produce pears;

they bear only apples. True Christians will be characterized by the fruit of the Spirit, not works of the flesh. While it is true that not every Christian matures as he or she ought to, every genuine child of God will grow and bear fruit to some extent; this is evidence of salvation (Jas. 2:17). There are various possible reasons for a lack of maturity. The sluggish believer may not be spending time in the Word of God as he or she ought, due to a preoccupation with temporal things and activities. Others may be grieving the Holy Spirit through unconfessed sin. A lack of growth in a believer may well be caused by either or both reasons. Yet, some who profess the name of Christ may not be truly saved; these are like the stony and the thorny ground upon which the gospel seed fell in the parable the Lord told about the sower (Matt. 13:1-8). Their outward presentation looks good for a while, but because there was never any root of faith in their hearts, in time they are shown to be counterfeits.

Only the Lord knows the heart, and we can easily be fooled in this matter of true and false professions. However, as the Lord Jesus foretold (Matt. 7:17-23), there will be many on the Day of Judgment who will learn that *knowing* about the Lord and *doing* works in His name are not the same as *trusting* Him for salvation and *following* after Him. Those who know Christ as Savior do works of righteousness for Him (Matt. 7:21), while those who do not, work to be seen by others (Matt. 7:22). Humility and faithfulness are marks of a believer. A true profession of faith is evident, in time, by good and consistent fruit-bearing (2 Cor. 7:10). True believers may indeed fall from time to time, but there is a consistent testimony of God's life within them which cannot be hidden; a good tree bears good fruit.

As believers, we should heed scriptural limitations in judging others. We are permitted to judge those identifying with Christ who are committing immoral acts (1 Cor. 5) or embracing bad doctrine (2 Thess. 3:6, 14). Judgments must be rendered in such cases to encourage those in sin to repent and to limit the influence of their sin on others. Those walking with the Lord are to have no fellowship with those who are not (1 Cor. 5:11, 15:33); if an individual is out of fellowship with the Lord, it is impossible for that person to enjoy His fellowship with other Christians.

There are other aspects of the Christian's life that we are not to judge, however; only the Lord knows the heart. We are not to judge in the area of liberty (Rom. 14:3). This speaks of questionable activities not specifically prohibited by Scripture, which permits believers to have differing opinions on what is acceptable conduct. The motives of others are not to be judged (Matt. 7:1-5), nor the effectiveness of their ministry (1 Cor. 4:1-4). Paul knew that the flesh was biased, and, therefore, he did not judge the value of even his own ministry; this would be the Lord's responsibility. Lastly, we are not to judge the salvation of others, though there may be reason to be concerned for their souls (John 5:21-24). Only the Lord knows an individual's heart, and thus only He can render judgment in these matters. Paul reminds the Christians in Rome of this important truth:

> *Who are you to judge another's servant? To his own master he stands or falls. Indeed, he will be made to stand, for God is able to make him stand... For none of us lives to himself, and no one dies to himself. For if we live, we live to the Lord; and if we die, we die to the Lord. Therefore, whether we live or die, we are the Lord's* (Rom. 4:7-8).

The vision of the fig baskets shows that the Lord knows the hearts of men, that He knows who is His, that He knows who will be judged and who will be saved. Let us be cautious, then, not to usurp His authority. If no extension of Christ's authority has been given to the Church by Scripture, then it is best to leave the matter of judgment with the Lord. God's dealings with backslidden Judah show us that He is perfectly capable of judging offenses and rendering just punishment for sin.

Meditation

Jesus, Thou art all compassion; pure, unbounded love Thou art,
Visit us with Thine affection, enter every longing heart.
Firstfruits of Thy new creation, faithful, holy, may we be,
Joyful in Thy great salvation, daily more conformed to Thee:
Changed from glory into glory, till in heaven we take our place,
Then to worship and adore Thee, lost in wonder, love and praise.

— Charles Wesley

Seventy Years
Jeremiah 25:1-11

Jeremiah 25 is the capstone of all this prophet had been preaching to Judah. It is the thirteenth and final message, as organized in his book, before judgment fell on Jerusalem. This particular prophecy was delivered to the people during the fourth year of Jehoiakim and during Nebuchadnezzar's first year of ascension; thus, the likely date is 605 B.C. King Josiah had been killed in battle at Carchemish three years earlier. Jeremiah's message was first delivered audibly and then prior to Nebuchadnezzar's first attack on Jerusalem; later that year it was put in written format (v. 9).

At the commencement of this address, Jeremiah notes that he had been delivering the Word of God to the inhabitants of Judah for 23 years (vv. 2-3), and that, besides himself, God had sent other prophets also to warn them night and day (v. 4). How had the Jews responded to their call to repent and depart from wickedness (v. 5)? They had ignored God's warnings and chosen to continue in idolatry (v. 6). God would not withhold His righteous anger any longer – He would avenge Himself by using the Babylonians to decimate them (vv. 7-9). How long would the judgment last? Jeremiah indicated the interval: *"And this whole land shall be a desolation and an astonishment, and these nations shall serve the king of Babylon seventy years"* (v. 11).

The number seventy is associated with the nation of Israel in a special way throughout Scripture. Genesis 46 provides the first roster of the nation, which included the names of those in Jacob's family that traveled with him to Egypt. In all, sixty-six sons and grandsons are named. Counting Joseph and his two sons, who were already in Egypt, and Jacob himself, the total number of males composing the nation of Israel at this time was seventy (Gen. 46:5). There were seventy elders of Israel (Num. 11:16), seventy prophetic weeks determined upon Israel before their restoration (Dan. 9:24-27), and, during New Testament times, there were seventy members of the Sanhedrin, and seventy witnesses sent out to Israel by Christ (Luke 10:1). This thread can also be seen in the book of Jeremiah; the prophet confirmed a twofold seventy-year prophecy concerning the nation of Israel: there would be seventy years of Babylonian captivity and seventy years of rest for the land (v. 11; 2 Chron. 36:21).

The seventy years of captivity began the very year that Jeremiah spoke the prophecy, coinciding with Nebuchadnezzar's first invasion of Judah and first deportation of Jews to Babylon in 605 B.C. The captivity portion of this prophecy was concluded seventy years later when the Babylonian empire fell to the Medes and Persians, and the Jewish captives were freed by King Cyrus; this was an event foretold two centuries earlier by Isaiah (Isa. 44:28-45:1). The prophet Daniel, who had been in that first group of captives, understood this event to be the fulfillment of Jeremiah's prophecy (Dan. 9:2).

The second portion of the prophecy of seventy years did not begin until Nebuchadnezzar's third invasion, when he initiated a siege of Jerusalem during King Zedekiah's reign. God commanded the prophet Ezekiel to record the exact date this occurred:

> *Again, in the ninth year, in the tenth month, on the tenth day of the month, the word of the Lord came to me, saying, "Son of man, write down the name of the day, this very day – the king of Babylon started his siege against Jerusalem this very day"* (Ezek. 24:1-2).

This date is the equivalent of December 13, 589 B.C in the Gregorian Calendar. Why did the Lord want the exact date of the beginning of the siege of Jerusalem identified? It was because it was the day that all agriculture stopped in Judah. The Babylonian army sowed fields with rocks, filled wells with debris, destroyed vineyards and fruit groves, and confiscated food stores outside of Jerusalem. When Nebuchadnezzar surrounded Jerusalem with his army, the land began to enjoy its overdue rest. There would be no planting or harvesting for the next seventy years.

One may wonder why the Lord would determine a seventy-year cessation from agricultural work. The Mosaic Law commanded that the Sabbath Day be set aside to rest and to honor God. The Jews, their slaves, and their beasts of burden were all to rest on the Sabbath Day.

Likewise, the Israelites were to honor a Sabbath Year. Every seventh year the fields, the olive groves, and the vineyards were to receive a full year's rest. Whatever grew naturally during this time was to be freely gleaned by the poor, and anything left would be God's provision for the beasts of the field. Certainly, the Sabbatical Year would remind the Jews that God owned the land they dwelled upon and that they were merely stewards of it (Lev. 25:23).

This was God's Law for the land; unfortunately, the Jews often ignored the Sabbath Year and, ultimately, God would severely judge them and extend seventy years of rest to the land. According to 2 Chronicles 35:14-21, the reason for the specific length of time was that exactly seventy years were due to the Lord as His portion (i.e. one-seventh of the 490 years the Jews did not honor the Sabbath Year). This judgment began on December 13, 589 B.C. and ended, according to the prophet Haggai, when the foundation of the temple was laid on the base previously completed. Like Ezekiel, Haggai recorded the exact day that the Lord lifted the forced agricultural rest:

Consider now from this day forward, from the twenty-fourth day of the ninth month, from the day that the foundation of the Lord's temple was laid – consider it: Is the seed still in the barn? As yet the vine, the fig tree, the pomegranate, and the olive tree have not yielded fruit. But from this day I will bless you (Hag. 2:18-19).

The Jews who returned from Babylon began to enjoy the benefits of the land again on December 17, 520 B.C. God caused one prophet to record the exact starting date and another, the precise ending date of the sabbatical period that the land would enjoy in order to prove that His Word stands sure for all time. A Jewish year is 360 days (Rev. 12:6, 14, 13:5; Dan. 12:7), meaning that there are 25,200 days in 70 Jewish years (i.e. 70 x 360 days = 25,200 days). Thus, as Sir Robert Anderson confirms in the tenth edition of *The Coming Prince*, the seventy-year period of rest that started on December 13, 589 B.C. ended on December 17, 520 B.C., the exact day that God restored the land to fruitfulness according to Haggai.[1] God kept His word to His people to the exact day. Just as Jeremiah predicted, the Jews were captives for seventy years and the land enjoyed seventy years of rest.

After the seventy years of captivity were over, God would judge the Babylonians as foretold in Jeremiah 50 and 51, which were likely written about the same time as Jeremiah 25 was. Babylon would be repaid for all her evil deeds (vv. 12-14). They had been God's chastening rod upon the backs of His people, but they were not guiltless; they were wicked pagans who were also deserving of judgment. But until the time of their punishment, the Lord would use them as a scourge upon the entire region. He would punish not only His people, but the surrounding nations also: Egypt to the south; Philistia to the west; Edom, Moab, and Ammon to the east. Also mentioned are the cities of Tyre and Sidon, north of Israel, and Dedan, Tema, and Buz in the northern part of the Arabian Peninsula (vv. 15-26). If God, because of the sins of His own people would decimate Jerusalem, the city containing the only temple where He could be worshipped, how could the surrounding nations expect to go unpunished for their sins (vv. 25-29)? They would not escape judgment. Rather, the Lord would permit the Babylonians to descend upon them like a mighty storm. Their lands would be filled with corpses and their leaders smashed like pottery. There was no escape from His vengeance; if they tried to flee, He would be like a prowling lion in hot pursuit of its prey.

There are no loopholes in God's judicial system. Those who reject God's Word and authority will be punished – He is no respecter of persons. The Lord Jesus said that His Father had committed the judgment of all men into His hands (John 5:22). At the Great White Throne judgment, justice will be administered in accordance with His Word: *"He who rejects Me, and does not receive My words, has that which judges him – the word that I have spoken will judge him in the last day"* (John 12:48). God will righteously judge all things according to His decrees; therefore, it behooves man to behave righteously now and to uphold the justice God demands against those who do not.

Meditation

And must I be to judgment brought, and answer in that day,
For every vain and idle thought, and every word I say?

192

Yes, every secret of my heart, shall shortly be made known,
And I receive my just desert for all that I have done.

How careful, then ought I to live, with what religious fear!
Who such a strict account must give for my behavior here.
Thou awful Judge of quick and dead, the watchful power bestow;
So shall I to my ways take heed, to all I speak or do.

— Charles Wesley

Not Worthy of Death
Jeremiah 26:1-24

The first twenty-five chapters of Jeremiah focus on God's forthcoming judgment on Judah because of their lack of repentance. In this section, Jeremiah briefly mentions the opposition to his messages and his dismay over the people's aggression towards himself, but those details are not prominent. However, the narrative of the next four chapters (Jer. 26-29) is written from the suffering prophet's perspective; Jeremiah provides us with a personal account of his conflicts with the inhabitants of Judah.

Jeremiah revisits the aftermath of the message he delivered on the temple mount (Jer. 7-10), during the early days of Jehoiakim's reign. The date of the message would be approximately 608 B.C. The contents of his third message were set forth in Jeremiah 7-10; now, however, he addresses the response of the people. The prophet apparently organized his book in this fashion in order to provide a prominent, continuous representation from chapters 2 through 25 of God's anger and pending judgment as a result of Judah's backsliding ways. As to not distract from this general theme, Jeremiah purposely withheld information concerning his own difficulties which ensued from his prophetic ministry. In this chapter, Jeremiah informs us that there were two responses to his message: some heeded Jeremiah's warning and defended him (vv. 17-24), while others hardened themselves against his message and sought to kill him (vv. 8-9).

Before examining the narrative of this chapter, a brief review of the temple message is warranted. The main theme was this: If the people repented, then God would not bring about the disaster He was planning, but if the Jews did not turn from their wicked ways, He would destroy the temple and Jerusalem (vv. 4-6). Jeremiah now documents how the people reacted to this message. As soon as he had finished delivering it, the false prophets, priests, and all the people

194

seized Jeremiah and demanded that he die for speaking against the temple and Jerusalem in the Lord's name. Jeremiah stood trial in the entrance of the New Gate and the princes (i.e. high ranking officials of the king) judged the case (vv. 7-11). H. A. Ironside describes the scene:

> Jeremiah is permitted to speak for himself. Without the slightest hesitation, and with no apparent concern for the outcome as to himself, he boldly declares, *"The Lord sent me to prophesy against this house and against this city all the words that ye have heard."* The message was not of the servant, but of the Lord, and the case is one of Judah versus Jehovah, whom they hypocritically professed to serve. If they disliked to hear threatenings of judgment and desolation there was a sure way to avoid their fulfillment. *"Therefore now amend your ways and your doings, and obey the voice of the Lord your God; and the Lord will repent Him of the evil that He hath pronounced against you"* (vv. 12, 13). Not by murdering the messenger, but by heeding the proclamation, could the wrath of Jehovah be turned aside.

> *"As for me, behold, I am in your hand: do with me as seemeth good and meet unto you."* Without a quaver in his voice or a sign of pallor on his cheek, he gives himself up to die if they are determined upon it. Nevertheless he warns them of the result. *"But know ye for certain, that if ye put me to death, ye shall surely bring innocent blood upon yourselves, and upon this city, and upon the inhabitants thereof: for of a truth the Lord hath sent me unto you to speak all these words in your ears"* (vv. 14, 15). It is the courage of one conscious of his own integrity, relying upon the justice of the Holy One. In a similar spirit did Robert Moffatt of Kuruman bare his breast for the savages' spears, and in like manner Paton of the New Hebrides fearlessly faced the enraged men of Tanna. So have thousands of devoted saints jeoparded their lives for the truth's sake, concerned far more for the ungrateful people to whom they ministered than for their own safety.[1]

In summary, Jeremiah provided a threefold defense of himself. First, he reminded the people that he was the Lord's prophet and that he had been sent by Him with the message they had heard. Jeremiah would have been a prophet for some seventeen years at this point, so they were well familiar with his credentials. Second, he reminded the people that his message was conditional in nature; God's judgment could be avoided if they turned back to Him. Third, he told the court that if they sentenced him to death, they would be guilty of the blood of an innocent man, an act that would only add to their condemnation (vv. 12-15).

It is interesting that verse 12 records that Jeremiah directed his defense directly to the princes. Although the priests and prophets had consistently rejected his message, the princes, on the other hand, were stirred by the prophet's warnings. Their consciences were still pliable, and they still possessed some aspect of hope for the future of their nation. For this reason, William Kelly explains, Jeremiah's warning to them contained an additional conditional clause:

> So Jeremiah speaks to all the princes and to all the people. He does not now remonstrate with the priests and the prophets; they were thoroughly hardened and sold to evil; but he does appeal to the princes on the one hand and to the people on the other, who, after all, were simple. … *"Therefore now amend your ways and your doings, and obey the voice of Jehovah your God; and Jehovah will repent Him of the evil that He hath pronounced against you."* Jeremiah's prophecies are more conditional than any other, save only that of Jonah. Indeed, they are more conditionally expressed than even Jonah's. Jonah did not put forward a condition: *"If you repent, God will spare Nineveh."* But Jeremiah does state the condition: *"If you repent, Jehovah will repent of what He means to do."*

> But the reason why Jeremiah's prophecies are more conditional is that, more than any of the other prophets, he alludes to the impending judgment of Israel and the nations by Nebuchadnezzar. And as this judgment was but a temporal one, a condition is attached to the prophecy. When the coming of the Lord Jesus Christ and the judgment that He will execute form the prominent topic before the mind of the Holy Ghost, no conditions of repentance are expressed. There God has distinctly before Him the consummation of the frightful apostasy of man — of the Jews, of the Gentiles, and, we can now add, of Christendom. Therefore inasmuch as the measure of the wickedness to be judged is certain, so the coming of the Lord to judge that wickedness is also certain. It is a fixed event,

and so far as I know, this coming in judgment is never stated conditionally. There is no warning, such as, *"If you repent, the Lord will not come."* It would in fact be a kind of dishonor to the Lord Jesus.[2]

The Lord longs for the wayward to repent and turn to Him; in some cases the consequences of rebellion are overshadowed by divine grace. However, there is a day coming in which the Lord will return and completely and thoroughly judge the wicked. In that day, no mercy will be shown. From this standpoint, Jeremiah's conditional message was good news indeed – God's judgment on Judah was not final; there was still hope for the future.

After considering the case against Jeremiah, the officials, the people, and the elders were of one mind – Jeremiah had not done anything worthy of death (v. 16). The elders reminded the people that there were cases of historical significance which proved that Jeremiah had not committed a crime by prophesying against the temple. For example, the prophet Micah prophesied the destruction of the temple seventy years earlier during the days of King Hezekiah (Mic. 3:12). Hezekiah did not sentence Micah to death for his message, but rather harkened to it and sought the Lord's favor; Jerusalem was spared because of the king's response to God's warning. These elders seemed to understand that the only way to avoid God's judgment was to listen to Jeremiah's message and follow the example of Hezekiah. Much to the dismay of the priests and prophets, Jeremiah's life was spared. Unfortunately, the people still did not heed his message (vv. 17-19).

Though Jeremiah's life had been spared, other godly prophets during this time were not so fortunate. The prophet Uriah is mentioned as an example. He delivered a message similar to that of Jeremiah (v. 20), but when King Jehoiakim heard his message, he sentenced him to death without a trial (v. 21). Uriah escaped the king's wrath by fleeing to Egypt, but Jehoiakim sent a delegation to Egypt, led by Elnathan son of Acbor, to extradite him back to Judah. As Elnathan was one of the officials present when Jeremiah's scroll was read and was one of three who pleaded with King Jehoiakim not to burn it (36:12, 25), it is questionable whether he personally agreed with his assigned task, but he carried out the king's command in any case. Uriah was brought back to Judah and executed with a sword. He received no honorable burial, but instead his body was thrown into the burial ground of the common people (v. 23).

Despite this situation, God had His people in positions of authority to protect Jeremiah. One such individual was Ahikam, the son of Shaphan (v. 24). He was determined not to allow the people to murder Jeremiah and, though he risked a social backlash, used his political clout to gain Jeremiah's release. The family of Shaphan, as Charles H. Dyer explains, had a significant role in the public affairs of Judah in years just prior to the Babylonian invasion:

> Shaphan was King Josiah's secretary who reported the findings of the Law to Josiah (2 Kgs. 22:3-13). Shaphan had at least four sons – three of which were mentioned in a positive way by Jeremiah (Ahikam, Gemariah, and Elasah). The fourth son, Jaazaniah, was the "black sheep" of the family; his presence among the idol-worshippers in the temple caught Ezekiel by surprise (Ezek. 8:11). Ahikam's son, Gedaliah, was appointed governor of Judah by Nebuchadnezzar after the fall of Jerusalem in 586 B.C.[3]

Shaphan honored the Lord by rearing up godly seed which would continue serving Him for generations to come (Mal. 2:15).

It is also noted that Shaphan's son Gemariah, along with Elnathan as mentioned earlier, urged Jehoiakim not to burn Jeremiah's scroll (Jer. 36:12, 25). Shaphan's son Elasah hand-carried Jeremiah's letter to the exiled Jews in Babylon (Jer. 29:1-3). Shaphan must have been a godly man to rear up three fine sons who lived for God and, indeed, raised their sons to do the same. The grandson of Shaphan through Ahikam was Gedaliah, a just and righteous governor over Judah. Micaiah, the grandson of Shaphan through Gemariah, convinced the princes of the importance of Jeremiah's scroll after hearing it read by Baruch (Jer. 36:11-26). It has been observed that the value of parenting is witnessed in one's grandchildren. To this end, Shaphan was a father who obtained a good heritage from the Lord; happy is the man who has a quiver full of such children (Ps. 127:3-5). God used Shaphan's legacy to confront wickedness and to save the life of His faithful messenger, Jeremiah. Seeing one's children and grandchildren going on for the Lord is one of the greatest privileges of our earthly sojourn.

Meditation

My people, give ear, attend to My Word, in parables new deep truths shall be heard;
The wonderful story our fathers made known to children succeeding by us must be shown.

Instructing our sons we gladly record the praises, the works, the might of the Lord,
For He hath commanded that what He hath done be passed in tradition from father to son.

Let children thus learn from history's light to hope in our God and walk in His sight,
The God of their fathers to fear and obey, and ne'er like their fathers to turn from His way.

— The Psalter

The Battle of the Prophets
Jeremiah 27:1-22

Apparently, in the summer of 593 B.C. (28:1), King Zedekiah held a secret conference in Jerusalem. One might ask why delegates from Edom, Moab, Ammon, and Phoenicia were all gathered in Jerusalem (v. 3). It is likely they were considering forming an alliance to oppose Babylonian aggression. This seems to be a logical conclusion given Jeremiah's message to the conference attendees, and that the Babylonian Chronicles record that Nebuchadnezzar had suppressed an attempted coup from within Babylon the previous year (which might explain the secret nature of the conference).

There apparently is a scribal error in verse 1, as Jehoiakim and not Zedekiah is referred to as king of Judah. Although a few Hebrew manuscripts do state that Zedekiah was king, most put Jehoiakim's name here. The internal evidence of the remainder of the chapter, however, clearly states that Zedekiah (3, 12, 28:1) was king at the time Jeremiah penned chapters 27 and 28. As the Septuagint omits Jeremiah 27:1, the discrepancy is best explained as a scribal error; perhaps the entire verse was inserted accidentally.

The secret meetings of men are not hidden from God, so He commanded Jeremiah to construct a yoke, a mechanical device used to hitch teams of oxen together for the purpose of pulling carts, plows, etc. (v. 2). Jeremiah was to put the yoke upon his own neck and then summon the delegations together to hear his message, which would then be relayed back to their superiors (vv. 3-4). He informed them that it was God who created the earth and formed life upon it and, thus, He alone ruled in the affairs of men (v. 5). The Lord had determined to use Nebuchadnezzar, His servant, to punish Judah and the surrounding nations. God had put the entire region under Nebuchadnezzar's jurisdiction; he controlled the land and therefore could despoil it at will. Given Jeremiah's decree, they all were commanded to willingly submit to Nebuchadnezzar (vv. 10-11).

The same message was then delivered in person to Zedekiah: *"Bring your necks under the yoke of the king of Babylon, and serve him and his people and live"* (v. 12). The message offered two possible outcomes based on the response of the audience: if it was heeded, they would survive, and if not, they would die (v. 13). The bottom line: no alliances against God's authority and His decrees would be tolerated. Jeremiah warned both the delegates and Zedekiah (vv. 9, 14) not to listen to their false prophets who were trying to convince their superiors that they could successfully defeat Babylon if an alliance was formed (v. 14). These prophets promised that their respective nations would not serve Nebuchadnezzar.

Having spoken to the foreign delegates and Zedekiah, Jeremiah delivered a similar message to the priests and common people of Judah (vv. 16-22). He again warned them against listening to the message of the false prophets. Apparently, some of these were saying that all of the temple vessels that were taken to Babylon with King Jehoiachin would soon be returned (v. 16). Jeremiah countered that not only would the temple vessels stay in Babylon, but all of the remaining temple furnishings would soon be hauled away also. Only after God's judgment was complete would He return the temple vessels back to Jerusalem (2 Kgs. 25:13-17; Ezra 1:7-11). The fulfillment of this prophecy would provide the people with irrefutable proof as to who were really prophets of God and who were imposters.

The certainty that all of his enemies would be shown to be fools, and that he would be honored as God's faithful servant must have encouraged Jeremiah's heart. Likewise, believers can rest assured that the Lord Jesus Christ shall judge the world in righteousness and reward His faithful saints. The mouths of the opposition will be stopped (Rom. 3:19), and all those who persecuted the Church will know the full fury of the Lord.

Every believer will enjoy the Lord in eternal bliss and glory, but some will appreciate the heavenly experience more than others. Paul knew the tie between suffering for Christ now and reigning with Him later. When Paul weighed all his troublesome experiences against his future with Christ, he concluded:

The Spirit Himself bears witness with our spirit that we are children of God, and if children, then heirs – heirs of God and joint heirs with Christ, if indeed we suffer with Him, that we may also be glorified together. For I consider that the sufferings of this present time are not worthy to be compared with the glory which shall be revealed in us (Rom. 8:16-18).

Our school days on earth are toilsome and often agonizing, but our groaning is not a useless thing in God's kingdom. Paul compares these to a woman in travail. Her suffering ends when her child is born. Likewise, one day we shall be delivered from the presence of sin and all its ugliness to experience the wonders of Christ's presence. Until that day, may we follow the examples of Jeremiah, Paul, and countless others and stay true to our calling in Christ and keep toiling for Him – it will be worth it!

Meditation

Onward, Christian soldiers, marching as to war,
With the cross of Jesus going on before;
Christ the royal Master leads against the foe;
Forward into battle, see His banner go.

Crowns and thrones may perish, kingdoms rise and wane,
But the Church of Jesus constant will remain;
Gates of hell can never against that Church prevail;
We have Christ's own promise, and that cannot fail.

— Sabine Baring Gould

The Broken Yoke
Jeremiah 28:1-17

Jeremiah continued the subject of the previous chapter, detailing his conflicts with the false prophets. One adversary in particular that adamantly opposed Jeremiah's message was Hananiah the son of Azur. As Hananiah was from Gibeon, one of the forty-eight cities allotted to the priests, it is quite possible that he, like Jeremiah, was from a family of priests (v. 1). His message directly contradicted Jeremiah's; he claimed that God would break the yoke of the Babylonians (v. 2). Though delivered at the temple, this declaration would no doubt encourage the foreign representatives to form an alliance against Babylon. He further stated that within two years all the temple articles and the exiled Jews (including King Jehoiachin) would return to Jerusalem (vv. 3-4).

This was a difficult situation; two recognized and respected prophets were claiming to speak for God, but had contradictory messages. Although Jeremiah would have preferred Hananiah's message be the one to come true, as indicated by Jeremiah's sarcastic "Amen," he knew Hananiah's message was a lie (vv. 5-6). Jeremiah reminded the people that "the test of a true prophet" was whether or not his word came to pass (vv. 7-9; Deut. 18:20-22). Hananiah's time-constrained declaration of complete deliverance in two years was a matter surely to be proven, one way or another.

Jeremiah reminded the people that other prophets like Hananiah had previously prophesied deliverance from oppressors and had been wrong. A furious Hananiah removes the yoke from off of Jeremiah's neck and breaks it as a public dramatization of the validity of his own message. Jeremiah said nothing more, but *"went his way"* (v. 11). Why did Jeremiah not publicly challenge Hananiah's actions? Was Jeremiah not God's man? Was not Hananiah a liar? William Kelly provides an answer to this question:

This self-restraint is a great lesson for us; the servant of the Lord shall not strive. The same man, Jeremiah, who had been like a brazen wall, who had resisted kings and prophets and priests to the face, now refuses to contend with the prophet Hananiah. The reason for his conduct is plain. Jeremiah did remonstrate, and warn while there was a hope of repentance or when long-suffering grace called for it, but where there was no conscience at work, where there was a false pretense of the name of the Lord, he simply goes his way. He leaves God to judge between prophet and prophet. If Jeremiah was true, Hananiah was false. He was perfectly sure that he was true himself. He allows, therefore, the word and the act of Hananiah to be before the consciences of the men of Judah, without adding a word of his own. He would have weakened his former testimony, if he had said one single word more.[1]

Jeremiah follows the wise counsel of Solomon; when an uncorrectable disposition exists, it is best not to answer a fool according to his folly (Prov. 26:4).

Shortly after his confrontation with Hananiah, *"the word of the Lord came unto Jeremiah"* (v. 12). Jeremiah was to inform Hananiah that he had broken a yoke of wood, but his lying message would cause the people to bear yokes of iron (vv. 12-13). God had determined to put yokes of iron about the necks of all the nations of that area, including Judah; they would all serve Nebuchadnezzar. Then Jeremiah rebuked Hananiah for falsely claiming to have a message from God. This offense was great – he had associated Jehovah God with a lie and caused the people to rebel against Him (v. 15).

Earlier, Hananiah had given a specific timetable associated with his prophecy; now, it was Jeremiah's turn to do the same. He informed Hananiah that he would die before the year passed (v. 16). The initial confrontation between the two happened in the fourth year and fifth month of Zedekiah's reign (v. 1), and Hananiah died that same year in the seventh month (v. 17), only two months after Jeremiah informed him of the death sentence upon his head.

Jeremiah and, more importantly, the Lord's honor had been vindicated. God's dealings with Hananiah showed that God knows all about those who oppress our testimony of Christ: *"And there is no creature hidden from His sight, but all things are naked and open to the eyes of Him to whom we must give account"* (Heb. 4:13). Hananiah's thoughts, speech, and actions were all open to God, and the Lord determined that he had lived long enough. The opportunity to repent had passed and his false prophecies would no longer be tolerated.

The actions of Hananiah remind us of the blatant opposition to truth that will exist just prior to the Tribulation Period. Scripture teaches us that in the latter days of the Church Age, Satan will reside comfortably in various branches of Christendom (Matt. 13:32). When His disciples questioned Him about signs indicating the end of the Church Age, the Lord Jesus warned, *"Take heed that no one deceives you. For many will come in My name, saying, 'I am the Christ,' and will deceive many"* (Matt. 24:4-5). Paul stated that there will be great apostasy in the professing Church just prior to the appearing of the Antichrist (2 Thess. 2:3-4).

From the time of Jeremiah until now, there have always been only two groups of people in the world: "saints" and "ain'ts." Saints are those individuals who, by faith, have trusted God's revealed truth and received a standing of righteousness in Christ; "ain'ts," so to speak, have not been justified through faith. God's endorsement of Jeremiah and judgment of Hananiah would be a source of comfort for all true prophets of God in Judah. God knows those who are His and marks a difference between His children and children of the devil, who are appointed to wrath (Eph. 2:2-3; 2 Pet. 2:17; Jude 13):

Much more then, having now been justified by His blood, we shall be saved from wrath through Him (Rom. 5:9).

And to wait for His Son from heaven, whom He raised from the dead, even Jesus who delivers us from the wrath to come (1 Thess. 1:10).

For God did not appoint us to wrath, but to obtain salvation through our Lord Jesus Christ (1 Thess. 5:9).

As mentioned earlier, there is a time of great trouble coming called the Tribulation, which will affect the entire world (Matt. 24:21). But as John acknowledged to the believers in the Church at Philadelphia, the Church will be brought home prior to the initiation of this time of wrath: *"Because you have kept My command to persevere, I also will keep you from the hour of trial which shall come upon the whole world, to test those who dwell on the earth"* (Rev. 3:10). The Greek preposition *ek* is rightly translated "keep ... from" in this verse; if the Lord wished to signify that He would preserve the Church *through* the Tribulation, the Greek preposition *dia* would be required. The Lord will keep the Church out of the Tribulation Period, not preserve her through it. The Church will not experience God's wrath as He judges the wicked during the Tribulation Period (1 Thess. 1:10, 5:9), but the wicked are fully conscious of who is judging them at this time – the Lamb (Rev. 6:15-17).

Stand for truth, dear believer; the Lord knows His own and He will sustain you until your service for Him is complete. Then you will enjoy His presence and watch Him judge those who resisted His truth. There is only one thing for the believer to fear on earth, and that is that he or she might pull back from living for Christ and experience shame at His appearing (1 Jn. 2:28). Jeremiah's example is a good one to follow: he stood fast in the face of great opposition and would not relent from speaking for God, giving a message that he knew could save lives. The fact that it was rejected by the majority did not discourage him from sharing it with others. The gospel message of Jesus Christ is vital to the salvation of millions of lost souls; may we also rejoice to share it.

Meditation

Sowing in the sunshine, sowing in the shadows,
Fearing neither clouds nor winter's chilling breeze;
By and by the harvest, and the labor ended,
We shall come rejoicing, bringing in the sheaves.

Going forth with weeping, sowing for the Master,
Though the loss sustained our spirit often grieves;
When our weeping's over, He will bid us welcome,
We shall come rejoicing, bringing in the sheaves.

— Knowles Shaw

Trouble in Babylon
Jeremiah 29:1-32

Not only did Jeremiah battle false prophets in Judah, he also had to confront them among the exiled Jews in Babylon. This chapter includes excerpts of letters that Jeremiah sent to Babylon shortly after the deportation of Jehoiachin, the queen mother, and some ten thousand other Jews in 597 B.C. (vv. 1-2). The first letter to the captives was carried by Elasah, the son of godly Shaphan, and Gemariah, the son of Hilkiah. Apparently, King Zedekiah sent these two men to Nebuchadnezzar on official business, and they agreed to deliver Jeremiah's letter to the exiled Jews there on their way (v. 3).

Contrary to the proclamations of false prophets (vv. 8-9), Jeremiah warned the exiled Jews not to expect a speedy return to their homeland. They should ignore anyone who spoke otherwise – they were not from the Lord. The Jews were instructed to erect homes, to plant gardens, to marry, and to have children (vv. 5-6). They were to settle into life while in Babylon, but without becoming absorbed into the Babylonian culture.

Since it was God who had enabled the Babylonians to overcome the Jews (v. 4), they were not to resist Babylonian authority; indeed, they were to cooperate and even pray for them (v. 7). The exiled Jews were to make Babylon their home until God brought them back to Judah after their seventy years of exile (v. 10). Their disposition in Babylon was not to be sour or morbid, but as William Kelly notes, they were to be happy in the Lord:

> They were to take from God all the circumstances. They were happily to trust in the Lord, but to do so as captives to Nebuchadnezzar. Nay, they were even to seek the good and peace of Babylon. Take wives for your sons, and give your daughters to husbands, that they may bear sons and daughters; that ye may be

207

increased there, and not diminished. And seek the peace of the city whither I have caused you to be carried away captives, and pray unto Jehovah for it.

Now souls not really bowing to God are always morbid, murmuring in their affliction, and avoiding the common duties of life. The [devout] do not shut their eyes to what is painful, nor are they insensible in their adversity. There would be no piety in ignoring the truth of things, but feeling the affliction, they seek grace from God to take the hardship from His hand with all patience.[1]

Jeremiah then comforted the people by reminding them that God had fond thoughts towards them and that in His timing would restore them in peace (v. 11). The Lord was doing exactly what He had promised to do centuries earlier before the Israelites inherited the land.

Moses warned the Israelites at that time that Jehovah would exile them if necessary to purge idolatry from the Promised Land. God had made good on His threat (Deut. 30:1-6). Moses also promised that if God did disperse them among the nations, He would indeed gather them back again into the land. This covenant with the Israelites was then conditional – they would be blessed if they obeyed God's commandments and punished if they did not (v. 9). However, God's covenant with Abraham, which promised blessing and protection to a future refined nation of his descendants, was unconditional (Gen. 12:1-3). Eventually, there would be a nation from Abraham's lineage, which would inherit all of the Promised Land (Gen. 15:18-21) and be highly esteemed and blessed by all nations (Gen. 12:3). Until that time, the same Scripture that promised chastening, Moses' Law, also guaranteed restoration: this would encourage the Jews to flee from idolatry and seek God with all their heart. When they did, God would return them to Judah and commune with them again (vv. 12-14). Through His prophet, God promised Judah, *"You will seek me and find me when you seek me with all your heart"* (Jer. 29:13). The Jews knew about Jehovah, but they did not know Him intimately. In application, A. W. Tozer explains why it is important for those who have trusted Christ as Lord and Savior to keep seeking after God:

Contemporary Christians have been caught in the spurious logic that those who have found him need no longer seek him. Come near to the holy men and women of the past and you will soon feel the heat of their desire after God. They mourned for Him, they prayed and wrestled and sought for Him day and night, in season and out, and when they found Him, the finding was all the sweeter for the long seeking.[2]

The great paradox of the Christian faith is that those who know the Lord Jesus Christ the best will be the ones who desire to seek Him more and to obey His Word.

Accordingly, the Jews were encouraged to listen and heed God's Word, rather than trust the lying prophets in Babylon who were predicting a soon return to Jerusalem. In fact, Jeremiah informed them that Jerusalem would not be a good place to reside in the near future. The exiled Jews thought that they were the unfortunate portion of the population; however, Jeremiah set the matter straight, explaining that those living in Jerusalem would suffer the most. The reason for this was that they had rebelled against the Lord and had not yielded to Babylonian rule; therefore, they would die by the sword, famine, or pestilence (vv. 15-19). Referring to his earlier illustration of the figs (24:1-2), Jeremiah likened the inhabitants of Jerusalem to rotten figs that were good for nothing and must be discarded.

The names of two particular false prophets among the exiled Jews are mentioned here: Ahab, the son of Koliah, and Zedekiah, the son of Maaseiah (v. 21). As mentioned earlier, a mark of a false teacher is sexual immorality, and these men fit the description; they continued in the sin of adultery (v. 23). They were predicting the downfall of Nebuchadnezzar, so God would turn these wicked prophets over to Nebuchadnezzar to be punished. When the king of Babylon heard of their propaganda among the people, he would see they were silenced; the text specifically states they would be burned alive (v. 22).

Another exiled Jew named Shemaiah also claimed to be a prophet of God, but yet vehemently opposed Jeremiah. Shemaiah had written a letter to Zephaniah, who was the chief officer of the temple in Jerusalem, requesting him to take action against Jeremiah. Shemaiah quoted a portion of Jeremiah's first letter to the captive Jews to bolster his position (v. 28). He considered Jeremiah to be a madman who falsely spoke in God's name and who should be publicly rebuked (v. 27). In his estimation, Jeremiah should not be allowed to speak at all, but rather should be placed in stocks and imprisoned (v. 26).

Rather than arrest Jeremiah, as his predecessor Pashhur had done a few years earlier (20:1-2), Zephaniah brought Shemaiah's letter to Jeremiah and read it to him. Perhaps Zephaniah remembered the fate of Pashhur after he had mistreated Jeremiah (20:3-5). Jeremiah had prophesied against him, and then Pashhur and his family were hauled to Babylon during the second deportation of Jews in 597 B.C. – God promised that his entire family would die in Babylon. Apparently, Zephaniah respected Jeremiah as a true prophet of God. He would later solicit counsel from Jeremiah on two different occasions on behalf of King Zedekiah (21:1; 37:3). Zephaniah was one of the many godly people who died with the wicked in Jerusalem during Nebuchadnezzar's third invasion (52:24-27).

The chapter closes with Jeremiah writing another letter to the Jewish captives in Babylon to expose Shemaiah for the fraud he was. Because he had caused the people to believe in lies and rebel against the Lord, he and his family would be judged. None of his descendants would return from Babylon to enjoy the good things God had prepared for His restored people (vv. 31-32).

It is likely that Jeremiah could have written more about his oppressors, but that might have drawn the reader's attention away from the seriousness of idolatry and wickedness to Jeremiah's personal exploits as a prophet of God. Four chapters suffice to demonstrate God's faithfulness to protect Jeremiah as He had promised to do and Jeremiah's faithfulness to his divine calling.

Jeremiah had a unique ministry to complete. Very few of us will be visited by the Lord as Jeremiah was and be audibly informed as to what our calling is. So how will we know what God desires us to do for Him? The first step is to know the revealed will of God as set forth in the commands of Scripture. Before we can possibly know God's purpose for our lives, we must be following His will in our lives; Paul instructs believers to *"be not unwise, but understanding what the will of the Lord is"* (Eph. 5:17). The will of God, as revealed in Scripture, is the same for all believers. This is where each Christian must initiate his or her quest to please God.

Ministry requires the preparatory work of building godly character, faith, and tenacity into an individual. Moses spent forty years in Egypt and then forty years on the backside of a desert before he was prepared for his ministry. John the Baptist was thirty years old before he became the *"voice of one crying in the wilderness."* Paul was saved approximately ten years before he was called into action, and a portion of that time was spent being taught by the Holy Spirit in the Arabian Desert. Before we can profitably engage in service, we must be broken to the will of God; otherwise, we are just disguising personal agendas as spiritual ministries.

> To accept the will of God never leads to the miserable feeling that it is useless to strive anymore. God does not ask for the dull, weak, sleepy acquiescence of indolence. He asks for something vivid and strong. He asks us to cooperate with Him, actively willing what He wills, our only aim His glory.

> — Amy Carmichael

The first step to brokenness is to know what the will of God is. That is, it is to understand what God's general will is for one's life. Here is a summary; each of the referenced passages below is directly tied to the phrase "the will of God":

1. Serve and please the Lord instead of men (Eph. 6:6).

2. Do not be conformed to the world (Rom. 12:2).

3. Put the ignorance of foolish men to silence by well-doing (1 Pet. 2:15).

4. Abstain from fornication (1 Thess. 4:3).

5. Give thanks in everything (1 Thess. 5:18).

6. Suffer for well-doing, rather than for evil-doing (1 Pet. 3:17).

7. Do not be controlled by the lusts of the flesh (1 Pet. 4:2).

Normally, when Scripture speaks of "the will of God," it explicitly states what it is; there is no mystery about it, for God has declared to us His will for our lives. As we learn to align our will with God's general will for us, we become more able to sense His specific calling. God grows people as He grows their ministries; otherwise their ministries would be a disaster rather than a good testimony of Christ. The lives of the false prophets in Jeremiah's day aligned with their evil messages. They were liars, evil brutes, and immoral men. Yet, Jeremiah was a just and honorable man; his pure character was consistent with the true message he conveyed. People who name Christ and live for the devil will never know what they are living for! But those who surrender themselves for Christ will gain a life worth living (Luke 9:24).

Meditation

He is no fool to give what he cannot keep, to gain what he cannot lose.

— Jim Elliot

The Time of Jacob's Trouble
Jeremiah 30:1-24

Chapters 30-33 pose a lovely interlude of hope and deliverance following what has been a steady stream of warnings and forecasting of doom. There can be little doubt that the prophet preferred to preach on the encouraging subjects of this section, and Jeremiah likely put his whole heart into the effort. After being delivered audibly, the message before them was to be written in a book. It contained a twofold prophecy pertaining to the Jews' return from Babylonian exile and their final national restoration with God during the Tribulation Period. The near term restoration of the Jewish nation was spoken of as "the days are coming" (v. 3), while its final restoration was specifically referred to as "that day" – a great day the like of which never was (vv. 7, 8). In the days coming, God would bring the Jews from Babylon back to the Promised Land, but not before those in Israel suffered great distress (vv. 3-5). The inhabitants would turn pale with fear. Jeremiah compares the anguish of men clutching themselves in panic to the travail of women in childbirth (v. 6). In a still future day, God will again return His people to Israel from among all nations (vv. 10-11). He has scattered them throughout the nations to punish them; indeed, they will be in a pitiful condition when He intervenes in the affairs of the world to bring them home once and for all (vv. 12-13). Jeremiah implies that they would suffer centuries of God's chastisement for their unfaithfulness to Him and their love of false gods (vv. 14-15). Through Christ (their future Governor), God promised to restore them to the land and to spiritually heal them, and to also punish those who had abused and despoiled them (vv. 16-17): *"And their governor shall come from their midst; then I will cause him to draw near, and he shall approach Me"* (v. 21). H. A. Ironside suggests that the governor who restores peace and order to Israel can be none other than the Lord Jesus Christ, who will be represented in

213

Israel during the Millennial Kingdom by a prince, a descendant of David:

> There seems to be good reason to believe that the "governor" here spoken of is the same as the prince referred to so frequently in the last five chapters of Ezekiel. (See Ezek. 44:3; 45:7; 46:2, etc.). He will, we gather, be a direct lineal descendant of David, and will be the earthly ruler, subject in all things to the glorified Immanuel. In this day of *"the restitution of all things spoken of by the prophets,"* the hearts of the people will have been fully turned to the Lord, that is, the spared remnant, for the apostate part of the nation will be destroyed in the great tribulation which is brought to our notice once more in the closing verses of this chapter.[1]

The "Time of Jacob's Trouble," which Jeremiah refers to as "that day" (v. 7), is said to come in "the latter days" (v. 24) and is a reference to the yet future Tribulation Period (Matt. 24:8-29). The Lord Jesus said that at no time before it, nor any time to come after it, will there have ever been such tribulation on the earth (Matt. 24:21). It is not a literal day, but a period of time in which Israel will suffer; yet, ultimately God will deliver them out of it (v. 7).

This period of immense tribulation for the Jewish nation is first introduced to us as a *type* in Genesis. During the days of Joseph, a devastating seven-year famine affected the whole land; this pictures the future seven-year Tribulation Period that would ravage the entire planet. When used metaphorically, *Egypt* speaks of "the world" in Scripture. Just as the nation of Israel was protected and preserved by God in Egypt during this severe seven-year trial, it will also be protected from the Antichrist during the Tribulation Period (Rev. 12).

According to the books of Exodus and Revelation, the plagues brought upon Egypt in the days of Moses will be similar to those unleashed upon the entire world during the Tribulation Period. For example, the fifth trump judgment will release from the bottomless pit armored locusts which sting like scorpions (Rev. 9:1-12); recall that locust ravaged Egypt in the eighth plague (Ex. 10:1-20). The second and third bowl judgments during the Tribulation Period turn all the ocean water and all the fresh water, respectively, into blood (Rev. 16:3-7). This reminds us of the events of Exodus 7:14-25, when

Moses turned the Nile into blood, which killed all life in the river. The fifth bowl judgment causes darkness throughout the Antichrist's kingdom (Rev. 16:10-11); Moses' ninth plague caused three days of intense darkness in Egypt (Ex. 10:21-29). Though the plagues and the seven-year famine brought devastation to Egypt, God preserved the Jewish nation through the hardship and then greatly blessed them afterwards. The antitype of this typological illustration has its fulfillment in the Tribulation Period. God will protect His covenant people from attempts of the Antichrist to exterminate them and then pour His blessings upon them afterwards in the millennial kingdom.

During the Tribulation Period, the wrath of the Lamb will be worldwide, not merely restricted to a single nation, such as Egypt. In Moses' day, God poured out His wrath upon the Egyptians because they abused the Hebrews and defied Him. God's judgment of Egypt is only a prelude to what the entire world will suffer during the Tribulation Period for the same two reasons. The Egyptian plagues furnished a striking prophetic forecast of God's future judgments upon the world!

The actions of Pharaoh's sorcerers picture future supernatural feats to be accomplished by the Antichrist and False Prophet during the Tribulation Period. These also will be performed through demonic power (Rev. 16:14). The interactions between the magicians and Moses demonstrated not only Jehovah's superior authority and power, as worked through Moses, but also the fact that Jehovah would judge the Egyptian gods and all who worshipped them. The same truth will be demonstrated during the Tribulation Period against all who follow the Antichrist and take his mark (Rev. 14:9-11, 19:20-21).

Another significant parallel between the events recorded in Exodus and those reported in Revelation (i.e. pertaining to the Tribulation Period) is the singing. The last mention of singing in the Bible is associated with the first song recorded in the Bible – it is the song of the redeemed Israelites after seeing their oppressors vanquished in the Red Sea (Ex. 15). In the book of Revelation, John describes the following heavenly scene:

And I saw something like a sea of glass mingled with fire, and those who have the victory over the beast, over his image and over his mark and over the number of his name, standing on the sea of glass,

215

having harps of God. They sing the song of Moses, the servant of God, and the song of the Lamb, saying:

> *Great and marvelous are Your works,*
> *Lord God Almighty! Just and true are Your ways,*
> *O King of the saints!*
> *Who shall not fear You, O Lord, and glorify Your name?*
> *For You alone are holy.*
> *For all nations shall come and worship before You,*
> *For Your judgments have been manifested* (Rev. 15:2-4).

This song is sung again, not by those just escaping death to begin a journey with Jehovah through the wilderness, but rather by those who will have suffered death at the end of their journey to escape the Antichrist on earth. These saints will choose to die rather than to bow to the Antichrist and to take his identifying mark. The heavenly inheritance sung of by the Israelites long ago will then be theirs to enjoy forever. Furthermore, God's own joy in His redeemed people is enthusiastically expressed in song directly after the Tribulation, and He will sing over His people (Zeph. 3:17).

The twelve Tribes of Israel were numbered when they departed Egypt under Moses' leadership. Similarly, during the first part of the Tribulation Period there will be 144,000 Jews (12,000 Jews from each tribe) who are counted and sealed to be witnesses for the Lord: *"And I heard the number of those who were sealed, one hundred and forty-four thousand of all the tribes of the children of Israel were sealed"* (Rev. 7:4). After these faithful Jews have completed their ministry in the Tribulation Period, we read:

> *Then I looked, and behold, a Lamb standing on Mount Zion, and with Him one hundred and forty-four thousand, having His Father's name written on their foreheads... They sang as it were a new song before the throne, before the four living creatures, and the elders; and no one could learn that song except the hundred and forty-four thousand who were redeemed from the earth. These are the ones who were not defiled with women, for they are virgins. **These are the ones who follow the Lamb wherever He goes.** These were redeemed from among men, being firstfruits to God and to the Lamb. And in their mouth was found no deceit, **for they are without fault before the throne of God** (Rev. 14:1-5).*

What the Jews first sang in Exodus after being redeemed and delivered from their oppressors in Egypt will be the song they sing before the Lord after being saved from the Antichrist.

Many of the Old Testament narratives which detail God's dealings with His covenant people also provide a prophetic blueprint for how He will accomplish their final conversion to Christ. It took the Babylonian exile and the destruction of Jerusalem and the temple to purge the Jews of idolatry in Jeremiah's day. Likewise, during the "Time of Jacob's Trouble," God will use immense suffering to open the eyes of the Jewish nation to the unsearchable riches in the Lord Jesus Christ. Through the Refiner's fire they will no longer be reprobate silver but will become purified silver which reflects the Refiner's own features. They will be established with God and blessed by Him forever!

Meditation

When through fiery trials thy pathways shall lie,
My grace, all sufficient, shall be thy supply;
The flame shall not hurt thee; I only design
Thy dross to consume, and thy gold to refine.

The soul that on Jesus has leaned for repose,
I will not, I will not desert to its foes;
That soul, though all hell should endeavor to shake,
I'll never, no never, no never forsake.

— John Rippon

An Everlasting Love
Jeremiah 31:1-9

Israel (speaking of the northern ten tribes) is not often addressed by name in Jeremiah's book, but this chapter begins with a proclamation of hope for the Northern Kingdom, which had been invaded and conquered by Assyria over a century earlier. Here, God promised to guide those who had survived the sword and had been displaced from the land; He pledges to intervene in a future day to end their exile and to secure national peace (vv. 1-2). Why was God eager to do this? He loved His people with an everlasting love and was continually drawing them to Himself through loving-kindness (v. 3).

Jeremiah then identifies three happenings that would characterize Israel's future joy at their restoration. First, the returning Jews would take up the tambourine and dance before the Lord and sing with gladness (vv. 4, 7). Second, the people would replant their vineyards on the hills of Samaria without the threat of attack or pillage. God would bless their harvest and they would again enjoy the fruit of their labor. Third, the Jews would be deeply committed to the Lord and freely come to Zion to worship Him when summoned by the watchmen stationed on the hills of Ephraim (v. 5).

The Lord promised to bring the Jews back to their homeland from all nations. Thus, this prophecy does not pertain merely to the return of Jews from their Babylonian or Assyrian exiles; it has a far more encompassing application. The prophet Ezekiel precisely identified when this promise would be fulfilled as after the battle of Gog and Magog near the end of the first half of the tribulation period (Ezek. 38:1-39:12). At that time, Israel will be back in their land, conquered in war (Ezek. 38:8). The land of Palestine became a Jewish state again in May 1948, a situation that was immediately and violently challenged by surrounding Arab countries. The land belonging to the

Jewish state was further expanded after their victory in the Six-Day War of 1967.

The process of bringing Jews back to Zion started in the early 20th century. It will be completed when all of the Jews are back in the land at the end of the Tribulation Period and they receive the Holy Spirit (Ezek. 39:28-29). The following chart shows the percentage of Jews worldwide that have returned to the land of Israel in recent years:

Year	Percent of Jews Worldwide Back in Israel[1]
1882	0
1900	1
1925	1
1939	3
1948	6
1955	13
1970	20
1980	25
1990	30
2000	37
2010	42
2014	44

The core Jewish population reached its peak just before WW2 at about 17 million, but was reduced to 11 million after Hitler's attempts to exterminate them. At the beginning of 2016, the core Jewish population was projected to be about 14.2 million worldwide, with 40 percent residing in the United States and 6,335,000 Jews (or about 44.6% of the world population) live in Israel. It is noted that Israel has the highest birth rate (an average of three children per woman) of any developed country in the world.

The order in which the Jews would return to Palestine is also prophetically predicted in Psalm 107:2-3 and Isaiah 43:5-6; the latter reads as follows:

Fear not, for I am with you; I will bring your descendants from the east, and gather you from the west; I will say to the north, "Give them up!" and to the south, "Do not keep them back!" Bring My sons from afar, and My daughters from the ends of the earth.

The precise order of return set forth in this verse (from the east, west, north, and then south) is reflected in recent history. The first wave of Jews to return to Palestine came from the eastern Arab countries. *Operation Magic Carpet* brought 49,000 Yemenite Jews to the new state of Israel from June 1949 to September 1950, and British and American transport planes made some 380 flights from Aden in a secret operation to bring these Jews home. The second wave came from Western Europe, especially Germany. The third wave came from Russia (the north) during 1980's to early 1990's; nearly one million Jews returned to Israel. It is noted that, since the year 2000, around 80,000 of these Jews have become disillusioned with the Zionist movement and returned to Russia. The fourth wave of Jews returning to Israel came from Ethiopia (the south).

Zephaniah 3:8-10 also predicted that when the Jewish nation became a reality again, the ancient Hebrew language would be revived and become the official language of the state. Prior to this event, the Jews spoke an impure form of the language called Yiddish. Besides a pure language, Ezekiel also predicted that the shekel would be reinstated as the common monetary unit in Israel (Ezek. 45:12-16). This prophecy also has now been fulfilled.

Another thing Scripture tells us about the new nation of Israel is that when the Jews returned to the land, it would become an agricultural icon.

Those who come He shall cause to take root in Jacob; Israel shall blossom and bud, and fill the face of the world with fruit (Isa. 27:6).

The wilderness and the wasteland shall be glad for them, and the desert shall rejoice and blossom as the rose (Isa. 35:1).

The agricultural prosperity of Israel today, including the flourishing forests there, has been another remarkable miracle. Seventy-five years ago, Israel was full of malarial swamps and deserts. Today the replanted forests are thriving and the Israeli agricultural production is amazing. Since May of 1948, cultivated land has increased from 165,000 to 435,000 hectares; also, irrigated land increased from fifteen to fifty-four percent between 1950 to 1984.

Israel's current agricultural prosperity, currency, official language, and the order of the return of Jews to Palestine were predicted over two millennia ago. God is bringing His covenant people home, just as He promised to do. Looking ahead, there are three more significant events that are prophesied to occur before the end of the Tribulation Period. It is possible that two of these prophecies may be fulfilled just prior to the Tribulation Period: namely, that the temple could be erected and the old system of animal sacrifices under the Law be put into practice again (Dan. 9:27; Matt. 24:15; 2 Thess. 2:3-7).

The third prophecy relates to the Jews enjoying a state of peace in Israel just before the battle of Gog and Magog around the midpoint of the Tribulation Period. Obviously, for this situation to occur, the prophecies of Jewish restoration to the land pronounced by Jeremiah would have been fulfilled. Both Jeremiah and Ezekiel provide prophetic details of this future event. It is noted that the Hebrew word *rosh* (v. 8), translated "chief," is the same Hebrew word used to describe the land of Rosh, which will attack Israel during the battle of Gog and Magog (Ezek. 38:1-2, 39:1). This land lies directly north of Jerusalem (Ezek. 38:6, 15), and one must travel between two seas to get there (Joel 2:20). It is noted that Moscow, the capital of Russia, is directly north of Jerusalem as one passes through Turkey (which is between the Black and Caspian Seas).

The Jews will be dwelling safely in unwalled villages when the attack comes from the north (Ezek. 38:8, 11, 14); they will be deceived into lowering their defenses while under the protection of the Antichrist's peace treaty (Dan. 9:27). Thankfully, the Lord will intervene and defeat the armies of Russia (Rosh), Eastern Turkey, Iran, Ethiopia, and Egypt (Ezek. 38; Joel 2:12-20). While Jerusalem itself will be saved at that time, the persecution of the Jewish people worldwide will have only begun. Before the Tribulation Period concludes, the Antichrist will slaughter two-thirds of all Jews worldwide (Zech. 13:7-8). However, the Lord Jesus Christ descends at the end of the Tribulation Period for the battle of Armageddon, where the Antichrist and the armies of the world that he has assembled will be completely obliterated (Zech. 14; Rev. 19).

The Bible has much to say about future events. Fulfilled prophecy is one of the evidences that the Bible is indeed God's Word to humanity. The prophecies just mentioned as well as others relate to the reestablishment of Israel as a nation. These are exciting times; we are seeing God's Word being fulfilled before our eyes. God is a promise-keeping God and by His everlasting love He is drawing His covenant people into His sovereign purposes for them. Their ultimate oneness with God will establish them in everlasting peace.

Thankfully, unlike the peace of the Jewish nation which is still future, the peace of God which surpasses all understanding is something that the Christian can enjoy today:

> *Be anxious for nothing, but in everything by prayer and supplication, with thanksgiving, let your requests be made known to God; and the peace of God, which surpasses all understanding, will guard your hearts and minds through Christ Jesus* (Phil. 4:6-7).

Isaiah put the matter this way, *"Thou wilt keep him in perfect peace, whose mind is stayed on thee: because he trusteth in Thee"* (Isa. 26:3; KJV). Nearness to God is the greatest defense against depression and the best means of promoting a stable mind. In a coming day the Jews will seek peace with the Antichrist and pay for that mistake dearly. True peace is found in God alone. There is but one hiding place for the threatened, one solace for the broken-hearted, and one salve for the wounded soul – the Lord Jesus Christ. Believer, stay near to Him!

Meditation

Peace, perfect peace, in this dark world of sin?
The blood of Jesus whispers peace within.
Peace, perfect peace, our future all unknown?
Jesus we know, and He is on the throne.
Peace, perfect peace, death shadowing us and ours?
Jesus has vanquished death and all its powers.
It is enough: earth's struggles soon shall cease,
And Jesus call us to Heaven's perfect peace.

— Edward Bickersteth

A Well-Watered Garden
Jeremiah 31:10-26

As captives, the Jews were led to Babylon, but how would they find their way back home after being freed? God promised to personally guide them home. He would lead them alongside streams of water to ensure they did not thirst and on level paths so they would not stumble (v. 9). What would they receive after their arrival in Israel? They would be blessed by the Lord with bountiful crops and multiplying flocks and herds (vv. 12-13). The nation would reap the abundance of the Lord as from a well-watered garden, and they would be completely satisfied with their God (v. 14). The Jewish captives returning from Babylon in 536 B.C. represent the future ingathering of Jews worldwide to the land of Israel during the Tribulation Period. They too will be abundantly cared for and greatly blessed by the Messiah after their trial is complete.

What did Jeremiah mean by the phrase, *"Rachel weeping for her children"* (v. 15)? There are several possibilities. Jeremiah may have been envisioning the children who were separated from their mothers during the Assyrian invasion of the Northern Kingdom in 722 B.C. Ephraim and Manasseh were the most prominent tribes in the Northern Kingdom, and the heads of both of these tribes were Rachel's grandsons through Joseph. Another possibility is that Jeremiah was making a prediction pertaining to Nebuchadnezzar's invasion of the Southern Kingdom, for Ramah, situated about five miles north of Jerusalem, became a staging point for the deportation of Jews to Babylon (40:1).

Whether the phrase refers to Israel, Judah, or both, the point is that women were deeply grieved about being separated from their children, whom they would never see again. In order to instill a sense of hope into the people (v. 17), Jeremiah contrasted this time of deep

223

sadness with a future time of great joy, for God would again return their children (speaking of their descendants) to their homeland (v. 16). Accordingly, Jeremiah was not to weep for those being deported, for God was accomplishing His purposes through Jeremiah's ministry, and he would be rewarded and his people would return to Israel in a future day.

It has been debated as to whether or not Jeremiah 31:15 is a prophesy relating to Herod's slaughter of male infants in the region surrounding Bethlehem at the time of Christ's birth (Matt. 2:16). Matthew connected Jeremiah's prophecy and this event:

> *Then was fulfilled what was spoken by Jeremiah the prophet, saying: A voice was heard in Ramah, lamentation, weeping, and great mourning, Rachel weeping for her children, refusing to be comforted, because they are no more* (Matt. 2:17-18).

The Greek word translated as "was fulfilled" in this verse is the aorist verb *pleroo* which means "to cram full," or "to complete," or "to verify."[1] It is the normal word that Matthew employs throughout his gospel account to speak of the verification or fulfillment of Old Testament Scriptures. His frequent use of Old Testament prophecy is for the purpose of supplying the Jews with evidence which proves that Jesus Christ is their Messiah and the rightful heir to the throne of David. Clearly, Matthew most often uses *pleroo* to indicate the actual fulfillment of an Old Testament prophecy, but in some cases, he uses the verb to indicate that the full potential of some Old Testament event had now been reached. For example, John the Baptizer did not want to baptize the Lord Jesus, but the Lord told John, *"Permit it to be so now, for thus it is fitting for us to fulfill all righteousness"* (Matt. 3:15). In other words, the fulfillment here is not a specific prophecy, but in accordance to a pattern witnessed in the Old Testament. In this sense the Old Testament type alludes to New Testament fulfillment, without being directly stated. It is the author's opinion that Jeremiah 31:15 *foreshadowed* the incident that Matthew wrote of, rather than predicted it. In the same way we might say, "The dog days of summer are nearly upon us," and then a few weeks later recall the expression during a brutally hot day. The saying does describe that day, but it describes other sweltering days also.

In either case, the Jews departed from Palestine in great sorrow. They had strayed from the path of righteousness and God severely punished them, but when they returned home, it would be in the spirit of humility, for the Jews would be repentant (vv. 19-20). The Jews were instructed to put up road signs and guideposts to mark their way to Babylon. This information would assist the displaced to later find their way back to their original towns and villages (vv. 21-22).

Verse 22 is one of the most difficult verses in Jeremiah to understand: *"For the Lord has created a new thing in the earth – a woman shall encompass a man."* The Hebrew verb translated "shall encompass" is *cabab* which means "to revolve about" or "to surround."[2] Some have suggested that this is a prophecy predicting the virgin birth of Christ. C. I . Scofield explains the reasoning for this thinking:

> Older exposition almost unanimously took the verse to predict the virgin birth of the Messiah. Their arguments are: (1) The "new thing in the earth" would require an event of unprecedented character. (2) The word "create" implies an act of divine power. (3) The term "woman" demands an individual rather than the entire nation. And (4) the word "man" is properly used of God (Isa. 9:6).[3]

While this verse may be a prophetic reference to the virgin birth of Christ, it does certainly describe how the Jews will behave when they return from Babylon – they will seek the Lord. It was appropriate for a man to court a woman to establish a marital relationship, not the other way around; but when the Jews return to the land from Babylon, they will be pursuing after God. However, this was not long lasting; a few years later the Jews withdrew from the Lord again. Jewish history and Biblical prophecy thus cooperate to point us even further into the future as to the meaning of verse 22. Albert Barnes explains that the saying better describes the behavior of the Jews after coming into the good of the New Covenant that God would establish with them:

> *A woman shall compass a man*, i.e. the female shall protect the strong man; the weaker nature that needs help will surround the stronger with loving and fostering care. This expresses a new relation of Israel to the Lord, a new Covenant, which the Lord will make with His people (v. 31).[4]

Certainly, this could only be realized as a result of a supernatural work in their hearts by their Husband of old.

Not only would the Lord restore the Babylonian captives to Himself, but He would bless them, the city of Jerusalem, and the temple, which sits upon the "mountain of holiness" (v. 23; Isa. 66:20). This particular scene of jubilation and blessing was short-lived, however, as the Jews again disobeyed the Lord and were scattered among the nations. The festive disposition of the Jews returning from Babylon would be a mere precursor to the future day when God would restore His covenant people to Himself permanently under the New Covenant. Under that covenant they will receive the Holy Spirit, obtain a clean heart, and never rebel against their God again. Then they will reap the full benefit of their well-watered garden and intimately know their God.

Meditation

O Christ, our God, who with Thine own hast been,
Our spirits cleave to Thee, our unseen Friend.
Make every heart that is Thy dwelling place
A watered garden filled with fruits of grace.

O grant us peace, that by Thy peace possessed,
Thy life within us we may manifest.
So shall we pass our days in holy fear,
In joyful consciousness that Thou art near.

— George Bourne

The New Covenant
Jeremiah 31:27-40

The Old Covenant could never make Israel a well-watered garden; a New Covenant was necessary and one that would result in supernatural transformation of the nation. Jeremiah introduced and developed this subject matter by employing three statements beginning with the word "behold;" each speaks of a separate future event. The first occurrence is found in verse 27: *"Behold, the days are coming, says the LORD, that I will sow the house of Israel and the house of Judah with the seed of man and the seed of beast."* Here the Jews were promised that, in a coming day, God would again sow the seeds of men and beast in the Promised Land (v. 27). The land would be decimated by the Babylonians and made unusable, but God would restore His covenant people back to the land in order to bless them and to care for them in that place (v. 28).

Apparently, some Jews felt that they had been wrongly judged by God for the sins of their forefathers and were bantering about a proverb: *"The fathers have eaten sour grapes, and the children's teeth are set on edge"* (v. 29). In short, the proverb insinuated that children suffered for the indulgences of their parents, while their parents escaped the consequences of their own wrongdoings. However, this was not the case; everyone will be rightly judged by God for his or her own sins (v. 30). For decades, Jeremiah and other prophets had summoned the Jews to consider their sin and its consequences, and to repent. Those in Babylon who were bantering about the proverb had no basis for complaint: they were not innocent and had, indeed, received mercy from God in that they were still alive.

The second injunction to "behold" relates to the Lord's promise to institute a New Covenant with the houses of Judah and Israel (vv. 31-32):

Behold, the days are coming, says the Lord, when I will make a new covenant with the house of Israel and with the house of Judah – not according to the covenant that I made with their fathers in the day that I took them by the hand to lead them out of the land of Egypt, My covenant which they broke, though I was a husband to them, says the Lord.

Jeremiah says that this would be an everlasting covenant resulting in eternal blessing to the Jews (32:40). This promise is understood to be literal, for God will erect an eternal city where the Jewish remnant will dwell (Isa. 48:2, 52:1). The prophet Ezekiel refers to the New Covenant as a *"Covenant of Peace"* with the Jewish nation (Ezek. 34:25). Isaiah proclaimed that through this covenant, *"Israel shall be saved in the Lord with an everlasting salvation"* (Isa. 45:17). Why was the New Covenant needed and how did it secure such blessing for Israel?

The writer of Hebrews informs us that this covenant was sealed by Christ's blood and would accomplish what the Old Covenant could not – propitiation for sins (Heb. 8:8). The Old Covenant was conditional in nature; the Jews had to keep God's Law to receive God's blessing (Ex. 19:5-8; Heb. 8:9). The New Covenant would be unconditional in nature and would be the means by which God would honor His covenant with Abraham, which was instituted by two immutable things – God's word and His oath (Heb. 6:13-18), neither of which can fail.

One may then wonder how the Gentiles could be brought into the goodness of the New Covenant, if it was strictly instituted between Jehovah and Israel. William Kelly addresses this question:

I do not say we, Christians, have got the new covenant itself, but we have got the blood of the new covenant. We have that on which the new covenant is founded. The new covenant itself supposes the land of Israel blessed and the house of Israel delivered, but neither the one nor the other has become true yet. The new covenant supposes certain spiritual blessings, namely, the law of God written in the heart and our sins forgiven. These spiritual parts of the new covenant we have received now, along with other blessings peculiar to Christianity, namely, the presence of the Holy Ghost and union with Christ in heaven which the Jews will not have. But nothing can be more evident than that this prophecy refutes the Jew when he imagines that it is a dishonor to the law for God to bring in anything better than what was enjoyed in the days of Moses.[1]

God, in His mercy, permitted the Gentiles to come into the blessing of the New Covenant as a second benefactor of His promise to bless Abraham's descendants (Eph. 2:14-3:8). Gentiles can only enter into the blessing of this covenant by following Abraham's example of trusting God's word by faith; in this way, they become spiritual descendants of Abraham and are able to partake of the spiritual blessings promised to his descendents (Rom. 4:11-17).

Through the New Covenant, God is able to righteously justify sinners, if they trust Christ alone for salvation (Rom. 4:23-25). Those who do so receive the gift of the Holy Spirit (John 14:16-17; 1 Cor. 12:12-13). Thus, through the gospel of Jesus Christ, those who were not God's people (the Gentiles) can become His children (Rom. 9:25-26). It is only by the power of the Holy Spirit that believers are able to both understand the law of God and to fulfill its righteousness (1 Cor. 2:11-15; Rom. 8:4-17).

Likewise, once Israel is fully restored to God at the end of the Tribulation Period, the Holy Spirit will ensure that they will never leave Him again for false gods; instead, they will continue in His Law. As a nation, they will receive the Holy Spirit, and He will give them a new heart (Joel 2:27-29; Ezek. 36:23-28). As a result, God's Law will be deep inside them (v. 33). In that day, all the Jews from the oldest to the youngest will intimately know Jehovah and identify Him as *"The Lord of Hosts"* (vv. 34-35). God cannot lie and His word is eternal, and so shall His blessing be towards His people (vv. 36-37).

The third and final "behold" statement relates to the Millennial Kingdom (v. 38): *"Behold, the days are coming, says the Lord, that the city shall be built for the Lord from the Tower of Hananel to the Corner Gate."* Jerusalem shall be a city built for the Lord, the religious center of the world, and the entire land of Israel shall be holy unto the Lord (vv. 39-40; Isa. 66:10-21; Zech. 14:17). The Millennial Kingdom of Christ will begin directly after the judgment of nations at the conclusion of the Tribulation Period (Matt. 25:31-46). Daniel informs us that there will be a 75 day interval between the destruction of the Antichrist at the battle of Armageddon and the beginning of the blessings of the Kingdom Age (Dan. 12:7-13; Rev. 17-21). But after all wickedness has been purged and the planet has been supernaturally revitalized, Jerusalem will be the seat of God's glory on the earth.

The Lord's Second Advent to the earth will conclude the period of time that the Gentiles were allowed to rule over Israel (Rom. 11:25). This event also coincides with the end of Israel's spiritual blindness (Rom. 11:7-14). When Christ came to the earth two thousand years ago, He removed the veil God had put over the Law (i.e. its full purpose was not disclosed until after Christ's ascension into heaven), but the Jews picked the veil back up and blindfolded themselves from the truth (2 Cor. 3:6-18). The purpose of the Mosaic Law was to show the Jews their sin (Rom. 3:20), and to point them to the solution – Christ (Gal. 3:24). At Calvary, Christ satisfied all of the judicial claims of the Law by subsitutionally dying in the place of sinners. By rejecting His kingdom gospel message, the Jews became locked into a state of blindness, a condition that Satan has worked to maintain (2 Cor. 4:4).

However, at Christ's Second Advent to the earth, the Jewish nation will recognize Him as their Messiah (Zech. 12:10). During the Tribulation Period, the Jewish nation shall be refined and restored to God at its conclusion (Rom. 9:27, 11:26-32). God will protect a remnant from the Antichrist's assault (Rev. 12:6-17), but during the refining process two-thirds of all Jews will be massacred (Zech. 13:7-8).

Until the Jewish nation receives the benefits of the New Covenant, the Lord Jesus Christ is building His Church which, although it includes both Jews and Gentiles, is chiefly composed of Gentiles. Moreover, God is bestowing blessings on Gentile believers to provoke the Jews to jealousy; this will ultimately result in their return to Him (Rom. 11:11-15). The Jews stumbled over Christ at His First Advent, and the blessing He offered them instead fell into the laps of the Gentiles, who were not even expecting it (Luke 20:9-16; Rom. 9:32). Thus, God would call a people that were not His people by covenant to be His children; He would bring them into the good of the New Covenant also (Hos. 1:10, 2:23; Rom. 9:25-26).

There are those who teach that God is done with the nation of Israel, and that the Church has replaced the nation of Israel in God's plan of blessing. However, it should be emphasized that the New Covenant, sealed by Christ's own blood, was not confirmed with Gentiles, but with the houses of Israel and Judah. God has sworn by His own name to complete what He promised Abraham He would do.

This truth was prophetically announced at the time of Christ's birth – He would be the one to achieve complete fulfillment of the Abrahamic Covenant (Luke 1:55). Simeon foretold that the infant Jesus Christ would be the revelation of God's goodness to the Gentiles and the glory of Israel (Luke 2:32). Anna proclaimed that He would bring redemption to Jerusalem (Luke 2:38). The priest Zechariah predicted that the Lord Jesus Christ would redeem His people, be a horn of salvation to Israel, deliver the Jews from all their enemies, and fulfill the covenant that God instituted with Abraham (Luke 1:67-80). *"My covenant I will not break, nor alter the word that has gone out of My lips"* (Ps. 89:34). Our God is a covenant-keeping God! Who but God could have ever devised a plan to show so much grace to a rebel race? We are undeserving of God's goodness, and He is undeserving of our rebel pride.

Meditation

O thank the Lord, the Lord of love;
O thank the God all gods above;
O thank the mighty King of kings,
Whose arm hath done such wondrous things.

— John Herbert

Is There Anything Too Hard for Me?
Jeremiah 32:1-44

By the time this chapter was written, Nebuchadnezzar had indeed invaded the land and besieged Jerusalem just as Jeremiah had prophesied years earlier. The events of Jeremiah 32 occurred in the tenth year of Zedekiah and the eighteenth year of Nebuchadnezzar, which puts the date somewhere between April and October of 587 B.C. (vv. 1-2), while Jerusalem was under siege. The siege of Jerusalem lasted about two and a half years, beginning in January of 588 B.C. and ending in July of 586 B.C.

The situation in Jerusalem was bleak; the siege was already deep into its second year. As one might expect, King Zedekiah did not appreciate Jeremiah discouraging the people with his prophecies of doom and gloom. The prophet was instructing the inhabitants of Jerusalem to give up the siege because no attempt to overcome the Babylonians would be successful. He also stated that, in the end, Zedekiah himself would be hauled off to Babylon as a captive. The king's reaction was an attempt to stifle God's mouthpiece by imprisoning him in the courtyard of the guard (vv. 3-5).

While in prison, the Lord informed Jeremiah that his cousin Hanamel, the son of Shalum, would soon come to visit him (vv. 6-7). The purpose for the visit was also revealed to Jeremiah; Hanamel would want Jeremiah to purchase some property from him. When Hanamel arrived, he requested that Jeremiah purchase a field in Anathoth. It is likely that the Babylonian occupation had put Hanamel and his family in a desperate situation, and he was looking for funds to sustain them through the hardship. Hanamel was following the Law, which allowed kinsmen to redeem (purchase) property to ensure that it remained in the family (v. 8; Lev. 25:25-28).

Anathoth was already under Babylonian control; thus, the field had little value. If the Lord had not told Jeremiah to purchase the

232

property, it is doubtful that Jeremiah would have, since at that time the land was under enemy occupation. However, Jeremiah agreed to purchase the field for seventeen shekels of silver (v. 9). Although the size of the field was not identified, this would be a meager price for even a small parcel of land, thus indication that the economic situation was desperate.

Jeremiah's payment for the land and Hanamel's signing of the deed was done in front of witnesses. There were two copies of the deed made, one copy would remain open so it could be read, while the second copy was bound and sealed as a permanent record of the transaction (vv. 10-11). Both copies were given to Baruch, Jeremiah's personal scribe and trusted friend (v. 12, 36:4).

What was he to do with these two copies of the deed? To ensure that the documents would be preserved for an extended period of time, Jeremiah instructed Baruch to place both documents into a clay jar. This would allow for their retrieval when God brought the Jews back to their homeland seventy years later (vv. 13-14). The purpose of this entire illustration was revealed in verse 15. God was declaring that in a future day, houses, fields, and vineyards would again be bought and sold by their Jewish owners. Such a scenario would only be possible if the region was no longer under the enemy's seige and if the Jewish captives had returned from Babylon. Jeremiah's purchase of this field was a prophetic analogy to encourage the Jews not to give up hope; God would restore them to the land and to Himself.

No doubt Hanamel's foretold visit was an encouragement to Jeremiah; it once again demonstrated God's abiding presence and was a reminder that, although he was in prison, God was in control. At this point, Jeremiah was incited to praise the Lord (vv. 16-19). He began by acknowledging God's sovereign authority, incomparable majesty, and holy character. God is the Creator of all and, thus, there is nothing too hard for Him, including building up and tearing down earthly kingdoms like Babylon. God's holy nature demands justice and that sin be punished. He is omniscient, knowing all the ways and workings of men. Accordingly, everyone will be judged for their own behavior by Him. Jeremiah realized that those who were persecuting him would be punished, and that he, God's prophet, would be rewarded for his faithfulness.

God had demonstrated His great power to His covenant people through signs and wonders since their very conception as a nation (Deut. 4:34). He had shown them His everlasting love by keeping His promise to Abraham, delivering them from their harsh Egyptian captivity and guiding them to the Promised Land, their inheritance (vv. 20-22). God had been very good to Israel, but the Jews had not reciprocated that goodwill; rather, they ignored God's Law once they had seized the land as their possession. God's holy nature could not permit this offense to go unjudged. It is because of this fact that Jeremiah was able to praise God in such trying times; in acknowledging the sin and just punishment of the Jews, Jeremiah exalted the character of God.

With this said, the prophet seemed to be perplexed as to just how God would accomplish all that He said He would. Jerusalem was in a hopeless situation. Siege ramps engulfed the walls of the city, ensuring that it would eventually fall. Beyond its walls the army of the enemy was encamped, bent on destruction. Jeremiah had just purchased a field in occupied territory, but he might well have wondered what would be left of Judah to come home to. Given Jeremiah's exaltation of God in the previous verses, it is doubtful that he questioned God's word or His workings in the situation. Instead, he recalled God's declaration to Abraham centuries earlier: *"There is nothing too hard for You"* (v. 17). Jeremiah acknowledged God's sovereignty; his questions here were only an expression of his own reservations about how the present catastrophe could ever result in restoration and blessing. From his perspective, the horrific state of affairs in Jerusalem and God's promises to bless it were a dichotomy (vv. 23-25).

God answered Jeremiah's prayer by first reminding him of His attributes and character: *"Behold, I am the Lord, the God of all flesh. Is there anything too hard for Me?"* (v. 27). The answer is obviously "no." In the remainder of this chapter, God reiterated what He had already promised. He would allow Nebuchadnezzar to destroy Jerusalem by fire, and He would allow the people to be slaughtered with the sword, famine, and pestilence because the idolatrous Jews had provoked Him to wrath (vv. 28-36). Yet, the Lord also stated that in a future day He would gather His people back to their homeland from among all nations and that He would be their God again (vv. 37-

38). This will be made possible through His New Covenant with them, which will accomplish what the Law could not: they will have a unified heart to obey and fear the Lord (vv. 39-40). In that day, God will rejoice over them and His people will inherit all that He has for them (vv. 41-44).

Jeremiah was not the first person in the Bible to whom the Lord asked the question, "Is anything too hard for Me?" In Genesis 18 the Lord visited another man of faith: Abraham. One-hundred-year-old Abraham prepared a meal for the Lord and His two angels. After dinner, the Lord spoke to Abraham, saying, *"I will certainly return to you according to the time of life, and behold, Sarah your wife shall have a son"* (Gen. 18:10). Sarah overheard this conversation and laughed within herself. It was a cynical and internal snicker of disbelief. Though there was no audible noise, the Lord asked why she laughed. No one but the Lord could know her thoughts. Yet, she denied laughing within herself. The Lord responded with a staggering question to assert one of the greatest expressions of truth in the Bible: *"Is anything too hard for the Lord?"* It is a rhetorical question with only one answer.

Twice during His conversation with Abraham the Lord declares, *"I will return unto you"* (Gen. 18:10, 14). These words have encouraged God's people throughout the ages not to lose heart. It is a promise that runs throughout the Scripture. The night before the Lord Jesus was crucified He comforted His disciples with similar words: *"And if I go and prepare a place for you, I will come again and receive you to Myself; that where I am, there you may be also"* (John 14:3). The final page of Holy Scripture declares three times, *"I come quickly"* (Rev. 22:7, 12, 20). For anyone else but the Lord of Glory to make such a promise would be presumptuous. Dear believer, do not lose heart; He is really coming back for you! "Is there anything too hard for the Lord?"

> *For ye have need of patience, that, after ye have done the will of God, ye might receive the promise. For yet a little while, and He that shall come **will come**, and **will not tarry**. Now the just shall live by faith: but if any man draw back, my soul shall have no pleasure in him* (Heb. 10:36-38; KJV).

Though God's people were discouraged and suffering at the hands of the Babylonians, God had not forgotten them. In fact, He bestowed them with a wonderful promise: *"For thus says the Lord: 'Just as I have brought all this great calamity on this people, so I will bring on them all the good that I have promised them'"* (v. 41). C. H. Spurgeon muses on what the latter portion of the verse means to believers today:

> How heart-cheering to the believer is the delight which God has in his saints! We cannot see any reason in ourselves why the Lord should take pleasure in us; we cannot take delight in ourselves, for we often have to groan, being burdened; conscious of our sinfulness, and deploring our unfaithfulness; and we fear that God's people cannot take much delight in us, for they must perceive so much of our imperfections and our follies, that they may rather lament our infirmities than admire our graces. But we love to dwell upon this transcendent truth, this glorious mystery: that as the bridegroom rejoices over the bride, so does the Lord rejoice over us. We do not read anywhere that God delights in the cloud-capped mountains, or the sparkling stars, but we do read that He delights in the habitable parts of the earth, and that His delights are with the sons of men.
>
> In what strong language He expresses His delight in His people! Who could have conceived of the eternal One as bursting forth into a song? Yet it is written, *"He will rejoice over thee with joy, He will rest in his love, He will joy over thee with singing."* As He looked upon the world He had made, He said, "It is very good"; but when He beheld those who are the purchase of Jesus' blood, His own chosen ones, it seemed as if the great heart of the Infinite could restrain itself no longer, but overflowed in divine exclamations of joy. Should not we utter our grateful response to such a marvelous declaration of His love, and sing, *"I will rejoice in the Lord, I will joy in the God of my salvation?"*[1]

The Lord wanted His people to understand that He had not forgotten them; indeed, it would be impossible for Him to do so. In fact, He delighted in them and longed to be reunited with them in a future day of blessing. The Lord Jesus has extended the same promise to the Church: let us be faithful and not give up hope – the Lord is coming for us (John 14:1-3). Maranatha!

Meditation

When silent falls the gushing tear, o'er cheeks grown pale with care;
And on the heart a cross is laid that seems too hard to bear,
Remember what our Lord has said, and trust, in weal or woe,
His holy Word, that changeth not, though uttered years ago.

When one by one our treasured hopes like autumn leaves decay,
And they who made our life most dear are borne from us away,
O look beyond the veil of time, where springs of comfort flow,
And trust His Word, that changeth not, though uttered years ago.

— Fanny Crosby

The Lord is His Name
Jeremiah 33:1-13

While imprisoned, Jeremiah received a second word from the Lord (v. 1). God reiterated His promise to both destroy Jerusalem and to restore it in the future. The chapter concluded with the Lord affirming His past covenants with David and with the Levitical priesthood (vv. 14-26). The authority of God's Word is the central theme of this chapter. The Lord Jesus said, *"For assuredly, I say to you, till heaven and earth pass away, one jot or one tittle will by no means pass from the law till all is fulfilled"* (Matt. 5:18). God always keeps His Word, and every detail of every promise will come to pass.

Jehovah began by reminding Israel of His personal name three times in verse 2: *"Thus says the Lord* [Jehovah] *who made it, the Lord* [Jehovah] *who formed it to establish it (the Lord* [Jehovah] *is His name)."* The Lord uses such repetition in Scripture to summon our attention to something important. What is the significance of God referring to Himself by His personal name? This question is best answered by reviewing the first instance God chose to reveal Himself by the name of Jehovah.

Moses' first encounter with Jehovah was before a bush that appeared to be in flames, but yet was not consumed by fire (Ex. 3:1-6). It was during this initial meeting that God promised to deliver His people from slavery and from Egypt through Moses' leadership (Ex. 3:7-10). After that disclosure, Moses asked the Lord, *"What is Your name?"* or by implication, "Who are You?" Usually, the first thing a person learns about someone is his or her name, and Moses needed to know whom he was to represent in Egypt. Moses' request indicated a shift in mental focus from his own lack of ability to God's power and authority; this is the first step in understanding the purposes of God in our life.

God's response to Moses' question was, *"I AM that I AM"* (Ex. 3:14). In preparation for their deliverance from Egypt and the wilderness experience to follow, God wanted His covenant people to know Him as "I AM." The Hebrew word *hayah* is used here to mean "I will be," and is a wordplay on the name *Yahweh* (Jehovah) in Exodus 3:15, which means "to be." Moses was to tell the children of Israel that I AM had sent him to them.

In the Old Testament, great significance is attached to personal names, for a name indicated not just the identity of a person but also their features, nature, or character. For example, Jacob lived up to his name "supplanter" – he was a trickster and a schemer. Esau's name related to the hairy appearance of his body at birth. Ezekiel was God's prophet to the discouraged Jews exiled in Babylon; his name means "God will strengthen." Likewise, God's names in Scripture reveal information about Him. His various names and titles in the Old Testament had substantial importance to His people, for many of God's names pertained to His relationship with them.

Yahweh, "the self-existent One," is found 6,828 times in the Old Testament; it may be translated as "Jehovah," but normally it is rendered as "the Lord" or "O Lord" (in many translations this Name appears with all letters in uppercase font - Lord). *Yahweh* is derived from the Hebrew tetragrammaton YHWH. As there are no vowels in the Hebrew written language, no one is quite sure how God's covenant name is to be pronounced. YHWH is considered to be so sacred by some Jewish rabbis that they often substitute another title for God rather than speak His personal name while reading the sacred scrolls. While reverence for the Lord is necessary, Jehovah did not want His name forgotten among His people.

Accordingly, the Lord repeatedly invoked His covenant name to Jeremiah to affirm His promise to crush Jerusalem and also to provide an invitation for His people to draw near to Him in a future day: *"Call to Me, and I will answer you, and show you great and mighty things, which you do not know"* (v. 3). It is an application befitting God's people throughout every dispensation of His working – the Lord blesses those who seek Him in truth with further understanding of Himself. The Lord Jesus extended a similar invitation to His disciples: *"He who has My commandments and keeps them, it is he who loves Me. And he who loves Me will be loved by My Father, and I will love him and manifest Myself to him"* (John 14:21). C. H. Spurgeon ponders what it means to be shown the great and mighty things of God by the Lord Himself:

> There are different translations of these words. One version renders it, "I will show thee great and fortified things." Another, "Great and reserved things." Now, there are reserved and special things in Christian experience: all the developments of spiritual life are not alike easy of attainment. There are the common frames and feelings of repentance, and faith, and joy, and hope, which are enjoyed by the entire family; but there is an upper realm of rapture, of communion, and conscious union with Christ, which is far from being the common dwelling-place of believers. We have not all the high privilege of John, to lean upon Jesus' bosom; nor of Paul, to be caught up into the third heaven. There are heights in experimental knowledge of the things of God which the eagle's eye of acumen and philosophic thought hath never seen: God alone can bear us there; but the chariot in which he takes us up, and the fiery steeds with which that chariot is dragged, are prevailing prayers. … Prevailing prayer takes the Christian to Carmel, and enables him to cover heaven with clouds of blessing, and earth with floods of mercy. Prevailing prayer bears the Christian aloft to Pisgah, and shows him the inheritance reserved; it elevates us to Tabor and transfigures us, till in the likeness of his Lord, as he is, so are we also in this world. If you would reach to something higher than ordinary groveling experience, look to the Rock that is higher than you, and gaze with the eye of faith through the window of importunate prayer. When you open the window on your side, it will not be bolted on the other.[1]

To lay hold of God's goodness by faith, one must rise above sensory knowledge and mental reasoning; obedience to revealed truth, then, becomes the only means of experiencing and knowing God in deepening degrees.

The situation in Jerusalem was getting worse; the houses near the royal palace were torn down to provide wood and stone to support the city's walls against the siege ramps. The Lord said that such desperate attempts to avoid defeat would fail; in fact, the spaces where the demolished houses had once stood would become a dumping ground for dead bodies (vv. 4-5). In verses 6-9, the Lord repeated His promise to heal the people and the city in a future day, which would include cleansing them from their sins and giving them a place of honor among the nations.

To further explain this transition from woe to blessing, the Lord issues two declarations, both of which are introduced by the phrase, *"This is what the Lord (Jehovah) says"* (vv. 10, 12). Initially, Jerusalem is described as *"a desolate waste,"* and *"without men or animals"* (v. 12). However, in a coming day the deserted streets of Jerusalem would be filled with people happily scurrying about the city engaged in the daily affairs of life. Worshippers would be heard at the temple praising God, sounds of joy would fill the air and joyful wedding celebrations would again be attended in Jerusalem. The surrounding towns and pasturelands would be restored with people, and shepherds would again count their sheep throughout Judah's hill country (v. 13). The entire scene pictures God's sheep restored to His care and protection in a future day.

> *Make a joyful shout to the Lord, all you lands!*
> *Serve the Lord with gladness;*
> *Come before His presence with singing.*
> *Know that the Lord, He is God;*
> *It is He who has made us, and not we ourselves;*
> *We are His people and the sheep of His pasture* (Ps. 100:1-3)

The psalmist understood that serving the Lord with gladness is only possible by personally knowing God. Accordingly, God invokes His personal name "Jehovah" several times in the thirty-third chapter of Jeremiah. In so doing, God was repeating the invitation first given to Moses in Exodus 3, that is, that His people draw near to Him and have communion with Him. Knowing God's personal names is really a prerequisite of knowing God Himself. To fabricate a conception of God through mental images, humanly ascribed names, or earthly forms is nothing less than pernicious idolatry. To approach God by any other name or way than what He has revealed in Scripture is vain religion. May we know and esteem God's various names, for in them He beckons us to draw near and know Him more deeply.

Meditation

Nearer, still nearer, while life shall last,
Till safe in glory my anchor is cast;
Through endless ages, ever to be,
Nearer, my Saviour, still nearer to Thee.

— Lelia Morris

The Branch of Righteousness
Jeremiah 33:14-26

"In those days" speaks of the future Kingdom Age under the rule of the Messiah. Verse 15 is the second time Jeremiah has referred to the coming Messiah as the Righteous Branch of David (23:5 being the first). God had promised that one of David's descendants would sit on his throne forever (v. 17; 2 Sam. 7:16). His authority would not be limited merely to Judah and Israel, but He would govern all the earth (23:5-6). This future Jewish Deliverer would be a righteous and a just King, and would sprout up as a branch from the loins of David. This means that accurate Jewish genealogies would be crucial to authenticate the Messiah's identity.

Like Jeremiah 33, Chronicles (one book in the Hebrew Bible) calls the Jews to remember the Levitical priesthood, which represented them before God (v. 21); to recall the glorious kingdom of David; and to anticipate the even more spectacular one to come. The extensive genealogies in 1 Chronicles 1-8 provide the means of connecting the Jews in Jeremiah's day to their initial forefathers, and paves the way for their connection to their future Messiah; *"so all Israel were reckoned by genealogies"* (1 Chron. 9:1).

The last book in the Hebrew Bible is *Chronicles*, so named by Jerome in his Latin translation; however, the Jews refer to *Chronicles* as "The Words of Days" (which they arrange as one book, rather than in two parts as in our Bibles). The Hebrew Bible arranges the Old Testament differently than in our Bibles, though the content is the same. The Jews commonly attribute the authorship of Chronicles to Ezra the scribe and, thus, place its writing during the latter portion of the Babylonian captivity and the initial stages of the Persian Empire. Regardless of his identity, the writer's focus was to awaken a small, struggling community of exiled Jews to their heritage in Jehovah. They had lost their perspective of being God's covenant people, His

243

chosen people on earth. They were a unique and distinctive social group and should have been elated by that reality.

When Chronicles is placed at the end of the Old Testament, a seamless transition is seen to Matthew, the first book of the New Testament. Chronicles contains the genealogies of Israel up to that point; the gospel of Matthew opens with a series of genealogies that provide the remaining connections to Christ, the Messiah. The opening sentence of Matthew both introduces the book's theme and explains its placement: *"The book of the generation of Jesus Christ, the Son of David, the Son of Abraham."* The principal topic of this gospel account is the direct fulfillment of the Davidic and Abrahamic covenants through Christ. These were unilateral covenants that God made with David and Abraham but until that time had never been completely fulfilled. For the Jews, the hope of permanent royalty from *a man after God's own heart* and the acquisition of the promissory blessing originally committed to *the friend of God* were paramount.

The genealogies of Matthew 1 served as proof to the Jews that Jesus, through Joseph, was a direct descendant of David and, thus, the legal and rightful heir to David's throne. As to not distract from his theme of covenant fulfillment, Matthew begins with Abraham, not Adam, in his rendition of Christ's genealogy. Luke's genealogy of Christ, however, is for a different purpose. Luke upholds Christ as the "Son of man," or more specifically, the "Son of Adam." In so doing, Luke shows Christ to be the "Last Adam," God's replacement representative of righteousness, and the literal fulfillment of the prophecy that the Messiah would come from the *"seed of a woman"* (Gen. 3:15-16). God thought it critical for mankind to understand that the Messiah would not be of the seed of fallen man, although His royal lineage would be established through a man, Joseph, back to David and through Solomon. The pair of New Testament genealogies accomplishes this: Luke focuses our attention upon the Lord's humanity derived from Mary through the power of the Holy Spirit, while Matthew demonstrates Christ's official authority through Joseph.

The Hebrew Bible concludes with genealogies from Adam up to the point in time in which God invoked 400 years of silence concerning His rebellious covenant people. This prophetic hush was broken with the announcement of the Savior's coming to earth. In Matthew 1, the genealogies pick up again after the centuries of silence and lead the Jews to their much-anticipated and predicted Messiah, the Lord Jesus Christ. He would be the literal fulfillment of God's promise to David: *"I will establish the throne of His kingdom forever"* (2 Sam. 7:13). Matthew provides the culmination of the story which Chronicles only partially disclosed, and bridges the remaining gap between the first Adam and the last Adam, who would restore righteousness and rule forever.

Jeremiah refers to the Messiah as *"the Branch of Righteousness to David"* (23:5-6, 33:17). As already mentioned, the branch speaks of that which would sprout from David; however, a second implication is equally clear – Messiah would be human. The humanity of Christ is sometimes symbolized by wood in Scripture, as it is in Noah's ark (Gen. 6), the tabernacle furnishings (Ex. 25-27), and Aaron's rod (Num. 17). Thus, Jeremiah's reference to the Messiah being a "Branch" confirms His humanity.

Before the ark could be constructed, building materials were needed; trees had to be cut down. The death of these trees pictured the humanity of Christ in that only through His sacrifice could spiritual life for man be secured. But since trees do not have blood, God is careful to apply some, in picture, to the ark that we not miss the fuller picture. The Hebrew word *kaphar* which is translated "pitch" in Genesis 6:14 is most often translated "atonement" throughout the Old Testament. Prior to Calvary, man's sin could only be atoned (covered) by the blood of animals through sacrifices. The fact that the ark was to be pitched from within and without further shadows the future suffering and sacrifice of Christ. From His wounds, redemptive blood would rudely and profusely coat his outer skin then drip and splatter upon the ground. The choice of words and the typology of Genesis 6 convey an image of a bleeding ark, thus, picturing the suffering Man of Calvary.

The furnishings of the Tabernacle, and, indeed, the Tabernacle itself, foreshadow Christ in symbolic form. For example, God commanded that the Ark of the Covenant, the Golden Altar of Incense, the Table of Showbread, and the boards that formed the walls of the tabernacle all be made of wood overlaid with gold. In the figurative sense, gold in Scripture speaks of purity and holiness. In the

Tabernacle, the gold and the wood combine to express the full deity and full humanity of Christ.

Another example of wood being used to picture the humanity of Christ is found in Aaron's budding and fruitful rod of Numbers 17. God used this miracle as a sign to affirm His selection of the High Priest and to confound other clan leaders who were aspiring for that office. The rod of each tribal leader was put with Aaron's rods before the Lord in the tabernacle. When Moses brought out the rods to the people the next day, Aaron's rod had budded, bloomed and yielded almonds (Ex. 17:8). Amidst all the other dead rods on the planet, God declares His Son, the Lord Jesus, as *"the resurrection and the life"* (John 11:25). Paul proclaimed that Christ was the first fruits from the dead; He is the first man to have experienced glorification, but a harvest of faithful souls is yet to follow (1 Cor. 15:20).

As shown earlier, the Old Testament speaks of the Messiah as a Branch in four ways which align with the unique vantage points of Christ in the four Gospels. The title "The Righteous Branch of David" aligns with Matthew's presentation of the Lord Jesus Christ as the One who fulfilled Scripture and was, therefore, the rightful heir to the throne of David. Jeremiah declares of Him:

That I will raise to David a Branch of righteousness; a King shall reign and prosper, and execute judgment and righteousness in the earth. In His days Judah will be saved, and Israel will dwell safely; now this is His name by which He will be called: THE LORD OUR RIGHTEOUSNESS (Jer. 23:5-6).

The books of Chronicles and Matthew, and indeed all of Scripture, draw our attention to this fact. In a future day, the Jews will come into the full understanding and appreciation of their Righteous Branch; indeed, the entire world will know Him.

Meditation

How bright appears the morning star,
With mercy beaming from afar!
The host of Heaven rejoices!
O righteous Branch! O Jesse's Rod!

Thou Son of Man, and Son of God!
We too will lift our voices,
Jesus! Jesus! Holy, holy! Yet most lowly!
Draw Thou near us:
Great Emmanuel! Stoop and hear us!

— Philip Nicolai

A Message for Zedekiah
Jeremiah 34:1-22

The events in this chapter precede those in Jeremiah 32 and 33 by one or two years (i.e. Jeremiah has not been imprisoned yet). By this time, even the sight of Jeremiah probably caused Zedekiah to cringe. God's prophet invariably prophesied against Zedekiah and his ongoing rebellion against Babylon. Jeremiah's visit on this occasion was no different than previous ones; he informed Zedekiah that Jerusalem would fall and burn, and that the king himself would not escape. He again foretold that Zedekiah would meet Nebuchadnezzar face to face before being hauled off to Babylon to be judged for his crimes (vv. 1-6). Jeremiah later recorded that all these things occurred in accordance with the prophetic edicts of God (Jer. 39:1-7, 52:7-11).

The situation was indeed desperate; Nebuchadnezzar's assault and siege of the fortified cities of Judah had been brilliantly successful, and only three cities remained in Judean control: Jerusalem, Lachish, and Azekah (v. 7). All the other cities, and in fact, the entire countryside was under Babylonian rule. The only glimmer of hope for Zedekiah in this dismal ordeal was that Jeremiah informed him that he would not die by the sword, but peacefully in Babylon. In fact, Jeremiah promised that Jewish survivors of the coming holocaust would ignite funeral fires to honor him and that they would mourn for him as for one who had died (v. 5).

An inscription written on a piece of potsherd in the ruins of Lachish has partly confirmed what Jeremiah wrote of the regional situation described in this chapter (the year is perhaps late 591 B.C., but more likely 590 B.C.). It was shortly after this time that a Judean soldier serving in a high outpost between Lachish and Azekah (signal fires could be seen by both cities at this location) wrote the following note to his commanding officer in Lachish: "And let my Lord know that we are watching for the signals of Lachish, according to all the indications which my Lord hath given, for we cannot see Azekah."[1] Apparently, Azekah was destroyed first by the Babylonians, and then Lachish fell sometime later, thus leaving only Jerusalem in Judean control.

In this chapter, Jeremiah not only spoke against Zedekiah, but he also had a rebuke for the people in general. The matter pertained to the enslavement of Jews by other Jews, which was prohibited by the Law (except for a maximum of six years to pay off a debt: Ex. 21:2-11; Lev. 25:39-55). Interestingly, perhaps in an attempt to gain God's blessing, King Zedekiah heeded this admonition and decreed that all slaves were to be freed. However, the upper crust of Jewish society apparently reneged on this commandment and later reinstated their fellow countrymen into slavery (vv. 8-11).

Given that Jerusalem was under siege, the most likely reason slavery existed was because people were selling themselves into it in order to feed their families. In this scenario, the Jewish slaves would have been in desperate circumstances indeed. The wealthier Jews could have demonstrated true repentance by forgiving the debts of their poor countrymen, not oppressing them further. Jeremiah stated that when they had set the slaves free, they had righted their wrong against the Lord. However, when they had reinstated slavery, they had profaned God's name because they willingly mocked their Sinai covenant with Him (vv. 12-16). God had a solution to match their rebellion. They had rescinded their promise to grant freedom to the slaves, so He would free the slaves from their owners, by the sword, pestilence, or starvation (v. 17). Of course, this was not the kind of liberation that the slaves or the slave-owners were hoping for. Jeremiah was using satire to better highlight the enormity of the coming judgment, which would be no respecter of persons.

To better explain why such an overwhelming judgment was deserved, Jeremiah provides a brief summary of the events which occurred at Sinai when God and the Israelites entered into a covenant. At Sinai, Moses slaughtered a calf and the covenant between God and the Israelites was sealed by blood. Moses had the people walk between the pieces of a parted calf to illustrate their agreement with God's covenant (vv. 18-19). What does this practice symbolize? It was the ancient eastern custom for two men making a binding agreement to kill an animal and split it in half. Instead of shaking hands or signing a contract, the two men would walk through the animal parts in front of witnesses. They were publicly proclaiming that, if they did not maintain the agreement they were entering into, the other party had the right to do to them as they had just done to the animal.

Genesis 15 supplies an example of this ancient custom. In obedience to God's command, Abram parted animals for the purpose just described. However, God did not ask Abram to walk through the animal pieces with Him. Instead, God caused a deep sleep to come over Abram, and God made a binding covenant with Himself to bless Abram (Heb. 6:13) – God passed between the animal pieces alone (Gen. 15:17). If Abram had walked with God through the midst of those animal pieces, the covenant would have been broken as soon as Abram failed God, and Abram would have had to die.

On Mount Sinai the Israelites had signified their complete devotion by walking through the parts of the calf, but had failed to keep their end of the covenant; now God would exact restitution. Their mutilated bodies would be strewn on the ground in the same way that the calf had been. Furthermore, Jeremiah told them that the birds and wild beasts would consume their rotting carcasses. They would not receive a decent burial, and there would be no grave markers for them to be remembered by. This intense prophecy was hard for the people to fathom, especially since Nebuchadnezzar had just withdrawn his army from Jerusalem.

Jeremiah warned, however, that their withdrawal was only temporary; God would bring them back and the siege would continue (vv. 21-22). God was going to destroy the city and make it desolate and there was nothing in heaven or earth that could stop that from happening. One can only admire the courage of Jeremiah to declare such a strong word from the Lord in such a spiritually corrupt and physically challenging time. Six centuries later, another Jew, Paul of Tarsus, would likewise declare his unwavering allegiance to declare God's Word to a lost world: *"For I am not ashamed of the gospel of Christ, for it is the power of God to salvation for everyone who believes, for the Jew first and also for the Greek"* (Rom. 1:16). The prophet Ezekiel was chosen by God to be a watchman to the Jews in Babylon. God warned him:

But if the watchman sees the sword coming and does not blow the trumpet, and the people are not warned, and the sword comes and takes any person from among them, he is taken away in his iniquity; but his blood I will require at the watchman's hand. So you, son of man: I have made you a watchman for the house of Israel; therefore you shall hear a word from My mouth and warn them for Me (Ezek. 33:6-7).

Despite the hostility of the lost, may each watchman for the Lord stand fast in the faith of Christ and declare God's message of love and truth to those who desperately need to hear it. God will not hold us guiltless if we withhold His words of life!

Meditation

Am I a soldier of the cross, a follower of the Lamb,
And shall I fear to own His cause, or blush to speak His Name?

Are there no foes for me to face? Must I not stem the flood?
Is this vile world a friend to grace, to help me on to God?

Sure I must fight if I would reign; increase my courage, Lord.
I'll bear the toil, endure the pain, supported by Thy Word.

When that illustrious day shall rise, and all Thy armies shine,
In robes of victory through the skies, the glory shall be Thine.

— Isaac Watts

251

A Man of God
Jeremiah 35:1-19

The timing of Jeremiah 35 jumps back nearly twenty years prior to the prophecy of the previous chapter. Jehoiakim, the son of Josiah, is said to be king, which dates this message somewhere between 609 and 605 B.C. Jeremiah was commanded to go to the Rechabites and to request that they accompany him to one of the side rooms of the temple (v. 2). These rooms were used for storage, to conduct meetings, and to provide living quarters for the priests (1 Kgs. 6:5; 2 Chron. 31:11; Neh. 13:7-9). Like Abraham, the nomadic Rechabites did not live in houses, but were tent-dwellers. They were descendants of the Kenites (1 Chron. 2:54-55) and normally dwelled in the wilderness of Negev (1 Sam. 15:6), but had been forced to move to Jerusalem after Nebuchadnezzar threatened the region in 598 B.C. (v. 11).

Key men from the clan followed Jeremiah to the temple (v. 3) and into the chamber of the sons of Hanan, who was the son of Igdaliah. This particular room was a place of prominence (v. 4). It was situated next to the chamber of temple officials and over the room of Maaseiah (who was one of the three temple doorkeepers). The Jews would view this room with the kind of awe that one today might associate with the Oval Office in the White House or the State Apartments in Buckingham Palace. The social clash of nomadic herdsmen standing in the presence of well-dressed and high-ranking civil officials would have been quite apparent, but this was to be part of Jeremiah's illustration.

Jeremiah put pots of wine and cups before the Rechabites and told them to drink, but they refused (v. 5). Why? Because their forefather Jonadab, the son of Rechab, had instructed them centuries earlier not to drink wine, nor build houses, nor plant fields or vineyards (vv. 6-10). Scripture reveals that Jonadab, who assisted Jehu in removing

252

Baal-worship from Israel (2 Kgs 10:15-27), was a godly man. H. A. Ironside explains:

> In 1 Chron. 2:55 we find the Rechabites numbered with the children of Judah. *"These are the Kenites that came of Hemath, the father of the house of Rechab."* It is through their valiant representative Jehonadab, the son of Rechab, that they first acquired special prominence. It was he who went out to meet Jehu after he had been anointed king of Israel by the nameless prophet sent by Elisha to Ramoth-Gilead. Having destroyed the vile house of Ahab, and likewise many of the house of Ahaziah king of Judah, Jehu was riding towards Samaria when *"he lighted on Jehonadab the son of Rechab coming to meet him: and he saluted him, and said to him, Is thy heart right, as my heart is with thy heart? And Jehonadab answered, It is"* (2 Kings 10: 15). Dramatically Jehu cried, *"If it be, give me thy hand."* Upon his doing so, he took him up with him into the chariot, saying, *"Come with me, and see my zeal for the Lord."*
>
> The conclusion is irresistible that Jehu already knew Jehonadab well as a man devoted to the worship of Jehovah, and an abhorrer of idolatry. The piety of his father Rechab is expressed in the name given to his son, the meaning of which is, "Jehovah freely gave." In company with the zealous but cruel king, Jehonadab is found commanding the search to see that no servants of Jehovah were mingled with the worshippers of Baal in the temple of Samaria, prior to their massacre at the order of Jehu. He is not again mentioned until we come down to our present chapter.[1]

Rechab had taught Jehonadab to fear the Lord and respect authority and this heritage had been passed down from generation to generation in their clan.

If Jeremiah knew the Rechabites would not drink wine, what was his purpose in setting it before them? This action was to demonstrate that, unlike the inhabitants of Judah, the Rechabites pleased the Lord because they respected God-ordained authority (v. 13). God honors those who are in a right relationship with His authority; He teaches us submission to Him through His various earthly authority structures. The Rechabites had obeyed the directions of their forefather Jonadab, and God promised to bless them because they had. Note that Jeremiah is not here affirming that Jonadab's prohibition of drinking wine and dwelling in houses was correct, but rather is commending his descendants for their submission to his command. Aside from their obedience, God was also pleased with the sojourning attitude that the Rechabites held towards life. The Rechabites did not invest or settle into a world condemned by God, but rather lived as if they were just passing through it. This is a good example for God's people to follow no matter what time period they sojourn in.

Rechab's forefather Abram was also known for his "passing through" disposition to life. In fact, it was this mindset that earned Abram the name *Hebrew* (Gen. 14:13). God's covenant people would later be called by this name. "Hebrew" means "the passenger," and beautifully encapsulates the pilgrimage of Abram and his alienation in a world estranged from God. Likewise, "Hebrew" signified the calling of Abram's descendants to be delivered out of Egypt and into God's presence. To be a Hebrew meant that you were a stranger in the world; thus, neither Egypt nor Babylon could ever be the resting place for God's people. The Rechabites were true Hebrews, and God was pleased with them. Their testimony of faithfulness provided a strong contrast to the unfaithfulness of Judah and is likely the reason that they are mentioned in this chapter.

It is interesting that, of all the temple rooms, Jeremiah led the Rechabites into the chamber of the sons of Hanan. Not much is known about Igdaliah, the father of Hanan, but Scripture does refer to him as *"a man of God"* (vv. 3-4). There are only twelve men in all of the Old Testament who earned that title. We are not told what Igdaliah did to earn such an honorary position in Scripture, but perhaps reviewing the lives of others who are also said to be men of God will be helpful in giving us an idea of what his lifestyle must have been like.

There are four individuals in the Old Testament who are acknowledged as men of God, although not identified by name: the man who rebuked Eli for his sons' wickedness (1 Sam. 2:27), the man from Judah who rebuked Jeroboam (1 Kgs. 13:1), the man who told Ahab that he would have the victory over the Syrians because they mocked God (1 Kgs. 20:28), and the man who told King Amaziah not to hire mercenaries out of Israel to battle Edom (2 Chron. 25:7). The fact that these men remained unnamed in Scripture suggests that their work for the Lord was more important than the recognition of men. Paul acknowledged that this is a good principle to govern how we serve the Lord: *"And whatever you do in word or deed, do all in the name of the Lord Jesus, giving thanks to God the Father through Him"* (Col. 3:17). Being heavenly minded ensures our earthly good.

There are eight other men who are specifically identified as men of God in the Old Testament: Moses (Deut. 33:1; Josh. 14:6), the Preincarnate Christ (Judg. 13:6), the prophet Samuel (1 Sam. 9:6), Shemaiah (1 Kgs. 12:22-23), the prophet Elijah (1 Kgs. 17:18), the prophet Elisha (2 Kgs. 1:9), King David (2 Chron. 8:14), and Igdaliah (v. 4). Igdaliah, introduced to us in this chapter of Jeremiah, probably met his death after the fall of Jerusalem at the hand of Nebuchadnezzar, who executed all the doorkeepers and high-ranking temple officials (52:24).

What made Igdaliah a man of God? First, he had apparently served the Lord faithfully in the temple. Second, he left a godly heritage; Igdaliah's grandsons were going on for the Lord also – they, like their grandfather, worked in the temple (v. 4). Igdaliah's example stood in stark contrast to Eli and Samuel, whose own children were wicked (so much so that Eli's sons were slain by God and Samuel's were rejected by the Israelites). Igdaliah was known as a man of God, and the conduct of his grandchildren testified to that fact.

The presence of the Rechabites in one of the most prominent rooms of God's house provided a visual rebuke to the disobedience of Judah. In contrast to the Rechabites, the Jews would not listen to God's prophets (v. 15), they would not turn from their evil ways (v. 16), and they would not repent of their idolatry (v. 17). Outwardly speaking, the Jews looked good, but inwardly they were rebels at heart and consequently deserved God's judgment. The Rechabites, on the other hand, had obeyed all the precepts of their forefather Jonadab. Because they had done so, God would honor and bless them. They were given this promise: *"Jonadab the son of Rechab shall not lack a man to stand before Me forever"* (v. 19). This not only meant that the Rechabites would survive the Babylonian invasion, but that there would also be some descendants of Rechab who would serve the Lord and be in communion with Him. May we too endeavor to pass along such a godly heritage to our children!

Meditation

Lord, who may abide in Your tabernacle?
Who may dwell in Your holy hill?
He who walks uprightly,
And works righteousness,
And speaks the truth in his heart;
He who does not backbite with his tongue,
Nor does evil to his neighbor,
Nor does he take up a reproach against his friend;
In whose eyes a vile person is despised,
But he honors those who fear the Lord.

— Psalm 15:1-4

The Burnt Scroll
Jeremiah 36:1-32

The events of this chapter follow shortly after those of the previous chapter, as Jeremiah identifies the date of his writing as the fourth year of Jehoiakim (v. 1). Jeremiah was instructed to write down Israel's and Judah's offenses against God and call them to repentance (v. 2). Perhaps after hearing the words of the scroll they would repent and turn to the Lord. If they did, God promised to forgive them their trespasses and to turn from His fierce wrath that was determined against them (vv. 3, 7).

Baruch was summoned by Jeremiah to write down his dictation and then to carry the scroll that he had written to the temple where he was to read it before the people (vv. 4, 6). Jeremiah had been constrained by God from going there personally (v. 5), perhaps because his earlier address at the temple had not been well received (7:1-5, 26:1-19).

A national fast was declared for the ninth month of the fifth year of Jehoiakim's reign (v. 9). Times of fasting were not commanded by the Lord in Israel's history, but fasts were occasionally practiced by the Jews, usually in response to a national emergency (v. 9; 2 Chron. 20:3). However, after the fall of Jerusalem, annual fasts were instituted to commemorate devastating national events (Zech. 7:5-6, 8:19). It was at this time that Baruch went to the temple and read the scroll aloud (v. 10). The fact that a year or more had transpired since Jeremiah had received the word of the Lord to write down suggests that the scroll may have been lengthy.

The reading of God's Word had a profound effect on Micaiah, the son of Gemariah and the grandson of Shaphan. As noted previously, Shaphan was an honorable man (2 Chron. 34). Micaiah immediately went to the officials of the priests and declared what he had heard. The response of the officials was commendable: they wanted to hear the Word of God for themselves, not merely Micaiah's rendition of it. This is a good practice for all God's people to follow. Baruch was summoned and led to a group of waiting priests. After Baruch read the contents of the scroll to them, he was questioned as to how he had obtained the scroll. Baruch told them that he had written down the very words that Jeremiah spoke as the Lord gave him revelation (vv. 17-18).

The Word of God penetrated deeply into the hearts of those listening to it. The priests keenly felt the significance and power of the message and were prompted to inform the king of what they had heard (v. 20). As God's priests and scribes, they had a duty to perform, despite the potential danger to themselves if the king became enraged. As a safety precaution against Jehoiakim's potential wrath, the officials instructed Baruch to find Jeremiah and to go into hiding with him (v. 19). This was a wise safeguard, considering that at that time Jehoiakim had already murdered the godly prophet Uriah for declaring the Word of God to him (26:20-23).

The priests put the scroll in the chamber of Elishama for safekeeping while they informed the king of the incident at the temple. The king sent Jehudi to retrieve the scroll. He returned with the scroll in hand and proceeded to read it aloud before the king (v. 21). It was wintertime and there was a fire on the hearth in the king's palace (v. 23). After reading three or four columns of the scroll, Jehudi, with the king's endorsement (v. 32), cut the scroll into pieces with a penknife and cast it into the fire (v. 23). Three godly priests (Elnathan, Delaiah, and Gemariah) pleaded with the king not to burn the scroll, but he did not listen to them (v. 25). The king and his officers were offended by the scroll's contents and did not fear divine retribution for its destruction (v. 24).

The king was enraged and sent out search parties to arrest Jeremiah and Baruch, but the Lord hid them from him (v. 26). While in hiding, Jeremiah was commanded to take another scroll and work with Baruch to reproduce the original words he had received from the Lord, along with an additional declaration that God would give him (vv. 27-28, 32). Verse 32 reads:

Then Jeremiah took another scroll and gave it to Baruch the scribe,
the son of Neriah, who wrote on it at the instruction of Jeremiah all

the words of the book which Jehoiakim king of Judah had burned in the fire. And besides, there were added to them many similar words.

Commenting on this verse, C. I. Scofield provides this observation as to how the book of Jeremiah came to be in its final form:

This verse explains the arrangement of Jeremiah's prophecy. As the exile came nearer, God commanded Jeremiah to write down the messages that He had already given orally (30:2) and to add to them new divine promises of return from exile and of other blessings in the more distant future (30:3, 10-11). Jehoiakim destroyed Jeremiah's scroll (36:23). God commanded Jeremiah to dictate a new scroll. Jeremiah did so, reproducing the contents of the previous scroll, which probably had been arranged in the order in which God had originally given them. But he added at the proper places certain other inspired discussions of the same subjects (36:32). Later on Jeremiah inserted messages received at later times but logically related to messages previously given, putting them at the appropriate places within the scroll already written [for instance chps 21, 24, 27-29, 32-34. Other messages given after the new scroll was written] were added in the order in which they were received, and these were followed by certain special sections (chps. 45-52). Thus the arrangement of the book is partly according to the time the messages were given, and partly according to the nature of the subject matter.[1]

In his autumn years, Jeremiah had likely accumulated many scrolls documenting various messages he had given throughout his ministry. These he arranged into a final book. In some cases, the Lord provided additional information to be included within the scrolls which had already been written.

Jeremiah began dictating to Baruch, who copied down his words. The new scroll revealed that God had placed a curse on Jehoiakim and his descendants for his arrogance of burning Jeremiah's scroll:

He shall have no one to sit on the throne of David, and his dead body shall be cast out to the heat of the day and the frost of the night. I will punish him, his family, and his servants for their iniquity; and I will bring on them, on the inhabitants of Jerusalem, and on the men of Judah all the doom that I have pronounced against them; but they did not heed (Jer. 36:30-31).

As mentioned previously, Jeremiah's prophecy concerning Jehoiakim is significant because God had promised David that one of his descendants would be on his throne forever (2 Sam. 7:12-16). According to Jeremiah, that descendant could not come through the royal line of Jehoiakim (v. 30). Jehoiachin, the son of Jehoiakim, reigned only three months before being removed by Nebuchadnezzar. Jehoiachin was judged by God for his wickedness and because of his father Jehoiakim's sin of defying God by burning Jeremiah's scroll.

Jeremiah also foretold that Jehoiakim would not have a proper burial, but that his carcass would be cast out on the open ground to rot. It would be exposed to the heat of the day and the frost of the night. The way in which Jehoiakim's body would be discarded was a prophetic analogy of the judgment coming upon his descendants, and, indeed, all the inhabitants of Jerusalem – the city would be destroyed and the rotting bodies of the inhabitants would adorn its ruins (v. 31).

This section of text serves as a warning to all believers not to change or ignore the Word of God. John warned that those who would add or subtract to his book, "The Revelation," would be plagued in life and severely judged in the afterlife (Rev. 22:18-19). However, John also promises a blessing to those who read Revelation and keep its words in integrity (Rev. 1:3). It is part of man's rebel nature to flavor, to change, or to dilute God's Word. Yet, all Scripture is inspired by God and will thus stand the test of time and human manipulation (2 Tim. 3:16). The Lord Jesus said every detail of God's Word will come to pass (Matt. 5:18); may we endeavor to heed God's Word without trying to twist it, flavor it, ignore it, or neglect it.

Meditation

Lord, Thy Word abideth, and our footsteps guideth;
Who its truth believeth light and joy receiveth.
When the storms are o'er us, and dark clouds before us,
Then its light directeth, and our way protecteth.
O that we, discerning, its most holy learning,
Lord, may love and fear Thee, evermore be near Thee!

— Henry Baker

260

The Return of the Chaldeans
Jeremiah 37:1-21

The exact timing of this chapter is unknown, but we do know that Zedekiah was on the throne of Judah and that Jerusalem was under siege by the Babylonians. Because we read that the Egyptian army was nearing Jerusalem in order to confront the Babylonians (v. 5), this chapter was likely written early in the siege, perhaps in 588 B.C. (Jerusalem would later fall in July of 586 B.C.). At any rate, it is clear that Jeremiah 37 occurs prior to Jeremiah 32 (which describes the latter months of the siege), as Jeremiah had not yet been imprisoned (v. 4).

Though Zedekiah had ignored Jeremiah's previous preaching (v. 2), he did send a delegation to Jeremiah to ask him to pray for the situation in Jerusalem (v. 3). Apparently, the Babylonians had lifted their siege in order to engage Pharaoh's approaching army. Perhaps Zedekiah thought that prayers offered by Jeremiah might convince God to grant favor to the Egyptians in battle. If the Egyptians could defeat the Babylonians, Jerusalem and all of Judah would be spared.

Not only did Jeremiah decline to pray for the Egyptians, but he informed Zedekiah that the Egyptians would be soundly defeated and driven back to their homeland. Furthermore, he declared that the Babylonians would return to besiege Jerusalem again and would eventually conquer the city and destroy it by fire (vv. 8-9). Even if Pharaoh should inflict heavy losses upon Nebuchadnezzar's army, nothing would alter God's edict in this matter (v. 10).

Shortly after the Chaldeans departed from Jerusalem to fight Pharaoh's army, Jeremiah embarked on a short journey to his hometown in the land of Benjamin *"to claim his property there among the people"* (vv. 11-12). This is not the same real estate transaction of Jeremiah 32, in which while in prison Jeremiah redeemed his cousin's field; that event had not yet taken place at this

261

time. Rather, it seems that Jeremiah had some money due him and he was going to collect it. However, he did not get past the gate of Benjamin exiting Jerusalem before being detained by Irijah, the captain of the guard. Jeremiah was accused of defecting to the Chaldeans (v. 13), a charge that Jeremiah adamantly denied (v. 14).

In any case, Jeremiah was arrested and brought before the officials, who beat him and imprisoned him in the house of Jonathan, a scribe (v. 15). Jeremiah was in prison for many days before he was summoned to a secret meeting with Zedekiah (vv. 16-17). The king asked Jeremiah, *"Is there any word from the Lord?"* (v. 17). This inquiry seems out of character, as Zedekiah had already rejected Jeremiah's previous prophetic word. It seems the Chaldeans had returned to Jerusalem (v. 19), and Zedekiah was desperate. He hoped for some new word of encouragement from the Lord. Yet, there was no new message; Jeremiah just confirmed what the king had already been told many times. God had not changed His mind – Jerusalem would fall to the Babylonians (v. 17).

Jeremiah defended himself as a prophet of God who served the king by confirming God's word to him. He had not done anything that justified imprisonment (v. 18). The king was sympathetic to Jeremiah's defense and his request not to be returned to the house of Jonathan, lest he die (v. 20). The urgency of the prophet's request would indicate that his living conditions in the house of Jonathan were quite poor. Instead, Zedekiah put Jeremiah in the court of the prison and commanded that he receive a daily piece of bread until the city's resources were gone (v. 21). Though this action would preserve the prophet's life, it highlights how terribly Jeremiah suffered to fulfill his God-ordained ministry.

Peter's exhortations to suffering Jewish Christians six centuries later confirm that God's people who choose to fulfill their calling in Christ will suffer for that commitment: *"Therefore let those who suffer according to the will of God commit their souls to Him in doing good, as to a faithful Creator"* (1 Pet. 4:19). Peter reminded them to follow the example of the Lord Jesus Christ, who was innocent of any wrongdoing but suffered patiently for righteousness (1 Pet. 2:21). Peter declared that God is pleased when we follow His example: *"For what credit is it if, when you are beaten for your faults, you take it patiently? But when you do good and suffer, if you take it patiently, this is commendable before God"* (1 Pet. 2:21). Suffering with the same attitude that Christ demonstrated pleases God the Father. In effect, one is saying, "Lord, this makes no sense to me, but I will bear this trial and allow You to judge the situation and mature me in the process." The wrath of man does not work the righteousness of God (Jas. 1:20); this means that believers would be better served to trust the Lord in such circumstances, rather than their passionate emotions.

We have learned from the life of Jeremiah and writings of Peter that God allows His people to suffer in life, even when they have done nothing wrong. Not only was God interested in dealing with the backsliding Jews, He was also intent on growing Jeremiah's own faith and spiritual maturity. And, James tells us, there are certain aspects of our faith which cannot be strengthened without enduring fiery trials. The virtue of patience is added by fire to our spiritual endurance and enhances our ability to serve Christ – that is, if we allow the Lord to have His way with us in the difficulties of our lives (Jas. 1:2-3).

During hard times, remembering God's promises will be a rich source of encouragement. One of these promises is that the Lord will never leave, nor forsake the believer (Heb. 13:5). He also will not allow us more testing than we can bear without providing grace or a way of escape (1 Cor. 10:13). Paul understood this promise to be true and sought to remind others of it. To the suffering Christians at Thessalonica he wrote, *"He who calls you is faithful, who also will do it"* (1 Thess. 5:24); and to Timothy he said, *"If we are faithless, He remains faithful; He cannot deny Himself"* (2 Tim. 2:13). This type of true and living trust in God repels doubt.

Paul also encouraged the Thessalonians to *"comfort the feebleminded, support the weak"* (1 Thess. 5:14). Often the faith of others is needed to strengthen the fainthearted (Heb. 11). Consequently, not only is the "shield of faith" a necessary part of a believer's spiritual armor but it can also be used to assist other believers to stand fast in the faith also (Eph. 6:16). The Romans used a leather-covered wooden shield (about four feet high and two feet wide) which could be connected on either side with the shields of other soldiers to create an impenetrable wall against incoming fiery darts and arrows. There is strength in numbers, and the faith of the many can "pull up" those wobbly-kneed believers who are stumbling under crushing loads (Gal. 6:2). Christians need each other, and we need each other's faith to carry on boldly for the Lord. We all suffer at times with mental weakness. Doubts pour over us like a flood. But praise God for those who will come alongside and lift our heads heavenward. Paul was one such person. He was put behind prison bars, but his faith could not be constrained. As a result, others were *"much more bold to speak the word without fear"* (Phil. 1:14). May our faith be focused on Christ and be a benefit to His body – the Church.

Although Charles Haddon Spurgeon is well known as the "Prince of Preachers," very little is said of his wife Susanna, who suffered many physical trials for nearly thirty years of her life. Once she wrote:

> At the close of a dark and gloomy day, I lay resting on my couch as the deeper night drew on ... and some of the darkness seemed to have entered into my soul. Vainly I tried to see the hand which I knew held mine, and guided my fog-enveloped feet along a steep and slippery path of suffering. "Why does my Lord ... so often send sharp and bitter pain? Why does He permit lingering weakness to hinder the sweet service I long to render?" For a while silence reigned, broken only by the crackling of the oak log burning in the fireplace. Suddenly I heard a sweet, soft musical note, like a robin beneath my window. Yet there was no robin. "It comes from the log on the fire," my friend exclaimed. The fire was letting loose the imprisoned music from the old oak's inmost heart! The oak had stored up the song in the days when all was well with him, but it took the flames of the fire to consume away the calluses of age to let it out again.[1]

Yes, dear beloved, *"count it all joy when you fall into various trials, knowing that the testing of your faith produces patience"* (Jas. 1:2-3). God is faithful and will remain faithful. Faith that is not tested will not be trusted when the trials come. The difficulties of life can draw us closer to God, make our character more like Christ's, and release a song of praise to Him from our hearts. Do not waste a good problem!

Meditation

Trials dark on every hand, and we cannot understand,
All the ways that God could lead us to that blessed promised land;
But He guides us with His eye, and we'll follow till we die,
For we'll understand it better by and by.

Temptations, hidden snares often take us unawares,
And our hearts are made to bleed for a thoughtless word or deed;
And we wonder why the test when we try to do our best,
But we'll understand it better by and by.

— Charles Tindley

Sunk in Mire
Jeremiah 38:1-28

The events of this chapter detail what are likely the harshest circumstances that Jeremiah had to endure during his entire ministry. Food stores in Jerusalem were gone and resentment against God's prophet was immense. These were the last days of siege; Jerusalem would fall into Babylonian hands in the very next chapter.

Having been removed from the house of Jonathan as he requested, Jeremiah enjoyed a certain amount of liberty while being confined to the courtyard of the prison. It is evident that he could preach God's Word to anyone who would listen, and he did just that. However, one day four high-ranking officials overheard Jeremiah speaking to the people (v. 1). He was telling them that unless they abandoned Jerusalem they would lose their lives; instead of resisting Nebuchadnezzar, they should surrender to him (vv. 2-3).

The officials were offended by this message and immediately informed Zedekiah that Jeremiah was sowing seeds of rebellion among the people. The conditions under the siege were terrible, and they argued that Jeremiah's message could easily lead to mayhem. The officers requested that Jeremiah be silenced by death to ensure he would no longer dishearten the people (v. 4). The king gave permission for the officials to do with Jeremiah as they pleased; he would not intervene (v. 5). By this time, Zedekiah was nothing but a political figurehead – Nebuchadnezzar controlled the area beyond the walls of Jerusalem, and within the city, officials plotted together to influence his decisions.

Having obtained the king's permission, the officials sought to murder Jeremiah. Apparently, they thought that death by the sword would be too swift; they wanted the prophet to suffer for a while before he died. There was a cistern in the courtyard of the guard. Cisterns in the city were usually cut into rock formations to collect rain water in the winter months, which could then be stored for summer usage. Albert Barnes notes the sophistication of the subterranean water network in Jerusalem at that time:

> Every house in Jerusalem was supplied with a subterranean cistern, so well constructed that the city never suffered in a siege from want of water. So large were they that when dry they seem to have been used for prisons (Zech. 9:11).[1]

The long drought had caused this cistern to dry up – there was only mud left in it. The cistern must have been deep as Jeremiah was lowered down into it by ropes (v. 6). Jeremiah sunk down in the mire. A human being would not live long in these conditions. With the cool mud and damp, chilly air siphoning off Jeremiah's body heat, hypothermia could result in a matter of hours. If the mud was not very deep, Jeremiah might have lived for a few days but eventually would die of dehydration and starvation.

Thankfully, an Ethiopian eunuch in the king's house called Ebedmelech heard of Jeremiah's plight, had pity for Jeremiah, and petitioned the king for his life (vv. 7-8). Ebedmelech may not have been this man's actual name; Ebedmelech literally means "servant of the king." This situation must have unfolded near the fall of Jerusalem, for the eunuch states that there was no more bread in Jerusalem (v. 9). After learning what his officials had done to Jeremiah, the king changed his mind (again) and sent thirty men with Ebedmelech to retrieve Jeremiah from the cistern (v. 10). Whether the king was moved by pity or guilt, we do not know, but H. A. Ironside makes the following observation about Zedekiah's erratic behavior:

> Again, Zedekiah, a typical changeling, whose mind is controlled by the last man who gains his ear, reverses his judgment. Ebed-melech is commanded, "Take from hence thirty men with thee, and take up Jeremiah the prophet out of the dungeon, before he die" (ver. 10). The king makes no confession of sin in thus having treated Jehovah's messenger; nor is there a word of apology to the prophet for the indignities so unrighteously heaped upon him after his pledged word as to provision for his comfort.[2]

On their way to the pit, Ebedmelech stopped at the king's house, located under the treasury, to obtain some old rags and worn-out garments (v. 11). These were lowered down to Jeremiah by cords. He was told to put them under his arms to reduce the rubbing of the cords when they lifted him to safety (v. 12).

Ebedmelech provides us with a good lesson in the practical care of God's people. Often when someone is in distress we want to do something before we fully think through the situation. We need to consider what is best for the person in the difficult situation. The lesson to be learned from Ebedmelech's example is that wisdom is required to minimize further hurt to the individual we desire to assist. He could have come to the cistern with ropes alone and rescued Jeremiah, but the prophet would have likely been injured in the process. Instead, Ebedmelech considered the situation and thought ahead, bringing padding to prevent the rope from chafing the prophet as he was extricated from the pit. A little forethought by Ebedmelech accomplished the task at hand in a way Jeremiah would most appreciate.

After being saved from the cistern, Jeremiah was held in the court of the prison (v. 13). Zedekiah sought a private meeting with Jeremiah in the third entrance of the house of the Lord (perhaps a corridor between the temple and the king's palace). The king wanted Jeremiah to reveal to him everything he knew about their present situation and to hold nothing back (v. 14). Although Jeremiah knew that his counsel would be wasted on the king because he would not heed it, he willingly told the king what he requested under the condition that Zedekiah take an oath to spare his life (v. 15). In response, Zedekiah swore that he would not put him to death nor hand him over to the officials again (v. 16).

Jeremiah repeated his previous "surrender and live, resist and die" message. God would keep Jerusalem from being burned and the king's family alive only if Zedekiah surrendered to Nebuchadnezzar. The king told Jeremiah that he could not surrender because he would be ill-treated by the Jews who had already joined the ranks of the Babylonians (v. 19). No doubt he feared these Jews would avenge themselves for past atrocities committed by the king. Jeremiah informed the king that God would not permit that to happen if he surrendered to the Babylonian army (v. 20). The prophet further warned the king that if he chose not to surrender, he would suffer the very ridicule that he wanted to avoid, for when he was brought out before Nebuchadnezzar as a prisoner, even his own harem would scoff at him (v. 22).

What would these women say? They would mock the king's gullibility; he listened to his supposed friends and trusted advisers who only led him into the pit of despair and who then deserted him there (v. 23). The king would watch his wives and children being led away by the Babylonians, and Jeremiah promised the king that he himself would not escape. Zedekiah commanded Jeremiah not to reveal to anyone else what he had told him (v. 24). As the two men may have been seen together by spies, Zedekiah gave Jeremiah an alibi to protect his life. This was necessary as the Judean princes were attempting to maintain a unified front against Nebuchadnezzar and were on the lookout for potential defectors. Perhaps, Zedekiah was trying to protect himself from suspicion as well. If questioned by any official, Jeremiah was to say that he had begged the king not to send him back to the house of Jonathan. Since Jeremiah had requested this of Zedekiah already (37:20), the prophet could use the alibi with a clear conscience.

Zedekiah's insight paid off, because some officials did learn of this secret meeting and inquired of Jeremiah concerning its purpose (v. 27). As a prophet of God, they would expect Jeremiah to tell the truth, and since no one else had heard the private conversation, they accepted Jeremiah's version of the story. Jeremiah remained a prisoner in the courtyard of the guard until Jerusalem fell (v. 28). Zedekiah, knowing the truth, failed to heed it because he feared men more than God; he was eventually brought low before the Babylonians.

Proverbs 29:25 reads, *"The fear of man brings a snare, but whoever trusts in the Lord shall be safe."* The real driving force behind the *fear of man* is what the writer of Hebrews describes as the *"fear of death,"* although the writer then acknowledges that Christ has released *"those who through fear of death were all their lifetime subject to bondage"* (Heb. 2:15-16). The fear of man is rooted in the dread of personal injury. Why did the Pharisees fear arresting Jesus Christ? It was not because they thought He was the Son of God, but rather because they feared a revolt of the people, which might do them harm (Matt. 21:26, 46).

The Lord Jesus said that believers should not fear anyone or anything but God Himself (Matt. 10:28). As the believer learns to fear and respect only the Lord, his or her mind is liberated to serve God as he or she is motivated by love. This occurs because *"there is no fear in love; but perfect love casts out fear, because fear involves torment. But he who fears has not been made perfect in love"* (1 Jn. 4:18). The judgment of our sin is past; consequently, believers are secure in Christ forever. In recognition of this, Christians are propelled to service not by a spirit of fear but out of love for the Lord; this gives our service value. While Christians should live in such a way as to not offend God's holy nature (Heb. 12:28), it is also understood that because Christ was judicially punished for their sins, they have eternal life in Him (John 10:28). World religions motivate their captives to serve their flawed agendas through fear tactics (e.g. the threat of eternal punishment), but this is not God's way.

It was not until Peter had settled the "death question" that he was made useful for the kingdom of God. He had forsaken all for the Lord (his occupation, his family, his home, etc.), but Peter learned on the night the Lord was arrested that this was not enough to live for the Lord. It seems Peter was willing to die for the Lord at the Lord's arrest: Peter risked his life and wielded his sword against overwhelming numbers in a misguided attempt to protect the Lord. Peter did not understand that the Lord needed no bodyguard to ensure His safety, for the arrest and the events that followed were completely in His control. However, only a few hours later, Peter, because of the fear of men, would vehemently deny the Lord Jesus. The lesson Peter would learn that night was that it is harder to live for the Lord than it is to die for Him.

A fearful believer will have a poor testimony for Christ. Peter learned this lesson the hard way, but after being restored to Christ, he preached a message after which 3,000 souls were won to Christ (Acts 2). How about you – are you willing to die to self daily in order to serve the Lord, or will you serve men because you fear them more than you reverence Christ? Joshua's appeal to the Lord's people 3,500 years ago is still valid today:

Now therefore, fear the Lord, serve Him in sincerity and in truth, and put away the gods which your fathers served.... But as for me and my house, we will serve the Lord (Josh. 24:14-15).

Until a believer settles the death question and resolves to die daily for Christ, he or she will find it difficult to live for Christ. When dictators die, their rule abruptly ends, but when Christians die, their reign begins! In effect, the believer who dies daily to live out the life of Christ is training for reigning.

Meditation

This Lamb is Christ, the soul's great Friend,
The Lamb of God, our Saviour;
Him God the Father chose to send
To gain for us His favor.
"Go forth, My Son," the Father saith,
"And free men from the fear of death,
From guilt and condemnation.
The wrath and stripes are hard to bear,
But by Thy Passion men shall share
The fruit of Thy salvation."

— Paul Gerhardt

271

Jerusalem Falls
Jeremiah 39:1-18

The fall and destruction of Jerusalem during the Babylonian invasion is one of the darkest pages of Jewish history. The elite social class and much of the general population were massacred, the city and temple burned, wells plugged up, vineyards destroyed, fields strewn with rocks. The entire region was decimated. The fortunate ones were hauled off to Babylon as slaves; the less fortunate were left to fend for themselves in an ongoing struggle for survival. The latter group was comprised of those who had previously defected to the Babylonians and the poor (vv. 9-10).

Chapter 39 brings to a climax all of Jeremiah's previous prophetic messages. The long-suffering patience of God is given over to righteous indignation. The glory of the Lord departs from the temple and Jerusalem. The city now falls into the hands of the Gentiles and is slated for destruction. Although the word "Jerusalem" means "the foundation of peace," perhaps no other city on earth has had such a long history of tribulation, tragedy, and sorrow as it has, a fact that clearly contradicts its name.

Jeremiah records when the siege of Jerusalem began (in the tenth month of the ninth year of Zedekiah's reign; v. 1), and when it ended (the ninth day of the fourth month of the eleventh year of Zedekiah; v. 2). The siege had lasted for two and a half years (i.e., if the years relate to Tishri and the months to Nisan). Verse 3 identifies several of Nebuchadnezzar's chief officers present at the time Jerusalem was captured. One officer was Nebo-Sarsekim. The record of this name is quite significant because in 2007, a Babylonian financial account was found among the British Museum's collection of 130,000 Assyrian cuneiform tablets, which documents the payment of 0.75 kg of gold to the temple in Babylon by Nebo-Sarsekim. The tablet is dated to the 10th year of the reign of Nebuchadnezzar II, 595 B.C., several years before the siege of Jerusalem. Jeremiah 39:3 identifies Nebo-Sarsekim as one of Nebuchadnezzar's generals present at the fall of Jerusalem in 586 B.C. Michael Jursa, an Assyriologist professor from Vienna, called the tablet the most important find in Biblical archaeology in one hundred years.[1] The fact that Nebo-Sarsekim lived at this time confirms this detail recorded by Jeremiah and is yet another indication of the reliability of Scripture.

When Zedekiah saw that the city was falling into Babylonian hands, he marshaled what soldiers he had left and fled eastward from the city (v. 4). As Jeremiah had already predicted, he did not escape, but was captured in the plains of Jericho and brought before the Babylonian king (v. 5). With Zedekiah watching, Nebuchadnezzar had the nobles of Judah executed and then he slew all of Zedekiah's sons (v. 6). This horrific scene would be the last thing Zedekiah would witness, for his eyes were then put out, and he was chained and taken to Babylon (v. 7). The rebels had hoped that God would do better than what He said He would do, and that they would somehow be spared on judgment day. Many today are hoping for the same impossibility, for what God speaks is a mere reflection of who He is – He cannot compromise His holiness.

The walls of Jerusalem, the royal palace, the houses of the people, and the temple were burned (v. 8). The intense heat crumbled the stone walls and consumed the cedar framings. Nebuchadnezzar did provide the impoverished of the land with a few fields and vineyards to help sustain them, but generally speaking, all agriculture in Judah ceased (v. 10). The land would now enjoy seventy years of rest to compensate for all the Sabbath years the Jews had ignored. The destruction of Jerusalem marked the beginning of a new era called *"the times of the Gentiles"* (Luke 21:24). This period of time continues even now, for although the Jews gained independence in May 1948 after 2,600 years of Gentile rule, they are still in a constant state of war with Gentiles. Daniel said that this would be the case until the Tribulation Period when at the battle of Armageddon, the *"the times of the Gentiles"* will end (Dan. 9:27; Luke 21:24; Rev. 11:2). The Lamb shall return from heaven to be the Victor and establish His covenant people in His presence forever.

Liberation day finally came to Jeremiah. He was set free from the courtyard prison and entrusted into the care of Nebuzaradan, the captain of the guard, by Nebuchadnezzar himself (v. 11). The captain was to serve Jeremiah and protect him from harm (v. 12). This open-ended, good-will gesture would allow Jeremiah to minister to the surviving Jews as he saw fit. To ensure that Jeremiah was well cared for, the captain entrusted him to the newly-appointed Jewish governor of the land, Gedaliah. Gedaliah would be the liaison between the Babylon authorities and the Jewish people. Jeremiah was free to move among the people and attend to their spiritual needs (v. 14). What would Jeremiah's message be to the surviving, but disheartened, remnant? The answer, as H. A. Ironside explains, is a timeless one:

> There is no day so dark but that the Lord will be the light of every soul that ceases from man and turns to Himself; no sorrow so great but that fellowship with Him will sweeten the bitter waters. In every trial He is near; in every hour of discouragement and gloom He abideth faithful still –"He cannot deny Himself." The little remnant left in the land might seem to be bereft of all that could make life worth living. But they had Himself, and they could call upon His name, knowing that if He had been faithful to His own holy character in chastening them for their sin, now bowels of mercy were moved for them when, in lowliness of mind and confession of their iniquities, they sought His face.[2]

When all else is lost in life, the believer still has the Lord and that makes life worth living!

Apparently, just before Jerusalem fell, Jeremiah had received a word from the Lord concerning Ebedmelech, the Ethiopian eunuch who risked his life to save Jeremiah from the cistern (38:7-12). The Lord told Jeremiah to pronounce a blessing upon him. Ebedmelech was not to fear the Babylonians, for God would not allow them to take his life (v. 17). Because he had acted bravely to do what was right, he demonstrated faith in the Lord and his life would be his reward (v. 18). Ebedmelech had been faithful to the Lord and the Lord rewarded him, and this the Lord promises to do for all those who are faithful to Him (1 Cor. 4:5).

At the Judgment Seat of Christ (2 Cor. 5:10; Rom 14:10-12), every believer will receive or lose rewards for those works done while on earth. Deeds which are done in Christ's strength and for His glory will be rewarded and that which is unprofitable for the kingdom of

God will be burnt up (1 Cor. 3:11-15), and we, when in the presence of Christ, will be glad they were. Therefore, let us not be self-serving, but *"whatever you do, do it heartily, as to the Lord and not to men, knowing that from the Lord you will receive the reward of the inheritance; for you serve the Lord Christ"* (Col. 3:23-24). Pleasing the Lord is the greatest privilege of our new life in Christ!

In this future day, the Lord Jesus Christ will judge His saints and reward them for their honorable service to Him. Besides those resounding words that every believer longs to hear, *"Well done, My good and faithful servant"* (Matt. 25:21-23), there are various rewards that the faithful will receive at the Judgment Seat of Christ. These rewards are called crowns, and though there are likely many other types of crowns, five are specifically mentioned in Scripture:

The Crown of Glory will be given to church elders who shepherd well (1 Pet. 5:4).

The Crown of Life will be given to those who endure trials because they love the Lord (Jas. 1:12).

The Crown of Rejoicing will be given to those who were soul-winners for Christ (1 Thess. 2:19; Phil 4:1); this crown may be more encompassing than this, such as reward for spiritual growth.

The Crown of Righteousness will be given to those who long for His appearing (2 Tim. 4:8).

The Incorruptible Crown will be given to those who control fleshly desires through the Holy Spirit (1 Cor. 9:25).

The rewards that are earned during this lifetime provide the believer with a greater appreciation for the Lord, a greater capacity to worship Him throughout eternity, and, indeed, a greater capability to enjoy heaven (Rev. 4:11). Paul clearly taught that some believers will shine more brightly than others in their eternal glorified bodies; this is a greater, an earned reflective glory of Christ (1 Cor. 15:40-42). What is truly done for Christ now translates into an eternal weight (or measure) of glory (2 Cor. 4:17). It is a common axiom, which C. T. Studd popularized, but believers should never grow weary of it: "Only one life and 'twill soon be past; only what's done for Christ will last." Believer, will your life count for eternity?

Meditation

Only one life to offer – take it, dear Lord, I pray,
Nothing from Thee withholding, Thy will I now obey.
Thou who hast freely given, Thine all in all for me,
Claim this life for Thine own, to be used, my Saviour,
Every moment for Thee.

— Avis B. Christiansen

The Land is Before You
Jeremiah 40:1-16

This chapter provides us with further details concerning Jeremiah's release from prison. Initially, he had been chained and led away with other captives to Ramah (v. 1). However, after being recognized, he was freed. Nebuchadnezzar was familiar with Jeremiah's prophecies (39:11-14); perhaps defecting Jews had informed him of the prophet's messages of Babylonian victory. Jeremiah's ministry had been validated when God had punished the Jews for their sins against Him, just as Jeremiah had prophesied. In any case, Nebuchadnezzar knew that Jeremiah was not a part of the rebellion against him. Consequently, the captain of the guard, Nebuzaradan, confirmed this understanding to Jeremiah, and released him (vv. 2-3). This captain then offered Jeremiah safe passage to Babylon under his care if the prophet desired to accompany him; however, if Jeremiah thought it best to remain in Judah, the captain told him, *"the land is before you"* (v. 4). Jeremiah was free to stay.

Jeremiah did decide to remain in the land. Nebuzaradan responded by providing Jeremiah with provisions and a gift before he himself departed to Mizpah. Following the destruction of Jerusalem, Mizpah became the new administrative center for the region. The captain, Nebuzaradan, also encouraged Jeremiah to live with the newly-appointed governor Gedaliah, who could supply Jeremiah's necessities and provide him with protection (v. 5). Jeremiah followed this advice and took up residence with Gedaliah (v. 6).

Gedaliah was a godly man who diligently worked to restore order to the land. Generally speaking, after a war is lost, there will be those who refuse to surrender their cause and who will continue to fight. Such was the case in Judah; bands of Jewish soldiers not captured by the Babylonians had established an underground resistance movement which threatened the security of the region. The governor knew that the last thing his people needed at that point was for Nebuchadnezzar to return to Judah with his army to root out these rebels.

To avoid the necessity of this, Gedaliah's solution was to offer amnesty for all soldiers who would lay down their arms and willingly submit to Babylonian rule (vv. 7-9). A number of notable soldiers met with Gedaliah to discuss the matter: *"Then they came to Gedaliah to Mizpah, Ishmael the son of Nethaniah, and Johanan and Jonathan the sons of Kareah, and Seraiah the son of Tanhumeth, and the sons of Ephai the Netophathite, and Jezaniah the son of the Maacathite, they and their men"* (v. 8). He asked that they, instead of pursuing a lost cause, help their people by gathering wine, oil, and summer fruits from the fruit trees and vineyards that Nebuchadnezzar had provided (v. 10). In fact, the governor offered the same amnesty to Jews hiding in Moab, Ammon, and Edom (v. 11). The response to this offer was well-received and many Jews ceased fighting and hiding, and turned their energies to gathering provisions for the winter months ahead.

Under Gedaliah's leadership the situation in Judah was improving. There was civil order, adequate food supplies, and no threat of extermination. However, not everyone approved of these social advances; in fact, Gedaliah was made aware of a threat upon his life. The fact that Johanan and the other captains of the soldiers informed Gedaliah of this plot is an endorsement of Gedaliah's character (v. 13). At first, they had resisted his authority, but they had been won over by his character and good leadership. These men were genuinely concerned for the one who had helped them and blessed them by his leadership.

The governor was told that King Baalis of the Ammonites had hired Ishmael to kill him; this Ishmael was the same prominent soldier who was among the delegation to discuss terms with Gedaliah, and who had received amnesty at his hand (v. 14). Such treachery seemed unlikely to Gedaliah. The Ammonites were in alliance with Judah; why would they want to murder him? It appears that the Ammonites were trying to buy more time to better prepare themselves against the Babylonians. Nebuchadnezzar had moved his army away from Jerusalem in order to lay siege on the city of Tyre in the north (Ezek. 29:17-18). After the fall of Tyre, he would most assuredly attack Ammon next. However, if there was social unrest in Judah, Nebuchadnezzar would first need to redeploy his army to secure

Jewish obedience (v. 15). In effect, this would tie up the Babylonian army for some time, giving Ammon a reprieve from attack. The king of Ammon must have concluded that the best means of creating chaos in Judah was to kill the man who had brought order to the region – Gedaliah.

Gedaliah dismissed the rumor (v. 16). However, Johanan, another captain who had previously met with Gedaliah to discuss terms of amnesty, clearly considered it a real threat. He met privately with the governor again, even volunteering to assassinate Ishmael himself to ensure that Gedaliah would suffer no harm at his hand. The governor was an honorable man and, not believing Ishmael to be treacherous, rejected this plan. Unfortunately, his disregard for this warning would lead to his death in the next chapter.

This situation highlights the fact that there was a "mixed multitude" in Judah at this time – some were faithful to the Lord and others were not. Such was ever the case in Israel's history, since the time they left Egypt under Moses' leadership. Two expressions describe the group leaving Egypt; they were *"a mixed multitude"* (Ex. 12:38), and they were *"the hosts of the Lord"* (Ex. 12:41). The Jews did not leave as "the hosts of Israel," for they had been purchased by blood; they were the Lord's possession. Unfortunately, the Jews did not depart from Egypt alone, for they came out as *"a mixed multitude."* It was this devilish contingency that continually stirred up the Lord's people to murmur and complain against the Lord (Num. 11:4).

Scripture represents Satan both as a threatening lion who is ready to devour God's people (1 Pet. 5:8), and as a cunning serpent who endeavors to deceive and trick them (Gen. 3:1). Through the ten plagues and the blood of the Passover lamb, the strong and brutal lion in Egypt had been thoroughly conquered by Jehovah. Defeated, the enemy now slithered along in the shadows of the departing nation; if he could not keep God's people in Egypt (the world), he would seek to ensure Egypt keeps to them. Through the "mixed multitude," Satan would corrupt the Israelites from within. C. I. Scofield identifies the following correlation with the Church today:

This mixed multitude, similar to unconverted church members in the present age, was a source of weakness and division then as now

(Num. 11:4-6). There had been a manifestation of divine power, and men were drawn to it without a change of heart (Luke 14:25-27).[1]

The "mixed multitude" caused the Israelites to murmur against the Lord and to doubt His goodness, from the time of Moses to the time of Jeremiah. Their presence in Judah at this time would cause division and disorder through the murder of Gedaliah. These ambassadors of evil are causing the same ill effects in the Church presently. Paul was fully aware of this ongoing threat in his day. After summoning the elders from Ephesus to meet with him at Miletus, Paul warned them of two dangers facing their local church:

> *Therefore take heed to yourselves and to all the flock, among which the Holy Spirit has made you overseers, to shepherd the church of God which He purchased with His own blood. For I know this, that after my departure savage wolves will come in among you, not sparing the flock. Also from among yourselves men will rise up, speaking perverse things, to draw away the disciples after themselves* (Acts 20:28-31).

Paul warns that if the local church is composed of a "mixed company," there will certainly be trouble. Opposition to the things of God is expected from those outside the local church, but when wolves incognito suddenly rise up from within the assembly, the attack and devastating consequences are often unanticipated. A wolf masquerading in sheep's skin is often hard to spot until it is too late. One matter is certain; a child of the devil in the midst of God's people will tend to stir up trouble in the local assembly. He or she will rob the assembly of peace, and try to introduce doctrines and practices which are unbecoming of God's people. Satan's goal is the same as it was in Moses' and Jeremiah's days: entice the flesh of God's people and draw them away from serving their God.

Gedaliah was naïve to the situation of his day. He could not believe that an individual who had received his help would reward him with such treachery. Gedaliah did not know how desperately wicked the human heart is (17:6), but he would soon learn how destructive the "mixed multitude" could be.

This is a lesson that elders of the local church should heed; they cannot relax in their care of God's sheep. Satan will continue to attempt to undermine any true work of God. For example, in Genesis 3, Satan attacked the word of God, in Job 1, Satan attacked the child of God, and in Matthew 4, Satan attacked the Son of God. Satan may use his undercover agents within or invoke a direct frontal assault on your church meeting. Until the Lord's return for the Church, the "mixed multitude" will always be among us, constantly looking for ways to wreak havoc among God's people. Beloved of the Lord, be alert and be constantly aware of this threat!

Meditation

And truly it is a most glorious thing
Thus to hear men pray and God's praises sing,
O how great comfort is it now to see—
The churches to enjoy full liberty.
And to have the Gospel preached here with power,
And such wolves repelled as all would else devour.

— William Bradford

Gedaliah Murdered
Jeremiah 41:1-18

The fall of Jerusalem in chapter 39 and the death of godly
Gedaliah in this chapter mark two solemn events in Jewish history.
Gedaliah had brought order to a chaotic situation. He had the unique
ability to unify people with different ideologies and enable them to
work together for the common good. His death led to many
unfortunate consequences.

The exact timing of the circumstances of Jeremiah 41 is
questionable. Jeremiah identifies that Gedaliah was murdered in the
seventh month, but the year is not mentioned (v. 1). We do know that
Nebuchadnezzar did return to Jerusalem in the twenty-third year of
his reign (i.e. 583 to 582 B.C.) and took 745 Jewish captives back to
Babylon (52:30). It is speculated that Gedaliah's murder would have
caused civil unrest in Judah which demanded the Babylonian king's
attention and would have provoked him to take this action. If this is
true, then Gedaliah would have governed Judah for three or four years
before being assassinated by Ishmael.

Ishmael and ten of his men came to Gedaliah under a banner of
peace. Gedaliah showed hospitality to his visitors by feeding them. It
was during or after this dinner that Ishmael and his men struck. Not
only did they murder Gedaliah, but they also slew all those in the
banquet hall, including the Babylonian soldiers dispatched to protect
Gedaliah (vv. 2-3; 2 Kgs. 25:25). The slaughter, likely in the evening,
was so complete that it went undetected until the next day (v. 4).

The day after the slaughter, Ishmael met eighty pilgrims coming
from the Northern Kingdom of Israel to Jerusalem with grain and
incense offerings for the Lord (v. 5). Although the temple was
destroyed, the Jews continued to worship at that site. There were three
fall feasts that fell in this seventh month and these Jews were being
obedient to God's Word – they had come in a spirit of brokenness to

worship the Lord. Ishmael and his men feigned to also have contrite spirits and joined the caravan (v. 6). As they walked together, Ishmael offered to take them to Gedaliah. This was an unexpected privilege and the pilgrims agreed. Once they entered Jerusalem, Ishmael and his men robbed and killed seventy of the men (v. 7). The only reason the other ten men were spared is that they bartered for their lives with additional supplies that were hidden in a field and were not within the caravan. Ishmael agreed not to kill them if they led him to the hidden cache of barley, wheat, oil, and honey (v. 8).

The bodies of Gedaliah, his companions, and the seventy men slaughtered the following day were disposed of in a large cistern. King Asa had constructed the cistern 200 years earlier as a defensive installation against the invading armies of Israel under Baasha's command (v. 9). It is unknown how many people in all were butchered in Mizpah by Ishmael and his men. Those who were not murdered were taken captive. This group included the king's daughters, court officials, soldiers, women, children, Baruch (43:3), and also Jeremiah (vv. 10, 16).

When Johanan learned of the slaughter, he mobilized all the men that he could find to pursue Ishmael, who was heading eastward to Ammon (v. 11). Moving prisoners and supplies is slow business and Johanan overtook Ishmael's entourage near the great pool at Gibeon (v. 12). In the confrontation, the captives were secured by Johanan (vv. 13-14). Two of Ishmael's men were captured or killed in the conflict, but Ishmael and eight of his men were able to evade their opponents (v. 15).

Johanan led his men and the liberated group of captives to Geruth Kimham, a town near Bethlehem, about ten miles south of Gibeon (v. 16). It was at this location that the group was able to rest, regroup, and discuss plans for the future. We learn that Johanan feared Nebuchadnezzar's retaliation for the death of his appointed governor Gedaliah, and the captain was determined to run for the shelter of Egypt (vv. 17-18). God's people were in a quandary as to what to do – should they remain in Judah or flee to Egypt? In the next chapter, we will learn that they sought counsel from the Lord. This is always the best course of action when God's written Word does not specifically address the dilemma we are facing.

The child of God is responsible for discerning between what is holy and what is evil, what is wise and what is foolish. What is holy and wise should be obeyed, and what is evil and foolish should be shunned. The matter of discerning between right and wrong behavior is dependent upon knowing the commandments of Scripture. Discerning between what is wise and what is foolish is often more complicated, and requires a knowledge of God's commandments, warnings, principles, promises, and the lessons learned from personal narratives in Scripture. In fact, the Lord addressed the matter of being wise and not foolish much more often than the matter of what is right and what is wrong, though the latter would be included in what is wise and foolish. Gaining discernment of what is wise and what is foolish requires prayer and Bible study, heeding godly counsel, and following the leading of the Holy Spirit in our lives.

Once a believer understands the mind of God in a particular situation, the real test is whether or not he or she will heed it. It is best to trust the Lord, even when we do not understand His ways: *"Oh, the depth of the riches both of the wisdom and knowledge of God! How unsearchable are His judgments and His ways past finding out!"* (Rom. 11:33). As God's way will always be the best path for us to follow in life, it behooves us to pause and seek His guidance when we do not know which way to turn. Such was the dilemma for Johanan and his band of followers. Not knowing what to do, they sought counsel from the One who knows all. But knowledge alone will never foster wise behavior: one must submit to truth to reap its reward.

Meditation

My span of life will soon be done,
The passing moments say;
As lengthening shadows over the mead
Proclaim the close of day.
O that my heart might dwell aloof
From all created things,
And learn that wisdom from above
Whence true contentment springs!

— Maria Cowper

284

Don't Go to Egypt
Jeremiah 42:1-22

After witnessing the Babylonians destroy Jerusalem and Judah as prophesied by Jeremiah, the Jews understood that they were suffering under the chastening hand of God. This realization caused them to petition to Jeremiah to pray to the Lord for guidance as to what they should do (vv. 1-3). Should they flee to Egypt or stay in the land? Jeremiah promised to inform the Jews of all that the Lord would reveal to him (vv. 4-5). He also affirmed the fact that they must obey the word of the Lord, whether they agreed with it or not, in order to obtain His blessing (v. 6).

Ten days later, Jeremiah received an answer to his prayer (v. 7). He summoned all the people together, from the least to the greatest, so that he could tell everyone God's answer at the same time: the Jews were to remain in the land (vv. 8-10). Jeremiah explained that it was God who had brought them down to the low estate they were currently in, and it was He who promised to build them back up again if they remained in Canaan. The people were not to be afraid of the Babylonians if they stayed in Judah (vv. 11-12). However, if they ventured into Egypt, the people were informed that God would not protect them there.

The Jews thought that by going to Egypt they would escape war and hunger (vv. 13-14). However, Jeremiah informed them that if they did choose to depart from the Promised Land, suffering would follow them into Egypt. There they would die either by the sword or by famine or by pestilence (vv. 15-17, 21-22). Furthermore, God promised to pour out His fury upon them if they did not heed His word on this matter (vv. 18-19).

Jeremiah closed his address to the people by reminding them that they were the ones who asked him to seek counsel from the Lord as to what they should do and that they had also agreed to do whatever the

Lord commanded, whether they thought it was the best solution or not (v. 20). Unfortunately, we learn in the next chapter that the people again defied the Lord by journeying to Egypt.

God's people will never solve their problems by diverting into Egypt (a picture of the world); rather, submitting to and trusting in God's Word is what brings direction and blessing. Looking back in Israel's history, we find that both Abram and Isaac thought Egypt offered the best solution to preserve their lives during separate famines. God intervened to keep Isaac in the Promised Land, but Abram would personally learn the practical consequences of descending into Egypt to resolve one's problems.

Not long after arriving in Canaan, Abram was faced with a famine and a choice (Gen. 12:10). Would he remain in the land divinely conferred to him for a possession or abandon it? Would he tarry and seek God's assistance through the trial, or would he seize personal control of the matter and search for help elsewhere? Abram chose to divert into Egypt to alleviate his problem. Egypt is a symbol of the world throughout Scripture. Samuel Ridout comments, "Alas, Abram did as we are all prone to do: he sought relief from all his difficulties, rather than profit by the trial."[1] This is our natural tendency when we experience trials; we want to flee from them, instead of allowing God to have His way in them. David put the matter this way, *"I would hasten my escape from the windy storm and tempest"* (Ps. 55:8). Abram, without God's direction, chose to run from the storm.

Scripture speaks of Abram going *"down"* to Egypt (Gen. 12:10), and when he forsook that land, Scripture speaks of him *"going up out of"* Egypt (Gen. 13:1). When pilgrims of God venture *"down"* into Egypt, a selfish desire to explore the world's system for aid and comfort is represented, while *"coming out"* of Egypt pictures their dependent reliance on God's faithfulness for the same. The specific terms used here reflect the spiritual direction of our lives. Abram had wasted years in Haran and now was set to squander more time in Egypt. Abram, apparently, did not consult God in this matter, and God chose not to intervene until the covenant plan was in jeopardy. Sometimes the best teacher in life is practical experience – failure can lead to understanding. Abram's trip *down* to Egypt would be a costly lesson. The granaries of the earth and manna from heaven are two vastly different spiritual diets – worlds apart!

First, his marriage was adversely affected by the journey. Perhaps Abram noticed lingering stares and admiring glances directed towards his beautiful wife as they journeyed through the promiscuous and pagan population. He had not anticipated this horrible situation and found himself confronted with a decision for which he was unprepared. Often Satan strikes a pernicious blow to God's unguarded servant through forcing quick decisions in the midst of ungodly company. Abram feared that these immoral descendants of Ham would murder him just to have his wife. To save his own neck, Abram was willing to compromise his wife. He simply informed Pharaoh that Sarai was his sister. She was indeed his half-sister, but Abram was implying that she was not his wife. This half-truth was nonetheless a blatant lie. It has been well stated: "When the devil encourages a half-truth, he wants people to believe the wrong half." How important and secure do you think Sarai felt? Her husband was supposed to provide for her and protect her, but instead he allowed her to be inducted into Pharaoh's house. Apparently, instead of defiling her, Pharaoh was considering marrying her. God alone would be the guardian of her purity and honor now.

Second, the pagan culture had a lasting influence on at least one member of his family, Lot. After their trip to Egypt, Lot was not satisfied with the simple life anymore. His mind had become compromised with worldliness, and in Genesis 14 and 19, we learn that his indulgent pursuit of worldliness led his family into moral disaster (2 Pet. 2:7-8).

Third, Abram came out of Egypt with a lot of "stuff" (Gen. 12:16, 13:2). The more stuff believers have, the more opportunities Satan is allowed to entangle and strangle us with things. The Lord strictly taught that His disciples must forsake all to follow Him (Luke 14:33). This was something that the disciples understood was necessary in order to serve Christ effectively, and they sacrificially obeyed (Matt. 4:22; Luke 5:11). Apparently, Abram came out of Egypt with more servants to help him manage all his stuff. There can be little doubt that these individuals brought their own gods with them. The Lord has called us to a life that is good and simple concerning evil (Rom. 16:19), and He asks us to be content with the necessities of life (food, clothing, shelter, etc. – 1 Tim. 6:6-10).

Fourth, Abram likely brought a servant girl named Hagar back with him from Egypt to be his wife's maid. It sounded like a good idea at the time; a young girl around the house could be a big help to Sarai. Yet, if Abram had not assayed into Egypt, there would have been no Hagar to tempt him in the matter of bearing the needed son. This seemingly unpretentious matter led to the unfolding of two nations (Jew and Arab), which have been venomously hostile towards each other ever since the beginning.

Certainly, if Abram had fully known the cost of journeying to Egypt to resolve his problems, he would have chosen to stay in the Promised Land. Believer, it is always better to yield to God's Word and trust our loving heavenly Father with our desperate circumstances, than it is to depend on secular wisdom or our own wherewithal to resolve the trial. Better to allow the Lord to have His way in your storm than to suffer the plagues of Egypt!

Meditation

I long ago left Egypt for the promised land,
I trusted in my Saviour, and to His guiding hand;
He led me out to victory through the great Red Sea,
I sang a song of triumph, and shouted, I am free!

You need not look for me, down in Egypt's sand,
For I have pitched my tent far up in Beulah land;
You need not look for me, down in Egypt's sand,
For I have pitched my tent far up in Beulah land.

— Margaret Harris

Proud Men
Jeremiah 43:1-13

Jeremiah had hardly finished declaring the Word of God when Azariah, Johanan, and other proud men spoke out against the message he had delivered to them (v. 1). They accused Jeremiah of speaking falsely, saying that he was not a prophet of God. Furthermore, they declared the prohibition against sojourning in Egypt was a lie, that God had not given such a command (v. 2). It seems strange that they had recognized Jeremiah as a true prophet in the preceding chapter, but now they rejected him.

These proud men accused Jeremiah's scribe, Baruch, of convincing Jeremiah to lie to them. What Baruch was to gain by this supposed action is not stated; perhaps they thought he was in alliance with the Babylonians. What is known is that these men did not want to be hauled away to Babylon as slaves, or worse, be slain by the Babylonians (v. 3).

Johanan commanded the people to ignore Jeremiah's message (v. 4), then proceeded to gather survivors throughout Judah to embark on a mass reverse exodus to Egypt (v. 5). The number of these refugees seems significant (v. 6), and Jeremiah was consequently forced to accompany these rebels to Egypt. Johanan disobeyed the clear voice of the Lord and led God's people to the city of Tahpanhes (v. 7). It was here that the Lord spoke to Jeremiah again (v. 8).

The prophecy that Jeremiah received pertained to Nebuchadnezzar's invasion of Egypt. What the Jews had tried to escape would follow them. As a symbolic act to get the Jews' attention, Jeremiah gathered several large stones and buried them in the clay under the brick pavement in the courtyard at the entrance of Pharaoh's palace. Pharaoh's main residence at this time was on the island of Elephantie situated in the upper Nile; therefore, the palace in which Jeremiah spoke must have been a lodging for Pharaoh when government matters caused him to visit the city. Jeremiah's stones were to mark the spot where Nebuchadnezzar would erect his throne and spread his royal canopy when he came to attack Egypt.

God would use the king of Babylon to burn Egypt's temples and judge her false gods. Nebuchadnezzar's sword would destroy many, and those fortunate enough to live would be taken to Babylon as captives. Babylon's various conquests are attested to in many books of the Bible (2 Kings, 2 Chronicles, Jeremiah, Ezekiel, and Daniel). What extra-biblical evidence is there that Jeremiah's prophecy concerning the invasion of Egypt actually occurred? Four Babylonian Chronicles were found in 1956 containing historical information dating as far back as 594 B.C. These tablets record the historical events associated with the rise of the Babylonians: the conquest of the Assyrians, Egyptians, and Judah. The Babylonian Chronicles confirm military events such as the battle at Carchemish against Egypt in 605 B.C., as also recorded in Jeremiah 46:2 and 2 Kings 24:7-17.

The Babylonian Chronicles do not verify Jeremiah's prophecy per se, but one fragmentary text has been found among them which states that Nebuchadnezzar invaded Egypt in 568 to 567 B.C.[1] Ezekiel, who was already in Babylon, also predicted that Babylon would invade Egypt. The date of his prophecy is April of 571 B.C., just three or four years before the Babylonian Chronicles state the event occurred (Ezek. 29:17). Both pieces of information do corroborate with Jeremiah's prophecy concerning Babylon's invasion of Egypt. The Lord had provided His people with ample information to do what was right, but proud leaders invariably cause the Lord's people to sin. Such leaders will do charitable acts and ooze flattering words in order to gain the loyalty of others. But in the end, proud and rebellious leaders cause God's people to turn away from Him (Prov. 8:13).

Paul warned his spiritual son Timothy of such false professors who had a form of godliness, but lacked the supernatural power to produce the real thing. People, without spiritual fortitude, engage in religious charades, which excel in leading God's people into folly. Paul provided a graphic character sketch of these people and how believers should react to their doings:

But know this, that in the last days perilous times will come: For men will be lovers of themselves, lovers of money, boasters, proud,

290

blasphemers, disobedient to parents, unthankful, unholy, unloving, unforgiving, slanderers, without self-control, brutal, despisers of good, traitors, headstrong, haughty, lovers of pleasure rather than lovers of God, having a form of godliness but denying its power. And from such people turn away! For of this sort are those who creep into households and make captives of gullible women loaded down with sins, led away by various lusts, always learning and never able to come to the knowledge of the truth (2 Tim. 3:1-7).

Paul then mentioned the names of Pharaoh's magicians, Jannes and Jambres, as examples of men with corrupt minds who resisted God's truth: *"Now as Jannes and Jambres resisted Moses, so do these also resist the truth: men of corrupt minds, disapproved concerning the faith; but they will progress no further, for their folly will be manifest to all, as theirs also was"* (2 Tim. 3:8-9). Paul used Jannes and Jambres as an object lesson to illustrate how people who have only a form of godliness resist divine truth. On this point, C. H. Mackintosh wrote:

> The method in which Jannes and Jambres withstood Moses was simply by imitating, as far as they were able, whatever he [Moses] did… The most satanic resistance to God's testimony in the world is offered by those who, though they imitate the effects of the truth, have but the "form of godliness but denying the power thereof."[2]

Those who have *"a form of godliness but deny its power"* are likened to slithering serpents *"who creep into households and make captives of gullible women loaded down with sins, led away by various lusts"* (2 Tim. 3:6). The threat to believers may come from false teachers embedded in Christendom or canvassing cult members. Many modern cults identify in pretense with the name of Christ, but they deny His Word, degrade His attributes, and lessen His importance as Savior by promoting a *good-works* message for salvation. Often these ambassadors of deception visit during the day when God's appointed protector of the home is absent, and the stress of caring for one's children and the home is at its highest. They slither in and secretly take the gullible captive.

Thankfully, believers do not have to be deceived by the Janneses and Jambreses of the world (i.e. those opposing divine truth). John instructed Christians, *"Believe not every spirit* [teacher]*, but test the spirits whether they are of God"* (1 Jn. 4:1-4). God's people who have a good knowledge of Scripture will be able to recognize and refute error. Besides His Word, God has provided another safeguard for believers so that they should not be deceived by the ensnaring arts of Satan's workers. John informed those to whom he was writing of an anointing that they had received at spiritual rebirth. There is no need to pray for this anointing; every believer has it already. This once received anointing provides the believer with spiritual discernment of what is true and what is false.

> *But you have an anointing from the Holy One, and you know all things* (1 Jn. 2:20-21).

> *These things I have written to you concerning those who try to deceive you. But the anointing which you have received from Him abides in you, and you do not need that anyone teach you; but as the same anointing teaches you concerning all things, and is true, and is not a lie, and just as it has taught you, you will abide in Him* (1 Jn. 2:26-27).

Within each believer is the wherewithal to sense with divine clarity what is of God and what is not. The Word of God guides believers into truth, and their anointing precludes them from embracing alternate versions of it.

Concerning the matter of distinguishing truth from evil deception, Luke endorsed the behavior of the Bereans as a good example to follow: *"These were more noble ... they received the Word with all readiness of mind, and **searched the Scriptures daily**, whether those things were so"* (Acts 17:11; KJV). When they were confronted with the gospel message, they sought to verify or disprove it by investigating Old Testament Scripture. Similarly, every child of God should be a Berean, proving what is true and identifying what is false by exploring the Word of God for answers (2 Tim. 2:15-16). There is no reason to be deceived by proud men who outwardly put on a good show; the Lord guides those who desire to be led. Unfortunately, the Jews followed Johanan to Egypt, instead of abiding with the Lord. Johanan had saved a few Jews from the hand of Ishmael, but now his pride would result in the demise of many. Satan will often feign a retreat in order to lure pride-blinded victims into his clutches.

Meditation

Saviour, I follow on, guided by Thee,
Seeing not yet the hand that leadeth me;
Hushed be my heart and still, fear I no future ill,
Only to do Thy will, my will shall be.

— Charles S. Robinson

Come Home
Jeremiah 44:1-30

The Lord did not want His people in Egypt where they would be further influenced by paganism. In Israel's infancy, Jacob and his family had made their way to Egypt during a severe famine so that all the tribes might be preserved together. Joseph had been sold into slavery through brotherly mischief, but God had protected and blessed him there. In Egypt, the nation would be preserved intact. Later, the Lord chose Moses to deliver the Hebrews from slavery and from Egypt so that they might have unhindered communion with God. After forty years in the wilderness, Joshua led the next generation of Israelites into Canaan to possess the land that had been promised to Abraham 400 years earlier. God promised that He would safeguard the nation in this Promised Land, if they would obey His Law. Yet, in time, the Jews grossly neglected God's Law and had now been punished for doing so.

Evidently a vast numbers of Jews, besides those led by Johanan, had relocated to Egypt just prior to or during the Babylonian invasion. Accordingly, the next message from Jeremiah was addressed to all the Jews who were sojourning in Migdol, Tahpahnes, and Memphis in the north of Egypt, as well as those living in the upper Nile region in the south. We understand that Jeremiah was not only interested in the Jews who had taken up residence in the northern and southern tips of Egypt, but that he was using a literary merism (see Jer. 2:10) to address all the Jews between those regions also. For example, we might use the merism, "We looked high and low," to indicate that we have searched everywhere for something.

Jeremiah reminded the Jews that their recent chastening was for the purpose of driving idolatry from them. But instead of repenting from that sin in Judah, they had fled to Egypt and were burning incense to false gods there. Consequently, they were in imminent danger of being further punished by God. Jeremiah beseeched them to return to the Promised Land and to be restored to Jehovah, who would bless them and protect them there (vv. 2-10). If they remained in Egypt, God would have no choice but to severely punish them by the sword and famine. What they had suffered in Jerusalem they would again experience in Egypt. What would be the consequences of further rebellion? Jeremiah foretold that most of the Jews in Egypt would die and that only a few fugitives would be able to return to Judah afterwards (vv. 11-14).

The Jews rejected Jeremiah's call to repentance; in fact, they blatantly declared that they were not trusting in Jehovah for their provision and protection in Egypt, but rather in the Queen of Heaven. The Queen of Heaven, as discussed in Jeremiah 7, is likely a reference to Ashtoreth, a pagan fertility goddess. Apparently, the Jewish women were honoring her with incense and drink offerings (v. 18). Their husbands refused to put an end to this long-standing practice of idolatry and thus endorsed the practice (vv. 15-19).

God's prophet pleaded with the people to turn from this gross sin, for if they did not, they would receive cursing instead of blessing from God. God had already demonstrated His intolerance for idolatry through severe chastening, and He would continue to scourge His people until they returned to Him (vv. 20-23). The people, however, would not heed the warning. Jeremiah then sarcastically implored them to be faithful to their vows to the Queen of Heaven, so that when judgment came there would be no question that Jehovah was the true God and that His word would stand forever. Again Jeremiah promised these rebellious Jews that nearly all of them would die in Egypt (vv. 24-28).

Throughout the centuries the Jews have demonstrated their propensity to live by sight and not by faith. We repeatedly see them lusting for signs and wonders in order to affirm God's presence and direction (Luke 11:16; 1 Cor. 1:22). In this case, Jeremiah obliged them with a sign: Pharaoh Hophra would be dethroned and handed over to his enemies, just as Zedekiah had been turned over to Nebuchadnezzar (vv. 29-30). According to the historian Herodotus, Pharaoh Hophra lost his throne in 570 B.C. after one of his generals, Amasis, staged a successful coup. With most of the army with Amasis, Pharaoh was defeated in battle and imprisoned. Later Amasis released Hophra to suffer the fury of the people; he was strangled to death. The timing of this incident, along with the prophecy of Nebuchadnezzar's invasion of Egypt (Ezek. 29:17), would substantiate that Jeremiah's sojourn in Egypt took place somewhere within the timeframe of 571 to 582 B.C.

It was unfortunate that the Jews would not heed Jeremiah's warnings. It provoked God to demonstrate that He would rather see His covenant people die than bowing to pagan gods. He had reserved for them a great inheritance in the Promised Land and, thus, could not tolerate their excursion in a pagan land. Those who survived His wrath would be chastened back to His land of testimony.

God's adverse attitude towards Egypt and its pagan culture was clearly demonstrated during Moses' encounters with Pharaoh centuries earlier. After God had punished Egypt with four plagues, Pharaoh agreed to allow the Hebrews to worship their God, but only if they remained in Egypt. Moses declined the offer. There were several problems with this proposition. First, it was not what God had commanded. It is not the dictates of a religious system or a secular movement which regulates the believer's worship and service, but the authority of God's Word. Moses would not compromise God's command on this matter and neither should the Church – the Bible is the Church's worship manual and the Holy Spirit its Leader.

Second, sacrificing animals in Egypt would create a problem for the Hebrews. The Egyptians thought many animals represented deities. For example, the Egyptians worshipped *Apis* – the sacred bull – as one of their premiere deities. If the Hebrews started sacrificing bullocks as burnt offerings to Jehovah, there would be a national riot, resulting in harm to the unarmed Hebrews.

Third, and most importantly, if they remained in Egypt, they would have to sacrifice to Jehovah the very objects of abomination, the animals which the Egyptians worshipped as gods. Worship influenced by paganism would be an affront to the God of the Hebrews. Consequently, Pharaoh's attempt to hoodwink the Jews to worship their God in Egypt failed.

Satan uses this same tactic today to convince the saved that it is acceptable to worship God in a doctrinally corrupt church. As foretold in Scripture, in the latter days of the Church Age, Satan will reside comfortably in various branches of Christendom (Matt. 13:32). Paul stated that there will be great apostasy in the professing Church just prior to the appearing of the Antichrist (2 Thess. 2:3-4).

But just as a departure from truth characterizes the false church, Spirit-led worship founded upon revealed truth is a mark of the true Church (John 4:23-24). The Holy Spirit guides believers into truth (John 16:13-14). On the other hand, Satan exercises his delegated authority to promote the corruption of truth. The Lord Jesus plainly acknowledged this fact while speaking to the Pharisees, who were the leaders of religious corruption in Christ's day:

> *You are of your father the devil, and the desires of your father you want to do. He was a murderer from the beginning, and does not stand in the truth, because there is no truth in him. When he speaks a lie, he speaks from his own resources, for he is a liar and the father of it* (John 8:44).

It is a pagan, under Satan's control, who initiates worship in and of himself. However, it is the Holy Spirit, not any human, who is to be the "worship leader" in the local assembly; His role is to guide believers into an ever deeper understanding of the truth concerning the Lord Jesus and the overall greatness and goodness of God. Only through Spirit-led worship, which will be completely founded in divine truth, can the believer offer any acceptable sacrifice of praise unto God.

Egypt was under the curse of God; the children of Israel had to come out from that which was corrupt and stand on holy ground with the Lord before they could offer acceptable worship to Him. Christ, speaking to His disciples, acknowledged that the same truth would apply to the Church: *"If you were of the world, the world would love its own. Yet because you are not of the world, but I chose you out of the world, therefore the world hates you"* (John 15:19-20). The believer has been called out of Egypt, and the Lord hates to see what is of Egypt in the believer's life (Jas. 4:4). Nothing has changed since the days of Moses or Jeremiah. God hates paganism and worldliness, because these oppose His order, His character, and His veneration.

Meditation

It was the Lord of hosts that led us out of Egypt's sand;
And He led us through the Red Sea by His mighty hand,
Never halting in the wilderness, but His command
Gave assurance we were able to possess the land.

When we crossed the river Jordan, in the land we found:
Wine and oil and milk and honey, richest fruits abound;
Sparkling fountains, and the showers come upon the ground;
We are able, Hallelujah! Let God's praise resound.

There's no thirsting for old Egypt, since we're in this way,
And we care not what the critics or the ten spies say;
For the land abounds in plenty, and we're here to stay,
Won't you come and join us, brother, enter in today?

— Kittie Suffield

Beware of Self-Seeking
Jeremiah 45:1-5

The events of this chapter correlate with those of Jeremiah 36. It was the fourth year of King Jehoiakim's reign and Jeremiah was busy dictating God's Word to Baruch who was recording it on a scroll (v. 1). Jehoiakim would later burn this scroll, which caused Jeremiah and Baruch to repeat the tedious exercise of writing God's messages to His people on a second scroll.

Apparently, Baruch was greatly discouraged by the contents of the scroll. God's severe punishment of His people was cause enough for grief, but he had been faithful to serve the Lord and it seemed unfair to him that God was adding pain and sorrow to his life. Baruch was worn out with groaning and could not steer his mind into God's peace. He had hoped that God would reward him for his faithfulness, but instead it seemed God was punishing him (v. 3).

Baruch's high expectations of reward and greatness clearly clashed with God's national plan *"to overthrow and build,"* and *"to uproot and plant"* (v. 4). God admonished Baruch to trust Him in the matter of dealing with the backsliding nation of Judah and not to be self-focused (v. 4). He was told that, while most Jews would lose their lives or become Babylonian captives, his own life would be reward enough for his faithfulness (v. 5). William Kelly identifies the valuable lesson for Baruch from this text, which is indeed a lesson that all believers should understand:

> Lowliness of mind always becomes the saint, but in an evil day, it is the only safety. Humility is always morally right, but it is also the only thing that preserves from judgment. I am speaking now not of God's final judgment, but of that which is executed in this world. Now it seems to me plain that Baruch had not learned this lesson. He had now to learn it. This was the word of the prophet to him at an earlier date — the fourth year of Jehoiakim.[1]

299

The low road is the pathway to divine blessing. God honors those who humble themselves and put their trust in Him, especially when it seems most appropriate to invoke personal rights in a dire situation (1 Sam. 30:1-8).

Certainly the placement of this account here in the forty-fifth chapter is out of place chronologically; we may wonder, then, why Jeremiah placed it at the end of his prophecies to Judah. It would seem that the message God delivered to Baruch some time prior to this is included here because it was the one God wanted the Jews to heed at the present time. Jeremiah 45 forms the capstone over all that God has decreed to His people and desires of them. His call can be summarized as, "Cling to My Word by faith and hope in Me alone for future blessing." This was the response that God wanted from His covenant people whether they were captives in Babylon, sojourners in Egypt, survivors in Israel, or servants of the Lord such as this prophet and scribe.

As H. A. Ironside explains, Baruch should not have been swallowed up in grief or expected greatness for merely doing his duty.

> In Baruch's case, it would seem that he felt the king's rejection of the Word of God as an insult aimed at himself and his master, rather than at the Lord who inspired the writing that was in the roll. The result was *sore* discouragement.... It was quite right that the son of Neriah should feel, and feel keenly, the wretched state of his people, and their departure from holiness and truth. Every godly soul must of necessity have thus felt. Jeremiah did, as we know; and Ezekiel, in vision, saw a mark placed upon the foreheads of the men who sighed and cried because of Jerusalem's abominations (Ezek. 9). This was pleasing to God, and indicated a chastened spirit and divine sensibilities. But the grief of Baruch is more personal, like that which threatened to consume the prophet himself, in chapter 15. It was prompted in large measure by disappointment. He had not received the recognition as Jehovah's servant and the amanuensis of Jeremiah that he looked for. Hence he faints in the day of adversity, because his strength is small. He has not yet learned to deny himself, which is quite another thing to merely being self-denying. This latter thing he knew: the former he has not yet reached.

Perhaps almost unknown to himself, and unseen heretofore even by Jeremiah, Baruch was seeking a measure of recognition from man.[2]

Why do faithful men and women of God become self-seeking at times? Though the exact expression "the sin nature" is not found in the Bible, Christians often use the phrase to describe the self-seeking disposition of our fallen state. Unchecked, the lusts of our flesh and the desires of our minds lead us into sin – we desire what is unlawful to have. In our natural state we cannot help but sin; we are born with a deep-seated malice against God. Paul called this *"the law of sin"* that dwelled within him (Rom. 7:17, 20, 23). In Eden, Adam acted outside of divine boundaries, and we inherited that same flesh nature from him: *"All we like sheep have gone astray; we have turned, every one, to his own way"* (Isa. 53:6). Though the flesh includes inherent safeguards to govern the operations of our bodies, the fallen nature inherited from Adam makes consistent proper control impossible (Rom. 7:15-18).

The flesh, governed by the fallen nature, is never satisfied; it wants more than what is reasonable or lawful. Solomon put it this way: *"The eye is not satisfied with seeing, nor the ear filled with hearing"* (Eccl. 1:8). This can be seen in all areas of life. For example, instead of drinking *"a little wine for [one's] stomach's sake"* (1 Tim. 5:23), the flesh longs to be drunk with wine (Eph. 5:18). This is because when a person is drunk, the restraining influence of reason is lost and it becomes easier for the flesh to rule the moment. Instead of eating what is necessary to maintain a fit body, the flesh engages in gluttony (Prov. 23:21, 28:7). Scripture exhorts us to dress modestly to avoid flaunting our bodies before others (1 Tim. 2:9; 1 Pet. 3:3), and not to seek to be the center of attention (Luke 14:8), but the flesh wants to be noticed and admired by others. The marriage covenant protects the sexual relationship between a husband and a wife, but unchecked cravings lead to fornication, which is a great offense against God (1 Thess. 4:3; Eph. 5:5), and against one's own body (1 Cor. 6:18).

Paul spoke of a law within his members (Rom. 7:23) which continued to oppose the *law of God* in his mind (i.e. his understanding of what God demanded of him). He referred to this nature as the *law of sin* (Rom. 7:25) and he knew it was an abiding evil presence within himself. There is no need to put a pre-conversion or post-conversion tag to Romans 7; an unregenerate person or a believer not walking in the Spirit will have this same difficulty that Paul describes. As Paul concedes, this ongoing battle could not be won through natural means:

> For I know that in me (that is, in my flesh) nothing good dwells; for to will is present with me, but how to perform what is good I do not find. For the good that I will to do, I do not do; but the evil I will not to do, that I practice. Now if I do what I will not to do, it is no longer I who do it, but sin that dwells in me (Rom. 7:18-20).

However, after conversion Christians should not be governed by the law of sin within them, but rather by the Spirit of God (Rom. 8:13). Moderation and self-control are a testimony to others that God is the One controlling a believer's actions (Phil. 4:5). Apparently, many in the church at Corinth did not have such a testimony because they were being controlled by their lusting flesh. In the opening verses of 1 Corinthians 3, Paul told them three times that they were "carnal." The Greek word normally translated as "flesh" in the New Testament is *sarx*, and Paul used this word as a modifier (*sarkikos*) to describe their carnal behavior – they were "fleshly." This carnal nature was governing their behavior within the assembly and, as a result, the testimony of the church was suffering.

It is important that a believer remember what God says about his old nature, the flesh. Everything God says about the flesh is *negative.* In the flesh there is *"no good thing"* (Rom. 7:18). The flesh profits *"nothing"* (John 6:63). A Christian is to put *"no confidence"* in the flesh (Phil. 3:3). He is to make *"no provision"* for the flesh (Rom. 13:14). A person who lives for the flesh is living a negative life. It is impossible for believers to do great things for God until they first cease to seek great things from themselves. This was God's message to Baruch.

Believers are to be spiritually-focused and to be sober-minded. This defeats self-focusing and self-desiring attitudes and precludes the mind from being easily shaken. An overly active or anxious mind will disturb the quietness of our spirit. Baruch was *"worn out with groaning"* and, consequently, could not find peace for his soul (v. 3).

If the spirit is not clearly heard, emotions or high-speed thinking may inhibit us from being properly guided by the Holy Spirit, the result of which is independent action in opposition to God. If the mind is settled, the direction of the spirit is clearly understood and spiritual reasoning prevails to align the will and the heart Godward.

Baruch was exhorted to adapt to God's thinking about Judah's situation and not to seek for himself what God had not promised. The entire land was under God's judgment, so it behooved Baruch not to invest in or seek a blessing from what was cursed. Believers must adopt the same attitude towards the world in which they live – it has been cursed by God and is destined to be burned with fire. Why invest into that which will be soon destroyed? It is better to invest one's life into what will endure forever, where neither moth, nor rust, nor thieves can diminish its value (Matt. 5:19-20). Those who choose to invest into eternity have the promise that *their works follow them* (Rev. 14:13). The Lord promises that a mind properly aligned with Christ's thinking will never be self-seeking or self-exalting, for such nonsense is repulsive to His character.

Meditation

O Jesus Christ, grow Thou in me, and all things else recede!
My heart be daily nearer Thee, from sin be daily freed.
More of Thy glory let me see, Thou Holy, Wise and True!
I would Thy living image be, in joy and sorrow, too.
Make this poor self grow less and less, be Thou my life and aim;
O make me daily through Thy grace, more meet to bear Thy Name!

— Johann Lavater

The Judgment of Egypt
Jeremiah 46:1-28

Having completed and arranged his compilation of prophecies pertaining to Judah, Jeremiah now turned his attention to God's judgment of the nations. Jeremiah's ministry had centered on being God's spokesman to Judah and Israel, but he had also been commissioned as a prophet to the nations (Jer. 1:5). The next six chapters record God's pronouncements of judgment on the nations surrounding Judah: Egypt (46), Philistia (47), Moab (48), Ammon (49:1-6), Edom (49:7-22), Syria (49:23-27), Kedar and Hazor (49:28-33), Elam (49:34-39), and Babylon (50-51).

These prophecies have all been fulfilled with the exception of some of the prophecies concerning Babylon that had both near-term and far-term implications; the latter relates to the still future Tribulation Period. John referred to the religious and economic system established by the Antichrist to rule the world as "Babylon" (Rev. 17 and 18). Babylon represents the religious world system that began under Nimrod and will have its final destruction during the Tribulation Period, just prior to the establishment of Christ's kingdom on earth.

Jeremiah 46 contains two distinct prophetic messages, uttered approximately eighteen years apart. The first, contained in verses 2-12, relates to the attempt made by Pharaoh-Neco to invade the provinces of Babylon to quell its rise to power after the fall of the Assyrian empire. The text describes the dramatic overthrow of the Egyptian forces by Nebuchadnezzar's invincible army. The remaining section of the chapter refers to a later judgment which, given the contents of Jeremiah 43 and 44, was likely spoken by the prophet after the remnant had taken up residence in Egypt. In this passage, Jeremiah foretells the destruction of Mizraim after the defeat of Pharaoh Hophra by Nebuchadnezzar. Hophra was the last Pharaoh to be referenced in the Bible. Hence, Egypt, her gods, her kings, and her idolatrous people were severely judged. They had defied Jehovah, the living and true God, and God had levied a devastating blow against their military might and political enterprises.

King Josiah was killed in battle against Pharaoh Neco in 609 B.C. (2 Kgs. 23:29). Jeremiah penned the first part of this message four years later, after Neco's army had been defeated by the Babylonians at Carchemish (605 B.C.). Jehoiakim was the king of Judah at that time. In this message, God sarcastically mocked the Egyptians, who arrayed themselves for battle against the Babylonian army. Their soldiers were mounted on horses and clad with armor; they clutched their shields and extended their spears high. But the Babylonian attack was so swift and so powerful that Pharaoh's troops quickly fell into disarray: *"they shall stumble, and fall"* (v. 6). An orderly retreat was not possible and the Egyptians were slaughtered (vv. 1-6). Donald Wiseman elaborates on what we learn of this massacre from *The Babylonian Chronicles*:

> Nabopolassar himself stayed in Babylonia for the same reasons, perhaps of age or health, which had prompted his earlier withdrawal from the field. Nebuchadnezzar, the crown-prince, therefore replaced him as commander-in-chief and led the undivided army in person on the march up the Euphrates to Carchemish itself.... The initiative and surprise of the attack is consistent with the high military reputation of Nebuchadnezzar. The Babylonian army crossed to the west bank of the Euphrates, apparently near Carchemish itself, engaged the Egyptians in hand to hand fighting first of all within the city, and later, perhaps, in the open country.... The Egyptian defeat was decisive, their troops being annihilated save for a remnant that early in the fray had escaped so quickly that "no weapon could reach them." Nebuchadnezzar's swift pursuit overtook these fugitives in the province of Hamath where they too were so utterly defeated, according to the chronicler who writes of these events with unusual feeling, that "not a man escaped to his province of Hamath;" this may well imply attacks on scattered groups rather than on a compact force and include pursuit operation all down the Egyptian's homeward road towards the Mediterranean coast.[1]

Jeremiah's description of Neco's defeat aligned well with extra-biblical documentation. He stated that though Egypt amassed a huge army and desired to rise like the mighty Nile River in flood stage, they would not sweep across the land and conquer it. Why? Because the Lord's sword would take its vengeance on Egypt, and they would be slaughtered as a great sacrifice at the Euphrates River. Even if the Egyptians escaped as far as Gilead and obtained balm for their wounds, their efforts would be in vain – their wounds could not be cured. The nations would hear the cries of Egypt's shame and anguish (vv. 7-12).

Having foretold and explained God's dealings with Pharaoh at Carchemish, Jeremiah next prophesied the future invasion of Egypt by Babylon (vv. 13-19). As mentioned in the discussion on Jeremiah 43, Nebuchadnezzar likely invaded Egypt between 571-567 B.C. Jeremiah sounded the alarm for three northern cities in Egypt (Migdol, Memphis, Tahpanhes); these would be strategic cities which Babylon would attack. The Lord explained He was sending Nebuchadnezzar to Egypt to conquer it; the Babylonian general would stand high above Egypt in the same way that Mt. Tabor was the chief peak of southern Galilee. Tabor is situated approximately 11 miles southwest of the Sea of Galilee at the eastern end of the Jezreel Valley. Nebuchadnezzar's grandeur as a victor would be as magnificent as the view of Mt. Carmel from the Mediterranean Sea. Those living in Egypt were to pack their things and prepare themselves for their impending exile; the Babylonians were coming, and Memphis would be one of the first cities to be left in ruins (vv. 13-19). Pharaoh Neco likened himself to the mighty Nile River roaring across the land and sweeping away his enemies, but such a conquest would never be – the Babylonians were coming to Egypt.

Jeremiah used four similes to picture Babylon's then future attack on Egypt: a heifer bitten by a gadfly, fattened calves fit for slaughter, a fleeing serpent whose forest falls prey to the woodchopper's axe, and an innumerable horde of locusts which devour the land. Each metaphor illustrated that Egypt would be put to shame by the Babylonian army (vv. 20-24). God's judgment would not spare Pharaoh, his people, the Jews, or the gods of Egypt (v. 25). The Lord did promise, however, that the judgment of Egypt would not be permanent, and that the land would be again inhabited by the displaced Egyptians returning from Babylon (v. 26).

The Lord's promise to restore the exiled Egyptians back to their homeland is used as a reminder that God had also promised to return the Jews to Israel. The Jews were God's covenant people. He vowed not to utterly destroy them, but rather, after being chastened for their sins they would be restored and blessed in the Promised Land (v. 27-28). They are still waiting for this event to occur.

Presently, the Church also waits for the culmination of its redemption in Christ, that is, to be instantaneously caught up with Him into heaven and receive glorified bodies (1 Thess. 4:13-18; 1 Cor. 15:51-52). The Church has already been ransomed by blood, but the fullness of that redemption will not be realized until the Church is raptured to heaven. In that event, the same phenomenal power which defeated the power of hell at Christ's resurrection will be exercised to resurrect believers from Satan's domain, the world. Paul wanted the Christians at Corinth to understand this important truth, saying, *"Who delivered us from so great a death, and does deliver us; in whom we trust that He will still deliver us"* (2 Cor. 1:10). The Egyptians were to be punished and exiled, but they were to maintain hope for the future; God had promised to return them to their homeland. Likewise, the Church, with its heavenly citizenship, longs for her earthly labor and suffering to be complete so she may journey homeward, heavenward. She yearns for eternal bliss, glorious sights, and most of all, for the appearing of her Beloved, who will escort her home.

Meditation

Face to face with Christ my Saviour, face to face – what will it be,
When with rapture I behold Him, Jesus Christ, who died for me?

What rejoicing in His presence, when are banished grief and pain,
When the crooked ways are straightened, and the dark things shall be plain.

Face to face! O blissful moment! Face to face – to see and know;
Face to face with my Redeemer, Jesus Christ, who loves me so.

— Carrie E. Breck

The Judgment of Philistia and Phoenicia
Jeremiah 47:1-7

Jeremiah's second prophetic message against the nations is directed to the coastal regions of Philistia and Phoenicia. This message was delivered prior to Pharaoh Neco's push north to engage Babylonian armies in 609 B.C. (v. 1; 2 Kgs. 23:29-30).The Philistines dwelt directly to the west of the Judean foothills and had been the enemies of Israel since the days when Joshua led the Israelites into Canaan (Judg. 3:1-4). During the era of the Judges, the Philistines repeatedly attempted to expand their dominion by invading Jewish territory. The conflict raged back and forth for hundreds of years until King David subdued Philistia (2 Sam. 8). King Solomon continued to hold Philistia with a firm grip, but after the Jewish kingdom split during the reign of Solomon's son Rehoboam, the wrangling for superiority began again between these two people groups.

But judgment day had now arrived and Jeremiah informed the Philistines that the sword of the Lord would be against them (v. 6). Judgment would also fall upon the cities of Tyre and Sidon in Phoenicia because they assisted the Philistines in their assault against the Jews (v. 4). Jeremiah prophesied against the two chief cities of Philistia, Gaza, and Ashkelon: both would be decimated. As foretold, the Egyptians destroyed Gaza in 609 B.C., and Ashkelon fell to Nebuchadnezzar during his first invasion of the region in 605-604 B.C. The prophet likened the relentless attack of the Babylonians to the powerful torrent of a flooding river that would wipe out everything in its way. God would use the conflict between Egypt and Babylon to punish the Philistines; His sword would not be sheathed until Ashkelon and the cities of the seacoast were laid waste (v. 7).

What effect was this judgment to have on the Philistines? The people would shave their heads and cut themselves to express sorrow and grief. Cutting oneself to indicate remorse (such as in a funeral procession) or to show devotion to one's god was a pagan practice to which the Philistines were accustomed (1 Kgs. 18:28). However, Jehovah expressly forbade the Jews to mark, tattoo, or cut their flesh (Lev. 19:28). His people were to be a holy people and not adopt the practices of a wicked world. Why does God find such changes to one's appearance offensive? God designed and created each one of us the way we are; thus, it stands to reason that desiring to change what God has made without His permission is a form of rebellion. Every individual is a unique expression of His wisdom and sovereign purpose in time. Should we change what God has labored to put in place?

Many believers today seem to be unhappy with who they are in Christ. Our western culture has been strongly influenced by the world's valuation of beauty and the apparent need to augment one's outward appearance to comply with its carnal standards. Consequently, fortunes are spent on implants, tucks, lifts, tanning, coloring, highlighting, cosmetics, etc. We certainly should take good care of our bodies because they are God's temples, but much of what the world touts as attractive goes way beyond physical fitness or caring for one's skin and hair. This is to be expected, as the world's standard of beauty is quite different than the Lord's.

One's carnal flesh wants gratification and the bulk of its lusting is only skin-deep. Proverbs 20:29 states that the gray head testifies of acquired wisdom and that it is for this reason an older person is to be respected. Yet, as people age, many (including Christians) choose to color and hide their gray hair, the very thing God states is a sign of respect and honor. Perhaps if there were more elderly people settled with the natural ramifications of aging, there would be more young people showing respect to them. The flesh wants to deny aging and cling to the appearance of youthfulness as long as possible. Why? So others will appreciate or perhaps lust after their outward form a bit longer. This "pride of life" mentality will eventually lead to sin – either in action or in thought. Peter declared that God considers a meek and quite spirit and the pursuit of godliness priceless (1 Pet. 3:3-4). It is character, and not one's physical features, which is profitable in the furtherance of the kingdom of God.

The simple fact is that all of us have frail bodies which are ever-progressing towards the grave. We do not need to hide or deny this fact; rather, we should be reminding ourselves of it. Our mortal existence is short and we had better learn to value the things of God and to trust Him in the affairs of life. This results in a life worth living – one that counts for eternity. James says our physical bodies are like a vapor (Jas. 4:14), and Peter, quoting the prophet Isaiah, likens the life of our flesh to the brevity of grass (1 Pet. 1:24). Should we decorate what God says is fading and hide what He says is a sign of wisdom? We need to be reminded of how brief our sojourn on earth is and that our bodies are failing lest we waste what little time we do have living for ourselves and not for eternity. Let us not deny the obvious reminders of our frailty to become cosmopolitan believers. The lost must see our spiritually revitalized inner man – not our decorated outer man. The former calls them to Christ, while the latter endorses their misplaced priorities in life!

Babylon represents the world, so why would God's covenant people want to impress those in the world with their outward beauty? Jeremiah rebuked the Jews for trying to influence their Babylonian invaders with their outward appearance: *"Though you clothe yourself with crimson, though you adorn yourself with ornaments of gold, though you enlarge your eyes with paint, in vain you will make yourself fair"* (Jer. 4:30). God values the internal over the external: *"For which cause we faint not; but though our outward man perish, yet the inward man is renewed day by day"* (2 Cor. 4:16). May we long to be more like Christ and adorn ourselves with virtuous behavior and good deeds, rather than investing in what fades and will eventually die.

Meditation

My heart is withered like the grass, and I forget my daily bread;
In lonely grief my days I pass and sad my thoughts upon my bed.
My foes reproach me all the day, my drink is tears, my bread is grief,
For in Thy wrath I pine away, my days are like a fading leaf.

The Lord, exalted on His throne, looked down from heaven with pitying eye
To still the lowly captive's moan and save His people doomed to die.
All men in Zion shall declare His gracious Name with one accord,
When kings and nations gather there to serve and worship God the Lord.

— Paraphrase of Psalm 103 (Unknown)

The Judgment of Moab
Jeremiah 48:1-47

Looking back into Jewish history, we learn that Moses gave two and a half tribes permission to settle on the eastern side of the Jordan River, rather than within the land of Canaan. This agreement required the two and a half tribes to assist in the military campaign in Canaan. One of those who took up residence on the eastern plateau was the tribe of the Reubenites, who settled in the cities of Nebo and Kiriathaim (Num. 32:37-38; Josh. 13:19). These cities and others in the region were later captured by the Moabites, descendants of Lot through an illicit relationship with the older of his two daughters (Gen. 19:37). Judgment is here pronounced on the two cities previously mentioned, along with Misgab, which, although unknown to us, may have been another strong fortress within Moab (v. 1). Just as Moab had overcome the Reubenites and occupied the region which had been designated to them, God would now remove the Moabites from the land.

Furthermore, Jeremiah prophesied that the plotting of Moab's downfall would occur within its capital city of Heshbon (v. 2). Heshbon had been the capital of Sihon, king of the Amorites, until the Israelites conquered it during the Exodus (Num. 21:25-29). Moab later took the city from the tribe of Reuben who had rebuilt it (Num. 32:37). God's judgment would fall upon Heshbon and the entire region. Specifically mentioned are those in the town of Madmen; its inhabitants would be silenced (v. 2). Weeping would resound throughout the hills of Moab.

Wailing fugitives would flee southward to Horonaim and then on to Luhith hoping to find safety (vv. 3-6) Though the Moabites would try to escape judgment, God would bring destruction into every town and valley (v. 8). Just as the Jews had been exiled to Babylon, so the surviving Moabites, even their national god Chemosh (1 Kgs. 11:7) and his official priests, would be carried away also (vv. 7, 9-10).

In their entire history, Moab had never experienced the harsh reality of invasion and exile (v. 11). But now, it was necessary to remove the "dregs" from Moab in order to improve the quality of the nation. Dregs are sediments which accumulate in the bottom of a jar or bottle containing fermenting wine. If these are not removed within a certain period of time, the dregs will permit the wine to become too sweet and will eventually spoil it. The only way to improve the wine's flavor and aroma is to remove the dregs from the developing wine. Likewise, Moab's moral flavor and proud disposition were undesirable, but God would remove her dregs to remedy that condition (vv. 11-13).

Jeremiah decreed that Moab's destruction would be swift; her mighty warriors in whom she had great confidence would not be able to withstand the onslaught of the Babylonians. In the end, her scepter (speaking of her dominion in the region) would be broken. Jeremiah then dryly summoned the surrounding nations to come and console Moab at the time of her calamity (vv. 14-17).

The Lord vowed to fight against Moab's chief city of Dibon as part of His strategy to humble the inhabitants of the entire region. People traveling northward from the southern city of Arier (near the Arnon River) would stop and inquire of those fleeing from Dibon what had happened to the city. When the information of Dibon's destruction was brought back to Arier, the whole land, from north to south, would be filled with mourning. Indeed, Jeremiah specifically listed eleven Moabite cities which would be destroyed by the Babylonians (vv. 18-24).

Jeremiah utilized two metaphors to illustrate Moab's doom: the horn and the arm. First, he declared, *"the horn of Moab is cut off"* (v. 25). When used symbolically in Scripture, the word "horn" represents power or strength, which is typically associated with authority. An animal uses its horns (or antlers) to protect itself or to substantiate its territory in the wild, either by fighting or by making rubbings. The Antichrist is described by Daniel as being a "little horn" who is granted dominion to rule the world for seven years (Dan. 7:8-27). In Revelation 5 the Lord Jesus is thus described as a Lamb with seven horns. Since seven is the number of perfection and completeness in

Scripture, we understand that these seven horns figuratively represent the Lord's omnipotence, or perfect power.

Second, Jeremiah asserted Moab's arm would be broken. Figuratively speaking, an arm is used to symbolize strength in Scripture. Isaiah uses the metaphor over a dozen times in his writings to convey the concept of God's strength to deliver when no one else can (e.g. Isa. 59:16; see also Ex. 6:6). Men often arm wrestle to pit their strength against one another, but in this contest, Moab would be so powerfully defeated that his arm would snap. God would show Moab no mercy – overwhelming devastation was coming to their land. Afterwards Moab would be disdained by onlookers in the same way that people despise a drunkard who falls and wallows in his own vomit (v. 26).

Why was God set on punishing Moab? The next several verses inform us of the reason: Moab magnified himself against the Lord (vv. 26, 42). Moab was exceedingly proud, arrogant, and high-minded (v. 29). More than a century earlier, the prophet Isaiah proclaimed the same truth, saying, *"We have heard of the pride of Moab – He is very proud"* (Isa. 16:6). Pride has been the downfall of many people. Commenting on the evidences and effects of pride, Matthew Henry writes:

> We must be clothed with humility; *for the proud in spirit* are those that cannot bear to be trampled upon, but grow outrageous, and fret themselves, when they are hardly bestead. That will break a proud man's heart, which will not break a humble man's sleep. Mortify pride, therefore, and a lowly spirit will easily be reconciled to a low condition.[1]

> He that has a low opinion of his own knowledge and powers will submit to better information; such a person may be informed and improved by revelation: but the proud man, conceited of his own wisdom and understanding, will undertake to correct even divine wisdom itself, and prefer his own shallow reasonings to the revelations of infallible truth and wisdom. Note, we must abase ourselves before God if we would be either truly wise or good: *For the wisdom of this world is foolishness with God,* v. 19.[2]

True humility is selfless behavior that honors the Lord and longs to serve others. From Genesis to Revelation, the Bible declares God's contempt for pride and commitment to judge it. As the proverb says, *"Pride goes before destruction and a haughty spirit before a fall. Better to be of a humble spirit with the lowly, than to divide the spoil with the proud"* (Prov. 16:18-19). Both James and Peter proclaim that *"God resists the proud, but gives grace to the humble"* (Jas. 4:6; 1 Pet. 5:5). Solomon wrote, *"When pride comes, then comes shame; but with the humble is wisdom"* (Prov. 11:2). The psalmist declared, *"The sacrifices of God are a broken spirit, a broken and a contrite heart"* (Ps. 51:17). The opposite of pride is a broken spirit and a contrite heart.

To be broken before the Lord is to be a qualified recipient of His grace. Our failures should lead to personal brokenness, which should then cause us to cast ourselves upon the Lord in a way that we were hesitant to do beforehand. Our victories, won by His grace, only prompt us to praise His name! The outcome of testing, then, is that the believer knows and trusts the Lord with a greater patience and confidence than he or she had before. This is why the Lord longs for us to come to Him with all of life's burdens.

The Lord Jesus gave this invitation: *"Come to Me, all you who labor and are heavy laden, and I will give you rest. Take My yoke upon you and learn from Me, for I am gentle and lowly in heart, and you will find rest for your souls. For My yoke is easy and My burden is light"* (Matt. 11:28-30). May we learn of Him and be like Him, for He is meek and lowly in heart. Let us remember God's promise: *"A man's pride will bring him low, but the humble in spirit will retain honor"* (Prov. 29:23).

The story of Moab has a happy ending. Moab was known for its vineyards, and though God "harvested" the land, in a manner of speaking, He promised to restore the fortunes of Moab in the "days to come" (v. 47). Historically speaking, what Babylon left in Moab was later seized by the Arabians from the east (Ezek. 25:10). For the most part, the Moabite people lost their identity and were acculturated into other societies. Consequently, the term "days to come" is likely a reference to the Millennial Kingdom of Christ in which the curses of the earth will be removed and a time of peace, prosperity, and righteousness will be enjoyed by all who live on the earth. At that time, the fortunes of Moab will be restored to the land and be enjoyed by the remaining descendants of Moab and whoever else may co-inhabit the region. God judges pride, but once lowliness is learned, His grace lifts us heavenward.

Meditation

With broken heart and contrite sigh,
A trembling sinner, Lord, I cry;
Thy pardoning grace is rich and free:
O God, be merciful to me.

Far off I stand with tearful eyes,
Nor dare uplift them to the skies;
But Thou dost all my anguish see:
O God, be merciful to me.

— Cornelius Elven

The Judgment of Ammon and Edom
Jeremiah 49:1-22

In chapter 49, Jeremiah levies prophetic judgments against Ammon (vv. 1-6), Edom (vv. 7-22), Damascus (vv. 23-27), Kedar and Hazor (vv. 28-33), and Elam (vv. 34-39). Ammon and Edom will be addressed in this devotion, and Kedar, Hazor, and Elam will be discussed in the next.

The Judgment of Ammon (vv. 1-6)

The people of Ammon were descendants of Lot through his youngest daughter; thus, they were kin to the Moabites. They dwelled just to the north of Moab on the eastern side of the Jordan River. Though Ammon forged an alliance with Judah during Zedekiah's final rebellion against Nebuchadnezzar, the nations had been in frequent conflict with each other since the time the Israelites entered Canaan. Their interactions followed a turbulent course. Recall that it had been the Ammonites who had conspired with the Jewish captain Ishmael to murder godly Gedaliah, even though Ishmael had previously pledged to forego such mercenary activities (40:14).

Why was Ammon to be judged? Through the presentation of several rhetorical questions in this passage, two main reasons for punishment become apparent. First, Ammon had taken possession of several cities belonging to the tribe of Gad (v. 1). God had used the Assyrians to chasten idolatrous Israel in 722 B.C. Many Jews were consequently taken captive and exiled to Assyria at that time; the Ammonites took advantage of the situation and expanded their territory by invading the troubled land of Israel. Since the Jews were no longer there to defend their inheritance, the Ammonites determined that their land was free for the taking. They were wrong – the land had been allotted to the tribe of Gad by Jehovah, and foreign intrusion would not be tolerated. It is further declared that their god,

Molech, whom the Ammonites brought with them into Gad's inheritance, would be removed from the land (v. 3). God's disciplinary judgment against His people was measured for their offense; He would not allow the Ammonites to take advantage of the situation or to add further hardship to His covenant people.

The second indication for judgment was that, like the Moabites, the Ammonites were a proud people. They trusted in their vast wealth, gloried in their valleys, and felt they were invincible (v. 4). However, God would show them that they were not impregnable; indeed, their capital city of Rabbah would be reduced to rubble by the Babylonians. Additionally, the Israelites would drive the Ammonites out of the Jewish cities they had settled in (v. 5). However, as with the Moabites (48:47), God vowed to eventually restore the fortunes of the Ammonites (v. 6). This promise, as explained in the previous discussion regarding the Moabites, relates to the Millennial Kingdom of Christ.

The Judgment of Edom (vv. 7-22)

The Edomites were the posterity of Jacob's twin brother Esau, who settled in the region south of Moab and just east of the Dead Sea. The sibling conflict that began after Esau sold Jacob his birthright, for a bowl of bean soup, continued among their descendants. The Edomites were a heathen nation that loathed the Jews, their fraternal brothers (Ezek. 35; Obad. 15-16). The Jews, for their part, were not fond of the Edomites either.

Apparently Edom, especially the city of Teman in central Edom, was known for its wisdom (v. 7). Eliphaz, one of Job's three miserable counselors, was from Teman (Job 2:11). As he announced Edom's judgment, Jeremiah warned the merchants from Dedan to flee Edom and return to their homeland in the northern part of the Arabian Peninsula, southeast of Edom (v. 8). Jeremiah invoked two word pictures to express the completeness of God's forthcoming judgment upon Edom. First, God promised to pick the vines of Edom clean; not a single grape would be overlooked. Second, though thieves were limited to steal only what they could carry away, God (the rightful owner of the vineyard) would strip Edom of all her riches. Both images convey the same thought: in contrast to grape-pickers and thieves who normally leave something behind, God was determined to divest Edom of *all* her wealth and completely deflate her pride (v. 9). Yet, God was not without mercy; as an expression of this, He would not claim the widows' and orphans' rations as part of His judgment (v. 11).

Jeremiah posed a logical statement for the Edomites to consider: if the Lord was determined to cause the surrounding nations, who had no fraternal ties with the Jews, to drink from His cup of wrath, how much more judgment did the Edomites deserve for oppressing their own distant kin (v. 12)? Although the Edomites felt they were secure in their defenses, God would assemble His forces from among the nations and reduce them to a whisper of a nation (vv. 13-14). Like the cities of Sodom and Gomorrah in Abraham's day, their cities would be destroyed and become uninhabitable (vv. 17-18). The Lord would be like a great lion upon the flock of Edom; no shepherd would be able to withstand Him as He devoured the flock and destroyed the pasture of Edom (vv. 19-22). Jeremiah also likened the Lord to a majestic eagle swooping down upon its prey, speaking of His attack on Bozrah in northern Edom which would be sudden and decisive (v. 22).

Jeremiah explains why God's wrath would be poured out on the Edomites: *"Your fierceness has deceived you, the pride of your heart, O you who dwell in the clefts of the rock, who hold the height of the hill! Though you make your nest as high as the eagle, I will bring you down from there,' says the Lord"* (v. 16). Edom's pride had summoned God's judgment; they were high on themselves, but God would bring them low.

Unlike Egypt, Moab, and Ammon, Edom was not promised a future inheritance or restoration. In fact, history records that in the years following the Babylonian invasion, the Nabateans drove the Edomites westward from their land into southern Judah. The descendants of the Edomites became known as the Idumeans. According to Josephus, the Idumeans became subject to John Hyrcanus I, a Maccabean, in 125 B.C. and were forced to accept Judaism; thus the Edomites ceased to be a distinct people.[1] Today, there are still remnants of the Moabites and Ammonites living in their respective regions; this cannot be said of the Edomites.

Why were the Edomites destined to lose their distinction as a people? The answer to this question originates in Exodus 17 and is then confirmed elsewhere in Scripture: the Edomites represent something which continues to oppose God and must therefore be eliminated. After crossing the Red Sea, the Israelites were brought into the wilderness by Moses. There they suffered an unprovoked attack by the Amalekites (Edomites). Amalek was the grandson of profane Esau, *"who for one morsel of food sold his birthright"* (Heb. 12:16). Consequently, both Esau and Amalek are used in Scripture to picture the lusting flesh which continues to war against God's people.

Under Joshua's leadership and Moses' intercession on the mount, Amalek was soundly beaten, but not destroyed, the following day. This was to illustrate that the war against the Amalekites (picturing the conflict with the flesh nature) would rage on from generation to generation (Ex. 17:16). Likewise, the believer's flesh lives on and must be defeated again and again for the Christian to be a witness for Christ in the world, since the deeds of the flesh oppose God. Paul understood what would happen if he did not keep his flesh under control – he would suffer a shipwrecked testimony for Christ.

> *And everyone who competes for the prize is temperate in all things. Now they do it to obtain a perishable crown, but we for an imperishable crown. Therefore I run thus: not with uncertainty. Thus I fight: not as one who beats the air. But I discipline my body and bring it into subjection, lest, when I have preached to others, I myself should become disqualified* (1 Cor. 9:25-27).

Victory over one's flesh requires the removal of that which entices the flesh to dissatisfaction and, as Paul says, a willingness to land blows against one's own carnal appetites. To keep the flesh in subjection requires constant discipline, no matter how mature one is in Christ. Such is the believer's conflict until glorification; then, every soldier of the cross will have the final victory. Moreover, at the Judgment Seat of Christ, those who took this challenge seriously will be rewarded with an imperishable crown.

After Israel defeated the Amalekites, God promised Moses: *"I will utterly blot out the remembrance of Amalek from under heaven"* (Ex. 17:4). This realization seems to be the best explanation for why the Edomites would cease to exist as a people, in contrast with the Egyptians, Moabites, and Ammonites who were promised restoration.

319

The Edomites (Amalekites) are a figure of the sinful flesh nature, and this is to have no part in Christ's future kingdom. At the Great White Throne Judgment, God will completely do away with any wicked thing throughout all His new creation; sinful flesh will no longer exist in God's kingdom and all believers will be eternally thankful for its eradication!

Meditation

Dear dying Lamb, Thy precious blood shall never lose its power
Till all the ransomed church of God be saved, to sin no more.
Be saved, to sin no more, be saved, to sin no more;
Till all the ransomed church of God be saved, to sin no more.

— William Cowper

The Judgment of Damascus, Kedar, Hazor, and Elam

Jeremiah 49:23-39

The Judgment of Damascus (vv. 23-27)

Syria's major cities of Hamath, Arpad, and Damascus were quite dismayed by the advance of the Babylonian army. The anxiety of Damascus, the capital of Syria, over the pending attack was likened to that of a woman's labor pains before she gives birth. Furthermore, the mighty fortress of Ben-hadad (named after the dynasty that ruled Damascus during the 9th and 8th centuries B.C.) would also be destroyed and its soldiers silenced (i.e., killed).

Writing two centuries earlier, the prophet Amos also described the overwhelming destruction of Damascus and that her fortifications would be burned (Amos 1:4). Though Jeremiah does not specifically list the crimes of Damascus, the city had often meddled in Jewish affairs (1 Chron. 18:5; Isa. 7:1) resulting in much harm to God's people.

The Judgment of Kedar and Hazor (vv. 28-33)

Kedar was a nomadic clan of Ishmaelites who lived in the Arabian Desert. They were known for their flocks of sheep (vv. 28-29; Isa. 60:7), for their commerce (Ezek. 27:21), and for having a warlike mentality (Ps. 120:5-6). As with the other nations, God would use Nebuchadnezzar to destroy Kedar and Hazor, which was apparently its chief city. This Hazor is not the same city Joshua conquered in northern Israel a millennium earlier. Those living in Hazor were warned not to trust in their barred city gates, but to flee and hide themselves in deep caves.

The Babylonians were coming, and they would despoil Kedar of its flocks, camels, and goods (v. 29). These nomadic people probably

321

thought that Nebuchadnezzar would not bother them in their remote desert location, but that would not be the case. God had decreed that the tents of Kedar would be destroyed and that *"Hazor shall be a dwelling for jackals, a desolation forever"* (v. 33). Though many of the cities destroyed by Nebuchadnezzar were rebuilt, Hazor was not to be one of them; in fact, we have no archeological evidence to even indicate where the location of this city once was. Its judgment was swift, thorough, and complete!

The Judgment of Elam (vv. 34-39)

The prophecy against Elam was decreed early in the reign of Zedekiah, perhaps 597 B.C. Elam was situated east of Babylon in what is now known as Iran. The inhabitants of Elam were famous for their skill in archery (Isa. 22:6), but that expertise would not impede their conquerors, who were not identified. Elam's bow would be broken – its people scattered upon the face of the earth. The Babylonian Chronicles provide some historical evidence that Nebuchadnezzar conquered Elam in 596 B.C. However, since Elam later became part of the Persian Empire, which eventually overthrew the Babylonians, it would seem that this prophecy concerning Elam has a future meaning. God would not use the Babylonians to subdue Elam, but instead He would put His own throne there to ensure its subjection in "the latter days" (v. 39). At that time Elam's submission to the Lord will also include the restoration of her material prosperity. As in the prophecies regarding Egypt, Ammon, and Moab, Elam was promised blessing during the Kingdom Age under Christ's rule.

Tribulation Judgments

Many of the prophecies against the nations listed in Jeremiah 46-51 preview what is to come during and after the Tribulation Period. Believers in the Church Age should find of interest the events leading up to the fulfillment of these prophecies, since the Church will be removed from the earth just prior to the beginning of the Tribulation Period.

Before the Kingdom Age commences, the Lord Jesus will descend to the earth to war against the Antichrist and his armies in the Megiddo Valley. His victory will deliver Jerusalem from the Antichrist's invading armies (Zech. 14). After the Battle of

Armageddon, the nations will be gathered and judged (Matt. 13:47-50, 25:31-46); all those following the Antichrist will be killed (Rev. 19:20-21). Those who did not take his mark will be allowed to enter Christ's kingdom on earth – this will conclude *"the time of the Gentiles"* (Rom. 11:25; Rev. 11:1-2).

God will judge the nations for their wickedness, and refine and restore the Jewish nation to Himself during the seven-year Tribulation Period. There will be twenty-one specific judgments by God upon the earth. The Antichrist and the powers of darkness will also be rampant upon the earth, destroying and killing. In the book of Revelation, this horrific holocaust is quantified. In chapter 6, we are told that one-fourth of the world's population will die from pestilence, war, and famine. Chapter 9 states that one third of mankind will be destroyed by fire. Two hundred million soldiers will be annihilated at the battle of Armageddon (Rev. 9:16). Moreover, in Chapters 7, 13, and 20, we learn that an innumerable host of people from all nations will be martyred by the Beast for not worshipping him and receiving his mark.

If we understand the old Hebrew names correctly, Ezekiel 38 and 39 speaks of Iraq, Iran, Egypt, Germany, and Turkey coming with Russia (*Rosh*) to attack Israel during the middle portion of the Tribulation Period – these armies will be annihilated by Christ's intervention through nature. A remnant will be allowed to escape to the north back into Russia (indicated as the land between the Black and Caspian Seas, see Joel 2:19-20). Zechariah 13:8-9 confirms that two-thirds of the Jews will die during the Tribulation Period. Only a small Jewish remnant will survive the refining fire of the Tribulation Period and be restored to God as His chosen people (Rom. 11). There will be numerous other judgments upon the earth that will also cause death and misery. The bottom line is that earth will not be the place to be during the Tribulation Period, as perhaps eighty percent of the world's population will perish.

Throughout the Tribulation Period, God, through His judgments, will take away from man what man has ignorantly claimed as his own. For example, natural man has labored, stolen, cheated, murdered, etc. in order to gain wealth, power, prestige, and sensual gratification. However, conditions in this epic period of time will be such that death will be welcomed; even life's basic necessities of food and drinking water will be scarcely found (Rev. 6:6, 8:10-11). By the end of the Tribulation Period, man will have nothing. God will demonstrate His control over all things and then purify the earth in order to usher in the Kingdom Age (Dan. 2:35, 44-45; Rom. 8:21). During this era, the earth and all its inhabitants will enjoy a thousand years of blessing under Christ's rule. What will the Kingdom Age be like? From Isaiah 2:1-5 and 66:20, we learn that Jerusalem shall be the religious center of the world. Christ will reign from there and all the nations will come there to praise, worship, and learn of Him. There will be no war or violence, only peace. All the earth shall see the glory of the Lord Jesus. Isaiah 4:2-4 informs us that the Jews who live through the Tribulation will gaze upon Christ (the Branch of the Lord) and appreciate His splendor, glory, fruitfulness, and beauty. So great will be the glory of the Lord upon the earth that there will be no need for the sun or moon to illuminate it (Isa. 60:18-20).

At this time, strange phenomena in nature will be observed throughout the earth. The wolf and the lamb shall dwell together, as will the kid of the goat with the leopard, and the calf with the lion (Isa. 11:6-7). Small children shall play by the home of the asp and at the adder's den without being afraid (Isa. 11:8). The glory of the Lord will be displayed upon the world as abundantly as *"the waters cover the sea"* (Isa. 11:9). These circumstances, though wonderful, should not be confused with the eternal state in which there is a new heaven and earth. There are several clear distinctions between the Kingdom Age and the Eternal State. For example, the seas and oceans we know today will still be present during the Kingdom Age, but there will not be any sea in the new earth (Rev. 21:1). The new heaven and earth will not be created until after the Kingdom Age is concluded, Satan's last rebellion on earth is quelled (Rev. 20:7-10), and the planet we live upon today is destroyed (Rev. 20:11; 2 Pet. 3:10). What a day of blessing it will be when the curses that were put upon the earth as a result of man's sin will be lifted. Seed casually scattered on a mountaintop will produce a great harvest. Weapons will be used as agricultural implements, and a spirit of peace and tranquility will rest upon the whole earth. All this and more Christ shall do: *"Even so come Lord Jesus"* (Rev. 22:20)!

Meditation

The Lord, that sits above the skies, derides their rage below;
He speaks with vengeance in His eyes, and strikes their spirits
    through.
"I call Him My eternal Son, and raise Him from the dead;
I make My holy hill His throne, and wide His kingdom spread.
"Ask Me, My Son, and then enjoy the utmost heathen lands:
Thy rod of iron shall destroy the rebel that withstands."
Be wise, ye rulers of the earth, obey the anointed Lord,
Adore the King of heavenly birth, and tremble at His Word.

— Isaac Watts

The Judgment of Babylon
Jeremiah 50:1-51:64

Jeremiah 50 and 51 present the climax of the judgment of the nations, with God taking vengeance on Babylon, the very rod of chastening He used to punish His people and other societies. Indeed, this pictures the culmination of divine judgment upon the nations during the Tribulation Period when Babylon, the originator of rebellion against God on earth, will be once and for all destroyed. Thus, the prophetic declarations of these two chapters are swirling with both near-term and far-reaching statements.

As we would expect, Jeremiah's prophecies pertaining to Babylon dovetail nicely with those of other prophets. For example, over a century earlier Micah foretold that the Jews in Judah would be exiled to Babylon and then later be delivered and brought back to the land of Israel.

Be in pain, and labor to bring forth, O daughter of Zion, like a woman in birth pangs. For now you shall go forth from the city, you shall dwell in the field, and to Babylon you shall go. There you shall be delivered; there the Lord will redeem you from the hand of your enemies (Mic. 4:10).

Bringing the Jews back to Israel would mean that another world empire would have to conquer the Babylonians in the near future. The prophet Daniel explains that indeed this was God's plan and He would use the Medes and the Persians to accomplish this feat (Dan. 7:5, 8:3, 20).

The prophet Habakkuk was a contemporary of Jeremiah; he prophesied in the years just preceding the Babylonian invasion. He had been wondering why God had not judged the wickedness of His people. When the Lord confirmed that He was about to do just that and would use the Babylonians to accomplish that task, Habakkuk was astonished. How could God use such a wicked nation as Babylon to punish His covenant people? In responding to Habakkuk's question, the Lord promised that He would also judge Babylon, but in a future day. In fact, there was a coming day in which God would ultimately rid the earth of her rebellion forever. It is understood, then, that Scripture has much to say about God's decrees against Babylon; some judgments have been accomplished already, while others are yet future.

Returning to Jeremiah 50 and 51, the difficulty for us is to sort out which of these timeframes Jeremiah is referring to throughout his prophecy. The whole Bible is an expression of divine truth. Our understanding of that truth is not gained by the private interpretation of any one particular Scripture (2 Pet. 1:20) but rather through the guidance of the Holy Spirit in comparing Scripture with Scripture (1 Cor. 2:13). By reviewing the whole of Scripture, the application of most of Jeremiah's statements pertaining to Babylon can be understood, while some remain a mystery as to their exact meaning.

From the book of Revelation, we learn that the Antichrist's political and economic system is identified with Babylon and will be destroyed by Christ at His second advent (Rev. 18). The religious aspect of this system, which the Antichrist will use to gain control of the world, will actually be eliminated by him during the middle portion of the Tribulation Period (Rev. 17). This event coincides with what is called "the Abomination of Desolation." At that time, the Antichrist will no longer tolerate the one-world religion he helped create; he will demand to be worshipped as god himself (2 Thess. 2:4-7). The Antichrist will destroy the last religious system of humanism, which began with Nimrod in Babylon of old: "*MYSTERY, BABYLON THE GREAT, THE MOTHER OF HARLOTS AND OF THE ABOMINATIONS OF THE EARTH*" (Rev. 17:5). This religious system is responsible for the death of millions of God's people throughout the course of human history – the harlot, as John describes her, is literally *"drunk with the blood of the saints"* (Rev. 17:6).

With this understanding, we now turn our attention to the passage at hand. Jeremiah begins by proclaiming that Babylon would be attacked and conquered by an army from the north and that Babylon's chief deity Bel, also known as Marduk, would not be able to avert the calamity. The city of Babylon itself would be laid waste (i.e. destroyed by fire – 50:32) and uninhabited, and the nation as a whole would be put to shame (50:13). The Babylonians would be filled with terror and suffer the same fate that they had inflicted on so many others. God had used Babylon as an instrument of chastening, but they were a pagan nation also deserving of judgment for their own wickedness and atrocities against their fellow man.

The question, then, is, Have these prophecies already been fulfilled or do they have a future application? History records that the Medes and the Persians under the command of Cyrus conquered the city of Babylon in 539 B.C. However, extra-biblical documentation of this conquest does not confirm the descriptions Jeremiah and Isaiah provide of Babylon's destruction or their prophecy that the city would be uninhabitable (Isa. 13:17-22; Jer. 50-51). Reviewing what we know of ancient Babylon, how it fell to the Persians, and what became of the city afterwards will be helpful in substantiating this conclusion.

The Greek historian Herodotus (fifth century B.C.) recorded the following information about ancient Babylon at the time of its conquest:[1]

- The city was in the form of a square (each side was fourteen miles in length).
- The outer brick wall surrounding the city was 56 miles long, 300 feet high, 25 feet thick, and had a base that extended 35 feet below the ground.
- An inner wall of 75 feet in height was behind the first wall.
- The city had 250 towers that were each 450 feet high.
- The Euphrates River flowed through and around the city which provided it with a deep and wide moat for protection.
- Access to the city was gained either through ferry boats or a half-mile-long bridge which had drawbridges that were closed at night.
- The city had eight massive gates leading to the inner city, plus another hundred brass gates.
- The streets of Babylon were paved with stone slabs 3 feet square.
- Within the city was a great tower (a ziggurat) and fifty-three temples, including the "Great Temple of Marduk."

328

The famous walls of Babylon were indeed impenetrable. The only way into the city was through its gates or by the Euphrates River, which flowed through submersed passages in and out of the city. On this last point, the Babylonians had built metal grids at each point where the river flowed in and out of the city to prevent underwater intrusions. However, while Babylon was under siege, Cyrus' corps of engineers devised a way of diverting the Euphrates River away from Babylon. Persian troops were placed at strategic points around the city, waiting until the water level dropped. The plan was executed on the evening of a Babylonian feast (Dan. 5). At the appropriate time, Cyrus' engineers diverted the Euphrates river upstream, which caused it to drop to or below "mid thigh level on a man," according to Herodotus. With the water level brought down, Cyrus' soldiers were able to enter the city by marching under the gated walls. The Persian army swiftly conquered the outer city while most of the Babylonians were still feasting in the city center, oblivious to the breach and invasion force.[2]

At the time Babylon fell, Nabunaid (Nabonidus) shared its kingship with his oldest son Belshazzar. The Nabonidus Chronicle provides the exact date in which Cyrus conquered Babylon: "In the month of Tashritu on the fourteenth day, October 10, 539 B.C., the Persian forces took Sippar; on the sixteenth day, October 12, 'the army of Cyrus entered Babylon without battle'; and in the month of Arahsamnu, on the third day, October 29, Cyrus himself came into the city."[3] Thus, Babylon fell to the Persians on October 12, 539 B.C.

Two hundred years prior to these events, the prophet Isaiah foretold by name the man whom God would use to defeat the Babylonians: Cyrus. He would punish the Babylonians, end the Jewish exile, and initiate the rebuilding of the temple in Jerusalem (Isa. 44:28-45:4). But did Cyrus destroy the city of Babylon by fire? Was it uninhabited afterwards, as Jeremiah prophesied? The answer to these questions is, "No." Cyrus used Babylon as a Persian outpost, but through the centuries Babylon gradually lost its political influence throughout the Persian Empire. The population of Babylon declined over the next two centuries and, ultimately, the city was dismantled under the Greek Empire to provide building materials for other cities. In short, Jeremiah's prophesies concerning the method of Babylon's destruction have yet to be fulfilled.

When one compares the historical evidence and the specific declarations of Isaiah and Jeremiah, it becomes evident that many of their prophecies pertaining to the fall of Babylon remain unfulfilled:

- Babylon's walls and foundations were not suddenly thrown down into heaps (Jer. 50:15, 22, 26, 51:8, 44).
- Babylon was not destroyed by fire, like Sodom and Gomorrah (Jer. 51:25, 30, 32, 40, Isa. 13:19).
- Babylon was not conquered by a northern army (Jer. 50:3, 9, 41, 51:48) – the Persians came from the east.
- Babylon was not conquered by an army composed of a conglomeration of many nations (Jer. 50:9, 41, 46).
- Babylon was not made uninhabitable after it was conquered (Jer. 50:3, 45, 51:37; Isa. 12:20-21).
- The inhabitants of Babylon, including the Jews, did not flee from the city before its capture by the Medo-Persian army (Jer. 50:8, 51:5-6); in fact, we know from Scripture that Daniel and other Jews remained in the city (Dan. 5:28-6:3).
- Through the destruction of Babylon, the Jews were brought back to their homeland (Jer. 50:4-5, 19), but did not enter into *"a perpetual covenant"* with God that would never be forgotten (Jer. 50:5).
- Although the sword of the Lord was certainly against Babylon through the hand of Cyrus (Jer. 51:11), the promised Great Redeemer who would bring peace to Israel has not yet come (Jer. 50:34-37).

We conclude that the events related to Babylon's capture in the sixth century B.C. and its eventual demise centuries later do not conform to the specific prophecies of Isaiah and Jeremiah. To date, for example, Babylon has never been destroyed by fire. Since the Lord says that it must be destroyed by fire, the rebuilding of a city known as "Babylon" is guaranteed (Rev. 18:10). Another prophecy regarding Babylon in Jeremiah 51:26 further substantiates this point: *"They shall not take from you a stone for a corner nor a stone for a foundation, but you shall be desolate forever."* Reliable evidence shows that at least six cities contain building materials which originally belonged to ancient Babylon. Hillah, which is near ancient Babylon, was built almost entirely from its ruins. Over two hundred years after its fall to Cyrus, one of Alexander the Great's successors,

Seleucus, nearly demolished ancient Babylon to obtain resources to build a new city some 30 miles away.[4] According to the Bible, when Babylon is destroyed by fire, it will never be inhabited again, nor will debris from its ruins be profitable for reuse. Since this type of destruction has yet to occur, when might the fulfillment of this prophecy come to pass?

Two clues are found in Jeremiah 50:19-20, which declares that Israel would regain Bashan as a possession and no iniquity will be found in either Judah or Israel. Bashan (the Golan Heights in northeastern Israel) did not become a Jewish possession until after the Six Day War of 1967. Thus, the fulfillment of the destruction of Babylon by fire must be after 1967, after Israel had regained Bashan. Moreover, we know that the Jews will walk with the Lord in a state of righteousness only after they have been brought into the good of the perpetual covenant (50:5) by trusting Jesus Christ as their Savior and receiving the Holy Spirit. This will be a national event occurring at the end of the Tribulation Period (Ezek. 36:24-27). These clues, then, point to a yet future fulfillment of Jeremiah's prophecy concerning the judgment of Babylon.

A third clue is found in Revelation 18. John informs us that Babylon will be: destroyed suddenly (Rev. 18:8, 10, 17, 19), destroyed by fire (Rev. 18:8-9, 18), completely destroyed (Rev. 18:21), and remain uninhabited forever (Rev. 18:22). Indeed, John reconfirms much of what Jeremiah and Isaiah predicted concerning Babylon's final destruction seven to eight hundred years earlier. Whether the Babylon spoken of in Revelation 18 refers to an entire kingdom or a specific city is unknown, but it is noted that Saddam Hussein began rebuilding the city of Babylon upon its ancient foundations in 1983. However, after the Iraq War and the deposition of Hussein from power, much of the construction work ceased and the site has become merely a tourist attraction. The city was never fully established; perhaps it will be before all that is connected with Babylon is wiped out during the Tribulation Period.

Returning to the events in Jeremiah's day, why did God promise to punish Babylon? Two main reasons are given in the book of Jeremiah. First, God avowed, *"I will bring judgment on the carved images of Babylon"* (Jer. 51:47). God hates paganism; it robs Him of His rightful honor as Almighty God, Lord Supreme, and Creator of

All. Second, He promised, *"I will repay Babylon and all the inhabitants of Chaldea for all the evil they have done in Zion in your sight"* (Jer. 51:24). The Jews are the apple of God's eye, His covenant people. Zechariah proclaimed that any nation which persecutes the Jews will ultimately be judged by God: *"For thus says the Lord of hosts, 'He sent Me after glory, to the nations which plunder you; for he who touches you touches the apple of His eye'"* (Zech. 2:8). Babylon would be no exception.

Looking into the future, why will the Lord Jesus Christ destroy wicked Babylon at His second coming? Because the anti-God spirit that started in Nimrod's time will ultimately culminate with the political and religious system of the Antichrist in the Tribulation Period. As previously mentioned, this rebel movement has been responsible for the deaths of millions of God's people: *"In her* [Babylon] *was found the blood of prophets and saints, and of all who were slain on the earth"* (Rev. 18:24). God will judge all those who have oppressed and persecuted His people down through the ages. In Jeremiah's day, the fall of Babylon signaled that the time of Jewish chastening had ended, that it was time for the Jews to return to Israel, and that they would enjoy God's protection and blessing there. The future fall of Babylon will indicate the same things, only ever so much more so.

The exiled Jews in Babylon would have understood Jeremiah's prophecies concerning the fall of Babylon and their return to Zion to pertain to them personally. But we have the advantage of more scriptural revelation concerning the future of Babylon and the benefit of history to more fully understand what Jeremiah was writing about – the final destruction of Babylon during the Tribulation Period. Certainly the soon-coming restoration of the Jews to their homeland after Cyrus captured Babylon was in the mind of God, for Jeremiah had before proclaimed that truth many times. However, the spiritual unification of the Lord Jesus Christ with His covenant people after He destroys all that Babylon stands for is what thrills the heart of God and is what is the chief view of this passage of Scripture. Perhaps this longing is no better expressed than in the words of Hosea after buying back his adulterous wife Gomer (who represents Israel) from a slave auction: *"And I said to her, 'You shall stay with me many days; you shall not play the harlot, nor shall you have a man –so, too, will I be toward you'"* (Hos. 3:3). How the Lord desires to be with His people and for His people to walk with Him!

Babylon symbolizes a world system that opposes God and denies Christ's headship. The Lord's severe judgment of Babylon corresponds to the judgment of all brought under her influence. During the Millennial Kingdom of Christ, the ideologies of Babylon will have no place on the earth. All those following the Antichrist in rebellion against God will be put to death and their souls will be bound in Hades while they wait for their final judgment (Rev. 14:9-11, 19:20-21).

On the day that God destroys this planet, all the wicked will be resurrected before God's Great White Throne and be judged by the Lord Jesus Christ (John 5:25-29; Rev. 20:11-15). In one act of glorification, these former rebels will bow the knee to Jesus Christ and confess Him as Lord (Phil. 2:10-11). Afterwards, these condemned individuals (in resurrected bodies) will be cast into the Lake of Fire which will burn forever and ever (Rev. 20:10, 15, 21:8). This ends the Kingdom Age and the period of time known as *"the Day of the Lord,"* which was initiated with the Tribulation Period (1 Thess. 5:2; 2 Thess. 2:3; 2 Pet. 3:10).

"The Day of God" begins after the present earth is destroyed, and God creates a new heaven and new earth (Rev. 21:1-2; 2 Pet. 3:12). This is the eternal state of perfection and righteousness, in which God's people (in glorified bodies) will enjoy endless fellowship and bliss with the Lord forever (Rev. 21-22). In fact, the Lord will create a vast city, with the dimensions of a 1,500-mile cube and called the "New Jerusalem," as a permanent dwelling place for His bride (Rev. 21).

Although the specific outworkings of Jeremiah's prophecies concerning Babylon may be debatable given our current incomplete understanding, God's ultimate judgment of the wicked and eternal fellowship with those justified by faith is indisputable. Through the Lord Jesus Christ, God is able to utterly save, to preserve blameless, and to eternally bless those who will exercise faith in His revealed Word.

But He, because He continues forever, has an unchangeable priesthood. Therefore He is also able to save to the uttermost those who come to God through Him, since He always lives to make intercession for them. For such a High Priest was fitting for us, who is holy, harmless, undefiled, separate from sinners, and has become higher than the heavens (Heb. 7:24-26).

Given such a great High Priest and Savior, the writer of Hebrews implored his audience not to pull back, but to press forward through persecutions and trials to further the cause of Christ. In fact, perseverance is a mark of a true believer: *"For yet a little while, and He who is coming will come and will not tarry. Now the just shall live by faith; but if anyone draws back, My soul has no pleasure in him"* (Heb. 10:37-38). As the Jews in Jeremiah's day learned the hard way, drawing back from the goodness of the Lord serves to cover one's face in shame. They cried, *"We are ashamed because we have heard reproach. Shame has covered our faces, for strangers have come into the sanctuaries of the Lord's house"* (Jer. 51:51). It grieved the Jews that the very privileged station that only they, as God's covenant people, were extended, had succumbed to being trampled upon by strangers. The House of God was no longer considered a holy place, but rather, the common abode of strangers. C. H. Spurgeon applies this situation to Christendom today in the form of a warning to the House of God (i.e. the Church; 1 Tim. 3:15):

In this account the faces of the Lord's people were covered with shame, for it was a terrible thing that men should intrude into the Holy Place reserved for the priests alone. Everywhere about us we see like cause for sorrow. How many ungodly men are now educating with the view of entering into the ministry! What a crying sin is that solemn lie by which our whole population is nominally comprehended in a National Church! How fearful it is that ordinances should be pressed upon the unconverted, and that among the more enlightened churches of our land there should be such laxity of discipline. If the thousands who will read this portion shall all take this matter before the Lord Jesus this day, he will interfere and avert the evil which else will come upon His Church. To adulterate the Church is to pollute a well, to pour water upon fire, to sow a fertile field with stones. May we all have grace to maintain in our own proper way the purity of the Church, as being an assembly of believers, and not a nation, an unsaved community of unconverted men.[5]

The believer has an upward calling in Christ (Phil. 3:14). With the promise of the Lord's imminent return before us, may we all stand fast in the faith and press forward for the cause of Christ. For some, death will be the doorway into Christ's presence, but for many others, it will be the rapture of the Church; they will be suddenly summoned from all toiling and suffering to stand before Him. What will it be like to be instantaneously translated from a sin-cursed planet into the eternal bliss of God's glory? What will it be like to later return to the earth with Christ for the establishment of His glorious kingdom and to witness Him being honored by all? Maranatha!

Meditation

Look, ye saints! the sight is glorious: see the Man of Sorrows now;
From the fight returned victorious, every knee to Him shall bow;
Crown Him, crown Him, crown Him, crown Him,
Crowns become the Victor's brow, crowns become the Victor's
    brow.

Hark, those bursts of acclamation! Hark, those loud triumphant
    chords!
Jesus takes the highest station; O what joy the sight affords!
Crown Him, crown Him, crown Him, crown Him,
King of kings and Lord of Lords! King of kings and Lord of Lords!

— Thomas Kelly

The Fate of Jerusalem
Jeremiah 52:1-23

Jeremiah 51 concluded with these words: *"Thus far are the words of Jeremiah"* (51:64). Accordingly, we understand that Jeremiah did not write chapter 52. Rather, this chapter was written later and included as a parenthetical explanation of the events in Jeremiah 39. In other words, Jeremiah 52 is a historical appendix of certain events of which Jeremiah has already spoken. In regards to the date Jeremiah 52 was written, we know it had to be after 561 B.C., as it records Jehoiachin's release from prison in that year (v. 31). Albert Barnes discusses the origin of this chapter and reason for its inclusion in the text of Jeremiah:

> An historical appendix to the Book of Jeremiah, giving details of the capture of Babylon additional to those contained in chapter 39. The last words of the foregoing chapter affirm that Jeremiah was not the author, and the view adopted by most commentators is that this chapter is taken from the 2nd Book of Kings, but that the person who added it here had access to other valuable documents, and made several modification in it, the principal being the substitution of the account of those led captive by Nebuchadnezzar (vv. 28-30), for the narrative given in 2 Kings 25:22-26.[1]

This chapter recounts the destruction of Jerusalem and the temple, and the slaughter of those in the city at that time. The writer also addresses the fate of the Jewish survivors and the deposed King Jehoiachin, who had been exiled to Babylon.

Why, then, was this chapter added to Jeremiah's earlier writings? Perhaps the best explanation is that it showed Jeremiah's prophecies had come true. Jeremiah had prophesied that Jehoiachin would not be put to death by Nebuchadnezzar, but rather that he would be exiled to Babylon and remain there all of his days (22:26). Jehoiachin was released after thirty-seven years of imprisonment and invited to eat at the king's table the rest of his life (vv. 31-34). This positive disposition towards him by the Babylonian king would encourage the Jews that their time of exile was nearly over and they too would eventually receive favor from their Gentile captors. In summary, Jeremiah 52 vindicated Jeremiah, who had suffered greatly for his prophecies, and served to encourage both the Jewish remnant in Jerusalem and those in exile not to give up hope.

Verses 1-16 recount the fall of Jerusalem and Zedekiah's attempt to escape the Babylonians as recorded in Jeremiah 39:1-7. Just as Jeremiah had predicted, Zedekiah was captured and taken in chains to Babylon (38:14-23). Next, the destruction of Jerusalem is described (vv. 12-16). Again, Jeremiah's prophecies (e.g. 22:7) had come true; the temple, the royal palace, and the surrounding houses were destroyed by fire.

The next portion of chapter 52 (vv. 17-23) directly relates to Jeremiah's earlier confrontation with the false prophet Hananiah. He had withstood Jeremiah and contradicted the prophet's prediction that the remaining furnishings of the temple would be hauled to Babylon (27:19-22). Hananiah had countered this claim by saying no more of the temple fixtures would be taken away, and that in fact all those that had already been removed would be quickly returned (27:16). The writer of this chapter acknowledges that Jeremiah was correct, detailing the immense undertaking of the Babylonians to transport the remaining temple furnishings back to Babylon.

Even the massive bronze laver and two copper pillars from Solomon's temple were confiscated. Boaz and Jachin, the names of the two pillars, each stood 35 feet tall with their capitals (27 feet without) and were nearly six feet in diameter. The bronze laver held 2,000 baths (around 12,000 gallons) of water and measured about 7.5 feet high and 15 feet in diameter (2 Kgs. 7:23-26). Timothy Paine calculates that each of the two pillars weighed about 89 tons, and that the bronze laver with its twelve sculpted bronze bulls would have weighed a bit less than 44 tons. He also estimates that the bronze altar with its fourteen large castings weighed approximately 270 tons.[2] Moving these articles would obviously be a very difficult matter. When Jeremiah proclaimed the temple would be stripped and destroyed, it seemed to be an impossible statement, but in fact, it was exactly what the Babylonians did.

Another confirmation of Jeremiah's ministry is validated in the remaining verses of this chapter. Jeremiah had repeatedly told the people that if they did not surrender to Nebuchadnezzar and live as captives under his rule, they would die in Jerusalem by the sword, pestilence, or famine. The Jews had rejected Jeremiah's prophecy and stiffened their necks against the Babylonians. After suffering through a drought and a siege that lasted two and a half years, many in Jerusalem died before the Babylonians even took the city. Most of the inhabitants of Jerusalem at the time of its fall were slaughtered. To substantiate that Jeremiah's declaration had come true, the writer provides a partial roster of influential Jews that were beaten and then executed in Riblah by Nebuzaradan, the captain of the guard: Seraiah (the chief priest), Zephaniah (the priest next in rank), the three temple doorkeepers, the officer in charge of the soldiers, seven royal advisers, and the chief officer in charge of conscripting the people and sixty of his men (vv. 24-26). The word of the Lord spoken by Jeremiah had come true.

The exile of those Jews surrendering prior to the fall of Jerusalem and those surviving its destruction was also foretold by Jeremiah on many occasions. The first deportation was in 605 B.C. when Nebuchadnezzar initially invaded Jerusalem; the prophet Daniel and his three young companions were among these early exiles (Dan. 1). The second deportation of Jewish captives occurred in 597 B.C. after Nebuchadnezzar put down Jehoiachin's rebellion. Ten thousand Jews were taken to Babylon at that time, among whom was the prophet Ezekiel (2 Kings 24:14). The following year, the eighteenth year of Nebuchadnezzar's reign, 3,023 Jews were transported to Babylon (v. 29). A fourth deportation of Jews occurred shortly after the destruction of Jerusalem in 586 B.C. This group consisted of a large portion of the Jewish survivors, along with those who had surrendered to Nebuchadnezzar prior to Jerusalem's ruin (2 Kgs. 25:11). A fifth group of captives were exiled to Babylon after Nebuchadnezzar returned to Jerusalem to restore order after the murder of his appointed governor Gedaliah (v. 30). This event occurred in Nebuchadnezzar's 23rd year as king (582 B.C). The writer of this chapter records that 745 Jews were exiled at that time. It is likely there were more Jewish deportations than these, but the above record, as set down in Scripture, is sufficient to prove that God's Word through Jeremiah was fulfilled.

Extra-biblical documentation also agrees with the Word of God on these matters. As previously mentioned, the Babylonian Chronicles corroborate the biblical details of Nebuchadnezzar's invasions into Israel. Also, the Cyrus Cylinder, which was discovered in 1879 AD, records the Persian King Cyrus's overthrow of Babylon and his subsequent release of the Jewish captives. We should note that the Bible not only documents these events in detail, but actually, two centuries before his birth, prophesied about Cyrus by name, specifying how God would use him to defeat the Babylonian empire, release the Jewish captives, and then assist them in rebuilding the temple in Jerusalem (Isa. 44:29-45:1). Another example of external biblical evidence to confirm the accuracy of Jeremiah's statements is found in the Lachish Letters, which were discovered between 1932 and 1938 AD in a place twenty-four miles north of Beersheba. These ancient documents described the attack and siege of King Nebuchadnezzar on Jerusalem in 586 B.C. Both extra-biblical and biblical evidence confirm the truth of Jeremiah's prophecies.

Conclusion

Each of Jeremiah's prophecies foretelling God's judgment on His people served both as a warning not to forsake Him and a promise of blessing for obedience. Jeremiah's messages against the nations gave God's covenant people hope for the future – that there would be an end to their punishment and that those who oppressed them would themselves be judged. May the Church learn from Israel's mistakes: comfort promotes complacency, which leads to compromise, and ultimately results in carnal behavior. Just as the greatest rivers on earth begin with a tiny trickle of water, the first step in forsaking the Lord begins with a simple decision which promotes ease or neglects to take action against sin. The Jews learned that their backsliding ways caused them, in time, to first forsake and then forget the Lord altogether. Take heed, believer; do not let it happen to you!

Meditation

Lord, we would never forget Thy love,
Who hast redeemed us by Thy blood,
And now, as our High Priest above,
Dost intercede for us with God.

We would remember we are one
With every saint that loves Thy name,
United to Thee on the throne,
Our life, our hope, our Lord the same.

Lord, we are Thine, we praise Thy love,
One with Thy saints, all one in Thee,
We would, until we meet above,
In all our ways remember Thee.

— James G. Deck

Lamentations

Overview of Lamentations

Jeremiah was a firsthand witness to the destruction of Jerusalem by the Babylonians in 586 B.C. After forty years of ignored prophetic ministry, one might think that Jeremiah would feel vindicated that God had done exactly what Jeremiah said He would do. However, retribution for wrongs committed against him was not at the forefront of Jeremiah's contemplations. Rather, he penned Lamentations as a sorrowful postscript to his previous book. James Vernon McGee describes the nature of the book:

> This book is filled with tears and sorrow. It is a paean of pain, a poem of pity, a proverb of pathos. It is a hymn of heartbreak, a poem of sadness, a symphony of sorrow, and a story of sifting. Lamentations is the wailing wall of the Bible.[1]

Lamentations contains five elegies, which lament the desolation of the nation and its capital city, Jerusalem, the very location that God had chosen to exalt His name among the nations. Jeremiah wants his readers to understand: No matter how enticing and thrilling sin may be, it ultimately results in grief, misery, and death.

Theme

The passionate sympathy that Jeremiah conveys for Israel in Lamentations is reflective of God's remorse over the necessity of punishing His wayward people. In this sense, the tears of the prophet have their ultimate culmination in the lamenting of the Lord Jesus over the city of Jerusalem shortly before His crucifixion (Matt. 23:37-39). As in the days of Jeremiah six centuries earlier, God's covenant people were rejecting God's offer for deliverance (in this case, His own Son and their Messiah). Accordingly, they would experience His displeasure and stern chastening hand again. God then permitted the

Romans to destroy the temple and much of Jerusalem in 70 A.D. The temple has never been rebuilt, and will not be until the time of Jacob's Trouble (the Tribulation Period), as previous predicted by Jeremiah (Jer. 30:7).

Literary Form

Several of the psalms (e.g. 111, 119, and 145) have an alphabetical acrostic form of construction. Psalm 119 is the most familiar example; it is divided into twenty-two sections, one for each letter of the Hebrew alphabet. Jeremiah employs a similar alphabetic literary form in the first four chapters of Lamentations. The fifth chapter is not an alphabetic acrostic, although it does contain twenty-two verses, as do chapters 1, 2, and 4. Chapter 3 contains sixty-six verses composed of twenty-two alphabetical verse groupings (i.e., each verse in a triad begins with the same Hebrew letter). The stylistic arrangement of the fifth chapter is unique and produces a metered cadence prompting soberness (i.e., each verse commences with a bitter lament and concludes with a softer reply).

Outline

The following is a simple outline of Lamentations:

Chapter 1 – The Desolation of Jerusalem
Chapter 2 – The Lord's Anger
Chapter 3 – Jeremiah's Response
Chapter 4 – The Siege of Jerusalem
Chapter 5 – A Sorrowful Prayer

Devotions in Lamentations

The Desolation of Jerusalem
Lamentations 1

The theme of Lamentations, the sorrow of sin, reflects the divine ramifications of ignoring God's prophetic warnings recorded in Jeremiah's first book. God's covenant people had embraced lifeless idols instead of Jehovah and had then sought assistance from foreign powers to escape His chastening hand. Now the Jewish people were destitute, despised, and helpless.

Lamentations, an epilogue to the book of Jeremiah, poses two conclusions that the Jews should deduce from their agonizing experience: First, "the wages of sin is death" – a holy God must judge willful disobedience, especially spiritual infidelity. Second, God is faithful to His Word; consequently, in His timing, He would forgive and restore Israel to a position of splendor and blessing because of His covenant promise to do so.

As onlookers of Israel's calamity, we are permitted to contemplate the longsuffering and loyal nature of God in dealing with His wayward children. H. A. Ironside suggests that such exposure to the heart of God should greatly encourage believers in all ages to express their sorrows to One who alone can triumph over them for His glory; this is what Jeremiah does in Lamentations:

It should be a matter of deep interest for the child of God, in any dispensation, to know that there is One above who notes with compassion all of his sorrows, and is afflicted in all his afflictions. Nothing could demonstrate this more clearly than the incorporation, as a part of the Holy Scriptures, of the expressions of the heart-sorrows of Jeremiah as he beheld the overwhelming woes of his people, and the desolations of the Holy City. These feelings were

345

right and proper—nay, produced by the Spirit of God in the heart of His servant Jeremiah. He, the God of Israel, was no cold, indifferent spectator of the anguish, humiliation and pains of the people of His choice. His holiness demanded that He chasten them for their iniquities; and He had used the king of Babylon to that end, but His heart was grieved for them still, as a loving father is sorely pained in his own correction of a wayward son. He greatly valued, therefore, the soul-exercises of His grief-stricken prophet, and has seen fit to place his lamentations on record for our instruction and comfort.[1]

In his first of five laments, Jeremiah surveys the desolation of Jerusalem from two vantage points. First, an outside observer testifies of the widespread desolation of the city (vv. 1-11). Second, a personified Jerusalem calls out to those passing by to observe her horrific situation; perhaps someone will show compassion to her (vv. 12-22). However, Jeremiah notes five times the reality of their dismal condition: *"She has none to comfort her"* (vv. 2, 9, 16, 17, and 22).

The Onlooker's Perspective

The outside observer first describes the horrific scene in Jerusalem (vv. 1-7) and then why the city suffered such vast desolation (vv. 8-11). After recalling the past splendor of Jerusalem, as a premier city among the nations, the observer likens its smoldering ruins to a widow in mourning. For indeed most of her inhabitants were now dead or enslaved in foreign lands (v. 1). Personified Jerusalem wept bitterly, but there was no one to comfort her; not only had her previous lovers abandoned her, but they had also become her enemies (v. 2). This regretful outcome had been foretold by Jeremiah more than forty years earlier (Jer. 3:1, 4:30).

Judah's calamity declares a somber warning for all saints of all ages: When God's people fail to maintain separation from worldliness and the promiscuous ways of the wicked, as God demands, He is obliged to give His people up to wander aimlessly among the lost until so sickened by their practices and the consequences of sin that they want nothing else but God. This scenario repeatedly occurred throughout Israel's history and it also has marked much of the Church Age. For this reason Paul sternly admonishes believers:

Do not be deceived: "Evil company corrupts good habits." Awake to righteousness, and do not sin; for some do not have the knowledge of God. I speak this to your shame (1 Cor. 15:33-34).

Returning to the text, the observer more specifically describes the calamity that all of Judah had suffered (vv. 3-6). The roads leading into Jerusalem were no longer filled with pilgrims coming to the temple to commemorate the feasts of Jehovah (v. 4). Rather, many of these past worshippers had become slaves in Babylon (vv. 3, 5). Most of her leaders were slain, but some had fled like hunted prey into the wilderness to escape their pursuers (v. 6). Besides the physical and religious desolation of Jerusalem, her remaining inhabitants also suffered the mental anguish of recollecting their lost wealth and status previously enjoyed and also of being constantly ridiculed in their present dismal state (v. 7).

Why Judgment Came

After revealing the panoramic plight of Jerusalem, Jeremiah affirms why God so severely punished the city: *"Jerusalem has sinned gravely"* (v. 8) and *"She did not consider her destiny"* (v. 9). If the Jews would have considered Solomon's search for significance and happiness in Ecclesiastes, they would have realized that living for the moment is to chase after fleeting pleasure. Such selfishness can never yield the deep satisfaction of knowing and being blessed by God.

Rather, the Jews chose to abandon Jehovah for vain religiosity. Accordingly, the Lord permitted a pagan nation to desecrate and destroy His temple and then carry its sacred vessels to Babylon (v. 10). More than twenty years before the temple's destruction Jeremiah confirmed God's judgment was coming on Judah for her vain religious practices. Of particular offense to God was the Jews' notion that they were invincible because they had the temple (Jer. 7:4). The temple was viewed as a "good luck charm" which would protect the nation. Apparently, the structure, having been disassociated from Jehovah, was itself regarded as a bastion of safety (i.e. the people trusted in a man-made building to protect them rather than the One it honored). However, God had now decisively shown that He valued obedience more than any humanly-built structure.

347

The second offense mentioned by Jeremiah is that the people preferred to rely on their own resources to sustain them during the long famine and Babylonian siege. Instead of obeying Jeremiah's prophetic decree to surrender the city and live, they chose to reject God's word and trust in their own political wherewithal. The utter folly of this decision became evident during the long siege which was compounded by draught conditions – there was more silver and gold in Jerusalem than bread to eat (v. 11).

Jerusalem Pleads

In the latter half of this first lament, Jeremiah transitions from the outsider's testimony of Jerusalem's devastation (vv. 1-11) to how a personified Jerusalem felt about her dire state (vv. 12-22). Jerusalem first solicits bystanders to take note of her desperate condition (vv. 12-19) before pleading with the Lord to do the same and recompense her enemies (vv. 20-22).

A bewailing Jerusalem implores all who have witnessed her destruction to carefully listen to her as she explains her horrific plight: *"The Lord has inflicted* [us] *in the day of His fierce anger"* (v. 12). In His righteous jealousy, Jehovah, as promised, had poured out His fury upon Jerusalem for her adulterous ways (Jer. 3:8; Ezek. 16:32). Jerusalem now acknowledges that what happened to her was not by chance, but rather Jehovah had moved Nebuchadnezzar to invade Judah to chasten them, His people.

Recalling the specifics, Jerusalem poetically describes God's fourfold attack: First, *"from above He has sent fire into my bones,"* perhaps speaking of lightning strikes into the city (v. 13). Second, *"He has spread a net for my feet"* to entrap her wayward inhabitants to ensure their punishment (v. 13). Third, *"the yoke of my transgressions was bound; they were woven together by His hands, and thrust upon my neck,"* hence indicating that she was bound to serve Babylon (v. 14). Fourth, *"the Lord has trampled underfoot all my mighty men in my midst"* (v. 15). The Lord had beckoned invaders from the north to gather up Jerusalem's inhabitants like grapes to be crushed in a winepress. Indeed, the Jewish people had been cruelly trodden down under the feet of a Gentile army in God's winepress.

Now Jerusalem was like a barren widow stretching out her hands in desperation to anyone who would look upon her predicament, but no one was obliged to assist her (vv. 16-17). Even in her deplorable condition, her neighbors (now her enemies) had no pity for Jerusalem; rather, they shunned and despised her as some putrid thing to be discarded. Though desiring mercy and help from anyone who might render assistance, Jerusalem does not question God's righteous ways in dealing with her. She had gotten what she deserved and she knew it: *"The Lord is righteous, for I rebelled against His commandment"* (v. 18). She confessed to her onlookers that because of her proud vanity she had been deceived by her foreign lovers (political allies) to embrace their false gods and commit spiritual adultery (v. 19).

After confessing her sins to others, Jerusalem was prompted to cry out to God to notice their agonizing situation and take action. Divine chastening had brought about its desired result in Jerusalem, her admission of sin: *"I have been very rebellious"* (v. 20). Realizing that she deserved all that God had called her to endure was a bittersweet experience. True repentance is always appreciated by God, but to realize that all their sorrows had resulted from their own defiance was a bitter realization.

Having come to grips with her own sin, Jerusalem petitions the Lord to recompense to their aggressors the same kind of judgment that they had received (vv. 21-22). She then pleads: *"Bring on the day You have announced, that they may become like me"* (v. 21). "The day" speaks specially of "the Day of the Lord" widely prophesied in the Old Testament as a time when Jehovah would intervene in a visible and powerful way to judge the wicked on earth. In its final application, the Day of the Lord emphasizes Israel's final deliverance from all future Gentile oppression.

This latter meaning is predominately posed throughout the New Testament and speaks specially of the Tribulation Period (1 Thess. 5:1-5) and the millennial reign of Christ (2 Pet. 3:10). The Day of the Lord concludes with the destruction of the earth and the subsequent Great White Throne judgment of the wicked, which then ushers in the Day of God or the eternal state (2 Pet. 3:12). While in her desperation, Jerusalem longed for the Day of the Lord during the Babylonian captivity. However, God's vindication of His covenant people would not occur at that time; rather, their final salvation would continue to be hoped for in the coming centuries. In God's grand plan, Jewish deliverance would be achieved when God chose to vindicate His Son, the Lord Jesus Christ, and establish His kingdom on earth. This will occur at the conclusion of the Tribulation Period. In Christ alone will the Jewish people finally escape shame, oppression, and death. In this chapter, we learn that rebellion against God to temporarily achieve one's way is much too costly.

Meditation

Afflicted saint, to Christ draw near –
Thy Savior's gracious promise hear,
His faithful Word declares to thee,
That as thy days thy strength shall be.

— John Fawcett

The Lord's Anger
Lamentations 2

In the first lament, both the unconcerned onlooker and a personified grief-stricken Jerusalem testified to the utter ruin of the city. In the second dirge, the focus shifts from the consequences of Israel's rebellion to the One offended by her infidelity – the Lord. God is longsuffering and patient, but steadfast Jewish waywardness and the rejection of His prophetic warnings provoked His anger to action. His eternal love for His covenant people was thus expressed in jealous retribution with the goal of restoring communion with them.

Having spent much time with the Lord, Jeremiah also keenly felt God's own hurt and displeasure over Israel's infidelity. William Kelly suggests that this is the reason why the prophet Jeremiah was divinely prompted to pen Lamentations:

> It has been noticed that the solitude of Jerusalem is the prominent feeling expressed in the opening of these elegies. Here we shall find its overthrow spread out in the strongest terms and with great detail. Image is crowded on image to express the completeness of the destruction to which Jehovah had devoted His own chosen people, city, and temple; the more terrible, as He must be in His own nature and purpose unchangeable. None felt the truth of His love to Israel more than the prophet; for this very reason, none could so deeply feel the inevitable blows of His hand, obliged as He was to be an enemy to those He most loved.[1]

In first ten verses of the lament, the prophet is connecting the injury inflicted upon God's own heart by Israel's worldliness and defiance with His righteous response of punitive correction (i.e., the destruction of Jerusalem):

How the Lord has covered the daughter of Zion with a cloud in His anger! He cast down from heaven to the earth the beauty of Israel, and did not remember His footstool in the day of His anger (v. 1).

The Old Testament contains over 200 direct and approximately another 150 implied references to divine anger. Throughout the Bible, God's anger is associated with the unrighteous conduct of His creatures that possess a free moral will, namely angels and humans: *"God is angry with the wicked every day"* (Ps. 7:11). Anger is an emotion, not a behavior; it can prompt righteous indignation or sinful acts (e.g., rage, resentment, bitterness). But God's anger never causes Him to sin, for He is holy in nature and cannot sin (Ps. 30:4, 111:9). *"For the righteous Lord loves righteousness"* (Ps. 11:7). His very essence defines what is righteous – what is apart from God is unholy (Isa. 45:5-7). Accordingly, Scripture reveals God's anger as a righteous emotion in response to unholy conduct and affirms that anger itself is not a sin.

Since God's anger and His behavior resulting from His anger are always righteous, we can learn much from Him concerning how we should control this powerful emotion. We observe that God is not an angry God by nature but must be provoked to anger (Deut. 4:25, 9:18). Indeed, His anger has a building up time before causing Him to act (Ex. 4:14; Num. 11:1). Thankfully, He is slow to anger (Ps. 103:8-9, 145:8), His anger does not endure (Ps. 30:4-5, 103:9), and He is quick to forgive (Ps. 86:5). In summary, God provides us a perfect example to follow concerning how to managing anger to accomplish what has His approval.

Anger must have an immediate God-honoring purpose, or it is to be released. This is a fundamental rule of anger management – my anger must have a **present righteous purpose,** or it must be dismissed until such a time as it can immediately and righteously serve God. Once righteous anger has served God, it also must be relinquished. Anger is too strong of an emotion to contain or control for a long period of time – eventually, we will serve the flesh, and in so doing, we sin against God (Ps. 37:7-8; Eccl. 7:9). From time to time, all of us will be confronted with circumstances that prompt our anger. The challenge is to ensure that our anger will honor God and not needlessly hurt others or serve ourselves. While in close fellowship with the Lord, the power of the Holy Spirit will effectively control and mold our anger to accomplish the righteousness of God.

Jeremiah ensures that his Jewish audience understands that it was the Lord who dismantled their city, their strongholds, their dwellings, and their palaces because He had been provoked to wrath by their willful sin (vv. 1-5). He had removed *"every horn of Israel"* (v. 3). Those of social influence and political power, who had guided the people in the rebellion, were taken away. (This included not only the royal family, but other civil leaders also.) The judgment on Judah had been so widespread that the remaining Jews likened God's displeasure against them to that of a raging fire or of a ruthless invading army (vv. 4-5). But each of these analogies is connected with the associated expression of "like" or "as," meaning that God was really not their enemy though their rebellion compelled Him to act as though He were. As a result, the Jews had no strength or hope; all they could do was weep and lament over their miserable condition.

Not only was God's anger directed towards the city, but He also had torn down His own temple: *"He has done violence to His tabernacle, as if it were a garden"* (v. 6). The poetic language here is hard to understand from our modern perspective (i.e., a farmer does not till under a huge building with a plow). Charles H. Dyer explains the likely meaning of the expression:

> The word for "dwelling" (*sok*) is a variant spelling of the word for "booth" (*sukah*). The thought expressed by Jeremiah is that God tore down His temple (His place of meeting) in the same way a farmer would tear down a temporary field hut or booth used to provide shade during a harvest.[2]

In God's righteous indignation He destroyed the very place that He chose to commune with His people and to receive their gifts, praise, and worship. The temple was being desecrated by those feigning devotion to Jehovah but who were secretly embracing false gods; He would have none of it. His anger over fake devotion and meaningless religiosity was decisively conveyed through its obliteration. Afterwards the people wept bitterly at the ruins of the temple; there would be no more feasts or sacrifices – all that God had previously instituted in His Law was put away (v. 7). The reality of what Ezekiel had witnessed in a prophetic vision a few years earlier was now evident; the glory of the Lord had departed from Jerusalem (Ezek. 10). An offended Jehovah had chosen not to dwell among, nor commune with, His treacherous people.

In executing judgment, the Lord removed Israel's stalwart leaders who the people had trusted in for protection (v. 8). Furthermore, the king and the princes surviving the holocaust were exiled among the nations. Furthermore, there would not be priests ministering in the temple or expounding the Law of God; nor would the prophets be receiving communication from God (i.e., visions; v. 9). Obviously, Jeremiah was still speaking for the Lord, but the loss of Israel's leadership and God's overall silence in the wake of such devastating judgment caused the Jews much remorse. The stunned and destitute survivors could do nothing more than to cover themselves with sackcloth and their heads with dirt while they sat speechless on the ground (v. 10). There had been so much death and loss that even the faintest glimmer of hope could not be found among God's people – they were all alone and despised by all.

Surveying the catastrophic aftermath of God's judgment on Jerusalem drained Jeremiah's tears; they were *"poured on the ground"* for his countrymen (v. 11). In his first book, Jeremiah freely discloses his personal remorse and revulsion concerning the plight of Judah. He cried, *"Oh, that my head were waters, and my eyes a fountain of tears, that I might weep day and night for the slain of the daughter of my people!"* (Jer. 9:1). Jeremiah made no attempt to hide his empathy or his tears for his people. Hence, he became known as "the weeping prophet" (4:19-26, 8:18-22, 13:17, 15:18, 20:7-18). He knew that they would not repent and that a terrible judgment was coming upon them. In Lamentations, we again find Jeremiah weeping for the people he loved suffering in the aftermath of divine retribution (vv. 11-19).

The scene of distraught parents unable to feed and care for their starving children and the inability of anyone to comfort the fainthearted was too much for the prophet to bear (vv. 12-13). Jeremiah was grieved that the people had rejected God's warnings and rather chose to believe the fanciful flattery of the false prophets promising good things to come (v. 14). The fact that Israel's enemies now proudly rejoiced over her downfall and mocked their once beautiful and joyful city further burdened Jeremiah's heart (vv. 15-16). This prompted Jeremiah to instruct his countrymen not to listen to such boasting and to remind them that it had been God who brought about their calamity because of their stubborn sin (v. 17). The prophet then tells them to pour out their hearts in sincerity to the Lord – tell Him of their grief, needs, longings, and regrets (vv. 18-19).

National revival would not come for another fifty years, but the tearful prayers of this frantic remnant were the seeds of the coming spiritual awakening. Their prayers lacked spiritual wisdom, but they were desperate for God to do something nonetheless. The ruined testimony of the Church today should likewise cause us to humble ourselves before the Lord and urgently beseech Him to visit us with a fresh manifestation of power. Even a few seriously-minded Christians consecrated to God and desperate for Him alone can affect a tremendous work of God in our time.

> When God intends a great mercy for His people, the first thing He does is to set them a-praying.
> — Matthew Henry

Jeremiah had cried out to the Lord and he instructed Jerusalem to do the same. The lament then concludes with her inhabitants pleading with God to notice their terrible plight (vv. 20-22). The famine coinciding with the long Babylonian siege of Jerusalem caused a severe food shortage in Judah. Many Jews were starving and some had resorted to cannibalism to survive. Hence, Jerusalem's inhabitants ask the Lord: *"Should the women eat their offspring?"* (v. 20). Perhaps they thought that by appealing to God's high morality they would provoke His pity and prompt His assistance to end what surely offended Him. Yet, man's depravity has ruinous consequences and if God always sought to alleviate the harsh sting of sin, human morality would only worsen. Moses had previously warned that the divine consequences of idolatry would be so severe that parents would resort to eating their own children to live. Cannibalism of the worst sort had occurred in Jerusalem just as Moses had forewarned centuries earlier (Lev. 26:27-29).

Next, Jerusalem reminded God that His priests and prophets were slain by Babylonian soldiers in His sanctuary – surely this insult deserved divine retribution against their mocking oppressors. Furthermore, the city was defiled with the rotting corpses of children and the aged, butchered by savage soldiers; should not the Lord be disgusted by this detestable sight (v. 21)? While it is true that the Lord was repulsed by the distressful conditions in Jerusalem, His lack of immediate intervention indicated His greater displeasure over Judah's sin, and that He would not remove their hardships until true repentance and spiritual revival had occurred. God knew exactly what would be necessary to purge the Jewish nation of her idols and He skillfully brought about every punitive detail to achieve that objective.

To ensure that the prayers of the spiritually despondent did not cast doubt on God's infallible character, Jeremiah closes this dirge by again reminding his audience that it was the sword of the Lord that had fallen on them: *"In the day of the Lord's anger there was no refugee or survivor"* (v. 22). Beginning with Moses and then the pre-exile prophets, God repeatedly warned His people what the consequences of idolatry and rebellion would be. Therefore, it would be expected that a holy and just God must honor His own word and execute judgment for the glory of His own name.

Meditation

It is my conviction that we are never going to have a revival until God has brought the church of Jesus Christ to the point of desperation.

— Stephen Olford

Jeremiah's Response
Lamentations 3

In this elegy, Jeremiah acknowledges that the rebellious Jewish nation, though preserved by God had not experienced His protection. The futility of human sin and its sorrowful repercussions in the first two chapters is here interrupted by the prophet's own testimony and personal reflections. Chapter 3, framed by the darkness of sin in the surrounding chapters, is the bright spot of this literary work. It continues to follow the alphabetic acrostic form of the previous two chapters but in a triplet format (i.e., three verses for each Hebrew letter). Besides being three times as long as the other chapters, this chapter also commences with a first-person narrative; this format stands in sharp contrast with the aloof, rhetorical "How" that initiates chapters 1, 2 and 4.

While much of this chapter represents Jeremiah's personal testimony to God's faithfulness throughout his arduous ministry, he does identify with his countrymen and their horrific trial (e.g., vv. 40-46). Jeremiah was burdened to teach the Jewish nation what he had learned through experience: God has His way during seasons of affliction so do not despair, but rather hope in His faithfulness. In this sense, Jeremiah is a representative of the nation and in this chapter he is trying to lead his fellow countrymen into a deeper understanding of God's unfathomable ways.

This long chapter can be divided into three segments: Jeremiah's testimony of God's faithfulness (vv. 1-18), what Jeremiah had learned through suffering (vv. 19-40), and how he wanted the nation of Israel to respond to this information (vv. 41-66). The prophet's goal is to instill hope in the minds of a distressed Jewish remnant such that they will seek the Lord in prayer and wait on Him for deliverance and restoration.

357

Jeremiah had experienced much affliction in the execution of his prophetic office. Though he had suffered much hardship, Jeremiah used metaphoric language to express this fact rather than mentioning specific details. His allegorical explanations show that he has no desire to glory in His afflictions; instead, he wanted to highlight the joyous outcome of what God accomplished through them.

Jeremiah could have spoken of many challenging and often life-threatening events during his ministry: Besides the plot of the citizens of Anathoth (Jer. 11:18-13), Jeremiah suffered much verbal abuse (Jer. 18:18), he was assaulted and chained by the priest Pashhur (Jer. 20:1-3), the priests and prophets sought to kill him (Jer. 26:7-24), King Jehoiakim burned Jeremiah's scroll and then ordered him to be arrested (Jer. 36:22-26), Jeremiah was struck by the priests and then imprisoned (Jer. 37:15), and in a final attempt on his life, the princes dropped Jeremiah into a deep pit where he sunk down into the mire (Jer. 37:11-38:13). Yet, in each of these trials and many others not mentioned above, God faithfully protected His prophet. Jeremiah knew of God's faithfulness in a unique way and he longed for others to experience His goodness during arduous trials also.

This is not to say that Jeremiah was not confused at times about God's ways. In fact, it seemed that God had turned His hand against Jeremiah to cause him to stumble in the darkness at times, even though he desired to commune in the light with Him (vv. 1-3). Indeed, there were seasons of adversity in which Jeremiah suffered tremendous physical and emotional trauma (vv. 4-6). During these bleak times, the prophet recalled feeling hemmed in by a wall of hopeless circumstances and wondered why God did not respond to his prayers (vv. 7-9). At such times, it seemed to him that God was like a bear or lion seeking to devour him as prey or that he had become the target for God's vexing darts (vv. 10-12). Jeremiah now understood that as a representative of the Jewish nation, he had been appointed to suffer adversity in the will of God with his countrymen. And indeed, he did. Invoking colorful imagery, instead of specifics, he describes being trampled underfoot, being forced to eat the bitter herb of gall, having his teeth broken by gravel, rolling in ashes, being laughed at and mocked, and being robbed of peace and prosperity for most of his life (vv. 13-18).

Because Jeremiah's sufferings were directly connected with Judah's chastening, he was able both to sympathize with his people and to inspire them to seek after the same solace he had found during arduous circumstances – trusting in God alone (vv. 19-40).

Difficult trials often cause God's people to suffer spiritual despondency. Even Jeremiah, during a moment of despair said, *"my strength and my hope have perished from the Lord"* (v. 18). But after calling on God to remember his past afflictions (v. 19), Jeremiah also recalled God's past faithfulness to enable him to persevere through adversity (v. 20). Jeremiah had learned through experience that God's children should never feel hopeless, for they were always established in God's eternal love and His promises:

Through the Lord's mercies we are not consumed, because His compassions fail not. They are new every morning; great is Your faithfulness. "The Lord is my portion," says my soul, "therefore I hope in Him!" The Lord is good to those who wait for Him, to the soul who seeks Him. It is good that one should hope and wait quietly for the salvation of the Lord (vv. 22-26).

Yes, God had punished Judah for her idolatry and unfaithfulness, but He could not reject or discard His covenant people. He could not undermine His unconditional promises to them despite their poor behavior. Centuries earlier, the Lord, speaking through the psalmist, pledged His eternal devotion to Israel:

If his sons forsake My law and do not walk in My judgments, if they break My statutes and do not keep My commandments, then I will punish their transgression with the rod, and their iniquity with stripes. Nevertheless My loving-kindness I will not utterly take from him, nor allow My faithfulness to fail. My covenant I will not break, nor alter the word that has gone out of My lips. Once I have sworn by My holiness; I will not lie to David: His seed shall endure forever, and his throne as the sun before Me; it shall be established forever like the moon, even like the faithful witness in the sky (Ps. 89:30-37).

What Jeremiah is teaching us is that the work of God and His association with it is more important than the personal consequences received for being obedient to the will of God. Jeremiah was obedient to the will of God, yet he gained a better understanding of God's character and His ways by suffering with God while He accomplished His purposes in Judah. The Hebrew word for the phrase "His compassions" in verse 22 is *racham*, which relates to the cherishing impulses that a woman has for the fetus in her womb. This is the type of divine tenderness that Jeremiah had consistently experienced.

It had cost Jeremiah much to go on with God, but He deemed the entire ordeal as profitable given what he had gained – greater understanding of the sovereignty and faithfulness of God. In the integrity of his heart, Jeremiah experientially knew and could emphatically declare: *"His compassions fail not. They are new every morning; great is Your faithfulness."* This should be the response of God's people in any age and in all circumstances, suggests H. A. Ironside:

> How precious the faith that, at such a time, could so speak! And what tried saint can truthfully say otherwise? Only when the soul is out of the presence of God does it seem as if His chastisements were too severe, and in part undeserved. No self-judged believer ever yet failed to own that he was far from *receiving* the full reward of his deeds. Rather, it seems as though God's grace leads Him to overlook even serious failure, and to correct but in part. *"His compassions fail not."* The rod is never directed by a cold, indifferent heart. He feels as no other can for the people of His choice, the children He loves. Every morning witnesses fresh evidences of His loving-kindness.[1]

Jeremiah had been faithful to His God-given commission and God had kept His promise to remain with Jeremiah while he fulfilled his calling: *"'For you shall go to all to whom I send you, and whatever I command you, you shall speak. Do not be afraid of their faces, for I am with you to deliver you,' says the Lord"* (Jer. 1:7-8). Jeremiah had remained under divine authority and therefore experienced God's favor and protection his entire life.

Christians today are also called by God to labor with Christ in ministry (1 Cor. 3:5-9), but we must choose to walk with Him in the light to receive His abundant resources (1 Jn. 1:6-7). If we choose to abide in darkness and disobedience, we do so alone, for the Lord cannot abide with us there. He does not leave us at such times; rather, we depart from His fellowship. If we walk in accordance to revealed truth, we will appreciate the Lord's communion, and like Jeremiah rely on His promises, such as, *"I will never leave you nor forsake you"* (Heb. 13:5).

After pondering the blessings of the Lord's abiding presence, the writer of Hebrews was further emboldened to serve the Lord: *"So we may boldly say: 'The Lord is my helper; I will not fear. What can man do to me?'"* (Heb. 13:6). As in Jeremiah's day, there will be times during the Church age that only a few faithful believers will choose to walk with the Lord, while many in the Church swerve from the truth. Because all believers are in the same Body, the faithful will also suffer the Lord's displeasure and chastening. Thankfully, Paul reminds us even *"if we are faithless, He remains faithful; He cannot deny Himself"* (2 Tim. 2:13). This bestows all believers a wonderful confidence in God: He expresses His eternal love in all forms of our sufferings.

Our affliction may be the consequence of our own sin (Heb. 12:6), or for personal refinement (Jas. 1:2-3), or to prepare us for further blessing (Job 42:12), but it is always for the glory of God (John 11:4). Thus, Paul could confidently write: *"For I consider that the sufferings of this present time are not worthy to be compared with the glory which shall be revealed in us"* (Rom. 8:18). In this sense, Paul and Jeremiah are teaching us that suffering for righteousness better prepares believers for heaven! Accordingly, there is a "ministry of suffering" which all believers must engage in to some degree, as Jeremiah puts it: *"It is good for a man to bear the yoke in his youth"* (v. 27). However, the choice as to how we bear it will determine our fruitfulness to God and His blessings to us. A humble disposition which expects sorrow and difficulties to better enter into the eternal good that God longs to accomplish through us is the right attitude. According to Jeremiah, believers possessing genuine faith can be silent and hope in the Lord during times of suffering (vv. 28-29).

No pain, no palm; no thorns, no throne; no gall, no glory; no cross, no crown.

— William Penn

Given what Jeremiah had learned through hardship, he wanted his countrymen to understand several principles associated with their chastening. First, God was faithful to His word, both to punish their rebellion and to bless their obedience (vv. 25-30). Therefore, since God had been faithful to execute the curses promised to rebellious Israel (Deut. 28:15-68), He could also be trusted to heal and restore His people for willful submission to His Word as promised (Deut. 28:1-14, 29:9-13, 30:1-2). Second, God's chastening for sin was temporary and was tempered by His mercy, to bring about the most advantageous result (vv. 31-32). Third, while God could rejoice in the outcome of their chastening, He derived no satisfaction in afflicting His people; it hurt God to injure His people (v. 33). Fourth, God does not approve of suffering caused by injustice (vv. 34-36). Fifth, God's discipline of His people is to accomplish His sovereign purposes in them; God is always in full control of what happens to those He loves (vv. 37-38). Sixth, Israel's affliction resulted from their sin and was administered to turn them back to the Lord (vv. 39-40).

Jeremiah's main point in this central section of the poem is that God has not been cruel to him or Israel in all that had befallen them; rather, God was displaying His immense love to His people and His faithfulness to His word. There was not one calamity that His people had suffered that He had not endorsed: *"Who is he who speaks and it comes to pass, when the Lord has not commanded it?"* (v. 37). This meant that God was familiar with and concerned about every detail of their lives and had acted with the same degree of intimacy in affecting what was best for them. Hence, Jeremiah asserts that there was no room for complaining to God, especially when they were in distress for their own sins (v. 39). Rather, God's faithfulness should cause His wayward people to reflect, examine themselves, and confess their sins: *"Let us search out and examine our ways, and turn back to the Lord"* (v. 40). Jeremiah's prayer in the final section of this chapter flows out of this exhortation (vv. 40-66).

Why had the Jews experienced God's anger but had not received His pity (v. 43)? Why did God not regard Israel's prayers (v. 44)? Why did the nations consider God's people as a pot of reeking scum to be cast aside (v. 45)? What had prompted all Israel's ruin and destruction (vv. 46-47)? God's people were suffering because they had not lifted their hearts and hands heavenward and confessed their transgressions to God that they might be pardoned (vv. 41-42). To complain to God about one's chastening without admitting one's guiltiness is a poor prayer indeed, suggests William Kelly:

> There are times when it does not become the saint to seek a deprecation of a chastening – where, if prayer were ignorantly so made, it were a mercy that it should not be heard. And so it was for Jerusalem then. The divine sentence must take its course, however truly God would prove His care of the godly under such sorrowful circumstances.[2]

All God's people must realize that it is pointless to petition God for anything while persisting in sin. The child of God who does not seek God's face has no right to seek His favor. Jeremiah understood that God chastens His people for the intended purpose of bringing them to repentance and restoring them to a state of blessing and fellowship with Him. Matthew Henry explains God's process of chastening to achieve restoration with His people:

> God is able to multiply men's punishments according to the numbers of their sins and idols. But there is hope when sinners cry to the Lord for help, and lament their ungodliness as well as their more open transgressions. It is necessary, in true repentance, that there be a full conviction that those things cannot help us which we have set in competition with God. They acknowledged what they deserved, yet prayed to God not to deal with them according to their deserts. We must submit to God's justice, with a hope in His mercy. True repentance is not only for sin, but from sin.[3]

Jeremiah knew that only through true repentance and not just sorrowing over sin's consequences would God's people experience spiritual refreshing. David understood this same reality through personal experience, as he explains in Psalm 38: Suffering severely under the chastening hand of the Lord, David petitions the Lord to temper His anger with mercy and to pardon him for his offense. David did not attempt to hide his sin, but readily confessed his foolishness; he was miserable night and day, and was also suffering from a debilitating illness because of his transgression. He knows that his pitiful state, brokenness, and deep sighing were fully visible to the Lord.

The psalmist does not deny his sin, nor that he is justly suffering because of it, but rather confesses it before the Lord and pleads for God to rescue him from his vicious enemies who are planning his destruction. The situation was desperate, God's discipline had served its purpose, and David now entreats the Lord to not forsake him, but instead be his Savior. Both Lamentations 3 and David's example teach us not to ignore sin, but to confess it to God, and to not complain about His just recompense for our stupidity. Such repentance should never be repented of, for restored fellowship with God should be cherished (2 Cor. 7:10).

In verse 48, Jeremiah shifts from exhorting his countrymen to repentance to his own ministry of brokenness and intercession before the Lord on their behalf:

> *My eyes overflow with rivers of water for the destruction of the daughter of my people. My eyes flow and do not cease, without interruption, till the Lord from heaven looks down and sees. My eyes bring suffering to my soul because of all the daughters of my city* (vv. 48-51).

The principle Jeremiah typifies here is of great importance in understanding the work of prayer that believers in close communion with the Lord can accomplish on the behalf of those not enjoying the same nearness to God. It is the Christian's identification with those who have failed and the Christian's privileged position in Christ that enables the righteous man or woman of God to have an effectual prayer life. As also witnessed in the lives of Moses, Daniel, and Nehemiah, those who practice righteousness and have found grace in the eyes of God will be prompted to identify with others who need God's grace. James puts the matter this way: *"Confess your trespasses to one another, and pray for one another, that you may be healed. The effective, fervent prayer of a righteous man avails much"* (Jas. 5:16). May every true worshipper of God engage in the important work of interceding for others!

Jeremiah, a righteous man who had received the grace of God and witnessed His glory, made effectual intercession to God on behalf of people who desperately needed His help. His contact with God prompted him to pray for others. True worshippers of God, then, will be marked as men and women who are compelled to pray for others. Those who are content to know the Lord superficially will not be burdened to intercede for others.

After promising to pray for his fellow countrymen until they had experienced God's forgiveness and refreshing, Jeremiah reflected on God's faithfulness in his past circumstances, as an example for them to consider. Jeremiah had suffered with all Judah because of sin, but he had cried out to the Lord for reprieve and was delivered (vv. 52-55). From the lowest pit of despair, Jeremiah had called out to the Lord. The Lord heard His prophet's cries for help and drew near to him and spoke these words of comfort, *"Do not fear"* (vv. 52-57). As a representative of Israel, Jeremiah was saying that if the nation followed his example of sincerely crying out to the Lord, they too could receive His assistance and indeed redemption (v. 58).

Because Jeremiah was in fellowship with the Lord and doing His will, he had complete confidence that God would vindicate him before His enemies (vv. 58-63). Jeremiah reminded the Lord that he had suffered much at the hands of false prophets and obstinate Jewish leaders; he now asks God to render vengeance upon those who had mocked him, plotted against him, and committed wrongs against him (vv. 64-66). He petitioned: *"Repay them, O Lord, according to the work of their hands"* (v. 64) and *"In Your anger, pursue and destroy them"* (v. 66).

After forty years of suffering in a ministry which mostly ignored or rejected his preaching, it would be natural for any servant of the Lord to desire vindication. David's imprecatory prayers in Psalms 35 and 71 and Nehemiah's call to judge those opposing his wall-building effort (Neh. 4:4-5) are similar to Jeremiah's request here. Such imprecatory prayers express the acceptable mindset of a Jew living under the Law, but not the proper recourse for a Christian living under grace. Believers today are not under "an eye for an eye" economy of the Law; rather, the Lord Jesus instructs us to *"love your enemies, bless those who curse you, do good to those who hate you, and pray for those who spitefully use you and persecute you"* (Matt. 5:44). In the Church Age, the grace of Christ is reigning, and, having experienced His unmerited favor, believers are responsible to

365

manifest that same grace to others. The reason Jeremiah's prayers seem categorically harsh to us is because we are viewing them in the light of the New Testament revelation.

While Scripture does record the prayers of the righteous pleading for immediate wrath upon their enemies, this protocol is not endorsed during the Church Age. In the Age of Grace, Christians should desire their adversaries to experience God's grace and be saved, not destroyed. Though the Lord Jesus and Stephen suffered at the hands of their oppressors, both prayed that God would not judge at that time those who had ill-treated them (Luke 23:34; Acts 7:60). The Lord instructed His disciples, His apostles in the Church Age, to pray for and show love to their enemies; perhaps some would repent and be saved (Luke 6:27-35). Such kindness demonstrates God's love in action and can soften the hardest of rebel hearts. Thus, Christians are not to seek the destruction of their persecutors, but are rather to pray for their salvation. Believers are to overcome evil deeds by reflecting Christ in generous acts of righteousness (Rom. 12:19-21).

Though we cannot directly relate to Jeremiah's heartaches, his sufferings, or even his punitive prayers, we can agree with him that without God, suffering would be a most miserable experience! It is only through Him that our human misery can have a foreknown and profitable outcome. He ensures the result of our suffering can accomplish a greater good; hence, like Jeremiah, we can be thankful for God's faithfulness in all our hardships (Rom. 8:28; Eph. 5:20).

Meditation

We were promised sufferings. They were part of the program. We were even told, "Blessed are they that mourn."

— C. S. Lewis

Many men owe the grandeur of their lives to their tremendous difficulties.

— C. H. Spurgeon

The Siege of Jerusalem
Lamentations 4

This dirge is tied with the cause and effect relationship of the one in chapter 2. The former highlighted the reason for God's righteous anger against Jerusalem and her idolatrous inhabitants. In this elegy, Jeremiah provides a contrast of the conditions in Jerusalem before and after God's indignation (vv. 1-11); the prophet then explains why God permitted the Babylonians to destroy the city (vv. 12-20), and concludes with a call of her vindication (vv. 21-22).

In former days, the inhabitants of Jerusalem, *"the precious sons of Zion,"* were considered as precious gold and fine gems adorning the city, but in the aftermath of judgment they were esteemed no better than clay pots (vv. 1-2). These pots were common vessels formed from the plentiful clay in the region and hence had little worth. During the siege Jewish mothers had treated their children worse than jackals. At least these despised scavengers nursed their young, but the people of Jerusalem had become like an ostrich that abandons her offspring to fend for themselves (vv. 3-4). The Lord used this same metaphor to remind Job that the ostrich is unconcerned as to where she lays her eggs, that is, she is apathetic about the proper care and safety of her young (Job 39:14-15). Sadly, the children of all social classes suffered starvation and disease during the siege and there was nothing that grief-stricken parents could do to alleviate their desperate situation.

Because of their own famished condition, the mothers of Judah were not able to nourish their children. From this text, H. A. Ironside provides this insightful application for the Church to consider today:

> Unspeakably sad is the state of God's people when their assemblies are not like nurseries where newborn babes and young saints can find nourishing food such as is suitable for them. It is to be feared

367

the needs of the lambs are often forgotten; and, alas, oftener still there is nothing to feed them with because all is parched and dry. If older saints are living for the world, it is small wonder that the babes languish and succumb at last to the withering influences about them, so far as their joy and testimony are concerned.[1]

Indeed, the young in Jerusalem wasted away in misery and death because of the spiritual despondency of their parents. May believers today learn from their mistake and avoid the same repercussions.

The first stanza ends with Jeremiah concluding that Jerusalem's condemnation had been worse than that of the perverse city of Sodom in the days of Abraham (Gen. 19:24): *"The punishment of the iniquity of the daughter of my people is greater than the punishment of the sin of Sodom"* (v. 6). Sodom's judgment was unexpected, swift, which meant that there had been no time to seek assistance to avert it. In contrast, Jerusalem's punishment for rebellion had been prophesied for years, but rather than repenting, the Jews sought help from Egypt to end their siege and deliver them from the Babylonians. Regardless of what Judah did, Jehovah was in control and their reluctance to yield to Him only added to their sorrows and suffering.

The second stanza is a reverberation of the previous one, but with more focused intensity. Jeremiah refers to Jerusalem's *"Nazirites"* (literally, "consecrated ones") in verse 7. Based on the nation's response to Jeremiah's, Habakkuk's, and Ezekiel's warnings, it is doubtful that there were many Jews during this era committing to a Nazirite vow of devoted consecration. Hence, Nazirites likely refers to Israel's princes or leaders rather than those who had initiated a vow, the point being that God's vengeance fell on everyone, no matter their social class, civil status, or level of consecration to God.

Not only did the Jewish children suffer during the siege, but even the well-maintained bodies of the elite shriveled and became discolored by protracted starvation (vv. 8-9). So severe was the situation that normally compassionate mothers resorted to cooking and eating their own children (v. 10). Moses had sternly warned that this would be a horrific consequence of idolatry (Deut. 28:56-57), one that had unfortunately occurred several times in Israel's history (e.g., 2 Kgs. 6:26-29). Hence, the second stanza concluded with a glaring summary as to why Jerusalem had experienced such devastation:

God's wrath had been poured out against His people because of their prolonged willful rebellion against Him (v. 11).

The solemn tenor of verse 11 is then further explained in verses 12-20, as Jeremiah supplies three specific reasons for the siege. Why would the impenetrable walls of Jerusalem be breeched by invaders (v. 12)? Because her prophets did not speak for God and led the people astray, her priests were perverse in executing their office, and her judges perverted justice and shed the blood of innocent people (v. 13). Most of these leaders were slaughtered during the fall of Jerusalem, but those surviving were now despised; they were likened to blind lepers wandering aimlessly about the streets and countryside (vv. 14-16). No one respected them or wanted to be near them; their counsel was pointless, their presence loathed, and their authority despised.

Besides the corruption of Israel's leaders, the second reason given for Jerusalem's siege is Israel's reliance of foreigner assistance, rather than heeding the calls of the prophets to surrender to Babylon (vv. 17-19). Early in Jeremiah's prophetic ministry, he warned that when the Babylonians arrived in Judah, they would despoil the Jews of their crops, flocks, vineyards, and fruit trees. The Jews would have no food supplies left to sustain themselves. The Babylonians would lay siege to their fortified cities and use starvation to cause their inevitable surrender, and Jehovah would teach them submission by forcing them to render service to their conquerors in Babylon (Jer. 5:17-19). Both Jeremiah and Ezekiel promised that if the Jews would surrender to God's chastening by surrendering to Nebuchadnezzar, their lives would be spared; they would still suffer servitude in Babylon but be spared death (Jer. 37:6-10; Ezek. 29:6-7). However, the Jewish leaders rejected God's word and sought assistance from Egypt. This effort proved futile against the armies of Babylon who were *"swifter than eagles in the sky"* in capturing their prey.

The third reason for the siege was the stiffed-necked response of the one *"anointed of the Lord"* to rule over Jerusalem, speaking of King Zedekiah (v. 20). Zedekiah repeatedly ignored Jeremiah's warnings, and then, when Jerusalem was near collapse, the king abandoned his people in the city and tried to secretly flee to Ammon through Babylonian controlled territory. He was caught in the enemy's traps. Nebuchadnezzar had all of Zedekiah's sons killed in his sight before blinding the king and hauling him back to Babylon in chains. The one that Jerusalem had trusted in, as life's sustaining breath, could not protect her under the shadow of his authority.

Jeremiah ends his fourth dirge by reminding the *"daughters of Zion"* that their punishment would end and that they would be restored to Jehovah because of His everlasting covenant with Israel (v. 22). On the contrary, Edom, Israel's close neighbor to the southeast, had no such relationship with Jehovah and therefore could only expect His wrath for troubling His people. Moses's prophecy in Deuteronomy 30:7 is against all Gentile nations opposing Israel, but Edom is specifically named here because she greatly rejoiced at Jerusalem's collapse (v. 21).

In the closing chapters of the book of Jeremiah, God pronounces judgment on various Gentile nations. According to Jeremiah 49:7, Edom's enormous pride sealed their doom. Unlike Egypt, Moab, and Ammon, Edom was not promised a future inheritance or restoration by Jeremiah. In fact, history records that in the years following the Babylonian invasion, the Nabateans drove the Edomites westward from their land into southern Judah. The descendants of the Edomites became known as the Idumeans and were later forced to accept Judaism under the rule of Maccabean John Hyrcanus, in 125 B.C. The Edomites ceased to be a distinct people afterwards and were eventually absorbed into the Jewish culture.

Each of the previous three chapters concluded with a prayer, but this dirge ends by highlighting God's promise to restore and vindicate His covenant people. Perhaps this is because the entire next chapter is a sorrowful prayer of the surviving Jewish remnant which concludes the book.

Meditation

> Afflictions, though they seem severe,
> In mercy oft are sent;
> They stopped the prodigal's career,
> And forced him to repent.
> Tis thus the Lord His love reveals,
> To call poor sinners home;

More than a father's love He feels,
And welcomes all that come.

— John Newton

A Sorrowful Prayer
Lamentations 5

Jeremiah's final elegy, a mournful petition of the Jewish remnant, does not follow the acrostic pattern of the four previous lamentations. The prophet had already proclaimed that God was fully aware of the atrocities committed against His people:

To crush underfoot all prisoners in the land, to deny a man his rights before the Most High, to deprive a man of justice, would not the Lord see such things? (3:34-36).

The Lord had brought Babylon against idolatrous Judah to chasten her, but the Gentiles had gone too far in their mistreatment of the Jews. They took advantage of the situation and God would repay them. Hence Jeremiah begins the prayer of the remnant: *"Remember, O Lord, what has come upon us; look, and behold our reproach!"* (v. 1).

The Jewish survivors not only bemoaned the Babylonian occupation, but that their property had also been divided up and parceled out for foreign ownership (v. 2). Additionally, the Jewish people had no personal rights, nor anyone to protect them from injustice and the cruelty of their new Gentile taskmasters. Even strong men were as helpless as orphans and married women were as vulnerable as widows (v. 3). Their living conditions were harsh and there was no reprieve from the daily grind of slavery (v. 5). The Jews were even forced to buy their drinking water and firewood needed for cooking and heating from their captors (v. 4).

The remnant acknowledged that they were being punished for the fickle disposition of their forefathers, who politically aligned with various foreign powers (e.g. Babylon, Assyria, and Egypt) in an attempt to gain food and favor and escape God's retribution for their apostasy (vv. 6-8). As a result of past national sins, the Jewish remnant was experiencing terrible brutalities by vile, debased taskmasters. Besides these cruelties, the people were under the constant threat of nomadic marauders, who ventured from their desert hiding places to raid defenseless Jews (vv. 9-10).

After detailing personal sufferings, the narrative switches from a first-person to a third-person perspective to address the impact of captivity among various sectors of Jewish society (vv. 11-14). The first atrocities mentioned were against defenseless women and even young virgins who were ruthlessly raped by sadistic Babylonian soldiers (v. 11). The invaders especially vented their frustrations against the Jewish leaders, who had caused the people to rebel against Babylon, which resulted in the long siege. Jewish elders were hung by their hands and brutally tortured to death (v. 12). Additionally, because there was a shortage of domesticated animals (as these were eaten during the long siege), surviving young men and boys were enslaved and forced to do the work of beasts at millstones, in pulling carts, and in carrying loads of wood (v. 13). The elders no longer judged personal grievances at the gates of the city, nor did the young men play their musical instruments – there was nothing to joyfully sing about (v. 14). Gender, age, and social status meant nothing to the invaders – no one was spared and nothing, including decency, was sacred.

Jerusalem was smothered by a shroud of gloom, misery, and death. The thriving fortified metropolis of Jerusalem, which had once been a crown of glory and honor to the Jewish people, had become a fit habitation for only jackals and other wild animals (vv. 15-18).

After describing their miserable plight to the Lord (vv. 1-18), the remnant pleaded with the One who reigns forever to demonstrate Himself strong against the false gods of their invaders (v. 19). They realized that their pitiful situation was not because Jehovah was powerless against the gods of Babylon, but rather because He was accomplishing His sovereign purposes. This meant that He had the power to vindicate them and restore them to Himself. Therefore, their prayer was that He would not forget, nor forsake them for a long period of time, but act in their favor soon (v. 20).

Their specific prayer marks the desire of all true children of God who have experienced the Lord's chastening hand: *"Restore us to yourself, O Lord, that we may return; renew our days as of old"* (v. 21). In an attempt to receive immediate relief, they petitioned the Lord to act, unless He had utterly rejected them (v. 22). The Lord longs to answer the prayers of His people which are within His will (1 Jn. 5:14), but He does not confound His own word or holy character to do so. Jeremiah had promised seventy years of Jewish captivity and seventy years of agricultural rest for the land if the Jews continued to rebel against the Lord; this would be just compensation for the 490 years the Jews had not honored God's year of Jubilee edict (2 Chron. 36:21; Jer. 25:11).

Thankfully, the grief-stricken book of Lamentations, marked by the repetition of complaint and supplication, concludes with a ray of hope shining through the dismal gloom enveloping Jerusalem: Jehovah had not utterly rejected them; His eternal, unconditional covenant with Israel and David ensured that He could not forsake them. In fact, Jeremiah promised his countrymen that the Lord was watching over them in their captivity to ensure His wonderful plan for the Jewish nation would be achieved (3:21-30).

While the nation waited for God to refine them through chastening, they would find comfort in the Lord and hoping in His promises. While speaking with the Lord, the prophet Isaiah, also no stranger to suffering, declared to his countrymen the only solution that he had found for despair:

You will keep him in perfect peace, whose mind is stayed on You, because he trusts in You. Trust in the Lord forever, for in YAH, the Lord, is everlasting strength (Isa. 26:3-4).

The night before His crucifixion the Lord Jesus similarly informed His disciples of how to maintain a settled peaceful mind despite forthcoming hardships and persecutions:

Let not your heart be troubled; you believe in God, believe also in Me (John 14:1-2).

Peace I leave with you, My peace I give to you; not as the world gives do I give to you. Let not your heart be troubled, neither let it be afraid (John 14:27-28).

These things I have spoken to you, that in Me you may have peace. In the world you will have tribulation; but be of good cheer, I have overcome the world (John 16:33).

Like Isaiah, the apostles experientially learned that hoping in the Lord's promises and enjoying His peace were the best solution to squelching their anxieties and disappointments. Therefore, with the utmost confidence Peter could pass along to new generations of believers the secret of maintaining peace in their Christian experience – resting in the Lord:

Grace and peace be multiplied to you in the knowledge of God and of Jesus our Lord, as His divine power has given to us all things that pertain to life and godliness, through the knowledge of Him who called us by glory and virtue (2 Pet. 1:2-3).

Amen and Amen!

Be anxious for nothing, but in everything by prayer and supplication, with thanksgiving, let your requests be made known to God; and the peace of God, which surpasses all understanding, will guard your hearts and minds through Christ Jesus (Phil. 4:6-7).

Meditation

At all times praise the Lord;
His promises are sure;
What if thou doubt? His steadfast Word
Unchanging shall endure.
Praise Him when skies are bright,
And gladness fills thy days;
Heaven shames thee with its glorious light,
And calls thee to His praise.

Praise Him when clouds are dark;
True faith waits not to prove;
Though hope no brightening gleam may mark,
His meaning still is love.
Praise Him when drear and lone

The shadows around thee fall,
No eye upon Thy sins but One –
Fear not, He pardons all.

— John Howson

Appendix I

An Attempt to Arrange the Writings of Jeremiah in Chronological Order by H. A. Ironside.[1]

(a) Reign of Josiah (B. C. 641 to 610).
B. C. 629 Chapter 1: Jeremiah's call.
Chapters 2-6: Exhortations to Judah and Benjamin.

(b) Reign of Jehoahaz *(Shallum)* B. C. 610.
No specific portion in this brief reign of three months, but see Chapter 22:10-12.

(c) Reign of Jehoiakim (B.C. 610 to 599).
B. C. 610 Chapter 26: Arrest and Acquittal
607(?) Chapter 35: The Rechabites.
607 Chapter 36: The Roll Burned.
607 Chapter 45: The Word for Baruch.
607 Chapter 52: Seventy Years' Servitude Foretold.
607 Chapter 46: 1-12: Judgment on Pharaoh.
605 Chapters 18, 19: The Potter and the Clay.
605 Chapter 20: Jeremiah's First Imprisonment.
602 Chapter 13: The Linen Girdle.
602 Chapter 14: The Famine.
601 Chapters 15-17: Captivity Foretold.
600(?) Chapters 7-10: Judgments Predicted.
600 Chapters 11, 12: Exhortations.
600 Chapters 47-49: Against the Nations.

(d) Reign of Jehoiachin, or Coniah (Jeconiah).
B. C. 599 Chapters 22, 23: Unfaithful Shepherds.

(e) Reign of Zedekiah (B. C. 599-588).
599 Chapter 29: Letter to First Captives.
599 Chapter 24: The Good and Bad Figs.
598 Chapters 30, 31: Return Prophesied.
595 Chapter 27: Bonds and Yokes.
595 Chapter 28: Controversy with Hananiah.
595 Chapters 50, 51: Doom of Babylon.
591 Chapter 34: The Violated Covenant.

* May not have been written by Jeremiah and was likely added to the book later.

Endnotes

Preface
1. William Kelly, *Notes on Jeremiah and Lamentations*,
   http://www.stempublishing.com/authors/kelly/1Oldtest/jeremiah.html

Overview of Jeremiah
1. Edythe Draper, *Draper's Quotations from the Christian World* (Tyndale House Pub. Inc., Wheaton, IL – electronic copy)
2. W. G, Moorehead, *Studies of the Prophecies of Jeremiah*; p. 9: quoted from James Vernon McGee, *Thru The Bible Commentary Vol. 3*, (Thomas Nelson Publishers, Nashville, TN; 1983), p. 351

Jeremiah
Called to Serve
1. Matthew Henry, *Commentary on the Whole Bible, Vol. 6*, (Hendrikson Publishers, Peabody, MA; 1991), pp. 399-400
2. Oswald Chambers, *My utmost for his highest: Selections for the year* (Discovery House Publishers, Grand Rapids, MI; 1993), June 27

The Called Protected

I Remember You
1. Albert Barnes, *The Bible Commentary Vol. 5* (Baker Book House, Grand Rapids, MI; reprinted 1879), p.148
2. Kyle M. Yates, *Preaching from the Prophets* (Baptist Sunday School Board; 1953) p. 139
3. Dr. Howard Taylor, *Spiritual Secret of Hudson Taylor* (Whitaker House, New Kensington, PA: 1996), p. 367

Forsaken
1. Matthew Henry, *Commentary on the Whole Bible, Vol. 6*, (Hendrikson Publishers, Peabody, MA; 1991), p. 406
2. James Vernon McGee, *Thru The Bible Commentary Vol. 5*, (Thomas Nelson Publishers, Nashville, TN; 1983), p. 545-546

Roadside Lovers

1. Edythe Draper, op. cit.
2. G. Campbell Morgan, *Studies in the Prophecy of Jeremiah*, quoted from James Vernon McGee, *Thru The Bible Commentary Vol. 3*, (Thomas Nelson Publishers, Nashville, TN; 1983), p. 361
3. Claus Westermann, *Genesis 37-50 A Continental Commentary* (Augsburg Fortress Publishers, Minneapolis, MN; 1986), p. 54
4. Gerhard Von Rad, *Genesis – The Old Testament Library* (Westminster John Knox Press, Philadelphia, PA; 1995), p. 359
5. Ibid., p. 360

Two Sisters

1. H. A. Ironside, *An Ironside Expository Commentary: Jeremiah and Lamentations* (Shiloh Christian Library), p. 38
2. Rabbi David E. Lipman, *The Birth of Israel,*
http://www.myjewishlearning.com/israel/History/1948-1967/Birth_of_Israel.shtml

Break Up Your Fallow Ground

1. H. A. Ironside, op. cit., p. 41

Circumcise Yourself

Foolish Pagans

1. Edythe Draper, op. cit.
2. Ibid.

The Unknown Tongue

Full of Fury

1. Albert Barnes, op. cit., p. 167
2. Kyle M. Yates, op. cit., p. 141

The Temple of the Lord?

1. William Kelly, op. cit.
2. H. A. Ironside, op. cit., p. 46

The Queen of Heaven

1. Alexander Hislop, *The Two Babylons* (Loizeaux Brothers, Neptune, NJ; 2nd ed. - 1959), p. 21
2. Ibid., p. 22
3. Ibid., p. 70
4. Ibid., p. 88
5. Ibid., p. 69
6. Ibid., p. 21

The Queen of Heaven (cont.)
7. Ibid., p. 87
8. http://www.tkam.org/christmas.html

Cut Off Your Hair
1. C. I. Scofield, *Rightly Dividing the Word of Truth* (Loizeaux Brothers, Neptune, NJ; 1896), p. 12

No Balm in Gilead
1. Albert Barnes, op. cit., p. 172
2. H. A. Ironside, op. cit., p. 52

Guided by Imagination

Dumb Idols
1. A. P. Gibbs, *Worship* (Walterick Publishers, Kansas City, KS; 1950), p. 118

Correct Me

The Broken Covenant
1. William Kelly, op. cit.

The Suffering Prophet

The Wicked Way
1. H. A. Ironside, op. cit., p. 58

The Marred Belt

Smash the Jars!

Severe Drought

Famine to Famine
1. Albert Barnes, op. cit., p. 187
2. William Kelly, op. cit.

Take No Wife
1. William Kelly, op. cit.

The Deceitful Heart
1. Matthew Henry, op. cit., p. 521
2. Martyn Lloyd-Jones, quoted in *The Fight of Faith 1939-1981* by Iain H. Murray (Banner of Truth; 1990), p. 330

The Deceitful Heart (cont.)
3. David Bercot, *A Dictionary of Early Christian Beliefs* (Hendrickson Publishers, Peabody, MA 1998) p. 624

Keep the Sabbath
1. Albert Barnes, op. cit., p. 194
2. Irving L. Jensen, *Jeremiah, Prophet of Judgment* (Moody Press, Chicago, IL; 1966), p. 59

The Potter's Wheel
1. Albert Barnes, op. cit., p. 195
2. H. A. Ironside, op. cit., p. 90

The Kingdom

The Broken Vessel

Labor and Sorrow
1. Edythe Draper, op. cit., quoting Tim Hansel

I Fight Against You
1. William Kelly, op. cit.

Kings Beware
1. William Kelly, op. cit.

The Righteous Branch

False Prophets
1. Albert Barnes, op. cit., p. 194
2. William Kelly, op. cit.

Two Baskets of Figs
1. H. A. Ironside, op. cit., p. 117

Seventy Years
1. Sir Robert Anderson, *The Coming Prince;* Preface to the Tenth Edition http://www.WhatSaithTheScripture.com [last accessed March 28, 2017]

Not Worthy of Death
1. H. A. Ironside, op. cit., pp. 127-128
2. William Kelly, op. cit.
3. Charles H. Dyer & Dallas Theological Seminary, *The Bible Knowledge Commentary: An Exposition of the Scriptures* (Victor Books, Wheaton, IL; 1983-1985), p. 1163

The Battle of the Prophets
The Broken Yoke
1. William Kelly, op. cit.

Trouble in Babylon
1. William Kelly, op. cit.
2. A. W. Tozer, *The Pursuit of God* (Revell, Old Tappan, NJ; 1987), p. 16

The Time of Jacob's Trouble
1. H. A. Ironside, op. cit., p. 153

An Everlasting Love
1. http://heavenawaits.wordpress.com/jewish-return-to-israel-in-end-times

A Well-Watered Garden
1. James Strong, *New Exhaustive Strong's Numbers and Concordance with Expanded Greek-Hebrew Dictionary* (Biblesoft and International Bible Translators, Inc.; 1994), electronic copy
2. Ibid.
3. C. I. Scofield, *The New Scofield Study Bible* (Oxford University Press, New York: 1967), p. 804
4. Albert Barnes, op. cit., p. 224

The New Covenant
1. William Kelly, op. cit.

Is There Anything Too Hard for Me?
1. C. H. Spurgeon, *Morning and Evening: Daily Readings* (Logos Research Systems, Inc., Oak Harbor, WA; 1995), September 21 AM

The Lord is His Name
1. C. H. Spurgeon, op. cit., September 9 AM

The Branch of Righteousness

A Message for Zedekiah
1. James B. Priochard, Lachish Letter No. 4 from *Ancient Near Eastern Texts Relating to the Old Testament.* (Princeton University Press, Princeton, NJ, 3rd ed.; 1969), p. 322

A Man of God
1. H. A. Ironside, op. cit., p. 184

The Burnt Scroll
1. C. I. Scofield, op. cit., p. 812

The Return of the Chaldeans
1. L. B. Cowman, *Streams in the Desert* (Zondervan, Grand Rapids, MI), March 13

Sunk in Mire
1. Albert Barnes, op. cit., p. 241
2. H. A. Ironside, op. cit., p. 214

Jerusalem Falls
1. Nigel Reynolds, *Tiny Tablet provides Proof for Old Testament*, (Telegraph.co.uk; July 13, 2007), http://www.telegraph.co.uk/news/main.jhtml?xml=/news/2007/07/11/ntabl et111.xml
2. H. A. Ironside, op. cit., p. 224

The Land is Before You
1. C. I. Scofield, op. cit., p. 86

Gedaliah Murdered

Don't Go to Egypt
1. Samuel Ridout from A.W. Pink, *Gleanings in Genesis* (Moody Press, Chicago: 1922), p. 145

Proud Men
1. J. F. Walvoord, R. B. Zuck, & Dallas Theological Seminary, *The Bible Knowledge Commentary: An Exposition of the Scriptures* (Victor Books, Wheaton, IL; 1983-1985), p. 1190
2. C. H. Mackintosh, *Genesis to Deuteronomy* (Loizeaux Brothers, Inc., Neptune, NJ; 1972), pp. 174-175

Come Home

Beware of Self-Seeking
1. William Kelly, op. cit.
2. H. A. Ironside, op. cit., p. 248

The Judgment of Egypt
1. Donald J. Wiseman, Chronicle of Chaldean Kings (626-556 B.C.) in the British Museum (The Trustees of the British Museum; 1956), pp. 23-24

The Judgment of Philistia and Phoenicia

The Judgment of Moab
1. Matthew Henry, op. cit., Eccl. 7:7
2. Ibid., 1 Cor. 3:18

The Judgment of Ammon and Edom
1. Josephus, *Antiquities* 13.9.1; 15:4

The Judgment of Damascus, Kedar, Hazor, and Elam

The Judgment of Babylon
1. Herodotus Book 1: sections 178-186
2. Ibid., section 191
3. James B. Pritchard, *Ancient Near Eastern Texts Relating to the Old Testament* (Princeton University Press, Princeton, NJ; 1955), p. 306
4. David Down, *Investigator 17, 1991* (March): Reprinted courtesy of SIGNS OF THE TIMES 1983 Volume 98 Number 6).
5. C. H. Spurgeon, op. cit., August 18 AM

The Fate of Jerusalem
1. Albert Barnes, op. cit., p. 277
2. Timothy O. Paine, *Solomon's Temple* (H.H. & T. W. Carter, Boston; 1870), p. 98

Overview of Lamentations
1. James Vernon McGee, *Thru The Bible Commentary Vol. 3*, (Thomas Nelson Publishers, Nashville, TN; 1983), p. 425

The Desolation of Jerusalem
1. H. A. Ironside, op. cit., p. 307

The Lord's Anger
1. William Kelly, *Notes on Jeremiah and Lamentations*, chp. 2 http://stempublishing.com/authors/kelly/1Oldtest/LAMENT.html
2. Charles H. Dyer, op. cit., p. 1215

Jeremiah's Response
1. H. A. Ironside, op. cit., p. 327
2. William Kelly, op. cit., chp. 3
3. Matthew Henry, MHCC derived from *Matthew Henry Commentary Vol. 2* (MacDonald Pub. Co., Mclean, VA), p. 188

The Siege of Jerusalem
1. H. A. Ironside, op. cit., p. 338

385

A Sorrowful Prayer

Appendix I
1. H. A. Ironside, op. cit., pp. 355-356

www.ingramcontent.com/pod-product-compliance
Lightning Source LLC
Chambersburg PA
CBHW060238100426
42742CB00011B/1570